CONTEMPORARY COLLEGE READER

Joyce S. Steward

University of Wisconsin, Madison

Scott, Foresman and Company

Glenview, Illinois

Dallas, Tex.
Oakland, N.J.
Palo Alto, Calif.
Tucker, Ga.
London, England

Library of Congress Cataloging in Publication Data

Main Entry Under Title:
Contemporary College Reader.

Includes bibliographical references and index.
1. College readers.   2. English language—
Rhetoric.   I. Steward, Joyce S.
PE1417.C652   808'.04275   77–17317
ISBN 0–673–15084–4

3 4 5 6-RRC-84 83 82 81 80 79 78

Contents

2
Shaping Details: *Description* 19

3
Framing Events: *Narration* 54

4
Organizing Specifics: *Example* 96

6
Seeing Similarities and Differences:
Comparison and *Contrast*   154

7
Discovering Likenesses:
Analogy   183

3
Analyzing Reasons and
Results: *Cause* and *Effect*   203

9
Making Meanings Clear:
Definition   **239**

10
Sorting It Out:
Classification and *Division*   **270**

‖
Making a Telling Point:
Argument and *Persuasion* 309

Preface

"Few remember that to learn to read and write is one of the greatest victories in life," said the English novelist Bryher in her autobiography. Most writers are readers first; learning to write is inextricably related to learning to read. Repeatedly, famous writers acknowledge their debt to their reading. While Thoreau admonishes that it is vain "to sit down to write" without having "stood up to life," many pages of his *Journals* are given to comment on the writers whose books he constantly read. While writing acquires its uniqueness from personal experience, observation, and thought, inevitably it bears the mark of the writer's reading.

Reading is a major form of experience and observation. As a reader, the writer-to-be observes not only what is written, but how. Then, the choice of words and images, the formation of sentences, the shape of paragraphs, and the plan for the writing as a whole are all influenced by discoveries made before the reader becomes a writer.

The selections and the accompanying study materials in this text are offered to help college students become better writers. Most of the selections are modern, most are fairly short, and they exemplify the patterns conveniently identified as methods of development. They will, it is hoped, initiate thinking and discussion, generate subjects to write about, provide models of organization, and illustrate ways of using language.

A writer must first have something to say. Chapter 1 therefore emphasizes the necessity for observation and careful recording of personal experience. A writer's notebooks are not only records but workbooks; they not only preserve incidents and thoughts but also provide an outlet for testing ideas and experimenting with language. The writers represented in Chapter 1 speak personally and practically about getting started.

Chapters 2 and 3 offer examples of description and narration, not for the sake of picture and story alone but for the purpose of making a point about observation and experience. Included here are scenes, events, and ideas for readers to relate to, as well as vivid and original ways of describing and narrating for them to observe.

Chapters 4 through 10 present traditional expository methods. Patterns frequently merge and blur, and most pieces of writing are not developed by one mode alone. Nevertheless, many are organized by a recognizably dominant method, and it is often easier to learn principles of organization by tackling one major purpose, one method of development, at a time. In their college and postcollege writing, students will face situations where they need to exemplify, to trace a process, to compare and contrast, to explain causes and effects, to define, and to classify. Finally, Chapter 11 offers essays and articles written primarily to persuade. Certainly most writing is intended to some degree to elicit agreement from a reader, and many selections in the text have an argumentative edge. But this chapter attempts to provide special opportunities for the close examination of the reasoning and strategies of persuasion.

Formulating a plan, finding a system of organization, seems to give more trouble to the developing writer than does any other part of writing. To offer help here, the chapter introductions include brief examples—themes in miniature—where the principles governing each method become obvious. In addition, a marginal guide analyzing the organizational pattern accompanies the first selection in each chapter after the first.

Study questions following the selections emphasize "Content and Form" and "Special Techniques." The suggestions for "Generating Ideas" may be used for discussion as well as for writing assignments. The index beginning on p. 357 locates the rhetorical and grammatical features treated throughout the book.

It is perfectly possible to use the text by rearranging the order of chapters, or of selections. Chapter 1 is intended as a point of departure and a way of initiating discussion about writing. Chapters 2 and 3 probably belong together, either at the beginning of a course or at the end. In the chapters that treat exposition, consideration has been given to building skills, starting with the relatively easy and moving to the increasingly complex, but other orders are quite conceivable. Whatever the arrangement of the material, however, it is hoped that students will enjoy the reading and find in it both ideas and methods to stimulate and improve them as writers.

Many persons have contributed in quiet but infinitely valuable ways to this book. Professor Emeritus Ednah S. Thomas of the University of Wisconsin, always a friend, has been both inspiration and sensitive critic. Professor Eva M. Burkett of the State College of Arkansas contributed insights about materials and study questions. Mary Feirn, Abigail McCann, and Sally Hansen—teachers all—reacted to selections and to composition assignments. Several colleagues gave useful suggestions along the way: Carol Adams, Delaware Technical and Community College; Eltse B. Carter, Northern Virginia Community College; William Heim, University of South Florida; Catherine E. Moore, North Carolina State University; John A. Muller, University of Utah; Mary Northcut, Richland College; May L. Ryburn, College of DuPage; Nadine S. St. Louis, University of Wisconsin-Eau Claire; James M. Williams, Johnson County Community College; Peter T. Zoller, Wichita State University. Editor Stan Stoga patiently and helpfully put up with a writer constantly beset with overwork. And above all, perhaps, many students learning to write have unknowingly revealed the need for reading that illustrates both the *what* and the *how*—the content and the techniques—which should bring them some victories in the writing game. To all of these, my gratitude.

Joyce S. Steward
Madison, Wisconsin

1
Observing, Recording, Writing

Observing

"What a great idea! Why didn't I think of it?" Have you ever read a magazine article or an informal essay and thought that you could write about the same subject? Have you ever had the same experience, made similar observations, but never thought about turning the event or opinion into a subject for writing? Or have you lamented, "I just don't have anything to write about," and let it go at that?

Good writing is closely linked to good observation. "One man walks through the world with his eyes open, another with his eyes shut; and upon this difference depends all the superiority of knowledge which one man acquires over another," says a character in Charles Kingsley's *Madam How and Lady Why.* The sources for observing are everywhere. Watch the people around you. Notice the way they work, listen to what they say, see how they interact and how they solve problems. Study the natural world. Storms and droughts, sunsets and rainbows, birds and animals and plants—all are exciting if you observe them closely. Pay attention to the mechanical world. Automobiles lined up at a gas pump, a pocket calculator, a rusty windmill rattling away on an abandoned farm—any of these might spark an idea for a writer. Or find subjects to write about in the world of the arts: paintings and photographs, music and dance, films and television.

Printed material provides another source of observation, for reading enables you to gather information and to get acquainted with the thoughts and opinions of other people in other times and places. As you read, notice not only *what* writers say but also *how* they say it. Observe the pattern of their thoughts, the words they use, and the ways they put them together.

The biographies and memoirs of many professional writers attest to the value of observation. In "City Walking," essayist Edward Hoagland says, ". . . aiming to be a writer, I knew that every mile I walked, the better writer I'd be." Like the artist, the photographer, and the scientist, the writer must learn to observe. One of the greatest of American writers, Henry David Thoreau wrote this comment on observing in the notebook he kept for more than twenty years:

> There is no such thing as pure *objective* observation. Your observation, to be interesting, i.e., to be significant, must be *subjective.* The sum of what the writer of whatever class has to report is simply some human experience, whether he be poet or philosopher or man of science. The man of most science is the man most alive, whose life is of the greatest event. Senses that take cognizance of outward things merely are of no avail. It matters not where or how far you travel,—the farther commonly the worse,—but how much alive you are.—*Journal,* May 6, 1854

A student of the Harvard geologist and zoologist Louis Agassiz wrote the following reminiscence about learning to observe closely. Although it was written about 1875, its meaning remains the same today.

Samuel Scudder

Look Again, Look Again!

It was more than fifteen years ago that I entered the labo-   1
ratory of Professor Agassiz, and told him I had enrolled
my name in the Scientific School as a student of natural
history. He asked me a few questions about my object
in coming, my antecedents generally, the mode in which
I afterwards proposed to use the knowledge I might acquire, and, finally, whether I wished to study any special
branch. To the latter I replied that, while I wished to be
well grounded in all departments of zoology, I purposed
to devote myself specially to insects.

"When do you wish to begin?" he asked.   2

"Now," I replied.   3

This seemed to please him, and with an energetic "Very   4
well!" he reached from a shelf a huge jar of specimens
in yellow alcohol. "Take this fish," he said, "and look at
it; we call it a haemulon; by and by I will ask what you
have seen."

With that he left me, but in a moment returned with   5
explicit instructions as to the care of the object entrusted
to me.

"No man is fit to be a naturalist," said he, "who does   6
not know how to take care of specimens."

I was to keep the fish before me in a tin tray, and occa-   7
sionally moisten the surface with alcohol from the jar,
always taking care to replace the stopper tightly. Those
were not the days of ground-glass stoppers and elegantly
shaped exhibition jars; all the old students will recall the
huge neckless glass bottles with their leaky, wax-be-
smeared corks, half eaten by insects, and begrimed with
cellar dust. Entomology was a cleaner science than
ichthyology, but the example of the Professor, who had
unhesitatingly plunged to the bottom of the jar to produce
the fish, was infectious; and though this alcohol had a
"very ancient and fishlike smell," I really dared not show
any aversion within these sacred precincts, and treated
the alcohol as though it were pure water. Still I was conscious of a passing feeling of disappointment, for gazing
at a fish did not commend itself to an ardent entomologist.
My friends at home, too, were annoyed when they discov-

ered that no amount of eau-de-Cologne would drown the perfume which haunted me like a shadow.

8   In ten minutes I had seen all that could be seen in that fish, and started in search of the Professor—who had, however, left the Museum; and when I returned, after lingering over some of the odd animals stored in the upper apartment, my specimen was dry all over. I dashed the fluid over the fish as if to resuscitate the beast from a fainting fit, and looked with anxiety for a return of the normal sloppy appearance. This little excitement over, nothing was to be done but to return to a steadfast gaze at my mute companion. Half an hour passed—an hour—another hour; the fish began to look loathsome. I turned it over and around; looked it in the face—ghastly; from behind, beneath, above, sideways, at a three-quarters' view—just as ghastly. I was in despair; at an early hour I concluded that lunch was necessary; so, with infinite relief, the fish was carefully replaced in the jar, and for an hour I was free.

9   On my return, I learned that Professor Agassiz had been at the Museum, but had gone, and would not return for several hours. My fellow-students were too busy to be disturbed by continued conversation. Slowly I drew forth that hideous fish, and with a feeling of desperation again looked at it. I might not use a magnifying-glass; instruments of all kinds were interdicted. My two hands, my two eyes, and the fish: it seemed a most limited field. I pushed my finger down its throat to feel how sharp the teeth were. I began to count the scales in the different rows, until I was convinced that that was nonsense. At last a happy thought struck me—I would draw the fish; and now with surprise I began to discover new features in the creature. Just then the Professor returned.

10   "That is right," said he; "a pencil is one of the best of eyes. I am glad to notice, too, that you keep your specimen wet, and your bottle corked."

11   With these encouraging words, he added:

12   "Well, what is it like?"

13   He listened attentively to my brief rehearsal of the structure of parts whose names were still unknown to me: the fringed gill-arches and movable operculum; the pores of the head, fleshy lips and lidless eyes; the lateral line, the spinous fins and forked tail; the compressed and arched

body. When I finished, he waited as if expecting more, and then, with an air of disappointment:

"You have not looked very carefully; why," he continued 14 more earnestly, "you haven't even seen one of the most conspicuous features of the animal, which is as plainly before your eyes as the fish itself; look again, look again!" and he left me to my misery.

I was piqued; I was mortified. Still more of that wretched 15 fish! But now I set myself to my task with a will, and discovered one new thing after another, until I saw how just the Professor's criticism had been. The afternoon passed quickly; and when, towards its close, the Professor inquired:

"Do you see it yet?" 16

"No," I replied, "I am certain I do not, but I see how 17 little I saw before."

"That is next best," said he, earnestly, "but I won't hear 18 you now; put away your fish and go home; perhaps you will be ready with a better answer in the morning. I will examine you before you look at the fish."

This was disconcerting. Not only must I think of my 19 fish all night, studying, without the object before me, what this unknown but most visible feature might be; but also, without reviewing my discoveries, I must give an exact account of them the next day. I had a bad memory; so I walked home by Charles River in a distracted state, with my two perplexities.

The cordial greeting from the Professor the next morn- 20 ing was reassuring; here was a man who seemed to be quite as anxious as I that I should see for myself what he saw.

"Do you perhaps mean," I asked, "that the fish has sym- 21 metrical sides with paired organs?"

His thoroughly pleased "Of course! of course!" repaid 22 the wakeful hours of the previous night. After he had discoursed most happily and enthusiastically—as he always did—upon the importance of this point, I ventured to ask what I should do next.

"Oh, look at your fish!" he said, and left me again to 23 my own devices. In a little more than an hour he returned, and heard my new catalogue.

"That is good, that is good!" he repeated; "but that is 24 not all; go on"; and so for three long days he placed that fish before my eyes, forbidding me to look at anything else, or to use any artificial aid. "Look, look, look," was his repeated injunction.

25 This was the best entomological lesson I ever had—a lesson whose influence has extended to the details of every subsequent study; a legacy the Professor had left to me, as he has left it to many others, of inestimable value, which we could not buy, with which we cannot part.

26 A year afterward, some of us were amusing ourselves with chalking outlandish beasts on the Museum blackboard. We drew prancing starfishes; frogs in mortal combat; hydra-headed worms; stately crawfishes, standing on their tails, bearing aloft umbrellas; and grotesque fishes with gaping mouths and staring eyes. The Professor came in shortly after, and was as amused as any at our experiments. He looked at the fishes.

27 "Haemulons, every one of them," he said; "Mr. ——— drew them."

28 True; and to this day, if I attempt a fish, I can draw nothing but haemulons.

29 The fourth day, a second fish of the same group was placed beside the first, and I was bidden to point out the resemblances and differences between the two; another and another followed, until the entire family lay before me, and a whole legion of jars covered the table and surrounding shelves; the odor had become a pleasant perfume; and even now, the sight of an old, six-inch, worm-eaten cork brings fragrant memories.

30 The whole group of haemulons was thus brought in review; and, whether engaged upon the dissection of the internal organs, the preparation and examination of the bony framework, or the description of the various parts, Agassiz's training in the method of observing facts and their orderly arrangement was ever accompanied by the urgent exhortation not to be content with them.

31 "Facts are stupid things," he would say, "until brought into connection with some general law."

32 At the end of eight months, it was almost with reluctance that I left these friends and turned to insects; but what I had gained by this outside experience has been of greater value than years of later investigation in my favorite groups.

Recording

Get into the habit of keeping a record of your observations, of storing them in a notebook or journal. "When found, make a note of," says Captain Cuttle, a character in Charles Dickens' novel *Dombey and Son.* As a student, you no doubt have taken notes on the reading for your various courses. Perhaps you have also jotted down memorable passages, things that you like so well that you wish to recall them later. But you should also get into the habit of making notes on your experiences and on your observations of everyday life so that these too are preserved. It is sad not to be able to retrieve a lost idea that seemed brilliant when it flashed across your mind, or a forgotten fact or faded memory that you need to make a point in an argument or to illustrate a conclusion. The best way to store your observations is to keep a journal.

The journal habit has still another value. Just as you need to record observations—the material for writing— you need to practice putting thoughts on paper. Learning to write is more like learning to ski or to play the piano than it is like studying calculus or anthropology. Practice helps you discover ways to improve. Writing down ideas for your own use forces you to examine them. Putting thoughts on paper for someone else to read forces you to evaluate not only the content—what you say—but also the expression—how you say it. As soon as you have written a page or two, you become the reader of the material. And you can assess its clarity or its imprecision, its effectiveness or ineffectiveness in conveying your thoughts and impressions.

In the following two selections, Freya Stark and Joan Didion present differing views on recording their observations. Freya Stark, British author, traveler, and photographer, prefers to write down the *causes* of impressions and to let these particulars later suggest the emotions and sensations of the original experience. American writer Joan Didion (who is represented again on p. 113) concludes that it is more important to record subjective reactions to the things she observes. Yet Stark and Didion agree about the value of keeping a journal.

8

Freya Stark

On Travelling with a Notebook

1   I was walking, when the first Cyprus crisis was at its
height, among the narrow byways that hug the Athens
Acropolis, when three or four very small boys came round
a corner and asked me where I belonged, naming one
country after another. Having exhausted all they could
think of, they looked at me with horror when I said,
"Anglia," English. The eldest reached for a stone and they
all in chorus cried, *"Kyprus."* Not knowing any Greek
with which to argue, I took the first historic name that
came into my mind and said, "Pericles." The classic bond
held. "Themistocles" one little boy responded, and I added
"Alcibiades" for good measure. The little group instantly
adopted me and shepherded me through all the dangers
of their fellows, just out from school. This is years ago
now and I had forgotten the episode until I happened to
read the single word *Anglia* in a notebook of that day
and the whole picture with its fierce gay little figures and
the Acropolis hanging above them came back into my
mind. The notebook, with its single word, had saved it
from total oblivion.

2   A pen and a notebook and a reasonable amount of dis-
crimination will change a journey from a mere annual
into a perennial, its pleasures and pains renewable at
will.

3   The keeping of a regular diary is difficult and apt in
most lives to be dull as it plods through good and bad
at one even pace. But the art of the notebook is selective.

4   One's own sensations and emotions should be left out,
while the *causes* that produced them are carefully identified. These are usually small concrete facts not particularly spectacular in themselves, and a single word, as we
have seen, may recall them. In describing Venice or Athens for instance, it is useless to record the rapture: no
mere mention can renew it: but the cause—some shimmer
of light or shadow, some splash of the flat-prowed gondola

as its crest turns a corner, or a sudden vignette, or the Greeks reading their morning papers in the theatre of Dionysius—such concrete glimpses produced the delight in the first place and can recapture it in the notebook's pages. Colours, odours (good or bad), even apparently irrelevant details like the time of day, are far more evocative than a record of feelings, which represent the writer and not the scene and are, usually, a mere embarrassment in later reading.

I have notes for instance of the Persian tribes moving 5
to their summer pastures under the great tombs of their kings at Naksh-i-Rustum: the tumult of goats, camels and horses, the women's black turbans, the clanking of cooking-pots tied to the saddle, and some effect of dust and distance are jotted down; and the remembrance of that wide freedom, the immensity of the background in space and time, come back automatically with the mention of the sights that caused them.

A painter once told me how important it is in a quick 6
sketch that the few details one has time for should be put in with particular care; far from being less precise they should be more so, or the illusion of reality will fail. The same rule applies to notebook jottings. A painter like Edward Lear shows the same awareness in his diary as in his sketches, where the details of light and colour for which he had no time are scribbled in pencil at the side.

In poetry the process is fundamentally the same, but 7
is worked out more completely with the harmony of words. The everyday traveller's notebook stops short of this process: it is intended for himself alone, it touches a chord already familiar to him, and therefore need not concern itself with the facilities of language: it is reminiscent, not creative, and can be brief and quite unreadable. With a little practice in selection, a very few lines will hold the gist of a whole day's journey; and the writing of them is much less of a labour than one would suppose.

You can amuse yourself too by reversing the process 8
when you are reading. Pick out of any particular description the concrete things the author must have seen and remembered: they have an immediate and convincing authenticity. The psalmist's hills in the mirage of noon that "skip like lambs"—have we not seen them at the deserts'

edges?—or Keats's musk rose "the murmurous haunt of flies on summer eves."

9   From things seen and remembered the fancy soars into the abstract and wanders beyond the notebook's scope— though sometimes even there a simile or image may well be recorded: "wine-dark" one may fancy the young Homer writing, on some Aegean headland while his sight still held. No confines to the human thought have yet been recorded. But the notebook is not the patrimony only of the thinker: it is an "Open Sesame" for every holiday traveller who learns to select his adjectives carefully and pack them compactly, so that at any odd moment he may recapture the spell of his days.

Joan Didion

From On Keeping a Notebook

1   My first notebook was a Big Five tablet, given to me by my mother with the sensible suggestion that I stop whining and learn to amuse myself by writing down my thoughts. She returned the tablet to me a few years ago; the first entry is an account of a woman who believed herself to be freezing to death in the Arctic night, only to find, when day broke, that she had stumbled onto the Sahara Desert, where she would die of the heat before lunch. I have no idea what turn of a five-year-old's mind could have prompted so insistently "ironic" and exotic a story, but it does reveal a certain predilection for the extreme which was dogged me into adult life; perhaps if I were analytically inclined I would find it a truer story than any I might have told about Donald Johnson's birthday party or the day my cousin Brenda put Kitty Litter in the aquarium.

2   So the point of my keeping a notebook has never been, nor is it now, to have an accurate factual record of what

I have been doing or thinking. That would be a different impulse entirely, an instinct for reality which I sometimes envy but do not possess. At no point have I ever been able successfully to keep a diary; my approach to daily life ranges from the grossly negligent to the merely absent, and on those few occasions when I have tried dutifully to record a day's events, boredom has so overcome me that the results are mysterious at best. What is this business about "shopping, typing piece, dinner with E, depressed"? Shopping for what? Typing what piece? Who is E? Was this "E" depressed, or was I depressed? Who cares?

In fact I have abandoned altogether that kind of pointless entry; instead I tell what some would call lies. "That's simply not true," the members of my family frequently tell me when they come up against my memory of a shared event. "The party was *not* for you, the spider was *not* a black widow, *it wasn't that way at all.*" Very likely they are right, for not only have I always had trouble distinguishing between what happened and what merely might have happened, but I remain unconvinced that the distinction, for my purposes, matters. The cracked crab that I recall having for lunch the day my father came home from Detroit in 1945 must certainly be embroidery, worked into the day's pattern to lend verisimilitude; I was ten years old and would not now remember the cracked crab. The day's events did not turn on cracked crab. And yet it is precisely that fictitious crab that makes me see the afternoon all over again, a home movie run all too often, the father bearing gifts, the child weeping, an exercise in family love and guilt. Or that is what it was to me. Similarly, perhaps it never did snow that August in Vermont; perhaps there never were flurries in the night wind, and maybe no one else felt the ground hardening and summer already dead even as we pretended to bask in it, but that was how it felt to me, and it might as well have snowed, could have snowed, did snow.

How it felt to me: that is getting closer to the truth about a notebook. I sometimes delude myself about why I keep a notebook, imagine that some thrifty virtue derives from preserving everything observed. See enough and write it down, I tell myself, and then some morning when the world seems drained of wonder, some day when I am only going through the motions of doing what I am supposed to do, which is write—on that bankrupt morning I will simply open my notebook and there it will all be, a forgotten account with accumulated interest, paid passage back to the world out there: dialogue overheard in hotels and elevators and at the hat-check counter in Pavillon (one middle-aged man shows his hat check to another and says, "That's my old football number"); impressions of Bettina Aptheker and Benjamin Sonnenberg and Teddy ("Mr. Acapulco") Stauffer; careful *aperçus* about tennis bums and failed fashion models and Greek shipping heiresses, one of whom taught me a significant lesson (a lesson I could have learned from F. Scott Fitzgerald, but perhaps we all must meet the very rich for ourselves) by asking, when I arrived to interview her in her orchid-filled sitting room on the second day of a paralyzing New York blizzard, whether it was snowing outside.

5   I imagine, in other words, that the notebook is about other people. But of course it is not. I have no real business with what one stranger said to another at the hat-check counter in Pavillon; in fact I suspect that the line "That's my old football number" touched not my own imagination at all, but merely some memory of something once read, probably "The Eighty-Yard Run." Nor is my concern with a woman in a dirty crepe-de-Chine wrapper in a Wilmington bar. My stake is always, of course, in the unmentioned girl in the plaid silk dress. *Remember what it was to be me:* that is always the point.

Writing

Now what will you make of all this observing once you have recorded it? How will it become something significant for others to read? This is where your individuality comes in again. Just as your observations are yours alone, for no two people look at things in quite the same way, your shaping of these observations into a piece of writing is also unique.

For most people, ideas emerge when relationships become apparent, when a thread of meaning links several observations. For instance, you notice a raccoon killed on the highway, and you think, "His instincts did not adapt him to be aware of speeding cars." At the library, you go through a door that swings open automatically, and you bump a small child who has wandered away from his parents. Suddenly you have a subject for an essay on the encroachment of mechanical devices into our everyday lives. Or you find that a small fishing village you love to visit has been invaded by too many tourists, too much traffic. The experience could generate an essay contrasting the "two faces" of the town, as it once was and as it now is; or your paper might analyze the effects of the tourists on the town's economy. Someone once said that "ideas go in pairs," and that should happen for you if you observe closely and think about your experiences.

Translating your observations into writing is largely a matter of making choices. The first choice, of course, is the decision about what to write. After that comes the choice of which details to include and which to leave out. You should choose only those materials that develop and keep the focus on your main point and purpose. But many other choices are also involved. Should your idea be expressed implicitly or explicitly? What inferences can you draw from what you have observed? Is there sufficient evidence to carry your judgments persuasively? Should you interpret facts or let them stand by themselves? These are some of the questions you must ask yourself prior to, during, and even after you write—and you must answer them to your and to your readers' satisfaction.

After deciding what to include and what to omit, you must decide on the form and style you want, and that takes practice. Most writers do not write a piece once;

they write and rewrite it several times. E. B. White (see p. 86) says, "A writer does a lot of work the reader isn't conscious of, and never gets any credit." Writing is work, and doing it well brings satisfaction. Henry David Thoreau comments on this third step in the process: "No day will have been wholly misspent, if one sincere, thoughtful page has been written."

Thoreau's work illustrates the transforming of observations recorded in a notebook into writing of lasting significance. Compare the following two excerpts, the first a journal entry for October 8, 1852, and the second a rewritten version of the same experience, taken from *Walden* (1854).

Henry David Thoreau

From the Journals

As I was paddling along the north shore, after having looked in vain over the pond for a loon, suddenly a loon, sailing toward the middle, a few rods in front, set up his wild laugh and betrayed himself. I pursued with a paddle and he dived, but when he came up I was nearer than before. He dived again, but I miscalculated the direction he would take, and we were fifty rods apart when he came up, and again he laughed long and loud. He managed very cunningly, and I could not get within half a dozen rods of him. Sometimes he would come up unexpectedly on the opposite side of me, as if he had passed directly under the boat. So long-winded was he, so unweariable, that he would immediately plunge again, and then no wit could divine where in the deep pond, beneath the smooth surface, he might be speeding his way like a fish, perchance passing under the boat. He had time and ability to visit the bottom of the pond in its deepest part. A newspaper authority says a fisherman—giving his name—has caught loon in Seneca Lake, N.Y., eighty feet beneath the surface, with hooks set for trout. Miss Cooper has said the same. Yet he appeared to know his course as surely under water as on the surface, and swam much faster there than he sailed on the surface. It was surprising how serenely he sailed off with unruffled bosom when he came to the surface. It was as well for me to rest on my oars and await his reappearing as to endeavor to calculate where he would come up. When I was straining my eyes over the surface, I would suddenly be startled by his unearthly laugh behind me. But why, after displaying so much cunning, did he betray himself the moment he came to the surface with that loud laugh? His white breast enough betrayed him. He was indeed a silly loon, I thought. Though he took all this pains to avoid me, he never failed to give notice of his whereabouts the moment he came to the surface. After an hour he seemed as fresh as ever, dived as willingly, and swam yet farther than at first. Once or twice I saw a ripple where he approached the surface, just put his head out to reconnoitre, and in-

1

stantly dived again. I could commonly hear the plash of the water when he came up, and so also detected him. It was commonly a demoniac laughter, yet somewhat like a water-bird, but occasionally, when he had balked me most successfully and come up a long way off, he uttered a long-drawn unearthly howl, probably more like a wolf than any other bird. This was his looning. As when a beast puts his muzzle to the ground and deliberately howls; perhaps the wildest sound I ever heard, making the woods ring; and I concluded that he laughed in derision of my efforts, confident of his own resources. Though the sky was overcast, the pond was so smooth that I could see where he broke the surface if I did not hear him. His white breast, the stillness of the air, the smoothness of the water, were all against [him]. At length, having come up fifty rods off, he uttered one of those prolonged unearthly howls, as if calling on the god of loons to aid him, and immediately there came a wind from the east and rippled the surface, and filled the whole air with misty rain. I was impressed as if it were the prayer of the loon and his god was angry with me. How surprised must be the fishes to see this ungainly visitant from another sphere speeding his way amid their schools!

2   I have never seen more than one at a time in our pond, and I believe that that is always a male.

Chasing a Loon

1   As I was paddling along the north shore one very calm October afternoon, for such days especially they settle on to the lakes, like the milkweed down, having looked in vain over the pond for a loon, suddenly one, sailing out from the shore toward the middle a few rods in front of me, set up his wild laugh and betrayed himself. I pursued with a paddle and he dived, but when he came up I was nearer than before. He dived again, but I miscalculated the direction he would take, and we were fifty rods apart when he came to the surface this time, for I had helped to widen the interval; and again he laughed long and loud, and with more reason than before. He manoeuvred so cunningly that I could not get within half a dozen rods of him. Each time, when he came to the surface, turning

his head this way and that, he coolly surveyed the water and the land, and apparently chose his course so that he might come up where there was the widest expanse of water and at the greatest distance from the boat. It was surprising how quickly he made up his mind and put his resolve into execution. He led me at once to the widest part of the pond, and could not be driven from it. While he was thinking one thing in his brain, I was endeavoring to divine his thought in mine. It was a pretty game, played on the smooth surface of the pond, a man against a loon. Suddenly your adversary's checker disappears beneath the board, and the problem is to place yours nearest to where his will appear again. Sometimes he would come up unexpectedly on the opposite side of me, having apparently passed directly under the boat. So long-winded was he and so unweariable, that when he had swum farthest he would immediately plunge again, nevertheless; and then no wit could divine where in the deep pond, beneath the smooth surface, he might be speeding his way like a fish, for he had time and ability to visit the bottom of the pond in its deepest part. It is said that loons have been caught in the New York lakes eighty feet beneath the surface, with hooks set for trout,—though Walden is deeper than that. How surprised must the fishes be to see this ungainly visitor from another sphere speeding his way amid their schools! Yet he appeared to know his course as surely under water as on the surface, and swam much faster there. Once or twice I saw a ripple where he approached the surface, just put his head out to reconnoitre, and instantly dived again. I found that it was as well for me to rest on my oars and wait his reappearing as to endeavor to calculate where he would rise; for again and again, when I was straining my eyes over the surface one way, I would suddenly be startled by his unearthly laugh behind me. But why, after displaying so much cunning, did he invariably betray himself the moment he came up by that loud laugh? Did not his white breast enough betray him? He was indeed a silly loon, I thought. I could commonly hear the plash of the water when he came up, and so also detected him. But after an hour he seemed as fresh as ever, dived as willingly and swam yet farther than at first. It was surprising to see how serenely he sailed off with unruffled breast when he came to the surface, doing all the work with his webbed feet beneath.

His usual note was this demoniac laughter, yet somewhat like that of a water-fowl; but occasionally, when he had balked me most successfully and come up a long way off, he uttered a long-drawn unearthly howl, probably more like that of a wolf than any bird; as when a beast puts his muzzle to the ground and deliberately howls. This was his looning—perhaps the wildest sound that is ever here, making the woods ring far and wide. I concluded that he laughed in derision of my efforts, confident of his own resources. Though the sky was by this time overcast, the pond was so smooth that I could see where he broke the surface when I did not hear him. His white breast, the stillness of the air, and the smoothness of the water were all against him. At length, having come up fifty rods off, he uttered one of those prolonged howls, as if calling on the god of loons to aid him, and immediately there came a wind from the east and rippled the surface, and filled the whole air with misty rain, and I was impressed as if it were the prayer of the loon answered, and his god was angry with me; and so I left him disappearing far away on the tumultuous surface.

2   For hours, in fall days, I watched the ducks cunningly tack and veer and hold the middle of the pond, far from the sportsman; tricks which they will have less need to practise in Louisiana bayous. When compelled to rise they would sometimes circle round and round and over the pond at a considerable height, from which they could easily see to other ponds and the river, like black motes in the sky; and, when I thought they had gone off thither long since, they would settle down by a slanting flight of a quarter of a mile on to a distant part which was left free; but what beside safety they got by sailing in the middle of Walden I do not know, unless they love its water for the same reason that I do.

2
Shaping Details:
Description

In her novel *Their Eyes Were Watching God,* Zora Neale Hurston describes a time when a group of her characters "sat around on the porch and passed around the pictures of their thoughts" for the others to see. How do you pass around the pictures of your thoughts? By describing, as specifically as you can, those people, places, things, and events that have become a part of your thought because they have been a part of your experience. Description is a part of conversation, and of almost all writing. It is a part of autobiography, and will be a part of the writing you do about yourself; it is a part of storytelling, whether the story is fictional or real. And, as you will discover from the essays in this section, it is a part of exposition, writing that explains an idea or opinion. Passages of description are found in almost all exposition, from a personal essay to a scientific explanation to an argument. The amount of description will vary. Some paragraphs and sections of essays may be purely descriptive, while in other cases description may be the primary method by which the writer conveys ideas.

Regardless of the amount of description in an essay, the writer attempts to make the reader see, feel, and hear by *showing* rather than by merely *telling.* It is through the use of specific detail and concrete language that abstract ideas and half-formed thoughts can become vividly real. By showing sense impressions and the thoughts these impressions evoke—by painting pictures in words—the writer can make a forceful comment about an experience or condition in life.

Description ranges from the *objective,* or scientific, to the *subjective,* or impressionistic. The former is factual writing in which the writer treats with detachment the subject being described. In the latter, the writer steps in not only to record observations but also to present and sometimes to comment upon the feelings and attitudes aroused by an experience or scene, showing the reader both what it was like and how the writer reacted to it. The word *ranges* is important here, since description can be more or less objective, more or less subjective.

The purpose of the objective description is different from that of the more subjective one. In a description of a solar power system for the home or in the description of the fish that Agassiz wanted to elicit from Samuel Scudder, the purpose is practical and scientific. In such cases, the describer makes an accurate record of the phenomena observed and the relationships between them. You can find many such descriptions in textbooks, in encyclopedias, in direction-giving manuals on a variety of subjects. At the other extreme, the purpose for a purely impressionistic description may be the recording of a mood or the creation of a picture whose significance you wish to share.

Most descriptive writing falls somewhere in between these two extremes. No matter where it falls, however, the qualities of good description remain the same. Effective description depends on close observation, the careful selection of details, and precise language with which to paint the picture, whether it be objective or subjective. Furthermore, through the careful arrangement of the details and language, the writer unifies the picture so that it projects a *dominant impression.*

Notice the rich details and language in this paragraph:

> The fading sunlight came through chinks in the pepper trees and fluttered about upon the hard-packed earth, like a covey of yellow evening birds. The houses, though small, and almost all alike, because they were company-owned, were neat and whitewashed. Their porches were filled with large potted plants growing in cheerful red Hills Brothers coffee cans, or with smaller potted plants in green Del Monte peach cans. In some of the houses, the shades were drawn, for here people worked on shifts and one man's night might be his neighbor's day. A picket fence, also whitewashed, ran the length of the street, and each man had a private gate to his yard, weighted in such a manner with old springs and defunct batteries that it swung shut of itself and he need never give a thought to its closing. From under the pepper trees, the derricks were out of sight. It was only

the smell of oil—which was taste as much as smell—the sight of an occasional sump hole at the end of a side street, and the sound of the pumps that reminded Cress where she was. The sound of the pumps filled the air, deep, rhythmical, as if the hills themselves breathed; or as if deep in the wells some kind of heart shook the earth with so strong a beat that Cress could feel it in the soles of her feet as she walked along.—Jessamyn West, *Cress Delahanty*

The author herself never intrudes, never speaks as "I." Yet she is there, selecting and arranging to produce a vivid impression of a small California oil town. She places the plants not just in "flower pots" or "coffee cans" but in "cheerful red Hills Brothers cans" and "green Del Monte peach cans." She re-creates the sensory experience of the "smell of oil" and the "sound of the pumps," which "Cress could feel . . . in the soles of her feet." Such sharp details, concrete words, and language that conveys vivid sense impressions are all marks of good descriptive writing.

West's paragraph is also planned to give a sense of movement—the reader moves along the streets of the town, past the houses, gradually becoming aware of the constant rhythm of the oil pumps. The arrangement of the paragraph is spatial, but other paragraphs of description may move from a general impression to the supporting details, or from the details to a general impression, stated or implied. Note the movement in this paragraph from the author's description of his boyhood:

The kitchen was the great machine that set our lives running; it whirred down a little only on Saturdays and holy days. From my mother's kitchen I gained my first picture of life as a white, overheated, starkly lit workshop redolent with Jewish cooking, crowded with women in housedresses, strewn with fashion magazines, patterns, dress material, spools of thread—and at whose center, so lashed to her machine that bolts of energy seemed to dance out of her hands and feet as she worked, my mother stamped the treadle hard against the floor, hard, hard, and silently, grimly at war, beat out the first rhythm of the world for me.—Alfred Kazin, *A Walker in the City*

Both the choice and arrangement of details in description depend largely on the writer's point of view. Some description is clearly written from a physical point of view—from a single place of observation: an open window facing out on a noisy and crowded city street, a cliff overlooking an ocean, for example. The physical point of view can shift, especially in description that involves the passing of time. When this occurs, the writer must provide clear signals to indicate that time is passing. In other cases, however, the point of view is mental rather than physical. Here the writer not only presents details impressionistically, he also describes his reactions to and feelings about the scene. The paragraph by Kazin provides a good example of this kind of point of view.

Like the point of view, the language of description can vary; but it should be chosen for the exactness of both *denotation* (the literal meaning of a word) and *connotation* (the emotional overtones and shades of meaning of a word). West's reference to "red Hills Brothers coffee cans" is literal—denotative; but she uses the connotative word *cheerful* to lend an added meaning to the phrase. A great deal of descriptive language may involve *metaphors,* which are figures of speech that imply comparisons between apparently unlike things. When Kazin calls the kitchen a "machine that set our lives running," and when he says that his mother's "bolts of energy seemed to dance out of her hands and feet," he is using metaphors to make the reader see what the scene and the activity were like.

All these devices are used by writers to lend variety, power, and color to their descriptions. The essays in this section exemplify these and other techniques for passing around the pictures of your thoughts.

John J. Rowlands

John J. Rowlands (b. 1892), son of a Canadian lumberman, began his close observations of nature as a gold prospector in upper Ontario and Quebec at the age of eighteen. After working for the United Press as a reporter and eventually as manager of its Boston office, he became Director of News Services for the Massachusetts Institute of Technology. He now lives in Cohasset, Massachusetts. Rowlands has recorded his observations of nature in two ways: with words and with camera. His book *Cache Lake Country* (1947) is based on his travels in the trackless forests of northern Canada, a region that he has photographed extensively. In the following selection from *Spindrift* (1960), subtitled "From a House by the Sea," he vividly re-creates pictures with words.

Lonely Place

There are many kinds and varying degrees of loneliness, but the peculiar loneliness of a once-teeming place deserted and for the time forgotten can be found only in a seaside amusement resort on a cloudy Sunday afternoon in winter. Nothing but the warming sun of another spring can dispel the all-pervading sense of abandonment and desolation.

1
Generalization about loneliness, followed by an immediate focus on the amusement park (par. 1)

Crowded with strollers on summer evenings, the broad promenade that fronts the gaudy palaces in the World of Fun and Frivolity is deserted, and dirty drifted snow lies in the sheltered niches. Across the boulevard where a milk truck scurries to more lucrative fields lies the sea and miles of empty beach on which thousands come to bask and bathe in summer. The empty life-guard towers look out to sea; their boats are gone; no human being in sight. The wind and the waves alone are moving and the only sound is the sea.

2
General impression of the area (par. 2)

The merry-go-rounds are boarded up for winter, but in a shed the saddled animals, running lions and tigers, leaping deer, prancing ponies, a sedate goat, and one giraffe, are huddled close together as if for companionship

3
Initial block of specific details: the closed attractions (pars. 3–8)

---

and warmth. Just along the walk the cavernous mouth of the Tunnel of Love is closed, and the echoes of summer squeals of adventure within have long since died away.

4   The serpentine skeleton of "The Longest, Fastest, Steepest, Most Thrilling Roller Coaster on Earth" stands black against the winter sky, its cars in canvas shrouds below. Gone is the roar and the clatter of flying wheels and the screams of clinging riders.

5   A faded poster of a sinuous dancer, with its bold promise of exotic sights within, flaps in the wind, and next door shutters hide the counter of the ring-tossing game with its prizes of paunchy pandas, garish dolls, and slender canes. And the dodger who sticks his head through a canvas curtain to taunt his customers to hit him will not be heard again until the sun is high and warm.

6   The season is closed in the shooting gallery and some of the ducks on their endless belt, a deer, and a white rabbit still lie where they fell to the midnight shots on Labor Day night.

7   Through the grimy window of the saltwater taffy counter you see the cold steel arms of the taffy puller motionless and empty-handed. Somehow that brings back memories of the prickly feeling of spun sugar on the tongue. Then suddenly for a moment—or is it just the wind?—you hear the voice of a barker calling "Hurr-ree-ee, hurr-ree-ee, hurr-ree-ee, folks! See the harem girls in the Dance of Love! Strictly for adults only." But the platform with its gaudy backdrop from which he always makes his pitch is gone. Just the wind.

8   A sign painter's portrait of The Fattest Women in the Universe, a monstrosity on a stool, is all but obliterated by the wind and flying sand. Her hair is thin and her face is pale, but the smile still shows.

9   Beyond the boulevard near the long white bathhouse the bandstand is filled with drifted snow and flying rubbish, but the winds have

Area of description is widened (pars. 9–10)

swept the open places clean. The stark white guide-lines on the empty parking lot lie row on slanting row like the bleaching bones of huge fish.

Further along where the great ferris wheel stands with its seats swathed in canvas, a sign recalls the delights of fried clams, but now the vats are dry and the corn-meal bin is empty. The gray thing that scurries under the counter is just a rat.

10

Although it is near the freezing mark and the wind is rising you remember the cold satisfaction of frozen custard, "The Kind Your Mother Used To Make." And so it was, but the shop is dark and gloomy now. Gone are the smells of hot dogs, onions and hamburgers, frying fish and chips, hot popcorn and freshly roasted peanuts; and gone, too, the stench of hot exhaust gases from the cars that crawl through shimmering heat-waves on the boulevard.

11
Recollection of past odors (par. 11)

Here in the shadows of the deserted buildings of The World of Fun and Frivolity lurks a kind of loneliness found nowhere else, the solitude of sounds of life replaced by silence. Back from an August night comes the carefree tinny music of the merry-go-rounds and the chain songs from jukeboxes in the snack bars, and through it all the persistent and persuasive voices of the barkers. You hear again the cries of children weary and bewildered, the irresponsible laughter of men and their girls, and the sharp crack of rifles in the shooting-gallery. Now only the yowling of a cat and the roar of the sea are real.

12
Recollection of past sounds (par. 12)

High across the front of the buildings neon tubing that glows so warmly on a summer night is a cold and glassy maze, hiding the patterns of signs that can't be read until they glow again.

13
Recollection of past sights (pars. 13–14)

The steamboat pier, a stubby finger pointing across the bay toward the city, is fenced off and posted with "No Trespassing" warnings. No sign now of the silent old men who fish

14

from the cap-log all day long in summer. The blast of the steamer's midnight whistle, warning of the last trip back, is just another echo.

15

Contrasting pictures of open hot-dog stand and closed stands (pars. 15–16)

The wind is coming from the sea again and the drifting sand grits under your feet like sugar on a kitchen floor. It's cold and damp. Far ahead you glimpse a spot of neon-red. Its message when you reach it is "Hot Dogs." The tired-looking man nursing three weary-looking wieners on a hot plate slides up the window of his slot-in-the-wall booth. "No fish and chips this time of year," he tells you, "just dogs. Just dogs and piccalilli. No mustard."

16

The pizza-pie parlor just ahead is closed, of course, and there's nothing very hopeful in the next sign that offers a full-course shore dinner, "Chowder, clams and lobster, ice cream and watermelon" for two dollars. The place where creamy root beer once flowed from a huge cask with polished hoops has been replaced by an orange-drink fountain, but the big round globe is empty.

17

Conclusion: the only sign of life is an occasion for self-questioning (par. 17)

The day is getting close to darkness and the only other sign of life lies behind the headlights of a prowl car that slows down close to the curb to look you over. And with good reason. Why should anyone choose to walk The World of Fun and Frivolity on a Sunday afternoon in winter?

Discussing Content and Form

1. Point out specific details in the essay that are particularly successful in creating an atmosphere of loneliness.

2. How much of the description depends on the contrast of the winter scene to the memories of summer?

3. The number and the kind of details a writer of description gives help create the effect. How many closed attractions does Rowlands mention in paragraphs 3–8? Do you think he could achieve the same effect with fewer details? Why or why not?

4. Rowlands never appears in the description as "I," yet it is obvious that he is the observer and recorder of the entire scene. Why do you think he chose not to write in the first person? Who is the "you" referred to in paragraph 7 and in several paragraphs following that?

5. Even though the writer does not explicitly state that "I felt this way" or "I thought that way," he interprets the scene by selecting those details he wishes to include. Explain how this selection becomes a form of interpretation in the essay.

Considering Special Techniques

1. A writer usually organizes a piece of description to give it a feeling of movement, thus guiding the reader through a scene (or around an object) with some sense of order. Sometimes it seems the writer is actually pointing to the things the reader should notice. Using the marginal guides, trace the movement of the walker around the amusement park. What groupings and connections do you find among the details, even those within paragraphs?

2. Good description relies heavily upon sense impressions: seeing, hearing, tasting, touching, smelling. Writers try to convey what they sense in a way that will in turn awaken their readers' senses. In this essay, find examples of words and details that evoke each of the senses. Does one sense seem dominant? If so, which? Why is the park a particularly good subject for using a variety of sense impressions?

3. Rowlands' essay is characterized by many adjectives: "empty life-guard towers" *(par. 2);* "serpentine *skeleton" (par. 4);* "faded poster of a *sinuous* dancer" *(par. 5). What is the effect of the multiplicity of such words? Do you occasionally find the use of these adjectives repetitious? Explain.*

4. What is the effect of these concluding sentences from several of the paragraphs? Why are they placed as they are?
"The stark white guide-lines on the empty parking lot lie row on slanting row like the bleaching bones of huge fish" (par. 9).
"The gray thing that scurries under the counter is just a rat" (par. 10).
"Now only the yowling of a cat and the roar of the sea are real" (par. 12).

5. Words to learn and use: pervading *(par. 1);* sedate, cavernous *(par. 3);* sinuous *(par. 5);* swathed *(par. 10).*

Generating Ideas

1. Describe an amusement part or resort area as it is during the peak season. Try to evoke the various senses by using vivid details and sensory language.

2. Describe a type of amusement or attraction with which you are familiar.

3. Describe some of the people who operate rides, stands, and various sideshows in an amusement park or at a circus. Try to give details that capture not only their appearance but also their way of living.

4. If you have ever visited a national park or state park in the off-season, or if you have seen some resort area when few people were present, write a paper in which your choice of details is influenced by your feelings (loneliness, contentment, sadness, etc.) about the place.

5. Write a paper describing your school when most of the students have left it, either late at night or during a vacation break. If you can, include some details that show the contrasts between the quiet time and the busy one: "There are no empty soft-drink bottles and discarded coffee cups around the dark and silent vending machines." If you have never seen the campus during such a time, you might write from imagination.

Jamaica Kincaid

Jamaica Kincaid (b. 1949) is a native of St. Johns, Antigua, in the West Indies, where she attended the Princess Margaret School. Since 1974, she has been a reporter for the *New Yorker*'s "Talk of the Town," a regular feature that over the years has contained the work of several writers represented in this book, including Brendan Gill, E. B. White, and James Thurber. In the following selection from "Talk of the Town," Kincaid paints a vivid portrait of her subject with many well-chosen and specific details.

Junior Miss

Every year, fifty high-school seniors, representing our fifty states, compete in a televised national Junior Miss contest, sponsored by Eastman Kodak, Kraft Foods, and Breck Shampoo. The winner, America's Junior Miss, receives a ten-thousand-dollar scholarship to the college of her choice. Two days before New York's Junior Miss, Dawn Fotopulos, of Queens, was scheduled to go to Mobile, Alabama, to compete in the Junior Miss finals, she came over to Manhattan, accompanied by her mother, Mrs. William Fotopulos, and had her picture taken by the *News,* had a long lunch at the St. Regis, and was interviewed on three radio talk shows. When we first saw Miss Fotopulos, who is just under eighteen, she was standing near a rack of clothes in a shop on East Fifty-third Street, obliging the *News* photographer with the many poses he wanted her to assume. She was wearing a green blazer, green-and-white patterned wool slacks, and a white blouse. She has blue eyes, ruddy cheeks, and long light-brown hair that flips up around her shoulders. Except for a trace of mascara, lip gloss, and blue eye shadow, she wore no makeup, and except for a small pair of pearl earrings she wore no jewelry. After taking the shots in the store, the photographer told Miss Fotopulos that he wanted some shots of her walking down Fifth Avenue. On Fifth Avenue, he stood her a few yards in front of him and told her to walk toward him now—first slowly, then fast, then slowly again. He sat her on one of the large planters that line the Avenue, tilted her head forward, and told her to stay in that position. He told her to gaze into a shopwindow displaying an assortment of women's shoes. He told her to gaze into another shopwindow, which had an assortment of women's sports clothes. Altogether, the photographer took thirty-six pictures of Miss Fotopulos, and for every single one of them she smiled.

2   At lunch at the St. Regis, Miss Fotopulos had roast beef, lyonnaise potatoes, salad with French dressing, a glass of milk, and fruit cup. She said that she had never before been in a place like the St. Regis, or had lyonnaise potatoes. She said, "I feel it's a dream. I feel I'm Cinderella or something. All this special treatment. Everybody has been treating me as if I were something special. It's so much fun. When I entered this contest, I had no idea all this would happen. I found out about the contest in *Seventeen,* and I wrote away for the forms. I thought I wouldn't win, because I didn't have a local sponsor. I was a candidate at large. But this is not like a beauty contest. You don't have to wear a bathing suit. It mostly has to do with scholarship and poise and grace. I have a ninety-five-point-six average. I want to study medicine, and the money that I have already won will help me to do that."

3   Mrs. Fotopulos showed us a picture of her daughter wearing a long white sleeveless gown and carrying a bouquet of roses as she walked down a runway at the New York State contest, held in Syracuse, in February. Mrs. Fotopulos said, "She's made us so proud of her. You know, she has received a letter of congratulations from our state senator, and Governor George Wallace has sent her a letter welcoming her to the State of Alabama."

4   At the radio talk show we sat in on, the hostess told her the theme of the day: "Whether Our Idea of Mr. Right Has Changed or Not." She asked Miss Fotopulos questions like "Do you cook?" (Miss Fotopulos said yes), "Do you believe in Mr. Right?" (Miss Fotopulos said she thought that that might be a possibility), "Do you know who Bess Myerson is?" (Miss Fotopulos identified her as Miss America of 1945), "Do you have a pair of white gloves?" (Well, I have to, because of the pageant"), and "Have you ever been to a prom?" (Miss Fotopulos said she hadn't).

5   Then the hostess asked Miss Fotopulos, "How do you feel about kissing?"

6   When Miss Fotopulos didn't reply immediately, the hostess said, "You're representing New York State and you don't have a stand on kissing?"

"Well, that's kind of unfair," Miss Fotopulos said. "I ⁷ would never ask *you* how *you* feel about kissing."

Discussing Content and Form

1. What overall impression of the life of a Junior Miss do you get from paragraph 1? Which details give this impression?

2. Consider Kincaid's selection of details to describe the Junior Miss.
a. How would you characterize the girl from the details of her appearance in paragraph 1?
b. What does paragraph 2 add to your impressions of her as a person?
c. What impressions do you have of the mother from the details in paragraph 3?

3. The last paragraphs (4–7) outline the questions asked the Miss Fotopulos on a radio talk show.
a. What impression do you have of the line of questioning? How do the questions serve to comment upon contests of the Junior Miss type? What do they reveal about talk-show interviewers? About the type of audience?
b. Explain your reaction to the answers the girl gives. In what ways are these answers consistent with her appearance and behavior?

4. What does the writer think about both the contest and Miss Fotopulos? Explain your answer by referring to clues (or lack of them) in the selection.

Considering Special Techniques

1. In describing people, places, and events, a writer often leaves the generalizing to the reader. If the descriptions are concrete and vivid, the reader can usually infer accurate generalizations about the scene being presented.
a. Explain why "Junior Miss" does not contain any topic sentences, the traditional generalizing sentences around which details of paragraphs are often drawn.
b. Since Kincaid does not use generalizations, how does the piece achieve coherence and movement?

2. Examine the way in which Kincaid manages to convey the impression of all thirty-six of the photographer's shots without actually describing each one (par. 1).
a. Note the repetition of the patterns of the sentences that describe the actions of the photographer:

"On Fifth Avenue, he stood her . . . ."
"He sat her on . . . ."
"He told her to gaze . . . ."
"He told her to gaze into another . . . ."
What effect does the writer achieve through the use of such
repetition?

b.   Look even more closely at one of these sentences: "He sat
her on one . . . tilted her head . . . and told her . . . ." Here,
the accumulation of verbs contributes to the picture. What
effect does this accumulation convey?

3.   Find details that emphasize the impression that Miss Fotopulos is a "Cinderella" figure as she says. Discuss how the details
create one impression of the girl but another of the contest itself.

Generating Ideas

1.   You have probably attended or seen on television several
contests of the Junior Miss variety. Take any stand you wish
and explain why you approve or disapprove of such events.
Then write a description of one of them, giving your impressions by selecting details from your observation. After you have
written the two papers, write a paragraph summarizing the
differences between the two types of writing.

2.   Kincaid describes Miss Fotopulos' physical appearance,
clothing, makeup, behavior, and conversation. Create a "portrait in words" of someone you know, using as many of these
types of details as seem fitting.

3.   In a biographical or fictional work that you have read recently, examine one or more of the passages that give an impression of a person or a character. Write an analysis of the methods
used by the writer, paying particular attention to both the
amount and kinds of details.

4.   Select a famous portrait—one in a gallery or from a
collection of great paintings or photographs—as a model for a
verbal picture. (You might use a collection such as Edward
Steichen's Family of Man as a source.) What can you tell from
the picture about the personality or character of the person?
What do you think the person might say if he could talk about
himself?

5.   Choose some famous person, living or dead, whom you would
particularly like to know. Imagining that you and your "friend"
could meet, write a descriptive sketch about the meeting.

Josephine W. Johnson

Josephine W. Johnson (b. 1910) is a novelist, short-story writer, poet, and essayist. Very early in her career (1935) she won a Pulitzer Prize for her novel *Now in November,* a vividly realistic story of a Missouri farm family struggling for survival during the Depression. Her other works include *Winter Orchard and Other Stories* (1935), *Jordanstown* (1937), *Paulina: The Story of an Apple-Butter Jar* (1939), *Wildwood* (1946), *The Dark Traveler* (1963), *The Sorcerer's Son and Other Stories* (1965), and *Circle of Seasons* (1974). Her collections of poetry are *Unwilling Gypsy* (1936) and *Year's End* (1937). *The Inland Island* (1969), from which the following sketch comes, is a collection of personal essays that comment on natural and human change as Johnson observes it through the year on a southern Ohio farm.

April

In two days the great forsythia cage, a vast mound of green wickets hung sparsely with yellow bells of flowers, the first leaves fine as a mist, has become a wild monster. Hairy, green, bushy, green-toothed and horned. 1

The birds no longer perch forming delicate Japanese paintings of the old school. They disappear. Who knows what goes on inside, now. 2

A great hare, dark and slow, huge as a domestic rabbit gone wild, lumbers out. We do not have many rabbits. Wild housecats have taken toll. One morning long ago the black wild Persian stalked beneath a bush. He moved around the house, and five minutes later the yard was strewn with limp brown bodies. Wantonly destroyed, as only one was eaten. 3

April is an assault. Too much. Too much of everything. It begins with the toothwort, a modest flower related to the turnip. There is not much to say about it except that it is pretty and uninteresting and first. Like most wild flowers, if picked and brought inside, it droops and has a weedy negligible look, reminiscent of one's own thoughts, which seem fresh, honest, sparkling, rare, when rooted still in the cool brain cave, but in the open air, picked and presented, tend to appear dusty and weak, irrelevant to the human condition of flesh, brass, and blood. 4

5   The hillside near the creek is covered with hepatica,
a lovely flower. Hepatica, meaning the liver, is an ugly
name. The shape of the leaves does not resemble the liver
at all. (What doctor finding a mass of flesh shaped like
these leaves within the human would know what to do?
What is this? These lovely green leaves? There is no liver
here.)

6   The hillside is held up by clumps of flowers on hairy
stems. The petals lavender and white and pink and purple
and sometimes a rare, pale blue. The same spot of earth,
riddled with moss, snail shells, ferns, oak leaves, produces
this pale rainbow. They last very little longer than a rainbow, and, returning in a day or two, one finds no flowers,
only hard green pods and a crop of odd-cut leaves.

7   These spring pools of flowers, rising year after year in
the same place, are a recurring joy that never fails. It is
one of the joys of living for years in the same place. This
is not limited to wild land, nor to large places, but few
stay long enough even on one small spot, or care enough
to plant the reoccurring seed and know this seasonal
miracle.

8   In the north pasture, the title "pasture" by courtesy only
now, a pool of mint rises each spring, a lavender pond
filled with bees, great bumblebees, small yellow bees, and
the brown furry bees like winged mice. It is filled with
the humming of the bees and the spicy smell of the mint
leaves (leaves rich, green, convoluted as seashells) and
the pool widens into a wider pool of white pansy violets,
like a foam at the far edges. The wild pansies are separate
and move in the wind.

9   This is the view from the woodchuck's den above the
draw. His porch is well beaten down, paths lead to it under
the raspberry hoops. Wrens sputter around on the ravine
rocks and broken crockery from the old rabbit hutches.
All this view is probably wasted on his stupid dogginess.
Unless, like Pythagoras [1], he thinks of the violet leaves
as spinach. The morning sun warms his front porch, the
mists over the cool stones withdraw. I think of him coming
out and contemplating this fresh April world, the smell
of broken mint, the violets moving in the morning breeze,
the trilling sounds of wrens before the day has brought

---

[1] Greek philosopher of the sixth century B.C.; although little is known about him,
many tales are told of his supernatural powers.

their spirits down. But in good truth he is not emerging that early, and if it is a cold day, he is not emerging at all. He is concerned about mating, if he is through hibernating, and thereafter (four weeks to be exact) the mate has two to eight blind, hairless young.

It was time for the fat old lady to leave in late March. Holing up with any of the creatures has about lost its charm by then. The smell of woodchuck holes on warm days drives out our old dream of dozing through winter in dark woodchuck dens.   10

An intermittent rain this morning, now ceasing. The quail are very shrill. Soggy but nervous. The woods are still bare except for the thousand limp umbrellas of the buckeyes—a low border holding up the hill. Spent time yesterday winding up the tents of caterpillars, shoving the flabby silk masses down in the earth. They squash green. Hateful. Hateful. Slashed at briars. An enormous ache in my head. A rage against my limitations.   11

This delicate shaking carpet of wild flowers! Ferns, violets, squirrel corn, bluebells, spring beauties, bloodroot leaves, wild poppies. All at once and together. And above the red trillium the red lilies of the papaws.   12

Goldfinches arrived. A mad twittering like a zoo full of canaries. Invisible. Finally saw a goldfinch separate from the gold-green tassels of the ash, the gold-green bunchy leaves. Finches seem paler close to the eye.   13

Rain and thunder this morning. Wish it would wash all the damn caterpillars away. They unwind in reels before my eyeballs at night. They look like phlegm on the trunks of the trees, clothing the branches. The very clouds look like their tents.   14

Now the sun has come out on a wet wash. The dogwood blossoms in the draw are dazzling. One drop of rain blazes up. The doves start their depressing cooing. What is the bird that keeps crying "Zooder-zeeee"? A whippoorwill last night was almost raging. Those cool, fierce calls!   15

The buckeye has yellow pyramids . . . thatches . . . stacks. The Ohio buckeye is *Aesculus glabra.* The extract from its bark will irritate the cerebro-spinal system of humans. (To what purpose and what end?) Its pollination is by bees. The horse chestnut is *Aesculus hippocastanum.* Alcohol from seeds is made, or can be made. The whole vegetative world is full of stuff like that. Poisons galore.   16

17   Tried to clear a path to the last great oak through the interlocking fiendishness of rusting barbed-wire fence and wood soft as cardboard. Roots of Virginia creeper vines booby-trapped the path. Old rotting tree held the old rotting fence in place. Put down the wire clippers. Came back and it had black walnut in its jaws—foraging in my absence.

18   This curious passion to tidy, tidy, tidy, tidy—lives . . . leaves . . . trees . . . emotions . . . house . . . surface . . . weeds . . . lawns . . . minds . . . words . . . endless sweeping, clipping, washing, arranging.

19   Lachesis,[2] the measurer, was young once, a terrible young woman.

20   The worms are unspeakable today.

21   What is the composition of this delicate shaking carpet of flowers, this blanket which the old king will tear away? Squirrel corn, like bleeding hearts, but waxy, white-grey-bluish; leaves fine-cut as ferns. The honey-and-hyacinth fragrance lifts the heart. The windflower, the anemone, the wind that opens the petals, blows the petals away. The yellow wild poppy bursting from its prickly buds; the shaking bells of the Greek valerian, the bluebells. Lavender in our woods, delicate and deceptive, from *valere,* to be strong and powerful. And from its roots a drug, calming and carminative, also having tonic properties. Yellow trout lilies, white lilies, purple violets, yellow violets, white violets, and everywhere the red trillium. *Trillium sessile* and *erectum*—also known as wake-robin, toadshade, birthwort, squawroot and stinking Benjamin (and for good reason, as one knows who hunts a dead mouse or a nasty fungus smell and finds no source except this innocent and brick-red flower).

22   In the open fields the rich, edible leaves of winter cress, mustard or yellow rocket, *Barbarea vulgaris.* They are to be eaten on St. Barbara's day, in December, when tender, but the bitterness is too strong for most persons. Green satin shining leaves named after an early saint, "murdered by her pagan father for becoming Christian." She's turned the tables now. My bitterness is too strong for most persons. . . .

---

[2] One of the three Fates in Greek mythology, she measured the span of life and presided over the future.

Discussing Content and Form

1. What is Johnson's reaction to the coming of spring? Explain your answer.

2. In what sense is April (at least in a region of seasonal changes) "an assault" (par. 4)? Which details convey the impression of an assault?

3. How do the following passages convey the feeling of sadness that sometimes accompanies the appreciation of beauty?
a. "if picked and brought inside, it [the toothwort] droops and has a weedy negligible look, reminiscent of one's own thoughts . . . ." (par. 4)
b. "few stay long enough even on one small spot, or care enough to plant the reoccurring seed and know this seasonal miracle." (par. 7)

4. How does the "curious passion to tidy" (par. 18) relate to the coming of spring?

5. This selection is from a book which is an almanac of sorts, a personal reflection upon the changing seasons. You may notice that Johnson is not strict about keeping one kind of detail (flowers, plants, animal life, etc.) together in a single paragraph. Rather she organizes her impressions in a fashion that is almost random. Why does Johnson mix the kinds of details rather than treat all one type before turning to another? How does the lack of strict organization contribute to the effect of a personal observation?

Considering Special Techniques

1. Johnson's description abounds in metaphor—*saying one thing in terms of another, implying a comparison between two things that are actually unlike. Discuss the effectiveness of the following metaphors in particular, and examine any others you find.*
"forsythia cage" (par. 1)
"birds . . . perch forming delicate Japanese paintings" (par. 2)
"spring pools of flowers" (par. 7)
"limp umbrellas of the buckeyes" (par. 11)
"sun has come out on a wet wash" (par. 15)
Closely related to metaphor is simile—*the explicit statement of likeness between two unlike things, using* like *or* as *to make the comparison. In Johnson's essay, "they [caterpillars] look like phlegm on the trunks of trees" (par. 14) and "wood soft as card-*

board" *(par. 17)* are similes. Discuss the effectiveness of these, and examine any others you find.

2. *Johnson also relies heavily on the use of* images—*words and phrases that convey sense impressions. Here is an example of each type of image:*
Sight: *"green wickets" (par. 1)*
Sound: *"trilling sound of wrens" (par. 9)*
Touch: *"they squash green" (par. 11)*
Smell: *"spicy . . . mint leaves" (par. 3)*
Taste: *"edible leaves of winter cress" (par. 22)*
Find images that fuse two or more senses. For instance, what senses are involved in "The smell of woodchuck holes on warm days drives out our old dream of dozing through winter in dark woodchuck dens" (par. 10)?

3. *What is the effect of giving the botanical names for some of the flowers? Consider how the use of these names affects you as a reader and what it reveals about the writer.*

4. *Study the use Johnson makes of sentence fragments:*
"Too much. Too much of everything." (par. 4)
"Hateful. Hateful. Slashed at briars." (par. 11)
"Rain and thunder this morning." (par. 14)
"Poisons galore." (par. 16)
Relate the use of sentence fragments to the idea that April is "an assault." Why is this technique appropriate in description, whereas it might not be in analytical exposition?

5. *Words to learn and use:* sparsely *(par. 1);* wantonly *(par. 3);* negligible, reminiscent *(par. 4);* convoluted *(par. 8);* phlegm *(par. 14);* pollination, vegetative *(par. 16);* fiendishness, foraging *(par. 17);* carminative, fungus *(par. 21).*

Generating Ideas

1. *Many writers have described seasons, months, or shorter periods of the year in order to make a thoughtful or philosophical statement. The columnist L. E. Sissman describes November as "the unsung month," a pause between autumn and winter that "confers perspective on the more distant past and hence on the present and future." You are probably familiar with various reactions to the seasons: "I like spring—it gives a sense of starting over"; or "The world is most beautiful in autumn just before everything dies." Choose a month or season to describe. Use specific, vivid details to lead to a statement about the meaning of the time for you or for people in general.*

2. *If you have gardened or if you have an interest in plants, try one of these topics:*

a. *In paragraph 20, Johnson says that the "worms are unspeakable today." Develop a paper about the pests that must be dealt with by gardeners.*

b. *Obtain copies of a seed catalog, or of a magazine such as* Better Homes and Gardens, Sunset, *etc., which offers suggestions for planting and maintaining gardens. Write a paper describing an outdoor setting you would like to create. Make your writing as objective as you can, using botanical names for the plants, for example.*

3. *Observe the activities of an animal (either domesticated or wild) or of a bird for about a half hour. Write a paper describing exactly what the object of your observation did—how it moved, played, ate, slept, etc.*

4. *People often develop strong attachments to the land or to a particular area in which they have lived or which they have visited. If you have felt this strong pull, write an essay describing the area and the attraction it has for you.*

5. *Use paragraph 18 concerning the urge to "tidy, tidy, tidy" as the basis for a paper about compulsive housekeeping or lawn maintenance. Or write about "tidying" such things as lives, emotions, and minds.*

Brendan Gill

Brendan Gill (b. 1914) is a novelist, playwright, poet, and biographer. A regular contributor to the *New Yorker* since 1936, he was its film critic from 1961 to 1967 and has been theater critic since 1968. Among his publications are *The Trouble of One House* (1950), for which he won a National Book Award, *The Day the Money Stopped* (1957), *A Book of Cole Porter Lyrics and Memorabilia* (1971), *Tallulah* (1972), *The Malcontents* (1973), and *Ways of Loving: Two Novellas and Eighteen Stories* (1974). He lives in New York City and Connecticut.

With Gill's volume of memoirs entitled *Here at the New Yorker* (1975), he joins such writers as James Thurber and E. B. White in chronicling the history and the colorful personalities involved in the publication of the *New Yorker*. In "Disorder at the *New Yorker*" (editor's title), Gill gives a description of physical surroundings that are quite out of keeping with the sophisticated appearance of the magazine itself.

Disorder at the *New Yorker*

1   When I came to work for the *New Yorker,* I was assigned to a nasty, interior cell, just big enough to contain a desk, a chair, a wooden hatrack, and me. For some reason, the hatrack was in excellent condition, but the desk and chair were barbarously scarred and battered and, in the case of the chair, unsafe; one of its legs had worked loose in its socket and had been wired, not by an expert craftsman, to the other three legs, in an intricate but insecure arrangement of picture wire and twisted coat hangers. When one sat in the chair, it listed sharply to the left and gave off a loud singing sound. Plainly, the furniture had been bought at second hand, for, hard as reporters notoriously are on the tools of their trade, the furnishings of my cell would scarcely have reached such a state of decrepitude in the twelve or thirteen years since the magazine had been founded. If it was wonderful that these articles could already have been so ruinous, what is even more wonderful is that many of them are still in use today. They are disgusting and immortal, and, observing them as I write these words, I cannot fail to have mixed feelings at the thought of their so easily outlasting me.

2   The typewriter I was given bore a notable accumulation of coffee, grease, and other stains. I had the uneasy feeling

that some invisible germ of life was in culture deep inside the machine, as if in a dish of agar-agar in some secret laboratory of the permanently soiled. Here and there, the lacquer of the typewriter had been eaten through to the bare metal by cigarettes left burning upon it, and one of my predecessors had laboriously etched out, perhaps with a paper clip, the initial letter of the typewriter's name; it was no longer "ROYAL" but "OYAL," and I could feel the loss. Another and more ominous oddity was that when one typed an "s," it invariably came out a "w." Thiw led to wingular effectw on my prowe. And these effects were all the more painful to me because I was by nature the neatest of typists. Moreover, as a beginner on the staff I was especially eager to create a favorable impression by handing in faultlessly typed copy. It turned out that if my typewriter had allowed me to do so, it would have been a waste of time; indeed, it might have been considered a black mark against me, because nearly everyone on the magazine took pride in following Ross's bent and typing as badly as possible, editing in the typewriter by hunt and peck as I was later to hear of young moviemakers editing in the camera. Ross's fiercely X'd out passages were the manifestations of canny second thoughts, contradictions introduced and then cancelled, gropings in the name of his sacred rubric "Nothing is indescribable."

The only attractive equipment supplied to me was the 3 copy paper. It was cheap and soft to the touch and it came in a cheerful shade of lemony yellow. We used only that yellow paper in the office until, just over ten years ago, the day came when copy was transmitted to the printer not by messengers but by closed-circuit TV; our new gadgetry required us to adopt a white paper of greater weight than the old, smoother and somehow less willing to accept the benefaction of the word.

My cell was a far cry from the conventional good taste 4 of the study at Old Toll Gate Farm, with its Alken prints and shining brass on the hearth and the bookshelves full of first editions of Henry James, all signalling, so I then proudly assumed, "Brilliant young author at work here." My cell at the magazine struck me as signalling something like "Derelict old author at a total loss here," for I sensed that, young and old, many a writer had sat in the cubicle before me and had vanished forever into that Sheol where all Ross's failed "Jesuses" might be imagined as dwell-

ing—Perth Amboy, perhaps, or the grim fringes of Bridgeport. ("Jesus" was the office corruption of "genius," the
epithet that Ross applied to every promising reporter he
discovered in the early days of the magazine and upon
whom he would immediately thrust the fugitive honor
of the managing editorship.)

5   To make matters worse, the walls of my cubicle, which
was one of four identical cubicles forming a small square
in the dark heart of the building, were of a particularly
unpleasant kind of frosted glass and of skimpily painted
wood; everyone else appeared to be favored with offices
that had soundproof walls of solid cinder block and plaster
and that had at least a single window apiece. Recently,
I asked Hawley Truax, the man responsible for much of
the physical layout of the editorial department, how such
miserable cubicles had happened to come into existence.
"I found them," he said simply. In short, they, too, had
been picked up at second hand, like their wretched contents. For all I know, Hawley encountered them in a heap
of refuse on the street and dragged them single-handedly
up to the nineteenth floor.

6   My dismay was heightened at the start by my being
unaware that this was the note that had always been
struck at the magazine: squalor had come to be something
that members of the staff took considerable pride in. It
was as if the magazine, having decided that it could not
afford to be beautiful, had decided to be as ugly as possible;
in this perverse intention it may be said to have scored
an unbroken series of triumphs. The contrast between
the elegance of the actual magazine as it appears from
week to week and the circumstances in which the editors
produce the magazine has always startled the outside
world. It used to startle me as well, but by now I am nearly
as inured as my colleagues to the shabby discomfort in
which we pass our days. Paint peels from the walls;
chunks of plaster fall from the ceilings. On a high wooden
cupboard near my office someone affixed a sign reading
"This door does not open." That was years ago; the sign
darkens with age, the door remains closed upon no one
remembers what. Along the corridors are scattered remains that put one in mind of the sidewalk outside a tene-
ment house on the day of its demolition. One passes chairs
whose stuffings leap up in a tangle of uncoiled springs
and frayed webbing, bookcases ripped from a wall and

bristling with bent spikes, a stepladder with two of its steps missing, innumerable empty ten-gallon jars of Great Bear spring water, said to be filled not from any spring but from the faucet of the janitor's slop-sink on the twentieth floor, dusty framed clippings from newspapers and magazines of the nineteen-forties . . . .

It is a palimpsest of an office, a Dead Sea Scroll, and only a scholar learned in urban débris could do it justice. Most of us on the magazine are not scholars; besides, the singular trophies that surround us have grown invisible. A sort of therapeutic blindness spares us what is understandably an occasion for astonishment in strangers. Take the first object that is likely to call itself to your attention when you get off the elevator on the nineteenth floor. It is the same object that called itself to my attention when *I* got off the elevator on the nineteenth floor, almost forty years ago—a large, shallow brazier of Indian design, set upon carved and painted tabouret legs. The brass of which it is made glints but dully, through lack of polish; sometimes cigarettes are stubbed out in it, sometimes it is filled with rejected rejection slips, crumpled up and left behind by indignant would-be contributors. What is that brazier doing in what passes for our reception room? Well, it was an article of furniture that Ruth Fleischmann, wife of the publisher of the magazine, decided to get rid of in the twenties, when she was fixing over the Fleischmann house on East Seventy-fourth Street. The brazier represents the first and certainly the last attempt ever made to "decorate" the premises. No doubt it was brought down to the office by Mr. Fleischmann's chauffeur, who was probably thinking, "Good riddance to bad rubbish!" And if the magazine should last another fifty years, one can be sure that the brazier will still be found in its usual place, secure in the immortality of neglect.

7

Discussing Content and Form

1. Describe Gill's reactions to his office when he began work at the New Yorker.
a. Have his reactions changed since? Has the office changed? Support your answers with evidence from the selection.
b. How did Gill's office represent the place in general? What are the reactions of the other staff members to their surroundings?

2. How does Gill's office compare to his study at home? If you are familiar with the New Yorker, *in what ways is it surprising that its offices are so drab?*

3. From the description of his own cubicle, Gill widens the view to the offices in general, and finally to the entrance with its strange decoration. Why do you think he chose this arrangement rather than one which brings us in the front door? What would be the effect of starting with a description of the brazier in the corridor?

4. Gill pays particular attention to the typewriter and the copy paper. Why are these elements important? Relate the paragraphs (2 and 3) in which these are described to the comment made by Ross, the editor, that "Nothing is indescribable" (par. 2).

5. Find elements in this selection that seem to you humorous. How much of the humor depends on the unexpected or ironic?

Considering Special Techniques

1. Study Gill's selection of details to determine which are objective and which are subjective.
a. Which details seem to you most vivid in depicting the drabness of the offices? How would you react to working in this place?
b. What is the purpose of including such minute details as the loose leg of the chair, the defaced label on the typewriter, and the yellow copy paper?
c. How does Gill really feel about the place? Support your answer with specific words and phrases from the selection. For instance, why does he say that "squalor had come to be something that members of the staff took considerable pride in" (par. 6)?
d. Contrast Gill's reliance on interpretive generalizations with the lack of such authorial commentary in "Junior Miss." Do you think these interpretations are more appropriate in the description of the New Yorker *offices than in the other selection? Why or why not?*

2. Description often follows a spatial pattern, i.e., the writing gives the effect of a camera moving in space, picking up details as it swings from left to right, from door to window, etc. Find parts of Gill's description which are arranged spatially. Point out places where the arrangement seems random, giving the effect of disorder or casual observation.

3. Irony, *in its verbal sense, is a figure of speech expressing a meaning opposite to the actual intent. Irony in situations involves an unexpected twist, an outcome opposite to that which seems natural or appropriate. After describing his typewriter in paragraph 2, Gill gives an example of the kind of typing he says it produces. Closely examine the irony that is achieved by this detail.*

4. *Why do you think Gill calls the office "a palimsest . . . a Dead Sea Scroll" (par. 7)? (A palimsest is a parchment on which the writing has been erased and a new message written over the erasure.)*

5. *Discuss the choice of the word* therapeutic *as it applies to* blindness *(par. 7). What is ironic about the "rejected rejection slips" and about the attempt at decoration in the form of a second-hand brazier (par. 7)?*

6. *Harold Ross, the editor of the* New Yorker, *has been the subject of a great deal of writing by many people who worked for him, among them James Thurber (p. 294). Ross's abrupt hiring and firing of new talent as described in paragraph 4. Explain the association between Ross's terms "Jesuses" and "geniuses." What is ironic about disappearing to Perth Amboy or Bridgeport?*

7. *Words to learn and use:* ominous, manifestations, canny, rubric *(par. 2);* gadgetry, benefaction *(par. 3);* derelict, epithet *(par. 4);* squalor, perverse, inured, affixed, demolition *(par. 6);* palimsest, therapeutic, brazier, tabouret *(par. 7).*

Generating Ideas

1. *Write an objective description of a room, office, classroom, or place of business. Arrange the details in a spatial order, moving, for example, from left to right, top to bottom, door to window. Or you can arrange your details by "order of notice"—moving from the first item to catch your eye to the last.*

2. *Write a description contrasting two rooms, houses, public buildings, or other such places. Be sure to give several details about each, although you might, as Gill does in contrasting his* New Yorker *offices with his home study, use one of the contrasting items to throw light upon the nature of the other.*

3. *Write a satire or humorous piece about any struggles you have had with a typewriter, or about your learning to type. You might try giving the typewriter human characteristics, making it an enemy or a friend.*

4.   Today, a great deal of attention is given to creating attractive lounges or work areas in business offices, factories, hospitals, etc. Using description as part of your method, develop a paper on the effect such surroundings have upon the workers and visitors.

5.   Do some reading about Harold Ross and other famous members of the New Yorker *staff. Choose one of these personalities or one part of the history of the publication as the subject for a short documented paper.*

Herman Melville

Herman Melville (1819–1891) was little recognized during his lifetime, and only since the 1920s has been acclaimed as one of the greatest of American writers. Among his many works of fiction that have found a permanent place in our national literature, his masterpiece is *Moby-Dick; or, The Whale,* the epic of a literal and philosophical quest which transcends any attempt at literary classification.

Melville's early experiences as a sailor provided the background for many of his literary works, among them the sketches entitled *The Encantadas, or The Enchanted Isles.* The selection that follows is the first in this collection of ten descriptive sketches based on a voyage Melville made in 1841 to the Galapagos Islands in the Pacific.

The Enchanted Isles

Take five-and-twenty heaps of cinders dumped here and there in an outside city lot; imagine some of them magnified into mountains, and the vacant lot the sea; and you will have a fit idea of the general aspect of the Encantadas, or Enchanted Isles. A group rather of extinct volcanoes than of isles; looking much as the world at large might, after a penal conflagration.

It is to be doubted whether any spot of earth can, in desolateness, furnish a parallel to this group. Abandoned cemeteries of long ago, old cities by piecemeal tumbling to their ruin, these are melancholy enough; but, like all else which has but once been associated with humanity, they still awaken in us some thoughts of sympathy, however sad. Hence, even the Dead Sea, along with whatever other emotions it may at times inspire, does not fail to touch in the pilgrim some of his less unpleasurable feelings.

And as for solitariness; the great forests of the north, the expanses of unnavigated waters, the Greenland ice-fields, are the profoundest of solitudes to a human observer; still the magic of their changeable tides and seasons mitigates their terror; because, though unvisited by men, those forests are visited by the May; the remotest seas reflect familiar stars even as Lake Erie does; and in the clear air of a fine Polar day, the irradiated, azure ice shows beautifully as malachite.

But the special curse, as one may call it, of the Encantadas, that which exalts them in desolation above Idumea and the Pole, is, that to them change never comes; neither the change of seasons nor of sorrows. Cut by the Equator, they know not autumn, and they know not spring; while already reduced to the lees of fire, ruin itself can work little more upon them. The showers refresh the deserts; but in these isles, rain never falls. Like split Syrian gourds left withering in the sun, they are cracked by an everlasting drought beneath a torrid sky. "Have mercy on me," the wailing spirit of the Encantadas seems to cry, "and send Lazarus that he may dip the tip of his finger in water and cool my tongue, for I am tormented in this flame."

5   Another feature in these isles is their emphatic uninhabitableness. It is deemed a fit type of all-forsaken overthrow, that the jackal should den in the wastes of weedy Babylon; but the Encantadas refuse to harbor even the outcasts of the beasts. Man and wolf alike disown them. Little but reptile life is here found: tortoises, lizards, immense spiders, snakes, and that strangest anomaly of outlandish nature, the *iguana.* No voice, no low, no howl is heard; the chief sound of life here is a hiss.

6   On most of the isles where vegetation is found at all, it is more ungrateful than the blankness of Atacama. Tangled thickets of wiry bushes, without fruit and without a name, springing up among deep fissures of calcined rock, and treacherously masking them; or a parched growth of distorted cactus trees.

7   In many places the coast is rock-bound, or, more properly, clinker-bound; tumbled masses of blackish or greenish stuff like the dross of an iron-furnace, forming dark clefts and caves here and there, into which a ceaseless sea pours a fury of foam; overhanging them with a swirl of gray, haggard mist, amidst which sail screaming flights of unearthly birds heightening the dismal din. However calm the sea without, there is no rest for these swells and those rocks; they lash and are lashed, even when the outer ocean is most at peace with itself. On the oppressive, clouded days, such as are peculiar to this part of the watery Equator, the dark, vitrified masses, many of which raise themselves among white whirlpools and breakers in detached and perilous places off the shore, present a most Plutonian sight. In no world but a fallen one could such lands exist.

8   Those parts of the strand free from the marks of fire, stretch away in wide level beaches of multitudinous dead

shells, with here and there decayed bits of sugar-cane, bamboos, and cocoanuts, washed upon this other and darker world from the charming palm isles to the westward and southward; all the way from Paradise to Tartarus; while mixed with the relics of distant beauty you will sometimes see fragments of charred wood and mouldering ribs of wrecks. Neither will any one be surprised at meeting these last, after observing the conflicting currents which eddy throughout nearly all the wide channels of the entire group. The capriciousness of the tides of air sympathizes with those of the sea. Nowhere is the wind so light, baffling, and every way unreliable, and so given to perplexing calms, as at the Encantadas. Nigh a month has been spent by a ship going from one isle to another, though but ninety miles between; for owing to the force of the current, the boats employed to tow barely suffice to keep the craft from sweeping upon the cliffs, but do nothing towards accelerating her voyage. Sometimes it is impossible for a vessel from afar to fetch up with the group itself, unless large allowances for prospective leeway have been made ere its coming in sight. And yet, at other times, there is a mysterious indraft, which irresistibly draws a passing vessel among the isles, though not bound to them.

True, at one period, as to some extent at the present day, large fleets of whalemen cruised for spermaceti upon what some seamen call the Enchanted Ground. But this, as in due place will be described, was off the great outer isle of Albemarle, away from the intricacies of the smaller isles, where there is plenty of sea-room; and hence, to that vicinity, the above remarks do not altogether apply; though even there the current runs at times with singular force, shifting, too, with as singular a caprice. 9

Indeed, there are seasons when currents quite unaccountable prevail for a great distance round about the total group, and are so strong and irregular as to change a vessel's course against the helm, though sailing at the rate of four or five miles the hour. The difference in the reckonings of navigators, produced by these causes, along with the light and variable winds, long nourished a persuasion, that there existed two distinct clusters of isles in the parallel of the Encantadas, about a hundred leagues apart. Such was the idea of their earlier visitors, the Buccaneers; and as late as 1750, the charts of that part of 10 the Pacific accorded with the strange delusion. And this apparent fleetingness and unreality of the locality of the isles was most probably one reason for the Spaniards calling them the Encantada, or Enchanted Group.

11 But not uninfluenced by their character, as they now confessedly exist, the modern voyager will be inclined to fancy that the bestowal of this name might have in part originated in that air of spell-bound desertness which so significantly invests the isles. Nothing can better suggest the aspect of once living things malignly crumbled from ruddiness into ashes. Apples of Sodom, after touching, seem these isles.

12 However wavering their place may seem by reason of the currents, they themselves, at least to one upon the shore, appear invariably the same: fixed, cast, glued into the very body of cadaverous death.

13 Nor would the appellation, enchanted, seem misapplied in still another sense. For concerning the peculiar reptile inhabitant of these wilds—whose presence gives the group its second Spanish name, Galapagos—concerning the tortoises found here, most mariners have long cherished a superstition, not more frightful than grotesque. They earnestly believe that all wicked sea-officers, more especially commodores and captains, are at death (and, in some cases, before death) transformed into tortoises; thenceforth dwelling upon these hot aridities, sole solitary lords of Asphaltum.

14 Doubtless, so quaintly dolorous a thought was originally inspired by the woe-begone landscape itself; but more particularly, perhaps, by the tortoises. For, apart from their strictly physical features, there is something strangely self-condemned in the appearance of these creatures. Lasting sorrow and penal hopelessness are in no animal form so suppliantly expressed as in theirs; while the thought of their wonderful longevity does not fail to enhance the impression.

15 Nor even at the risk of meriting the charge of absurdly believing in enchantments, can I restrain the admission that sometimes, even now, when leaving the crowded city to wander out July and August among the Adirondack Mountains, far from the influences of towns and proportionally nigh to the mysterious ones of nature; when at such times I sit me down in the mossy head of some deep-

wooded gorge, surrounded by prostrate trunks of blasted pines, and recall, as in a dream, my other and far-distant rovings in the baked heart of the charmed isles; and remember the sudden glimpses of dusky shells, and long languid necks protruded from the leafless thickets; and again have beheld the vitreous inland rocks worn down and grooved into deep ruts by ages and ages of the slow draggings of tortoises in quest of pools of scanty water; I can hardly resist the feeling that in my time I have indeed slept upon evilly enchanted ground.

Nay, such is the vividness of my memory, or the magic of my fancy, that I know not whether I am not the occasional victim of optical delusion concerning the Galapagos. For, often in scenes of social merriment, and especially at revels held by candle-light in old-fashioned mansions, so that shadows are thrown into the further recesses of an angular and spacious room, making them put on a look of haunted undergrowth of lonely woods, I have drawn the attention of my comrades by my fixed gaze and sudden change of air, as I have seemed to see, slowly emerging from those imagined solitudes, and heavily crawling along the floor, the ghost of a gigantic tortoise, with "Memento * * * * *" burning in live letters upon his back. 16

Discussing Content and Form

1.   What impression does Melville give of the Enchanted Isles? Would you call this description predominantly objective or subjective? Explain by citing details from the sketch.

2.   After introducing the islands by comparing them to "five-and-twenty heaps of cinders" dumped in the vacant lot of the sea (par. 1), Melville devotes each of the next four paragraphs to one of the islands' chief characteristics: desolateness (par. 2), solitariness (par. 3), changelessness (par. 4), and uninhabitableness (par. 5). Using these terms as headings, list the images and details that illustrate each feature. How do these four characteristics serve to organize the entire sketch?

3.   In what sense are the islands "enchanted"? Why does Melville explain their name so fully (pars. 10–11)? What is the significance of the name Galapagos *(par. 13)? Which name is used today?*

4. Melville writes about the reptiles, the only animal life on the islands, in two separate passages (par. 5 and pars. 13–14). What is the purpose of the description in paragraph 5? How does the description in the other two paragraphs differ from the first in purpose and tone?

5. What effect does Melville say the islands had upon sailors? What is the dominant characteristic of the seas in the area?

6. Melville twice uses the word penal: *the "extinct volcanoes" look as the world might after "a penal conflagration" (par. 1), and the tortoises have a "penal hopelessness" (par. 14). In what way does the sense of penal entrapment haunt the last two paragraphs of the sketch? What is the significance of the word* Memento *burning upon the back of the tortoise (par. 16)?*

Considering Special Techniques

1. This selection is rich in images—words and phrases that evoke sense impressions. Classify the images that you find particularly effective, using the five senses for the headings. Here is a start.
Sight: *"abandoned cemeteries" (par. 2); "old cities . . . tumbling" (par. 2)*
Sound: *"wailing spirit" (par. 4); "chief sound . . . is a hiss" (par. 5)*
Touch: *"gourds . . . withering in the sun" (par. 4); "cracked by everlasting drought" (par. 4)*
Taste: *"dip the tip of his finger in water and cool my tongue" (par. 4)*
Smell: *"mouldering ribs of wrecks" (par. 8); "cadaverous death" (par. 12)*
We sometimes speak of images that involve more than one sense as being synesthetic. *Find several images from the description that evoke at least two senses simultaneously, e.g., "a torrid sky" (par. 4).*

2. Melville emphasizes the bleakness of the islands by employing several allusions, usually to other desolate regions. Allusions are references to people, places, and events taken from history, literature, the Bible, mythology, etc. One of Melville's biblical allusions is to Idumea, the land of Edom, a barren stretch along the Dead Sea. The passage concerning Babylon (par. 5) is adapted from the Bible (Jer. 51:37): "And Babylon shall become a heap of ruins, a haunt of jackals, a horror and a hissing, without an inhabitant." Melville also employs allusions to classical mythology, e.g., Plutonian *refers to the classical Greek god of the underworld.*

Find other examples of biblical and mythological allusions, in addition to several from Melville's own time. Discuss the effect of these. What do they add to the sketch? Do you ever feel excluded from their meaning? Why might the readers of Melville's time have found them more effective than today's readers do?

3.   *Find examples of the negative prefix* un *and of negative words such as* no, not, nor, nowhere, *etc. Be sure to note that at least three paragraphs open with such words. What is the effect of these negative words?*

4.   *Words to learn and use:* penal, conflagration *(par. 1);* unnavigated, mitigates, irradiated, azure, malachite *(par. 3);* torrid, wailing *(par. 4),* anomaly *(par. 5);* fissures, calcined *(par. 6);* haggard, oppressive, perilous *(par. 7);* multitudinous, capriciousness, suffice *(par. 8);* spermaceti *(par. 9);* reckonings *(par. 10);* malignly *(par. 11);* cadaverous *(par. 12);* appellation, aridities *(par. 13);* dolorous, suppliantly, longevity *(par. 14);* prostrate, languid, vitreous *(par. 15).*

Generating Ideas

1.   *Write a paper in which you describe a place that you have seen or an experience that you have had that presented a strange or unusual aspect of nature or of the past. Try to evoke for your reader the sense of eerieness that Melville produces with his picture of the Galapagos. For instance, did you ever get trapped in a deserted building? Have you visited a very old cemetery? Have you been lost on some country road at night?*

2.   *Write a paper in which you explain the fascination of "haunted house" stories, plays, or movies. You might recall some Alfred Hitchcock films or stories by Agatha Christie.*

3.   *In paragraph 3, Melville mentions the ice-fields of Greenland and the stark beauty of a polar day, although he himself was not an explorer in those regions. Read some of the descriptions written by Admiral Richard E. Byrd of his expedition to the South Pole; then write a paper comparing the techniques of Melville in this sketch and those of Byrd in his writings.*

3
Framing Events:
Narration

From the beginning of civilization people have used narration to relate imaginary events, to record the happenings of their personal and collective histories, and to illustrate or explain ideas. Some of the many forms narration has taken include pictures on cave walls, the ancient Greek epics, the fiction and fact of chronicle and parable in the Old and New Testaments, and the popular fiction and biography of today. Much storytelling involves fictional events about imaginary characters told for the sake of the story itself. These stories provide a release from everyday life and increase our awareness and understanding of experiences outside our own. Frequently, however, narration serves an expository function: an actual story is told primarily in order to explain or to lead to an idea or a realization. In such writing, the story does not exist for its own sake, but instead serves the ideas the author wishes to present.

Notice how this brief narrative serves to make a point:

> The founding father of the Rockefeller dynasty illustrated how giving money away, and yourself in the process, squares with making it in the first place. John D. Rockefeller was larger than life. The advisers he hired were quick to see that the empire he controlled was creating problems for him rather than solving them. They took him out of the line of fire by putting him into the spotlight as a giver—not a big giver, but a small one.
>
> Back in the days when a dime meant something, Rockefeller started his own version of the March of Dimes. A shrewd and cynical adviser named Ivy Lee sold Rockefeller the idea of just giving away dimes. The old boy complied by going up and down the country posing for pictures while

abitrarily giving dimes away to youngsters as an inducement to them to save money and duplicate his own success
story.

Of course, these dimes were not actually meant to do
anybody any good—except Rockefeller himself. The purpose of the scheme was to show that he was a part of life—
not larger than life—and to catch him in the act of doing
what comes naturally to everyone—giving.—Eliot Janeway,
Musings on Money

The author, an economist, uses this anecdote—a short
narrative incident—in a book about managing money. The
first sentence and the entire last paragraph make apparent the expository purpose for the narration they enclose.
Together, the three paragraphs comprise a narrative essay in miniature.

In examining the place of narration in exposition, it
is useful to understand the similarities between narration
and description, for many of the same considerations apply to both. To be successful, both must grow out of good
observation and selection from that observation. Description gives a vivid and exact picture of things as they appear; narration gives a vivid and exact picture of things
as they occur. Thus narration provides a moving picture.
Description involves careful arrangement in space; narration involves careful arrangement in time so that the
events are in logical sequence, usually chronological. With
description, the reader is asked to look; with narration,
to follow. Both show rather than merely tell, but narration
goes further than description to present events dramati-
cally. Like description, narration may carry meaning by
direct statement or by implication. For example, a writer,
through his narrator, may announce, "Now all of this
means . . . ."; or he may lead the reader to a certain conclusion by letting his ideas unfold implicitly rather than
explicitly.

Much of the narration that you include in your expository writing will be autobiographical, although this kind
of narration too should not be just a simple recounting
of events. Rather, your personal experience should become part of the development of an essay in which you
discover and interpret a meaning in those events. In the
following narrative account, the writer leads up to a realization about a father-son relationship, yet he never states
the point directly:

I remember the first time I cultivated corn. First, a trip across the field with Father showing me how. I walked behind him, and it all looked simple and easy. Father turned the team around at the end of the row and told me to take over. I looped the lines around my back, grabbed the handles, and yelled, "Get up!"

The horses jerked forward. The moist earth flew out to cover the young plants. The shovels hit a rock, and the handles were torn from my hands.

"Whoa!" Father yelled.

We went back and uncovered the plants.

"Look," Father said. "It's not a race. The only way a horse knows how fast you want him to go is by how you talk to him. You yelled. That means get out and go. Now, try again. Speak soft and easy."

I tried again. The team moved slowly along the row. Father walked behind, now and then saying "gee" or "haw" to the horses. I needed more hands. The handles vibrated and jerked like something alive as the feel of the land came up through them. I didn't dare let go to pull the horses right or left with the lines. I tried Father's "gee" and "haw" and again found that how I spoke was as important as what I said. I needed more eyes, too. I had to keep looking at the row up ahead and keep looking straight down at the same time to guide the shovels close to the plants. I also needed an eye in the back of my head to see how Father was reacting.

At the end of that first row, with the cultivator close against the woven wire fence, I breathed a sigh of relief and tried to turn the horses around onto another row. The horses couldn't seem to turn. I looked at Father. He was smiling. "You're going to have to back up a little. You've got the end of the tongue stuck through the fence."

When I finally got turned around, Father laid a hand on my shoulder. "You're on your own." He walked back toward the house. I watched him go. He never looked back to see how I was doing. That was important.—Ben Logan, *The Land Remembers*

In writing narration for expository purposes, you should keep several points in mind. First, select details carefully, giving just enough of the right kind to make your point. Becoming intrigued with telling the story for its own sake leads to the inclusion of too much detail or to digressions. With such overtelling, the point may be diminished or even lost. Of course, selection must be aimed at evoking interest, perhaps even at creating the same kind of suspense as the fiction-writer does. Even the briefest anecdote or narrative illustration should be lively and vivid. The details should help the reader identify with the characters and action, thereby sustaining interest and carrying the message at the same time.

Another important consideration is the choice of the point of view. Eliot Janeway tells his anecdote about Rockefeller without intruding himself, without using the first person *I*. Ben Logan, on the other hand, is writing about his own experience, and so he uses the first person. The first kind of viewpoint is most appropriate to objective and straightforward narration, while the second is best suited to subjective and impressionistic stories. Whatever the form or length of the narration, however, the important thing is to maintain a consistent viewpoint in telling the story.

Probably the most important point in narration is to arrange events in clear order, giving sufficient links to guide the reader through the action. One kind of link, or transition, is the word or phrase that indicates time. For instance, Ben Logan connects events with such phrases as "I remember the first time" and "At the end of that first row." A second "time link" can be found in the sequence of verbs: "I walked" and "it all looked" and "Father turned" set the time in the first paragraph, and after that all the events are recounted in the same past tense. The indicators of time and the sequence of verbs keep the events in order, whether the action is set in the past, the present, or the future.

Selecting details, maintaining a consistent point of view, and providing links to keep the sequence clear should lead to effective narration. But as with other types of writing, narration depends ultimately upon experience and observation. They are the source of material for creating the moving pictures that both illustrate and carry your ideas.

Maya Angelou

Maya Angelou (b. 1928) spent part of her early years in Stamps, Arkansas, with her grandmother, the "Momma" of the selection that follows. She has told the story of her childhood and her struggles to achieve maturity and success as a dancer, singer, actress, producer, and writer in three lively accounts: *I Know Why the Caged Bird Sings* (1970), *Gather Together in My Name* (1974), and *Singin' and Swingin' and Gettin' Merry Like Christmas* (1976). She has also written two volumes of poetry: *Just Give Me a Cool Drink of Water 'fore I Diiie* (1971) and *Oh Pray My Wings Are Gonna Fit Me Well* (1975). In the 1960s, Angelou acted as Northern Coordinator for the Southern Christian Leadership Conference organized by Dr. Martin Luther King, Jr. In "A Lesson in Living" (editor's title), taken from *I Know Why the Caged Bird Sings,* Angelou recalls one of the early influences that helped shape her career.

A Lesson in Living

1

Establishment of scene, followed by anticipatory statement (par. 1)

For nearly a year, I sopped around the house, the Store, the school and the church, like an old biscuit, dirty and inedible. Then I met, or rather got to know, the lady who threw me my first life line.

2

Details of Mrs. Flowers' appearance and actions (pars. 2–5)

Mrs. Bertha Flowers was the aristocrat of Black Stamps. She had the grace of control to appear warm in the coldest weather, and on the Arkansas summer days it seemed she had a private breeze which swirled around, cooling her. She was thin without the taut look of wiry people, and her printed voile dresses and flowered hats were as right for her as denim overalls for a farmer. She was our side's answer to the richest white woman in town.

3

Her skin was a rich black that would have peeled like a plum if snagged, but then no one would have thought of getting close enough to Mrs. Flowers to ruffle her dress, let alone snag her skin. She didn't encourage familiarity. She wore gloves too.

4

I don't think I ever saw Mrs. Flowers laugh, but she smiled often. A slow widening of her thin black lips to show even, small white teeth, then the slow effortless closing. When she chose to smile on me, I always wanted to thank her. The action was so graceful and inclusively benign.

She was one of the few gentlewomen I have ever known, and has remained throughout my life the measure of what a human being can be. 5

Momma had a strange relationship with her. Most often when she passed on the road in front of the Store, she spoke to Momma in that soft yet carrying voice, "Good day, Mrs. Henderson." Momma responded with "How you, Sister Flowers?" 6 Her relationship with Momma (pars. 6–10)

Mrs. Flowers didn't belong to our church, nor was she Momma's familiar. Why on earth did she insist on calling her Sister Flowers? Shame made me want to hide my face. Mrs. Flowers deserved better than to be called Sister. Then, Momma left out the verb. Why not ask, "How *are* you, *Mrs.* Flowers?" With the unbalanced passion of the young, I hated her for showing her ignorance to Mrs. Flowers. It didn't occur to me for many years that they were as alike as sisters, separated only by formal education. 7

Although I was upset, neither of the women was in the least shaken by what I thought an unceremonious greeting. Mrs. Flowers would continue her easy gait up the hill to her little bungalow, and Momma kept on shelling peas or doing whatever had brought her to the front porch. 8

Occasionally, though, Mrs. Flowers would drift off the road and down to the Store and Momma would say to me, "Sister, you go on and play." As I left I would hear the beginning of an intimate conversation. Momma persistently using the wrong verb, or none at all. 9

"Brother and Sister Wilcox is sho'ly the meanest—" "Is," Momma? "Is"? Oh, please, not "is," Momma, for two or more. But they talked, and from the side of the building 10 where I waited for the ground to open up and swallow me, I heard the soft-voiced Mrs. Flowers and the textured voice of my grandmother merging and melting. They were interrupted from time to time by giggles that must have come from Mrs. Flowers (Momma never giggled in her life). Then she was gone.

11
Mrs. Flowers is likened to fictional and film characters (pars. 11–13)

She appealed to me because she was like people I had never met personally. Like women in English novels who walked the moors (whatever they were) with their loyal dogs racing at a respectful distance. Like the women who sat in front of roaring fireplaces, drinking tea incessantly from silver trays full of scones and crumpets. Women who walked over the "heath" and read morocco-bound books and had two last names divided by a hyphen. It would be safe to say that she made me proud to be Negro, just by being herself.

12

She acted just as refined as whitefolks in the movies and books and she was more beautiful, for none of them could have come near that warm color without looking gray by comparison.

13

It was fortunate that I never saw her in the company of powhitefolks. For since they tend to think of their whiteness as an evenizer, I'm certain that I would have had to hear her spoken to commonly as Bertha, and my image of her would have been shattered like the unmendable Humpty-Dumpty.

14
First part of the narrative: events leading up to the visit (pars. 14–31)

One summer afternoon, sweet-milk fresh in my memory, she stopped at the Store to buy provisions. Another Negro woman of her health and age would have been expected to carry the paper sacks home in one hand, but Momma said, "Sister Flowers, I'll send Bailey up to your house with these things."

15
The invitation (pars. 15–16)

She smiled that slow dragging smile, "Thank you, Mrs. Henderson. I'd prefer Marguerite, though." My name was beautiful when she said it. "I've been meaning to talk to her, anyway." They gave each other age-group looks.

Momma said, "Well, that's all right then. Sister, go and change your dress. You going to Sister Flowers's." 16

The chifforobe was a maze. What on earth did one put on to go to Mrs. Flowers' house? I knew I shouldn't put on a Sunday dress. It might be sacrilegious. Certainly not a house dress, since I was already wearing a fresh one. I chose a school dress, naturally. It was formal without suggesting that going to Mrs. Flowers' house was equivalent to attending church. 17
The choice of a dress (pars. 17–18)

I trusted myself back into the Store. 18

"Now, don't you look nice." I had chosen the right thing, for once. 19
Discussion of the dress (pars. 19–31)

"Mrs. Henderson, you make most of the children's clothes, don't you?" 20

"Yes, ma'am. Sure do. Store-bought clothes ain't hardly worth the thread it take to stitch them." 21

"I'll say you do a lovely job, though, so neat. That dress looks professional." 22

Momma was enjoying the seldom-received compliments. Since everyone we knew (except Mrs. Flowers, of course) could sew competently, praise was rarely handed out for the commonly practiced craft. 23

"I try, with the help of the Lord, Sister Flowers, to finish the inside just like I does the outside. Come here, Sister." 24

I had buttoned up the collar and tied the belt, apronlike, in back. Momma told me to turn around. With one hand she pulled the strings and the belt fell free at both sides of my waist. Then her large hands were at my neck, opening the button loops. I was terrified. What was happening? 25

"Take it off, Sister." She had her hands on the hem of the dress. 26

"I don't need to see the inside, Mrs. Henderson, I can tell . . ." But the dress was over my head and my arms were stuck in the sleeves. Momma said, "That'll do. See here, Sister Flowers, I French-seams around the armholes." Through the cloth film, I saw the 27 shadow approach. "That makes it last longer. Children these days would bust out of sheet-metal clothes. They so rough."

28   "That is a very good job, Mrs. Henderson. You should be proud. You can put your dress back on, Marguerite."

29   "No ma'am. Pride is a sin. And 'cording to the Good Book, it goeth before a fall."

30   "That's right. So the Bible says. It's a good thing to keep in mind."

31   I wouldn't look at either of them. Momma hadn't thought that taking off my dress in front of Mrs. Flowers would kill me stone dead. If I had refused, she would have thought I was trying to be "womanish" and might have remembered St. Louis. Mrs. Flowers had known that I would be embarrassed and that was even worse. I picked up the groceries and went out to wait in the hot sunshine. It would be fitting if I got a sunstroke and died before they came outside. Just dropped dead on the slanting porch.

32   There was a little path beside the rocky road, and Mrs. Flowers walked in front swinging her arms and picking her way over the stones.

Second part of narrative: events during walk to Mrs. Flowers' house (pars. 32–39)

33   She said, without turning her head, to me, "I hear you're doing very good school work, Marguerite, but that it's all written. The teachers report that they have trouble getting you to talk in class." We passed the triangular farm on our left and the path widened to allow us to walk together. I hung back in the separate unasked and unanswerable questions.

34   "Come and walk along with me, Marguerite." I couldn't have refused even if I wanted to. She pronounced my name so nicely. Or more correctly, she spoke each word with such clarity that I was certain a foreigner who didn't understand English could have understood her.

Discussion of language (pars. 34–37)

35   "Now no one is going to make you talk—possibly no one can. But bear in mind, language is man's way of communicating with

his fellow man and it is language alone which separates him from the lower animals." That was a totally new idea to me, and I would need time to think about it.

"Your grandmother says you read a lot. Every chance you get. That's good, but not good enough. Words mean more than what is set down on paper. It takes the human voice to infuse them with the shades of deeper meaning." 36

I memorized the part about the human voice infusing words. It seemed so valid and poetic. 37

She said she was going to give me some books and that I not only must read them, I must read them aloud. She suggested that I try to make a sentence sound in as many different ways as possible. 38

Promise of books (pars. 38–39)

"I'll accept no excuse if you return a book to me that has been badly handled." My imagination boggled at the punishment I would deserve if in fact I did abuse a book of Mrs. Flowers'. Death would be too kind and brief. 39

The odors in the house surprised me. Somehow I had never connected Mrs. Flowers with food or eating or any other common experience of common people. There must have been an outhouse, too, but my mind never recorded it. 40

Third part of narrative: arrival and events at Mrs. Flowers' house (pars. 40–46)

The sweet scent of vanilla had met us as she opened the door. 41

"I made tea cookies this morning. You see, I had planned to invite you for cookies and lemonade so we could have this little chat. The lemonade is in the icebox." 42

It followed that Mrs. Flowers would have ice on an ordinary day, when most families in our town bought ice late on Saturdays only a few times during the summer to be used in the wooden ice-cream freezers. 43

She took the bags from me and disappeared through the kitchen door. I looked around the room that I had never in my wildest fantasies imagined I would see. Browned photographs 44 leered or threatened from the walls and the white, freshly done curtains pushed against themselves and against the wind. I wanted to gobble up the room entire and take it to Bailey, who would help me analyze and enjoy it.

45 "Have a seat, Marguerite. Over there by the table." She carried a platter covered with a tea towel. Although she warned that she hadn't tried her hand at baking sweets for some time, I was certain that like everything else about her the cookies would be perfect.

46 They were flat round wafers, slightly browned on the edges and butter-yellow in the center. With the cold lemonade they were sufficient for childhood's lifelong diet. Remembering my manners, I took nice little lady-like bites off the edges. She said she had made them expressly for me and that she had a few in the kitchen that I could take home to my brother. So I jammed one whole cake in my mouth and the rough crumbs scratched the insides of my jaws, and if I hadn't had to swallow, it would have been a dream come true.

47 As I ate she began the first of what we later called "my lessons in living." She said that I must always be intolerant of ignorance but understanding of illiteracy. That some people, unable to go to school, were more educated and even more intelligent than college professors. She encouraged me to listen carefully to what country people called mother wit. That in those homely sayings was couched the collective wisdom of generations.

Fourth part of narrative: Mrs. Flowers' "lesson in living" (pars. 47–53)

48 When I finished the cookies she brushed off the table and brought a thick, small book from the bookcase. I had read *A Tale of Two Cities* and found it up to my standards as a romantic novel. She opened the first page and I heard poetry for the first time in my life.

49 "It was the best of times and the worst of times . . ." Her voice slid in and curved down through and over the words. She was nearly singing. I wanted to look at the pages. Were

they the same that I had read? Or were there notes, music, lined on the pages, as in a hymn book? Her sounds began cascading gently. I knew from listening to a thousand preachers that she was nearing the end of her reading, and I hadn't really heard, heard to understand, a single word.

"How do you like that?" 50

It occurred to me that she expected a re- 51
sponse. The sweet vanilla flavor was still on my tongue and her reading was a wonder in my ears. I had to speak.

I said, "Yes, ma'am." It was the least I could 52
do, but it was the most also.

"There's one more thing. Take this book of 53
poems and memorize one for me. Next time you pay me a visit, I want you to recite."

I have tried often to search behind the so- 54
phistication of years for the enchantment I *Summary of the sig-
so easily found in those gifts. The essence es-* *nificance of the visit
capes but its aura remains. To be allowed, no,* *(par. 54)*
invited, into the private lives of strangers, and to share their joys and fears, was a chance to exchange the Southern bitter wormwood for a cup of mead with Beowulf or a hot cup of tea and milk with Oliver Twist. When I said aloud, "It is a far, far better thing that I do, than I have ever done . . ." tears of love filled my eyes at my selflessness.

On that first day, I ran down the hill and 55
into the road (few cars ever came along it) *Final part of narra-
and had the good sense to stop running before* *tive: the return
I reached the Store.* *home and various
reactions to the visit
(pars. 55–59)*

I was liked, and what a difference it made. 56
I was respected not as Mrs. Henderson's grandchild or Bailey's sister but for just being Marguerite Johnson.

Childhood's logic never asks to be proved 57
(all conclusions are absolute). I didn't question why Mrs. Flowers had singled me out for attention, nor did it occur to me that Momma might have asked her to give me a little talking to. All I cared about was that she had made tea cookies for *me* and read to *me* from her

favorite book. It was enough to prove that she liked me.

58   Momma and Bailey were waiting inside the Store. He said, "My, what did she give you?" He had seen the books, but I held the paper sack with his cookies in my arms shielded by the poems.

59   Momma said, ":Sister, I know you acted like a little lady. That do my heart good to see settled people take to you all. I'm trying my best, the Lord knows, but these days . . ." Her voice trailed off. "Go on in and change your dress."

Discussing Content and Form

1. What in the narrative explains Angelou's statement that Mrs. Flowers "threw" her a "life line"?

2. Which details reveal Mrs. Flowers' qualities as a gentlewoman?

3. We sometimes speak of adults as "role models" for children or young people. In what ways was Mrs. Flowers a model for Angelou?

4. Why was Angelou embarrased over Momma's behavior with Mrs. Flowers? How is that embarrassment epitomized in Angelou's correction of Momma's improper grammar (par. 10)?

5. In light of Angelou's fame as an actress and writer, explain the significance of Mrs. Flowers' admonition about speaking well: "Words mean more than what is set down on paper" (par. 36). Do you agree that it is important to be "intolerant of ignorance but understanding of illiteracy" (par. 47)? Why or why not?

6. How important were books to the writer as a child?

7. This selection is not a short story but an autobiographical account that culminates in a significant point. Nevertheless, it is blocked out in a series of scenes or incidents just as short stories frequently are. Note how the incidents fit together. How does the writer catch and build interest? How does she resolve the tensions built up throughout the account?

8. Angelou's narrative involves persons comparable to characters in fiction. It is less important that these people are real than that they seem real. Which details make the persons in the narration seem lifelike? How does the writer make you feel about Momma, Mrs. Flowers, and herself?

Considering Special Techniques

1. Characters from fiction and persons from biography and autobiography are presented not only through the writer's direct comments but also through their actions, their speech, and the comments of other characters. Show how Angelou uses each of these methods in her presentation of Mrs. Flowers and Momma. Show how the same methods paint a picture of Angelou herself.

a. Why does speech play an important part in revealing the personalities of the people in the selection?

b. Point out two or three incidents that are particularly revealing of character. You might begin with paragraphs 25–31, the examination of the dress. What does this incident contribute to our understanding of the three persons involved?

c. What do the details concerning books reveal about Mrs. Flowers and her young guest?

2. What makes the dialogue in the selection effective? How does the writer distinguish between her grandmother and Mrs. Flowers? (Consider both grammatical patterns and word choice.) What does the dialogue between the two women reveal about their relationship? Why does Angelou say, "It didn't occur to me for many years that they were as alike as sisters, separated only by formal education" (par. 7)?

3. Angelou makes effective use of similes *(stated comparisons) and* metaphors *(implied comparisons). Make a list of the similes and metaphors that you find particularly vivid. You might begin with these:*
"I sopped around the house . . . like an old biscuit, dirty and inedible" (par. 1).
"One summer afternoon, sweet-milk fresh in my memory . . ." (par. 14).

4. Paragraph 47 lists the "lessons in living" through the use of several phrases constructed according to the same pattern. In the second sentence, "She said that" establishes the pattern. How do the two sentence fragments, both beginning with that, *fit the pattern of the second sentence? Why do you think Angelou chose to express her ideas in two fragments rather than in full sentences?*

Generating Ideas

1. Write a paper telling about a meeting or a series of meetings with someone who has been an influence in your life. Or relate a sequence of events that led to some "lesson in living."

2. Explain why role models are important to young people. Although you may find incidents helpful in developing your explanation, you need not write narration.

3. Dialogue is one of the best methods for revealing one's thoughts and feelings. Imagine or draw from real life two persons who are concerned with similar things, ideas, events, etc., but who have different perspectives about them. Write a narrative in which they meet and talk about their beliefs. Here are a few examples:
A trucker and a tourist talk about the use of their C.B. radios.
A salesperson and a prospective buyer talk about a new car.
A person with a great deal of formal education and one with little discuss the value (or the lack of it) of a college degree.
A social worker who has no children and a mother who has several talk about day-care centers.

4. Write a short autobiographical narrative telling of some embarrassment that you have suffered. Try to make your experience as vivid as Angelou does her feelings about her grandmother's grammar and about being told to show Mrs. Flowers the seams in her dress.

John Updike

John Updike (b. 1932), besides being one of the best known among current American novelists, is the author of numerous short stories, magazine articles, poems, essays, and reviews. He started writing while attending Harvard, where he edited the undergraduate humor magazine *Lampoon.* After attending Oxford University's Ruskin School of Drawing and Fine Art on a fellowship, he became for a time a staff writer on the *New Yorker,* and some of his work has continued to appear there. His novels include *The Poorhouse Fair* (1959), *Rabbit, Run* (1960), *The Centaur* (1963), for which he won a National Book Award, *Couples* (1968), and *A Month of Sundays* (1975). He has collected some of his prose pieces into two volumes: *Assorted Prose* (1965), from which "Eclipse" is taken, and *Picked-Up Pieces* (1975). In "Eclipse," Updike uses his narrative skill to comment philosophically on the feelings of precariousness that are aroused by an extraordinary or unnatural occurrence.

Eclipse

I went out into the backyard and the usually roundish spots of dappled sunlight underneath the trees were all shaped like feathers, crescent in the same direction, from left to right. Though it was five o'clock on a summer afternoon, the birds were singing good-bye to the day, and their merged song seemed to soak the strange air in an additional strangeness. A kind of silence prevailed. Few cars were moving on the streets of the town. Of my children only the baby dared come into the yard with me. She wore only underpants, and as she stood beneath a tree, bulging her belly toward me in the mood of jolly flirtation she has grown into at the age of two, her bare skin was awash with pale crescents. It crossed my mind that she might be harmed, but I couldn't think how. *Cancer?*

1

The eclipse was to be over 90 percent in our latitude and the newspapers and television for days had been warning us not to look at it. I looked up, a split-second Prometheus, and looked away. The bitten silhouette of the sun lingered redly on my retinas. The day was half-cloudy, and my impression had been of the sun struggling, amid a furious knotted huddle of black and silver clouds, with an enemy too dreadful to be seen, with an eater as

2

ghostly and hungry as time. Every blade of grass cast a long bluish-brown shadow, as at dawn.

3   My wife shouted from behind the kitchen screen door that as long as I was out there I might as well burn the wastepaper. She darted from the house, eyes downcast, with the wastebasket, and darted back again, leaving the naked baby and me to wander up through the strained sunlight to the wire trash barrel. After my forbidden peek at the sun, the flames dancing transparently from the blackening paper—yesterday's Boston *Globe,* a milk carton, a Hi-Ho cracker box—seemed dimmer than shadows, and in the teeth of all the warnings I looked up again. The clouds seemed bunched and twirled as if to plug a hole in the sky, and the burning afterimage was the shape of a near-new moon, horns pointed down. It was gigantically unnatural, and I lingered in the yard under the vague apprehension that in some future life I might be called before a cosmic court to testify to this assault. I seemed to be the sole witness. The town around my yard was hushed, all but the singing of the birds, who were invisible. The feathers under the trees had changed direction, and curved from right to left.

4   Then I saw my neighbor sitting on her porch. My neighbor is a widow, with white hair and brown skin; she has in her yard an aluminum-and-nylon-net chaise longue on which she lies at every opportunity, head back, arms spread, prostrate under the sun. Now she hunched dismally on her porch steps in the shade, which was scarcely darker than the light. I walked toward her and hailed her as a visitor to the moon might salute a survivor of a previous expedition. "How do you like the eclipse?" I called over the fence that distinguished our holdings on this suddenly insubstantial and lunar earth.

5   "I don't like it," she answered, shading her face with a hand. "They say you shouldn't go out in it."

6   "I thought it was just you shouldn't look at it."

7   "There's something in the rays," she explained, in a voice far louder than it needed to be, for silence framed us. "I shut all the windows on that side of the house and had to come out for some air."

8   "I think it'll pass," I told her.

9   "Don't let the baby look up," she warned, and turned away from talking to me, as if the open use of her voice exposed her more fatally to the rays.

Superstition, I thought, walking back through my yard, 10
clutching my child's hand as tightly as a good-luck token.
There was no question in her touch. Day, night, twilight,
noon were all wonders to her, unscheduled, free from all
bondage of prediction. The sun was being restored to itself
and soon would radiate influence as brazenly as ever—
and in this sense my daughter's blind trust was vindicated.
Nevertheless, I was glad that the eclipse had passed, as
it were, over her head; for in my own life I felt a certain
assurance evaporate forever under the reality of the sun's
disgrace.

Discussing Content and Form

*1.   What point does Updike make about the experience of
the eclipse? Is that point stated explicitly or is it merely implied? Explain.*

*2.   What is Updike's reaction to the experience? How is his reac-
tion different from or similar to the reactions of his wife
and his neighbor? What do their actions and Updike's conversation with both of them contribute to the point of the narration?*

*3.   What is the significance of the details concerning the baby?
How many times is she mentioned? What does returning to
her "as a good-luck token" in the last paragraph contribute to
the organization of the essay as well as to its meaning?*

4.   Why does Updike look at the sun?

*5.   In using narration to make a point, the writer must decide
how much interpretation of the story to give. What is the proportion of narration to the expository sections in the essay?
How much of the essay is descriptive?*

Considering Special Techniques

*1.   Updike italicizes two words—*Cancer *at the end of paragraph
1 and* Superstition *at the beginning of paragraph 10. What
is significant about the italics and about the placement of these
words?*

*2.   Point out words and phrases that evoke the atmosphere of
"strangeness" mentioned in paragraph 1. Why does Updike say
that "A kind of silence prevailed" (par. 1)? Explain what is
meant by a "split-second Prometheus" (par. 2). What does this*

comparison tell you about Updike's estimate of his own courage?

3. *What is the effect of including specific details about the trash: "yesterday's Boston* Globe, *a milk carton, a Hi-Ho cracker box" (par. 3)?*

4. *Sometimes an author repeats a detail or image in order to give his essay unity or to create a recurring picture that becomes a "motif." In paragraph 1, Updike says that "the spots of . . . sunlight underneath the trees were all shaped like feathers." In paragraph 3, the "feathers under the trees had changed direction." What is the effect of the repetition here? Find other examples of repetition that produces a similar effect.*

Generating Ideas

1. *Write a narrative in which you recount your experience (or that of someone you know) with a natural disturbance such as a tornado, blizzard, sandstorm, earthquake, or flood. Try to evoke in your reader the exact feelings you had by using details that capture the atmosphere surrounding the event.*

2. *Tell of some happening in which you (or people you know) were affected by a superstitious belief. Did you act differently because of it? Did your fear prove unfounded, or was it justified? For instance, have you ever known anyone who avoided walking under a ladder or crossing the path of a black cat?*

3. *If you ever had an experience in which a belief, an attitude, or a moral stance that you once held was challenged or changed drastically, write a paper using narration to explain what occurred and how the experience affected you. These suggestions may help you get started:*
A fear or realization that you were wrong about someone or something
A realization that a long-held wish could never come true
A marriage or divorce that affected your life
The discovery that many of your friends held a set of beliefs radically different from your own

Tom Wolfe

Tom Wolfe (b. 1931) has written extensively on many public figures and pop trends in contemporary American society. He holds a Ph.D. in American studies from Yale and was for a time a reporter for the *Washington Post* and a reporter and magazine-writer for the *New York Herald Tribune.* Since 1968, he has been a contributing editor for *New York* magazine. In 1965 he gained attention with his collection of trend-setting articles entitled *The Kandy-Kolored Tangerine-Flake Streamline Baby.* Since then he has published *The Electric Kool-Aid Acid Test* (1968) and three other volumes of essays: *The Pump House Gang* (1968), *Radical Chic and Mau-Mauing the Flak Catchers* (1970), and *Mauve Gloves & Madmen, Clutter & Vine* (1976). He analyzed the trends he and others set in *The New Journalism* (1973) and attacked contemporary art in *The Painted Word* (1975). He himself is a visual artist and has had two one-man shows of drawings.

"The Frisbee Ion" is from an article entitled "The Intelligent Co-ed's Guide to America," a commentary on what Wolfe calls the "O'Hare philosophers." These are intellectuals who Wolfe contends spend their time at O'Hare airport in Chicago, waiting for planes to fly them to profitable speaking engagements on college campuses where they preach their gloom-and-doom philosophies.

The Frisbee Ion

If you happen to attend a conference at which whole contingents of the O'Hare philosophers assemble, you can get the message in all its varieties in a short time. Picture, if you will, a university on the Great Plains . . . a new Student Activities Center the color of butter-almond ice cream . . . a huge interior space with tracks in the floor, along which janitors in green twill pull Expando-Flex accordion walls to create meeting rooms of any size. The conference is about to begin. The students come surging in like hormones. You've heard of rosy cheeks? They *have* them! Here they come, rosy-cheeked, laughing, with Shasta and 7-Up pumping through their veins, talking chipsy, flashing weatherproof smiles, bursting out of their down-filled Squaw Valley jackets and their blue jeans—looking, all of them, boys and girls, Jocks & Buds & Freaks, as if they spent the day hang-gliding and then made a Miller commercial at dusk and are now going to taper off with a little Culture before returning to the co-ed dorm.

They grow quiet. The conference begins. The keynote speaker, a historian wearing a calfskin jacket and hair like Felix Mendelssohn's, informs them that the United States is "a leaden, life-denying society."

2   Over the next thirty-six hours, other O'Hare regulars fill in the rest:

3   Sixty families control one-half the private wealth of America, and 200 corporations own two-thirds of the means of production. "A small group of nameless, faceless men" who avoid publicity the way a werewolf avoids the dawn now dominates American life. In America a man's home is not his castle but merely "a gigantic listening device with a mortgage"—a reference to eavesdropping by the FBI and the CIA. America's foreign policy has been and continues to be based upon war, assassination, bribery, genocide, and the sabotage of democratic governments. "The new McCarthyism" (Joe's, not Gene's) is already upon us. Following a brief charade of free speech, the "gagging of the press" has resumed. Racism in America has not diminished; it is merely more subtle now. The gulf between rich and poor widens daily, creating "permanent ghetto-colonial populations." The decline in economic growth is causing a crisis in capitalism, which will lead shortly to authoritarian rule and to a new America in which everyone waits, in horror, for the knock on the door in the dead of the night, the descent of the knout on the nape of the neck—

4   How other people attending this conference felt by now, I didn't dare ask. As for myself, I was beginning to feel like Job or Miss Cunégonde. What further devastations or humiliations could possibly be in store, short of the sacking of Kansas City? It was in that frame of mind that I attended the final panel discussion, which was entitled "The United States in the Year 2000."

5   The prognosis was not good, as you can imagine. But I was totally unprepared for the astounding news brought by an ecologist.

6   "I'm not sure I want to be alive in the year 2000," he said, although he certainly looked lively enough at the moment. He was about thirty-eight, and he wore a Madras plaid cotton jacket and a Disco Magenta turtleneck jersey.

7   It seemed that recent studies showed that, due to the rape of the atmosphere by aerosol spray users, by 2000

a certain ion would no longer be coming our way from the sun. I can't remember which one . . . the aluminum ion, the magnesium ion, the neon ion, the gadolinium ion, the calcium ion . . . the calcium ion perhaps; in any event, it was crucial for the formation of bones, and by 2000 it would be no more. Could such a thing be? Somehow this went beyond any of the horrors I was already imagining. I began free-associating. . . . Suddenly I could see Lexington Avenue, near where I live in Manhattan. The presence of the storm troopers was the least of it. It was the look of ordinary citizens that was so horrible. Their bones were going. They were dissolving. Women who had once been clicking and clogging down the Avenue up on five-inch platform soles, with their pants seams smartly cleaving their declivities, were now mere denim & patent-leather blobs . . . oozing and inching and suppurating along the sidewalk like amoebas or ticks. . . . A cabdriver puts his arm out the window . . . and it just dribbles down the yellow door like hot Mazola. . . . A blind news dealer tries to give change to a notions buyer for Bloomingdale's, and their fingers run together like fettucine over a stack of *New York Posts.* . . . It's horrible . . . it's obscene . . . it's the end—

I was so dazed, I was no longer wondering what the assembled students thought of all this. But just at that moment one of them raised his hand. He was a tall boy with a lot of curly hair and a Fu Manchu moustache. 8

"Yes?" said the ecologist. 9

"There's one thing I can't understand," said the boy. 10

"What's that?" said the ecologist. 11

"Well," said the boy. "I'm a senior, and for four years we've been told by people like yourself and the other gentlemen that everything's in terrible shape, and it's all going to hell, and I'm willing to take your word for it, because you're all experts in your field. But around here, at this school, for the past four years, the biggest problem, as far as I can see, has been finding a parking place near the campus." 12

Dead silence. The panelists looked at this poor turkey to try to size him up. Was he trying to be funny? Or was this the native bray of the heartland? The ecologist struck a note of forbearance as he said: 13

"I'm sure that's true, and that illustrates one of the biggest difficulties we have in making realistic assessments. 14

A university like this, after all, is a middle-class institution, and middle-class life is calculated precisely to create a screen—"

15 "I understand all that," said the boy. "What I want to know is—how old are you, usually, when it all hits you?"

16 And suddenly the situation became clear. The kid was no wiseacre! He was genuinely perplexed! . . . For four years he had been squinting at the horizon . . . looking for the grim horrors which he knew—on faith—to be all around him . . . and had been utterly unable to find them . . . and now he was afraid they might descend on him all at once when he least expected it. He might be walking down the street in Omaha one day, minding his own business, when—whop! whop! whop! whop!—War! Fascism! Repression! Corruption!—they'd squash him like bowling balls rolling off a roof!

17 Who was that lost lad? What was his name? Without knowing it, he was playing the xylophone in a boneyard. He was the unique new creature of the 1970s. He was Candide in reverse. Candide and Miss Cunégonde, one will recall, are taught by an all-knowing savant, Dr. Pangloss. He keeps assuring them that this is "the best of all possible worlds," and they believe him implicitly—even though their lives are one catastrophe after another. Now something much weirder was happening. The Jocks & Buds & Freaks of the heartland have their all-knowing savants of O'Hare, who keep warning them that this is "the worst of all possible worlds," and they know it must be true— and yet life keeps getting easier, sunnier, happier . . . *Frisbee!*

18 How can such things be?

Discussing Content and Form

1. What point does Wolfe want to make in his narration? Is his point explicit or implicit? Explain.

2. Describe the kind of reader Wolfe is trying to reach. Give reasons for your view.

3. Based on your experience, how accurate do you find Wolfe's description of the student audience?

4. What is your reaction to the problems discussed by the speakers? Which problem do you consider the most urgent and real? Can most of them be solved? Explain.

5.   *Is Wolfe in agreement with the "O'Hare philosophers" or with the student questioner? Support your answer by referring to the essay.*

6.   *In paragraph 17, Wolfe compares the situation of the student to that of the hero of* Candide, *a philosophical novel by Voltaire, published in 1759. Explain how irony functions in both situations. To what extent is the student's situation humorous? Is it also sad? Explain.*

7.   *What is the significance of the title "The Frisbee Ion"? Of using the word* Frisbee *at the end of paragraph 17?*

Considering Special Techniques

1.   *To what extent does the vividness of the descriptive and narrative sections of this selection depend upon the use of specific details? How much does the quantity of detail contribute to its overall effect?*

2.   *What is the function of the single sentence that comprises paragraph 2? Identify the two-fold function of paragraph 8. How does this paragraph contribute to the organization, and what does it reveal about Wolfe's attitude toward his subject?*

3.   *Wolfe frequently uses the dash, and he also uses three dots (four at the ends of sentences) as punctuation marks to separate phrases or even sentences. What does this kind of punctuation contribute to the movement of the narrative? What special effect is achieved by the punctuation in paragraph 16?*

4.   *The first three paragraphs of the narrative are in the present tense ("The conference is about to begin." "The decline in economic growth is causing. . . ."). In paragraph 4, Wolfe shifts to the past tense. Account for his use of the two tenses. Is the shift logical? Why or why not?*

5.   *Wolfe is a master of the precise phrase and comparison, and he often gives a humorous and vivid twist to his descriptions by using fresh and colorful images. Discuss the effect of the following phrases in particular, and find others that are equally effective:*
a.   *"a new Student Activities Center the color of butter-almond ice cream" (par. 1)*
b.   *"students come surging in like hormones" (par. 1)*
c.   *"with Shasta and 7-Up pumping through their veins" (par. 1)*
d.   *"fingers run together like fettucine" (par. 7)*

Generating Ideas

1. Write a narrative about a lecturer's visit to your campus. If you can, include several outstanding incidents as part of your paper. You might discuss the content of the lecture, describe student reactions, and record any questions and answers that were exchanged. Or, imagine yourself a guest lecturer, and write a narrative about your visit. Try to give vivid impressions of the campus, the students, and the reception given you.

2. If you have ever had a question misinterpreted by the person to whom it was directed, recount what happened. Here are some titles that may suggest an approach:
"A Question I Should Not Have Asked"
"No Questions, Please"
"Why Parents (Teachers) Refuse to Answer"
"Asked Out of Innocence"
"Answers by the Experts"

3. Write a paper about one of the catastrophes that so-called experts predict will befall the world in the next fifty years or so. Give reasons for believing or not believing in the prediction and its consequences. Here are some suggestions:
a. The depletion of fossil fuels
b. Thermonuclear war
c. A new Ice Age
d. The destruction of the earth's ozone layer from aerosol sprays
e. Worldwide starvation
   Or narrate an event which has brought home to you the possible truth of such predictions. For example, if you have experienced heavy smog over a city, you might write about your realization of pollution. If you have been through a power failure, you might write about "the day the energy gives out."

4. Using narration, present your own view of what life will be like in the year 2000.

5. Although the essay contains many examples of future catastrophes, it concludes with the idea that "life keeps getting easier, sunnier, happier" (par. 17). Create a dialogue or interview between two persons (real or imaginary) who hold these opposing views.

Nora Ephron

Nora Ephron (b. 1941) was educated at Wellesley and Briarcliffe and began her writing career as a reporter for the *New York Post.* Since 1968, she has been a free-lance writer, contributing numerous articles to such magazines as *Newsweek, New York,* and *Esquire.* Her writing, which is often humorous and satirical, and always penetratingly insightful, is chiefly about women. Two of her collections of essays are *Wallflower at the Orgy* (1970) and *Crazy Salad* (1975). In "The Hurled Ashtray" (from *Crazy Salad*), she presents in narrative form some of the confusion that she and other women feel about their relationship to men.

The Hurled Ashtray

I once heard a swell story about Gary Cooper. The person I heard the story from did this terrific Gary Cooper imitation, and it may be that when I tell you the story (which I am about to), it will lose something in print. It may lose everything, in fact. But enough. The story was that Gary Cooper was in a London restaurant at a large table of friends. He was sitting in a low chair, with his back to the rest of the room, so no one in the restaurant even knew that he was tall, much less that he was Gary Cooper. Across the way was a group of Teddy boys (this episode took place long long ago, you see), and they were all misbehaving and making nasty remarks about a woman at Cooper's table. Cooper turned around to give them his best mean-and-threatening stare, but they went right on. Finally he got up, very very slowly, so slowly that it took almost a minute for him to go from this short person in a low chair to a ten-foot-tall man with Gary Cooper's head on top of his shoulders. He loped over to the table of Teddy boys, looked down at them, and said, "Wouldja mind sayin' that agin?" The men were utterly cowed and left the restaurant shortly thereafter. 1

Well, you had to be there. 2

I thought of Gary Cooper and his way with words the other day. Longingly. Because in the mail, from an editor of *New York* magazine, came an excerpt from a book by Michael Korda called *Male Chauvinism: How It Works* 3

(Random House). I have no idea whether Korda's book is any good at all, but the excerpt was fascinating, a sort of reverse-twist update on Francis Macomber, as well as a pathetic contrast to the Gary Cooper story. It seems that Korda, his wife, and another woman were having dinner in a London restaurant recently. Across the way was a table of drunks doing sensitive things like sniggering and leering and throwing bread balls at Mrs. Korda, who is a looker. Her back was to them, and she refused to acknowledge their presence, instead apparently choosing to let the flying bread balls bounce off her back onto the floor. Then, one of the men sent over a waiter with a silver tray. On it was a printed card, the kind you can buy in novelty shops, which read: "I want to sleep with you! Tick off your favorite love position from the list below, and return this card with your telephone number. . . ." Korda tore up the card before his wife could even see it, and then, consumed with rage, he picked up an ashtray and threw it at the man who had sent the card. A fracas ensued, and before long, Korda, his wife, and their woman friend were out on the street. Mrs. Korda was furious.

4   "If you ever do that again," she screamed, "I'll leave you! Do you think I couldn't have handled that, or ignored it? Did I ask you to come to my defense against some poor stupid drunk? You didn't even think, you just reacted like a male chauvinist. You leapt up to defend *your* woman, *your* honor, you made me seem cheap and foolish and powerless. . . . God Almighty, can't you see it was none of your business! Can't you understand how it makes me feel? I don't mind being hassled by some drunk, I can take that, but to be treated like a chattel, to be robbed of any right to decide for myself whether I'd been insulted, or how badly, to have you react for me because I'm *your* woman . . . that's really sickening, it's like being a slave." Korda repeats the story (his wife's diatribe is even longer in the original version) and then, in a *mea culpa* that is only too reminiscent of the sort that used to appear in 1960s books by white liberals about blacks, he concludes that his wife is doubtless right, that men do tend to treat women merely as appendages of themselves.

5   Before printing the article, *New York* asked several couples—including my husband and me—what our reaction was to what happened, and what we would have done under the circumstances. My initial reaction to the entire

business was that no one ever sends me notes like that in restaurants. I sent that off to the editor, but a few days later I got to thinking about the story, and it began to seem to me that the episode just might be a distillation of everything that has happened to men and women as a result of the women's movement, and if not that, at least a way to write about etiquette after the revolution, and if not that, nothing at all. Pulled as I was by these three possibilities, I told the story over dinner to four friends and asked for their reaction. The first, a man, said that he thought Mrs. Korda was completely right. The second, a woman, said she thought Korda's behavior was totally understandable. The third, a man, said that both parties had behaved badly. The fourth, my friend Martha, said it was the second most boring thing she had ever heard, the most boring being a story I had just told her about a fight my college roommate had with a cabdriver at Kennedy Airport.

In any case, before any serious discussion of the incident   6
of the hurled ashtray, I would like to raise some questions for which I have no answers. I raise them simply because if that story were fed into a computer, the only possible response it could make is We Do Not Have Sufficient Information To Make An Evaluation. For example:

Do the Kordas have a good marriage?   7

Was the heat working in their London hotel room the   8
night of the fracas?

Was it raining out?   9

What did the second woman at the table look like? Was   10
she as pretty as Mrs. Korda? Was she ugly? Was part of
Michael Korda's reaction—and his desire to assert possession of his wife—the result of the possibility that he suspected the drunks thought he was with someone funny-looking?

What kind of a tacky restaurant is it where a waiter   11
delivers a dirty message on a silver tray?

What about a woman who ignores flying bread balls?   12
Wasn't her husband justified in thinking she would be
no more interested in novelty cards?

Did Michael Korda pay the check before or after throw-   13
ing the ashtray? Did he tip the standard 15 percent?

Since the incident occurs in London, a city notorious   14
for its rampant homoerotic behavior, and since the table
of drunks was all male, isn't it possible that the printed

card was in fact intended not for Mrs. Korda but for Michael? In which case how should we now view his response, if at all?

15   There might be those who would raise questions about the ashtray itself: was it a big, heavy ashtray, these people might ask, or a dinky little round one? Was it glass or was it plastic? These questions are irrelevant.

16   In the absence of answers to any of the above, I would nonetheless like to offer some random musings. First, I think it is absurd for Mrs. Korda to think that she and she alone was involved in the incident. Yes, it might have been nice had her husband consulted her; and yes, it would have been even nicer had he turned out to be Gary Cooper, or failing that, Dave DeBusschere, or even Howard Cosell—anyone but this suave flinger of ashtrays he turned out to be. But the fact remains that the men at the table *were* insulting Korda, and disturbing his dinner, as well as hers. Their insult was childish and Korda's reaction was ludicrous, but Mrs. Korda matched them all by reducing a complicated and rather interesting emotional situation to a tedious set of movement platitudes.

17   Beyond that—and the Kordas quite aside, because God Almighty (as Mrs. Korda might put it) knows what it is they are into—I wonder whether there is any response a man could make in that situation which would not disappoint a feminist. Yes, I want to be treated as an equal and not as an appendage or possession or spare rib, but I also want to be taken care of. Isn't any man sitting at a table with someone like me damned whatever he does? If the drunks in question are simply fools, conventioneers with funny paper hats, I suppose that a possible reaction would be utter cool. But if they were truly insulting and disturbing, some response does seem called for. Some wild and permanent gesture of size. But on whose part? And what should it consist of? And how tall do you have to be to bring it off? And where is the point that a mild show of strength becomes crude macho vulgarity; where does reserve veer off into passivity?

18   Like almost every other question in this column, I have no positive answer. But I think that if I ever found myself in a similar situation, and if it was truly demeaning, I would prefer that my husband handle it. My husband informs me, after some consideration, that the Gary Cooper approach would not work. But he could, for example, call

over the captain and complain discreetly, perhaps even ask that our table be moved. He could hire a band of aging Teddy boys to find out where the drunks were staying and short-sheet all their beds. Or—and I think I prefer this—he could produce, from his jacket pocket, a printed card from a novelty shop reading: "I'm terribly sorry, but as you can see by looking at our dinner companion, my wife and I have other plans."

I'm going out to have those cards made up right now.   19

Discussing Content and Form

1.   What is the relationship between the two narrative incidents with which Ephron opens her essay? What is her purpose in telling the two stories?

2.   In what sense is paragraph 5 a third narrative incident in which the author is involved?

3.   What are your reactions to the story about Gary Cooper? To the incident involving the Kordas? How do your reactions differ from those of the people to whom Ephron told the story (par. 5)?

4.   Account for the reaction of Mrs. Korda. Do her actions indicate that she is a feminist? Do you agree or disagree that she reduced the situation to "a tedious set of movement platitudes" (par. 16)?

5.   What do Ephron's comments indicate about her views of the male/female roles in the stories? What does she mean by the statement that "the episode just might be a distillation of everything that has happened to men and women as a result of the women's movement" (par. 5)? To what extent do you think Ephron is serious? Explain.

Considering Special Techniques

1.   A relevant and often amusing anecdote is frequently used as an opener for essays or articles. Comment on the effectiveness of the narrative techniques that Ephron uses. For instance, does she make the events of the stories dramatic? Does she interest you in the people involved as well as in the events? Is the dialogue true to life? Explain.

2.   Give your opinions of the tone and language of the essay. Make a list of terms that seem effective here but that might not be suitable in more formal writing. You might begin with "swell," "terrific," and "utterly" in paragraph 1.

3. *What is the effect of the one-sentence paragraph (2), "Well, you had to be there"?*

4. *Why does the writer resort to so many unanswered questions? What is the relationship of the repetition of questions to the main idea of the essay?*

5. *The allusions in this informal narrative are to actual people or to fictional characters that you probably can identify. For instance, Francis Macomber (par. 3) is the title character of an Ernest Hemingway short story. Macomber is killed by his wife while on an African safari; the author leaves it up to the reader to decide whether or not the shooting is accidental. Identify Dave DeBusschere and Howard Cosell (par. 16). How do you think they might have acted in Korda's position?*

6. *Other terms to explain:* Teddy boys *(par. 1);* chattel, diatribe, mea culpa *(par. 4);* rampant homoerotic behavior *(par. 14).*

Generating Ideas

1. *Take a stand favoring one of the opinions or actions presented in the essay, and write a paper explaining your views to a friend. These titles might help:*
"I Agree, Mrs. Korda!"
"Throw It Harder, Mike!"
"Good Going, Gary Cooper!"
"Like Nora's Friend, I Think It Boring"

2. *Recount an embarrassing incident you have observed, and draw some conclusions about what it is like to be placed in such an awkward situation. Or narrate an incident involving a public display of temper or bad manners; then draw your conclusions about such behavior. You might employ either a serious or humorous tone.*

3. *If you are a woman, relate an incident in which you felt that you were treated as an insignificant object by a man. If you are a man, write a narrative about circumstances that forced you, against your better judgment, to display masculine aggressiveness.*

4. *Write a paper dealing with one of these problems raised in the essay:*

a. *"some response does seem called for. . . . But on whose part?" (par. 17)*
b. *"I wonder whether there is any response a man could make in that situation which would not disappoint a feminist." (par. 17)*
c. *"where is the point that a mild show of strength becomes crude macho vulgarity; where does reserve veer off into passivity?" (par. 17)*

E. B. White

E. B. White (b. 1899) is one of America's finest prose stylists. He is known for his essays, editorials, and columns; he has also written verse. He revised and enlarged *The Elements of Style,* by his college professor William Strunk, Jr., a best-selling book for writers. Many readers, too, know and love his children's classics, *Stuart Little* (1945) and *Charlotte's Web* (1952). His essay collections include *Is Sex Necessary?* (with James Thurber, 1929), *One Man's Meat* (1942), *The Second Tree from the Corner* (1953), and *The Points of My Compass* (1962). In 1976 a collection of White's letters appeared, giving him what he describes as an "entirely different kind of exposure." Even the letters that White wrote as a very young boy reveal his gift for handling words, and the letters as a whole reveal the charm and humor that readers have appreciated in the essays.

For many years both White and his wife, Katharine Sergeant White, a *New Yorker* editor, were associated with that magazine. In 1938 they left Manhattan to live in their farmhouse on the coast of Maine. Some of White's best-known essays are based on his observations of life in the country. "Once More to the Lake" links his own boyhood summers in Maine with the experience of watching his son enjoy the same scene.

Once More to the Lake

August 1941

1   One summer, along about 1904, my father rented a camp on a lake in Maine and took us all there for the month of August. We all got ringworm from some kittens and had to rub Pond's Extract on our arms and legs night and morning, and my father rolled over in a canoe with all his clothes on; but outside of that the vacation was a success and from then on none of us ever thought there was any place in the world like that lake in Maine. We returned summer after summer—always on August 1st for one month. I have since become a salt-water man, but sometimes in summer there are days when the restlessness of the tides and the fearful cold of the sea water and the incessant wind which blows across the afternoon and into the evening make me wish for the placidity of a lake in the woods. A few weeks ago this feeling got so strong I bought myself a couple of bass h/oks and a spinner and returned to the lake where we used to go, for a week's fishing and to revisit old haunts.

I took along my son, who had never had any fresh water 2
up his nose and who had seen lily pads only from train
windows. On the journey over to the lake I began to wonder what it would be like. I wondered how time would
have marred this unique, this holy spot—the coves and
streams, the hills that the sun set behind, the camps and
the paths behind the camps. I was sure the tarred road
would have found it out and I wondered in what other
ways it would be desolated. It is strange how much you
can remember about places like that once you allow your
mind to return into the grooves which lead back. You remember one thing, and that suddenly reminds you of another thing. I guess I remembered clearest of all the early
mornings, when the lake was cool and motionless, remembered how the bedroom smelled of the lumber it was made
of and of the wet woods whose scent entered through the
screen. The partitions in the camp were thin and did not
extend clear to the top of the rooms, and as I was always
the first up I would dress softly so as not to wake the others,
and sneak out into the sweet outdoors and start out in
the canoe, keeping close along the shore in the long shadows of the pines. I remembered being very careful never
to rub my paddle against the gunwale for fear of disturbing the stillness of the cathedral.

The lake had never been what you would call a wild 3
lake. There were cottages sprinkled around the shores,
and it was in farming country although the shores of the
lake were quite heavily wooded. Some of the cottages were
owned by nearby farmers, and you would live at the shore
and eat your meals at the farmhouse. That's what our
family did. But although it wasn't wild, it was a fairly
large and undisturbed lake and there were places in it
which, to a child at least, seemed infinitely remote and
primeval.

I was right about the tar: it led to within half a mile 4
of the shore. But when I got back there, with my boy,
and we settled into a camp near a farmhouse and into
the kind of summertime I had known, I could tell that
it was going to be pretty much the same as it had been
before—I knew it, lying in bed the first morning, smelling
the bedroom, and hearing the boy sneak quietly out and
go off along the shore in a boat. I began to sustain the
illusion that he was I, and therefore, by simple transposition, that I was my father. This sensation persisted, kept

cropping up all the time we were there. It was not an entirely new feeling, but in this setting it grew much stronger. I seemed to be living a dual existence. I would be in the middle of some simple act, I would be picking up a bait box or laying down a table fork, or I would be saying something, and suddenly it would be not I but my father who was saying the words or making the gesture. It gave me a creepy sensation.

5   We went fishing the first morning. I felt the same damp moss covering the worms in the bait can, and saw the dragonfly alight on the tip of my rod as it hovered a few inches from the surface of the water. It was the arrival of this fly that convinced me beyond any doubt that everything was as it always had been, that the years were a mirage and there had been no years. The small waves were the same, chucking the rowboat under the chin as we fished at anchor, and the boat was the same boat, the same color green and the ribs broken in the same places, and under the floor-boards the same fresh-water leavings and débris—the dead helgramite, the wisps of moss, the rusty discarded fishhook, the dried blood from yesterday's catch. We stared silently at the tips of our rods, at the dragonflies that came and went. I lowered the tip of mine into the water, tentatively, pensively dislodging the fly, which darted two feet away, poised, darted two feet back, and came to rest again a little farther up the rod. There had been no years between the ducking of this dragonfly and the other one—the one that was part of memory. I looked at the boy, who was silently watching his fly, and it was my hands that held his rod, my eyes watching. I felt dizzy and didn't know which rod I was at the end of.

6   We caught two bass, hauling them in briskly as though they were mackerel, pulling them over the side of the boat in a businesslike manner without any landing net, and stunning them with a blow on the back of the head. When we got back for a swim before lunch, the lake was exactly where we had left it, the same number of inches from the dock, and there was only the merest suggestion of a breeze. This seemed an utterly enchanted sea, this lake you could leave to its own devices for a few hours and come back to, and find that it had not stirred, this constant and trustworthy body of water. In the shallows, the dark, water-soaked sticks and twigs, smooth and old, were undulating in clusters on the bottom against the

clean ribbed sand, and the track of the mussel was plain.
A school of minnows swam by, each minnow with its
small individual shadow, doubling the attendance, so
clear and sharp in the sunlight. Some of the other campers
were in swimming, along the shore, one of them with a
cake of soap, and the water felt thin and clear and unsub-
stantial. Over the years there had been this person with
the cake of soap, this cultist, and here he was. There had
been no years.

Up to the farmhouse to dinner through the teeming, 7
dusty field, the road under our sneakers was only a two-
track road. The middle track was missing, the one with
the marks of the hooves and the splotches of dried, flaky
manure. There had always been three tracks to choose
from in choosing which track to walk in; now the choice
was narrowed down to two. For a moment I missed terribly
the middle alternative. But the way led past the tennis
court, and something about the way it lay there in the
sun reassured me; the tape had loosened along the back-
line, the alleys were green with plantains and other weeds,
and the net (installed in June and removed in September)
sagged in the dry noon, and the whole place steamed with
midday heat and hunger and emptiness. There was a
choice of pie for dessert, and one was blueberry and one
was apple, and the waitresses were the same country girls,
there having been no passage of time, only the illusion
of it as in a dropped curtain—the waitresses were still
fifteen; their hair had been washed, that was the only
difference—they had been to the movies and seen the
pretty girls with the clean hair.

Summertime, oh summertime, pattern of life indelible, 8
the fade-proof lake, the woods unshatterable, the pasture
with the sweetfern and the juniper forever and ever, summer without end; this was the background, and the life
along the shore was the design, the cottages with their
innocent and tranquil design, their tiny docks with the
flagpole and the American flag floating against the white
clouds in the blue sky, the little paths over the roots of
the trees leading from camp to camp and the paths leading back to the outhouses and the can of lime for sprin-
kling, and at the souvenir counters at the store the miniature birch-bark canoes and the post cards that showed
things looking a little better than they looked. This was
the American family at play, escaping the city heat, won-

dering whether the newcomers in the camp at the head of the cove were "common" or "nice," wondering whether it was true that the people who drove up for Sunday dinner at the farmhouse were turned away because there wasn't enough chicken.

9   It seemed to me, as I kept remembering all this, that those times and those summers had been infinitely precious and worth saving. There had been jollity and peace and goodness. The arriving (at the beginning of August) had been so big a business in itself, at the railway station the farm wagon drawn up, the first smell of the pine-laden air, the first glimpse of the smiling farmer, and the great importance of the trunks and your father's enormous authority in such matters, and the feel of the wagon under you for the long ten-mile haul, and at the top of the last long hill catching the first view of the lake after eleven months of not seeing this cherished body of water. The shouts and cries of the other campers when they saw you, and the trunks to be unpacked, to give up their rich burden. (Arriving was less exciting nowadays, when you sneaked up in your car and parked it under a tree near the camp and took out the bags and in five minutes it was all over, no fuss, no loud wonderful fuss about trunks.)

10   Peace and goodness and jollity. The only thing that was wrong now, really, was the sound of the place, an unfamiliar nervous sound of the outboard motors. This was the note that jarred, the one thing that would sometimes break the illusion and set the years moving. In those other summertimes all motors were inboard; and when they were at a little distance, the noise they made was a sedative, an ingredient of summer sleep. They were one-cylinder and two-cylinder engines, and some were make-and-break and some were jump-spark, but they all made a sleepy sound across the lake. The one-lungers throbbed and fluttered, and the twin-cylinder ones purred and purred, and that was a quiet sound too. But now the campers all had outboards. In the daytime, in the hot mornings, these motors made a petulant, irritable sound; at night, in the still evening when the afterglow lit the water, they whined about one's ears like mosquitoes. My boy loved our rented outboard, and his great desire was to achieve single-handed mastery over it, and authority, and he soon learned the trick of choking it a little (but not too much), and the adjustment of the needle valve. Watching him I

would remember the things you could do with the old one-cylinder engine with the heavy flywheel, how you could have it eating out of your hand if you got really close to it spiritually. Motor boats in those days didn't have clutches, and you would make a landing by shutting off the motor at the proper time and coasting in with a dead rudder. But there was a way of reversing them, if you learned the trick, by cutting the switch and putting it on again exactly on the final dying revolution of the flywheel, so that it would kick back against compression and begin reversing. Approaching a dock in a strong following breeze, it was difficult to slow up sufficiently by the ordinary coasting method, and if a boy felt he had complete mastery over his motor, he was tempted to keep it running beyond its time and then reverse it a few feet from the dock. It took a cool nerve, because if you threw the switch a twentieth of a second too soon you would catch the flywheel when it still had speed enough to go up past center, and the boat would leap ahead, charging bull-fashion at the dock.

We had a good week at the camp. The bass were biting well and the sun shone endlessly, day after day. We would be tired at night and lie down in the accumulated heat of the little bedrooms after the long hot day and the breeze would stir almost imperceptibly outside and the smell of the swamp drift in through the rusty screens. Sleep would come easily and in the morning the red squirrel would be on the roof, tapping out his gay routine. I kept remembering everything, lying in bed in the mornings—the small steamboat that had a long rounded stern like the lip of a Ubangi, and how quietly she ran on the moonlight sails, when the older boys played their mandolins and the girls sang and we ate doughnuts dipped in sugar, and how sweet the music was on the water in the shining night, and what it had felt like to think about girls then. After breakfast we would go up to the store and the things were in the same place—the minnows in a bottle, the plugs and spinners disarranged and pawed over by the youngsters from the boys' camp, the fig newtons and the Beeman's gum. Outside, the road was tarred and cars stood in front of the store. Inside, all was just as it had always been, except there was more Coca-Cola and not so much Moxie and root beer and birch beer and sarsaparilla. We would walk out with a bottle of pop apiece and sometimes

11

the pop would backfire up our noses and hurt. We explored the streams, quietly, where the turtles slid off the sunny logs and dug their way into the soft bottom; and we lay on the town wharf and fed worms to the tame bass. Everywhere we went I had trouble making out which was I, the one walking at my side, the one walking in my pants.

12   One afternoon while we were there at that lake a thunderstorm came up. It was like the revival of an old melodrama that I had seen long ago with childish awe. The second-act climax of the drama of the electrical disturbance over a lake in America had not changed in any important respect. This was the big scene, still the big scene. The whole thing was so familiar, the first feeling of oppression and heat and a general air around camp of not wanting to go very far away. In midafternoon (it was all the same) a curious darkening of the sky, and a lull in everything that had made life tick; and then the way the boats suddenly swung the other way at their moorings with the coming of a breeze out of the new quarter, and the premonitory rumble. Then the kettle drum, then the snare, then the bass drum and cymbals, then crackling light against the dark, and the gods grinning and licking their chops in the hills. Afterward the calm, the rain steadily rustling in the calm lake, the return of light and hope and spirits, and the campers running out in joy and relief to go swimming in the rain, their bright cries perpetuating the deathless joke about how they were getting simply drenched, and the children screaming with delight at the new sensation of bathing in the rain, and the joke about getting drenched linking the generations in a strong indestructible chain. And the comedian who waded in carrying an umbrella.

13   When the others went swimming my son said he was going in too. He pulled his dripping trunks from the line where they had hung all through the shower, and wrung them out. Languidly, and with no thought of going in, I watched him, his hard little body, skinny and bare, saw him wince slightly as he pulled up around his vitals the small, soggy, icy garment. As he buckled the swollen belt suddenly my groin felt the chill of death.

Discussing Content and Form

1. In what sense are the first three paragraphs an introduction to the point made in paragraph 4: "I began to sustain the illusion that he was I, and therefore, by simple transposition, that I was my father"?

2. In the essay, White narrates in order to convey a central idea, to make a point not only about his experience but also about human experience in general. State his point in your own words. How does it relate to White's feeling of "transposition" expressed in paragraph 4? In succeeding paragraphs, find sentences that restate this idea. What special force does the last paragraph contribute?

3. White describes the lake as a "holy spot" and tells of his worries that it "would be desolated" (par. 2). Do you think he is sorry that he returned? Support your answer by referring to the essay.

4. White finds that fishing and swimming are unchanged, that the lake is still "enchanted" (par. 6), but that the middle track is "missing" from the road (par. 7). What is the significance of the change in the road? Why does White regret the loss of the "middle alternative"? What essential difference between nature and human beings is emphasized throughout the essay?

5. White says, "It seemed to me . . . that those times and those summers had been infinitely precious and worth saving" (par. 9). Do you think his son will feel the same way about the trip to the lake? Explain.

Considering Special Techniques

1. Most of White's paragraphs are tightly organized clusters of sentences that develop a single topic. Treating the first three paragraphs as the introduction, determine the general topic for each paragraph that follows.

2. Analyze the method of organization for paragraphs 10 and 12.
a. What use is made of contrast in paragraph 10? Note the linking phrases such as "In those other summertimes" and "But now the campers." Find other examples of such phrases in the essay.
b. Read the introduction to Chapter 7 on analogy and explain

how the comparison of the thunderstorm to a drama organizes paragraph 12. In what ways does a storm resemble a play?

3.   *White's writing furnishes many examples of what is sometimes called the* cumulative *sentence. Such sentences are made up of a main clause, or base, with an accumulation of modifying phrases added to enrich and enlarge the meaning and to make it more specific. The following sentence from paragraph 6 has three additions, each enlarging the idea expressed in the main clause:*
"We caught two bass,
> *hauling them in briskly as though they were mackerel,*
> *pulling them over the side of the boat in a businesslike manner without any landing net,*
> *and stunning them with a blow on the back of the head."*
In another cumulative sentence (par. 6), note how the added phrases tell something more about the school of minnows:
"A school of minnows swam by,
> *each minnow with its small individual shadow,*
> *doubling the attendance,*
> *so clear and sharp in the sunlight."*
Find other sentences in the essay where the details are added cumulatively to give increasingly specific information. Make an analysis of the first sentence of paragraph 8.

4.   *In paragraph 11, White shifts the form of the verbs from the simple past to the progressive form with the modal* would: *"We* would *be tired"; "the breeze* would *stir"; "Sleep* would *come." Why does he make this shift only in this paragraph?*

5.   *Why does the writer reverse the order of the second sentence in paragraph 9 and use it as the opener for paragraph 10?*

6.   *Explain the effect produced by these words and phrases: "a salt-water man" (par. 1); "the stillness of the cathedral" (par. 2); "this person with the cake of soap, this cultist" (par. 6); "the American family at play" (par. 8); "nervous sound of the outboard motors" (par. 10).*

Generating Ideas

1.   *Choose one of these subjects for an essay based on your experience or on those of others whom you know:*
A revisit to a place where you once lived
A storm and its effects on a town, resort area, etc.
A change in a family, in customs, or in a particular locale
A childhood journey or visit you made with an adult

2. *Write an essay about the "American family at play" as you know it. Use narrative incidents to illustrate your points. For example, if you think that families seldom take vacations nowadays, you will want to gather evidence to support your view.*

3. *White says the lake was "to a child . . . enchantment." Write of some spot or some experience that holds enchantment for you, trying to re-create in narration and description the emotional attachment you feel for the place.*

4. *Write a narrative about the visit to the lake as it might have appeared to White's son.*

4
Organizing Specifics:
Example

From experience and observation come the factual materials or examples that enable you to *show* rather than merely *tell* your reader what you mean. The difference between showing and telling is often the difference between writing that convinces and writing that merely presents generalizations which may or may not be convincing. Many people can make the same general statement in much the same words, but using personal observations gives writing the stamp of individuality and makes it ring true at the same time.

This chapter opens with a paragraph of generalization which needs some concrete support. That paragraph tells; this paragraph shows. Let us assume that you have in mind a generalization about the unusual stunts people perform on mountains. The following paragraph states this generalization, then lists many examples which give it powerful support:

> Mountains have always presented a stage for the offbeat and the record breaker. Longs Peak in the Rockies was in 1927 the scene of a summit marriage; three years later came the ascent by a five-year-old girl. The next year Francis W. Chamberlain got to the top on one leg and crutches, while in 1934 a marathon race up Mount Washington was held between three one-legged men. More conventional races have been run on scores of mountains from California's Mount Shasta to Scotland's Ben Nevis, where the speed of the locals has been pitted against visitors. A Japanese has skied down Fuji at 105 miles an hour, needing a parachute to bring him to a halt. On Yosemite's El Capitan, Rick Sylvester went one better, skiing down the summit slabs and parachute-jumping the remaining 1,000 meters. According to *The Alpine Journal,* he felt that climbs

he had made on the peak "no longer represented 'true adventure' as far as he was concerned, because they did not contain 'a large element of the unknown.' He therefore decided to undertake this sensational exploit, which perhaps has more in common with the circus than mountaineering, largely for the elements of uncertainty involved."—Ronald W. Clark, *Men, Myths, and Mountains*

This paragraph represents a very simple kind of organization, one that is frequently used in arranging examples. The opening sentence contains the controlling generalization for the paragraph. Such a sentence is sometimes called the *topic sentence,* and it frequently appears at the begining of a paragraph. The next two sentences each contain two examples, but the fourth sentence makes another general statement, one that is a little less general than that made by the first sentence. After that come two more examples: the first (about the Japanese skier) occupies one sentence, and the second (about Rick Sylvester) is expanded to fill the remainder of the paragraph. You can see that the writer has not only offered a great deal of specific support with the examples but he has also arranged those examples to build to the one he treats most fully, thus giving the paragraph both sufficient development and an emphatic conclusion.

Of course, the writer might have put his generalization in some position other than the first. And he might have used fewer examples or more, depending upon how many he thought would be both interesting and convincing. A fairly good rule of thumb in this kind of writing is to use about two-thirds to three-fourths of the space for examples and about one-fourth for generalizing, but there are no definite restrictions. In some single paragraphs, the general statement may not appear at all, but rather it may be implied. Whether explicit or implicit, the generalization is the point the writer wishes to convey by means of the examples.

We sometimes speak of the expanded example as an illustration, and in this paragraph the writer uses one such illustration from his personal experience to arrive at a statement about a word that he considers overused:

In *The New Yorker,* a few years ago, I described the rather haphazard way in which I first came to use the term "the Establishment," and tried to explain why it has made such an antic journey into the languages of I do not know how many countries. (A German scholar has told me that the correct translation of the word into German would contain at least seven syllables.) Not a day now passes when the phrase is not shouted, or whispered, back to me; and I have long since ceased to inquire what people mean by it. It seems to me now to have little or no meaning, and I rarely use it any longer.—Henry Fairlie, "The Language of Politics," *The Atlantic*

In long articles and essays, examples and illustrations may cover several paragraphs, all of them developing a section of general introduction or leading to one or more paragraphs of conclusion. And, of course, in such writing the sections developed by examples are usually combined with those developed by other methods. Frequently, however, the use of either short examples or longer illustrations dominates an entire selection. This is the primary method employed in the four essays in this chapter. Also, the development of an entire paper around illustrative details that support a generalization is often required in the essay questions given on tests: "Cite several examples of legal measures that have been used to control pollution of the Great Lakes"; "From the fiction we have studied, choose and discuss several examples of women who were forced by society to marry."

Whether the development by examples is long or short, "pure" or mixed with other methods, the same considerations apply. First, choose examples to fit both the purpose of the writing and the readers for whom it is intended. In writing about air pollution, for instance, it would not be suitable to introduce an example involving an oil spill in the Atlantic Ocean. The topic that is to be discussed sets limits around the choice of examples and rules out those that are marginally related. Similarly, in writing a letter to a newspaper about the dangers of pollution, you should include examples that are drawn from everyday life rather than from technical areas that would be suitable in a report for scientists. An example of the drainage problems at a local dump would serve the first audience, while examples dealing with the types and amounts of chemicals flowing into the Great Lakes might be more useful for the second.

Another major consideration—already mentioned in analyzing the paragraph about mountain climbing—is that of arrangement. When using several examples, you have to decide upon an order for placing them. At times a random or "the way things come to mind" order can be effective. (On p. 242, notice how Louis Untermeyer uses randomly placed examples to define metaphor.) However, if you are writing about dictators throughout the last two centuries of history, you might choose a chronological order, or perhaps an order of "least to most successful." If you want to give examples of the equipment needed to set up a home workshop, you could arrange the items in the order of the most essential to the least essential. If you want to discuss inexpensive vacations, you might begin with either the most or least costly trip of the group. Careful arrangement not only gives coherence to the paragraph or paper, thereby making it easy for the reader to follow, but it also allows for natural transition. In the paper on vacations, you could begin with an introductory phrase such as "The least expensive" and proceed to "The most costly but still relatively cheap," thus connecting the examples so smoothly that the reader hardly notices these linking devices.

Many old books on writing stipulated a "2–3–4–1" climactic arrangement for examples, suggesting that the second most interesting item be placed first and the best saved until last. (The numbers could, of course, be extended in the middle.) That rule seems rather rigid; but it might be worth using as a point of departure when you cannot decide on a more natural arrangement, especially for longer papers developed by a series of examples. Of one thing you can be sure with any arrangement. If the examples are suited to your purpose and interesting in themselves, they will both support your generalizations and provide the liveliness that is part of a vigorous style.

Charles Kuralt

Charles Kuralt (b. 1934) is best known for his CBS Television news feature "On the Road." Kuralt began his career in journalism with the *Charlotte* (N.C.) *News,* where he worked as a reporter from 1955 to 1957. He has been with CBS since 1957. Over the years, he has earned three major awards: the Ernie Pyle Memorial Award in 1956, and both the George Foster Peabody and Emmy awards for broadcasting in 1969. He is the author of *To the Top of the World* (1968) and of many articles derived from his work as a roving reporter whose chief interest is Americans and Americana. "The Great American Barbe-Queue" (editor's title) is in this same tradition of grassroots observation.

The Great American Barbe-Queue

1

Description of the old way of outdoor cooking (pars. 1–3)

An old refrigerator shelf was all you really needed.

2

That was your grill. You laid it on a circle of stones surrounding a bare spot on the lawn in the North Carolina backyard of my youth, started a charcoal fire under it, unwrapped a sirloin from the A&P, iced down a few bottles of beer in the wheelbarrow, and invited the neighbors over. After supper you sat talking quietly in the dusk until the mosquitoes got too bad. Contentment was within the grasp of anybody with an old refrigerator shelf.

3

I should have known something was going wrong when I came home from college to find that my own father had built a brick fireplace in the backyard, with a chimney. The neighbors admired it and set out to exceed it. That was twenty years ago.

4

Description of modern cooking equipment (pars. 4–5)

You, too, have noticed, I assume, how it all turned out. In this summer of our celebration, the electrical hum of the three-speed spit is heard in the land. It is revolving majestically over a four-wheel, gas-fired, smoke-controlled Adjustable Grid Patio Grill with a copper hood and a warming oven. The chef is wearing an apron with a funny saying on it. He is frown-

---

Originally entitled "Outdoor Cookery from Barbe to Queue," by Charles Kuralt from *Saturday Review,* June 26, 1976. Reprinted by permission of *Saturday Review.*

ing over his *caneton rôti aux pêches flambées,* trying to decide whether the sauce needs more Madeira. Contentment is not his.

For many years I have been traveling around America mooching meals from friends where possible and observing the decline of suburban serenity. I think the outdoor cooking machine has a lot to do with it. If we are ever going to win back our innocence, we have to rediscover the refrigerator shelf.

5

The pleasure of outdoor cooking used to be the simplicity of it. This is the ancestral secret of generations of American males that is in danger of being lost: *nothing you can do to a steak cooked outdoors can ruin it.*

6
Illustration of the simplicity of the older method (pars. 6–7)

A man (outdoor cooks are invariably men, for atavistic reasons having to do, I imagine, with knives and fire and ego) can thoughtfully marinate his steak for hours in a mixture of his own invention—wine vinegar, soy sauce, secret herbs, and tequila; then patiently wait for the coals to reach just the right color and temperature; then quickly sear the steak on both sides to contain its juices; then cook it by feel and by experience; he can do all these things—*or not*—and be certain of triumphant approval. "Good steak, George." "You cooked it just right, Daddy." They will say the same if he unwraps it half frozen, drops it on the grill, and remembers to pause in his drinking to turn it once.

7

But let this same man begin to believe himself a chef, acquire, in his pride, an outdoor cooking machine, and attempt dishes having to do with delicate sauces or, worse, flaming swords, and we would all be better off staying indoors. Indoors, Daddy disdains to help with the cooking. It is not cooking he loves; it is his machine.

8
Contrasting picture of the modern machine-oriented cook (par. 8)

There is still some good outdoor cooking going on in this country, but none of it needs machinery, and none of it comes from Escoffier.

9
Introduction to the examples of good outdoor cooking still to be found (par. 9)

First example (par. 10)

10 The first meal that comes to mind as I ruminate happily through my own recent memories of outdoor eating is a clambake last summer in Maine. Here is the authentic recipe for a clambake: dig a big hole in a beach. If you have a Maine beach to dig your hole in, so much the better, but any beach will do. Line the hole with rocks. Build a big fire on the rocks and take a swim. When the fire is all gone, cover the hot rocks with seaweed. Add some potatoes just as they came from the ground; some corn just as it came from the stalk; then lobsters, then clams, then another layer of seaweed. Cover the whole thing with a tarp and go for another swim. Dinner will be ready in an hour. It will make you very happy. No machine can make a clambake.

Second example (par. 11)

11 If there is a next-best thing to a Maine clambake, it is a Mississippi fish fry. I have a friend in Mississippi who is trying to keep Yankees from finding out that beneath the slimy hide of the catfish is concealed the flakiest, most delicate of all gifts from sea, stream, or farm pond. He is trying to keep it secret because there are not enough catfish to go around. I know he is my friend because he took me to a fish fry. You dip your catfish in seasoned flour, then in eggs, then in cornmeal, then into a bubbling pot of fat—that's all. Catfish fry happiest when accompanied in the pot by hush puppies. Hush puppies are cornmeal, flour, salt, baking powder, chopped onion, and ham fat, with enough beer worked in to hold them together. A few Baptists use water instead of beer. A fish fry is wonderful, with either wet or dry hush puppies.

Third example (par. 12)

12 Clambakes and fish fries are for fun. I went on a cattle roundup in West Texas this spring and found another brand of outdoor cooking that survives by necessity. Camp cooks are still much honored. They live by the principle that anything that can't be cooked in a heavy black iron skillet over live coals isn't worth

eating. Any of the good ones, given a campsite and one hour, can supply from one of those skillets beans, chili, stew, coffee, and even bread baked over the hot coals with additional coals heaped on the skillet lid. It is simple fare, always delicious, and more welcome to a hungry cowhand than anything Paul Bocuse ever created for jaded palates of the Continent.

I know some trout fishermen on the Upper Peninsula of Michigan who meet frequently at streamside to tell lies, play cribbage, and occasionally persuade some young brook trout that a fanciful floating speck of fur and feathers is actually a mayfly. They succeed often enough to eat well. Their specialty is mushrooms, grilled until their caps fill up with juices, served with a little salt, and washed down with bourbon out of an old tin cup. This is a meal I remember with reverence—mushrooms and bourbon—noble in its simplicity.

13
Fourth example
(par. 13)

From *barbe to queue,* the French said, to describe the roasting of a whole hog, from whiskers to tail. And thereby started an argument. Barbecue is one of those things Americans can't agree on, like nuclear power or Ronald Reagan. Midwesterners, to whom barbecue is any roasted meat with ketchup on it, think Midwestern barbecue is best. The best barbecue comes from a genius I know in Lexington, N.C., who merely anoints his hog with salt, pepper, garlic, sage, and a mysterious sauce, wraps it in burlap, buries it in coals, covers it with earth, and serves it in precious shreds hours later with hot corn bread and Brunswick stew. It's simple, he says.

14
Fifth example (pars.
14–15)

There are Southerners transplanted to New York who achieve almost the same result working with a hibachi on an apartment balcony. They know enough not to get too fancy with their barbecue sauce, whether swabbing it on a whole hog with a new broom in Lexington, N.C., or touching up a little pork tender-

15

loin with a watercolor brush twenty-three floors above Lexington Avenue.

16
Restatement of belief in the simplicity of the older method (pars. 16–17)

North, South, East, or West, cooking outdoors is a healing and a renewal for those smart enough to keep it simple. Hot dogs and hamburgers, than which nothing is more boring when cooked in the kitchen, become magical delights when grilled outdoors and eaten with your back against an oak tree. Spareribs, sausages, lamb chops, or chicken wings smoked indolently over a section of old stovepipe become greater than they are. Just being outdoors, it is truly said, enhances the flavor of just about everything, but it's not just that. *Is* there a better way of cooking fish than sautéing it, freshly caught, in butter, over a campfire? I have never discovered it. All you need is a fire, a fork, and a frying pan.

17

What you don't need is a machine.

18

Acknowledgment that, although machinery is unnecessary, it is here to stay (pars. 18–19)

But I know I am too late. You probably already have one. This is how far the al fresco escalation has gone: a man of my acquaintance, grown rueful and contemplative over the bigger and better outdoor cooking machines of his neighbors, watching their parties grow in size and sophistication, recently came upon a description of an Arab barbecue. A chicken, it seems, is stuffed into the stomach of a lamb, the lamb into the stomach of a cow, and the cow into the stomach of a camel. Roasting takes three days.

19

He's thinking about it. He says there's a machine at the hardware store that would do the job, but he can't find a camel in Scarsdale.

Discussing Content and Form

1.   Although Kuralt states his central message or meaning more than once, he makes it most explicit in paragraph 16: "cooking outdoors is a healing and a renewal for those smart enough to keep it simple."

a.   *Find the phrases and sentences scattered throughout the essay that state this point in other ways.*
b.   *Discuss ways in which Kuralt's message might be applied to other things besides cooking. Find hints in the essay that suggest this wider application.*

2.   The marginal guides divide the essay into sections, each of which adds a point or illustrates one of Kuralt's ideas. Explain how these divisions relate to an outline. How much of the material may be called "introduction"? How much is "conclusion"?

3.   Each section is developed by examples, but the most lengthy section is the one proving that the best outdoor cooking is natural (pars. 9–15).
a.   *Discuss the relationship between the examples and the paragraph divisions.*
b.   *What is the special significance of including examples from various parts of the country?*

Considering Special Techniques

1.   A writer must make a choice of the person *in which he wishes to write. He must decide whether to address the readers as "you," whether to make the writing more personal by using* I, *or whether to present his ideas and information strictly in the third person, thus conveying a more objective attitude.*
a.   *Why do you think Kuralt chose the second person for the opening of his essay? Is it a good choice? What would the difficulty be in sustaining this person throughout the essay?*
b.   *Beginning in paragraph 5, Kuralt shifts to the use of* I *in recounting personal experience. What does the use of the first person contribute to the tone of the essay?*

2.   Point out elements, other than the use of second- and first-person pronouns, that make Kuralt's style conversational.

3.   Point out several instances of Kuralt's humorous jabs at the American preoccupation with French cooking. What does this "put-down" contribute to the tone? Use the dictionary to check the accuracy of his information on the origins of the word barbecue *(par. 14).*

4.   Words to learn and use: atavistic, marinate *(par. 7);* indolently *(par. 16);* al fresco, escalation, rueful *(par. 18).*

Generating Ideas

1. *An observer of American life has jested that in our modern homes the bathrooms have moved indoors and the kitchens have moved out. Point out other examples of ironic changes in our homes, and use these to comment on the relationship between old and new life-styles. For instance, you might consider windows that do not open, fireplaces that do not provide heat, etc.*

2. *Write a paper in which you show how several modern conveniences have contributed to greater personal health and safety. You might use examples such as the dishwasher, vacuum cleaner, and the electric light.*

3 *Kuralt says that "Barbecue is one of those things Americans can't agree on, like nuclear power or Ronald Reagan." Using examples of various kinds, comment on the widely differing opinions Americans hold on a variety of subjects. Make your paper either serious or humorous, but be sure to state your main idea clearly. For instance, you might assert that disagreement is one of the great rights of a democratic society, or that our disagreements involve only small issues and that we agree on the big ones.*

4. *Kuralt defends American cooking. Choose another type of culinary art as a subject for an essay that contains many examples. For instance, you might discuss the pleasures of Chinese cooking, or the current vogue in health foods.*

5. *Write an essay about the modern fascination with machines or gadgets, developing your views by the use of examples. Try a title such as "Americans Will Buy Anything" or "New Wind-Ups for Grown-Ups."*

Studs Terkel

[Louis] Studs Terkel (b. 1912) grew up in Chicago and received bachelor's and law degrees from the University of Chicago. Never formally practicing law, Terkel has been at various times a playwright, actor, columnist, and radio-talk-show host. Out of his experiences in radio have come the ideas for *Division Street: America* (1966), *Hard Times: An Oral History of the Great Depression in America* (1970), and *Working: People Talk About What They Do All Day and How They Feel About What They Do* (1974), collections of taped interviews with people talking about various facets of their lives. In *Talking to Myself: A Memoir of My Times* (1977), Terkel uses the same method to reveal his own thoughts on a variety of subjects. In "Here Am I, a Worker," he selects several people he included in *Working* and organizes their comments to make his point.

Here Am I, a Worker

In our society (it's the only one I've experienced, so I cannot speak for any other) the razor of necessity cuts close. You must make a buck to survive the day. You must work to make a buck. The job is often a chore, rarely a delight. No matter how demeaning the task, no matter how it dulls the senses or breaks the spirit, one *must* work or else. Lately there has been a questioning of this "work ethic," especially by the young. Strangely enough, it has touched off profound grievances in others, hitherto silent and anonymous.

Unexpected precincts are being heard from in a show of discontent by blue collar and white. Communiqués are alarming concerning absenteeism in auto plants. On the evening bus the tense, pinched faces of young file clerks and elderly secretaries tell us more than we care to know. On the expressways middle-management men pose without grace behind their wheels, as they flee city and job.

In all, there is more than a slight ache. And there dangles the impertinent question: Ought there not be another increment, earned though not yet received, to one's daily work—an acknowledgment of a man's *being*?

Steve Hamilton is a professional baseball player. At 37 he has come to the end of his career as a major-league pitcher. "I've never been a big star. I've done about as

From *Capitalism: The Moving Target*, edited by Leonard Silk. Copyright © 1974 by Leonard Silk. Reprinted by permission of Quadrangle/The New York Times Book Co.

good as I can with the equipment I have. I played with Mickey Mantle and with Willie Mays. People always recognize them. But for someone to recognize me, it really made me feel good. I think everybody gets a kick out of feeling special."

5   Mike Fitzgerald was born the same year as Hamilton. He is a laborer in a steel mill. "I feel like the guys who built the pyramids. Somebody built 'em. Somebody built the Empire State Building, too. There's hard work behind it. I would like to see a building, say The Empire State, with a foot-wide strip from top to bottom and the name of every bricklayer on it, the name of every electrician. So when a guy walked by, he could take his son and say, 'See, that's me over there on the 45th floor. I put that steel beam in.' Picasso can point to a painting. I think I've done harder work than Picasso, and what can I point to? Everybody should have something to point to."

6   Sharon Atkins is 24 years old. She's been to college and acridly observes: "The first myth that blew up in my face is that a college education will get you a worthwhile job." For the last two years she's been a receptionist at an advertising agency. "I didn't look at myself as 'just a dumb broad' at the front desk, who took phone calls and messages. I thought I was something else. The office taught me differently."

7   Among her contemporaries there is no such rejection; job and status have no meaning. Blue collar or white, teacher or cabbie, her friends judge her and themselves by their beingness. Nora Watson, a young journalist, recounts a party game, Who Are You? Older people respond with their job titles: "I'm a copy writer," "I'm an accountant." The young say, "I'm me, my name is so-and-so."

8   Harry Stallings, 27, is a spot welder on the assembly line at an auto plant. "They'll give better care to that machine than they will to you. If it breaks down, there's somebody out there to fix it right away. If I break down, I'm just pushed over to the other side till another man takes my place. The only thing the company has in mind is to keep that line running. A man would be more eager to do a better job if he were given proper respect and the time to do it."

9   You would think that Ralph Grayson, a 25-year-old black, has it made. He supervises twenty people in the audit department of a large bank. Yet he is singularly

discontented. "You're like a foreman on an assembly line. Or like a technician sitting in a computer room watching the machinery. It's good for a person who enjoys that kind of job, who can dominate somebody else's life. I'm not too wrapped up in seeing a woman, 50 years old—white, incidentally—get thrown off her job because she can't cut it like the younger ones.

"I told management she was a kind and gentle person. They said, 'We're not interested in your personal feelings. Document it up.' They look over my appraisal and say: 'We'll give her about five months to shape up or ship out.' " 10

The hunger persists, obstinately, for pride in a man's work. Conditions may be horrendous, tensions high, and humiliations frequent, yet Paul Dietch finds his small triumphs. He drives his own truck, interstate, as a steel hauler. "Every load is a challenge. I have problems in the morning with heartburn. I can't eat. Once I off-load, the pressure is gone. Then I can eat anything. I accomplished something." 11

Yolanda Leif graphically describes the trials of a waitress in a quality restaurant. They are compounded by her refusal to be demeaned. Yet pride in her skills helps her through the night. "When I put the plate down, you don't hear a sound. When I pick up a glass, I want it to be just right. When someone says, 'How come you're just a waitress?' I say, 'Don't you think you deserve being served by me?' " 12

Peggy Terry has her own sense of pride and beauty. Her jobs have varied with geography, climate, and the ever-felt pinch of circumstance. "What I hated worst was being a waitress, the way you're treated. One guy said, 'You don't have to smile, I'm gonna give you a tip anyway.' I said, 'Keep it, I wasn't smiling for a tip.' Tipping should be done away with. It's like throwing a dog a bone. It makes you feel small." 13

Ballplayer. Laborer. Receptionist. Assembly-line worker. Truck driver. Bank official. Waitress. What with the computer and all manner of automation, add scores of hundreds of new occupations and, thus, new heroes and antiheroes to Walt Whitman's old anthem. The sound, though, is no longer melodious. The desperation is unquiet. 14

Perhaps Nora Watson has put her finger on it. She reflects on her father's work. He was a fundamentalist 15 preacher, with whom she had been profoundly at odds.

16   "Whatever, he was, he was. It was his calling, his vocation. He saw himself as a core resource of the community. He liked his work, even though his family barely survived, because that was what he was supposed to be doing. His work was his life. He himself was not separate and apart from his calling. I think this is what all of us are looking for, a calling, not just a job. Most of us, like the assembly-line worker, have jobs that are too small for our spirit. Jobs are not big enough for people."

17   Does it take another, less competitive, less buck-oriented society to make one match the other?

Discussing Content and Form

1. The introduction to this chapter stated that a general guideline to follow in developing a paper around examples is to use about two-thirds to three-fourths of the space for examples and about one-fourth for general statements. Is three-fourths of this essay devoted to examples? Where does Terkel provide introductory, interpretive, and concluding materials?

2. Why do you think Terkel includes so many examples? Would he be able to make his point with less proof? Why or why not? What examples, if any, do you think he could have omitted?

3. What effect is gained by naming the workers specifically? By quoting them directly?

4. In a selection such as this, not only the number but also the range of the examples is important. What age groups and backgrounds do Terkel's examples represent? What kinds of workers does he overlook? In answering, you might refer to the list that begins paragraph 14.

5. Beginning with paragraph 4, what is the basis for most of the paragraph divisions? Why does the pattern of organization, once it is established, require few transitional phrases to connect the paragraphs?

6. What does Terkel mean when he says that Sharon Atkins' contemporaries, people obviously in their early twenties, "judge her and themselves by their beingness" rather than by more traditional standards (par. 7)? What difference does he point out between the way younger and older generations view their jobs? How does he account for the difference?

7. *What attitudes are exemplified in the two waitresses, Yolanda Leif and Peggy Terry? Why might tipping be called demeaning?*

Considering Special Techniques

1. *Mike Fitzgerald, the steelworker, compares his work to that of Pablo Picasso, a well-known artist whose large metal sculpture is an attraction in Chicago, where Terkel lives. What special dimension does this comparison add to the picture of Fitzgerald?*

2. *A complex and subtle kind of comparison comes in the form of an* allusion *in paragraph 14, where Terkel says that "scores of hundreds of new occupations" should be added to "Walt Whitman's old anthem."*
a. *In alluding to a literary work, a writer expects a reader to be familiar enough with it so that he can see the relevance of the allusion. Read Walt Whitman's poem (the "old anthem") "I Hear America Singing," and compare the mood of the workers Whitman pictures to that of the people Terkel mentions.*
b. *Although relevant allusions are forceful and economical, they can also serve to limit the audience a writer hopes to reach. What is your feeling when you recognize an allusion? What feeling do you have when you fail to recognize such a reference?*

3. *Discuss the level of language in this selection. Comment on whether the essay is marred or enhanced by clichés such as these: "Unexpected precincts are being heard from" (par. 2); "has it made" (par. 9); "she can't cut it" (par. 9); "shape up or ship out" (par. 10); "puts her finger on it" (par. 15).*

4. *Words to learn and use:* increment *(par. 3);* acridly *(par. 6);* horrendous *(par. 11);* demeaned *(par. 12).*

Generating Ideas

1. *Consider Terkel's charge that America is a "buck-oriented society" and that the sound of its workers "is no longer melodious." Write a paper in which you cite examples of your own to prove or disprove this assertion.*

2. *Terkel says that American workers were once happy, or happier than they are now. Drawing on American social history for examples, write a paper proving or disproving this assumption.*

3. *Think of someone you know whose beliefs and life-style are similar to those of Nora Watson's father (par. 16). Develop a paper around that person's job and his or her feeling about the work. You might use one of Watson's lines or phrases for a title: "Jobs Are Not Big Enough"; "Looking for a Calling"; or "Not Just a Job." Or make such a line as "His work was his life" your controlling generalization.*

4. *Terkel says that the young judge people by their "beingness," and that they care less than older people about what a person does for a living. Use your experience to discuss the validity of this statement. Have you ever known young people who ask questions such as, "What does your father do?"*

5. *Terkel says that the "hunger persists, obstinately, for pride in a man's work" (par. 11). Project yourself into the future, and write a paper about the kind of job in which you feel you might have pride and happiness.*

Joan Didion

Joan Didion (b. 1934) is both a novelist and essayist. From 1956 to 1963, she was an associate editor for *Vogue* magazine; she now lives and writes in her native California. Her best-known novels are *Play It As It Lays* (1970) and *A Book of Common Prayer* (1976). Her essay collection *Slouching Toward Bethlehem* (1968) is the source for "Marrying Absurd" and for her personal reflections on keeping a journal in Chapter 1. Much of Didion's writing is aimed at revealing the troubled individuals whom she observes in the flamboyant and sophisticated world of southern California.

Marrying Absurd

To be married in Las Vegas, Clark County, Nevada, a bride must swear that she is eighteen or has parental permission and a bridegroom that he is twenty-one or has parental permission. Someone must put up five dollars for the license. (On Sundays and holidays, fifteen dollars. The Clark County Courthouse issues marriage licenses at any time of the day or night except between noon and one in the afternoon, between eight and nine in the evening, and between four and five in the morning.) Nothing else is required. The State of Nevada, alone among these United States, demands neither a premarital blood test nor a waiting period before or after the issuance of a marriage license. Driving in across the Mojave from Los Angeles, one sees the signs way out on the desert, looming up from that moonscape of rattlesnakes and mesquite, even before the Las Vegas lights appear like a mirage on the horizon: "GETTING MARRIED? Free License Information First Strip Exit." Perhaps the Las Vegas wedding industry achieved its peak operational efficiency between 9:00 P.M. and midnight of August 26, 1965, an otherwise unremarkable Thursday which happened to be, by Presidential order, the last day on which anyone could improve his draft status merely by getting married. One hundred and seventy-one couples were pronounced man and wife in the name of Clark County and the State of Nevada that night, sixty-seven of them by a single justice of the peace, Mr.

James A. Brennan. Mr. Brennan did one wedding at the Dunes and the other sixty-six in his office, and charged each couple eight dollars. One bride lent her veil to six others. "I got it down from five to three minutes," Mr. Brennan said later of his feat. "I could've married them *en masse,* but they're people, not cattle. People expect more when they get married."

2   What people who get married in Las Vegas actually do expect—what, in the largest sense, their "expectations" are—strikes one as a curious and self-contradictory business. Las Vegas is the most extreme and allegorical of American settlements, bizarre and beautiful in its venality and in its devotion to immediate gratification, a place the tone of which is set by mobsters and call girls and ladies' room attendants with amyl nitrite poppers in their uniform pockets. Almost everyone notes that there is no "time" in Las Vegas, no night and no day and no past and no future (no Las Vegas casino, however, has taken the obliteration of the ordinary time sense quite so far as Harold's Club in Reno, which for a while issued, at odd intervals in the day and night, mimeographed "bulletins" carrying news from the world outside); neither is there any logical sense of where one is. One is standing on a highway in the middle of a vast hostile desert looking at an eighty-foot sign which blinks "STARDUST" or "CAESAR'S PALACE." Yes, but what does that explain? This geographical implausibility reinforces the sense that what happens there has no connection with "real" life; Nevada cities like Reno and Carson are ranch towns, Western towns, places behind which there is some historical imperative. But Las Vegas seems to exist only in the eye of the beholder. All of which makes it an extraordinarily stimulating and interesting place, but an odd one in which to want to wear a candlelight satin Priscilla of Boston wedding dress with Chantilly lace insets, tapered sleeves and a detachable modified train.

3   And yet the Las Vegas wedding business seems to appeal to precisely that impulse. "Sincere and Dignified Since 1954," one wedding chapel advertises. There are nineteen such wedding chapels in Las Vegas, intensely competitive, each offering better, faster, and, by implication, more sincere services than the next: Our Photos Best Anywhere, Your Wedding on A Phonograph Record, Candlelight with Your Ceremony, Honeymoon Accommodations, Free

Transportation from Your Motel to Courthouse to Chapel and Return to Motel, Religious or Civil Ceremonies, Dressing Rooms, Flowers, Rings, Announcements, Witnesses Available, and Ample Parking. All of these services, like most others in Las Vegas (sauna baths, payroll-check cashing, chinchilla coats for sale or rent) are offered twenty-four hours a day, seven days a week, presumably on the premise that marriage, like craps, is a game to be played when the table seems hot.

But what strikes one most about the Strip chapels, with their wishing wells and stained-glass paper windows and their artificial bouvardia, is that so much of their business is by no means a matter of simple convenience, of late-night liaisons between show girls and baby Crosbys. Of course there is some of that. (One night about eleven o'clock in Las Vegas I watched a bride in an orange mini-dress and masses of flame-colored hair stumble from a Strip chapel on the arm of her bridegroom, who looked the part of the expendable nephew in movies like *Miami Syndicate.* "I gotta get the kids," the bride whimpered. "I gotta pick up the sitter, I gotta get to the midnight show." "What you gotta get," the bridegroom said, opening the door of a Cadillac Coupe de Ville and watching her crumple on the seat, "is sober.") But Las Vegas seems to offer something other than "convenience"; it is merchandising "niceness," the facsimile of proper ritual, to children who do not know how else to find it, how to make the arrangements, how to do it "right." All day and evening long on the Strip, one sees actual wedding parties, waiting under the harsh lights at a crosswalk, standing uneasily in the parking lot of the Frontier while the photographer hired by The Little Church of the West ("Wedding Place of the Stars") certifies the occasion, takes the picture: the bride in a veil and white satin pumps, the bridegroom usually in a white dinner jacket, and even an attendant or two, a sister or a best friend in hot-pink *peau de soie,* a flirtation veil, a carnation nosegay. "When I Fall in Love It Will Be Forever," the organist plays, and then a few bars of Lohengrin. The mother cries; the stepfather, awkward in his role, invites the chapel hostess to join them for a drink at the Sands. The hostess declines with a professional smile; she has already transferred her interest to the group waiting outside. One bride out, another in, and again the sign goes up on the chapel door: "One moment please—Wedding."

5   I sat next to one such wedding party in a Strip restaurant the last time I was in Las Vegas. The marriage had just taken place; the bride still wore her dress, the mother her corsage. A bored waiter poured out a few swallows of pink champagne ("on the house") for everyone but the bride, who was too young to be served. "You'll need something with more kick than that," the bride's father said with heavy jocularity to his new son-in-law; the ritual jokes about the wedding night had a certain Panglossian character, since the bride was clearly several months pregnant. Another round of pink champagne, this time not on the house, and the bride began to cry. "It was just as nice," she sobbed, "as I hoped and dreamed it would be."

Discussing Content and Form

1.   What is Didion's purpose in this selection? Her essay is a form of satire, *which presents human evil and foolishness as subjects for ridicule and laughter. Like other satirists, she intends to effect some change, at least in the reader's attitudes toward the behavior being presented. Does she expect to change the actions of the objects of her satire? Explain.*

2.   Didion never explicitly states the main point of her essay. What special significance, then, has the title of the selection?

3.   Make at least a rough count of the examples of absurd marrying. Explain why Didion provides as many examples as she does.

4.   Which details illustrate both the artificiality of Las Vegas and its bizarre role as a marriage mecca? Look closely at paragraph 2 in particular.
a.   In this paragraph, Didion generalizes about the city as "the most extreme and allegorical of American settlements, bizarre and beautiful." Yet even in the same sentence she adds examples to show the contradictions. What conclusions can you make about her style from the proportion of general statements and specific examples in this paragraph alone?
b.   Why does Didion call the city "allegorical"?
c.   What is meant by the statement that "Las Vegas seems to exist only in the eye of the beholder"? By the statement that it has no "historical imperative"?

5. *Which of the examples do you find amusing? How would you characterize the type of humor in the selection? To what kind of reader would Didion's brand of humor appeal?*

6. *Do you find the final example (par. 5) poignant or ridiculous? Explain your reaction.*

7. *Today there are more unconventional attitudes toward marriage than there were ten years ago when this article was written. Didion says that in Las Vegas "marriage, like craps, is a game to be played when the table seems hot." Discuss this statement, considering whether this idea may have spread to the rest of the country from this bizarre center for "marrying absurd."*

Considering Special Techniques

1. *Although paragraphs do not always contain a stated topic sentence, the sentences in a paragraph usually center on a single point or idea.*
    a. *Find or state the central point in each of the five paragraphs in this essay.*
    b. *After stating these points, discuss their relationship to an apparent outline or plan. Is the organization as random as one might at first think? Explain.*

2. *What special force is achieved by citing statistics (par. 1)? By giving place names (par. 2)? By including the advertisements (par. 3)?*

3. *Most of the references Didion makes are to actual people or instances. Identify, if you can, "Priscilla of Boston" (par. 2) and "baby Crosbys" (par. 4). Paragraph 5 contains an allusion to Dr. Pangloss, the elderly pedantic tutor in Voltaire's satiric novel* Candide *(1759). Pangloss is an incurable optimist who constantly reassures Candide and others that the world is beautiful despite many terrible misfortunes. How does this knowledge enrich the meaning of the reference?*

4. *One ingredient of satire is* verbal irony—*the use of words and phrases that, at first glance, seem inappropriate to the subject being considered. For instance, Didion satirizes Las Vegas by applying the terminology of business to what is usually a sacred and personal event: "the Las Vegas wedding industry achieved its peak operational efficiency . . ." (par. 1). Find other examples of verbal irony in the essay. What is the resulting tone?*

5. *Words to learn and use:* venality, obliteration, implausibility *(par. 2);* liaisons *(par. 4);* jocularity *(par. 5).*

Generating Ideas

1. *Satire ranges from the bitter exposure of human evil to the light and humorous revelation of weaknesses or follies. Write a short critical analysis (a single paragraph will do) in which you place Didion's satire where you think it falls along this spectrum. If you wish, mention other satiric writing that you find harsher or lighter as a way of supporting your judgment.*

2. *Choose some aspect of human behavior as a subject for a satirical paper. Shape your essay around several specific examples. Here are some possible subjects: overeating or any compulsive habit involving food; habitual cleaning or collecting; constant talking on the telephone.*

3. *Write a satire on some problem in an area or part of the country that you know; use as many specific examples as you can. Some suggestions: the traffic in a large city; the dullness of a small town; the artificiality of a suburb. Or you might gently poke fun at people's preoccupation with the climate: "Moving to Florida to escape the winter means coping with bugs and heat"; "If you go outdoors in Seattle, use a snorkel." The last two topics probably require a lighter touch, since these conditions really are not subject to the satirist's desire for change.*

4. *Didion speaks of the Las Vegas "devotion to immediate gratification" (par. 2). Consider the pursuit of gratification as you have observed it, and write a paper (satiric or serious) on that subject. Here are a few titles that may suggest approaches:*
"Promises, Promises"
"Bingo! The Lottery! The TV Giveaway Shows!"
"Cattle, Not People?" (see par. 1)
"I Want It Now!"
"A's, B's, or Drops"

Ashley Montagu

Ashley Montagu (b. 1905) was educated in England and Europe. After coming to the United States in 1927, he has taught at many universities here and lectured widely. A noted anthropologist and social biologist, he is also an expert on legal and scientific problems related to race and heredity, and he drafted the statement on race for UNESCO. He now lives in Princeton, New Jersey.

Montagu is the author of over forty books, including *Man's Most Dangerous Myth: The Fallacy of Race* (1942), *The Natural Superiority of Women* (1953), *The Cultured Man* (1958), and *The Science of Man* (1964). "Man-as-Killer in Fiction and Film" (editor's title), taken from his book *The Nature of Human Aggression* (1976), deals with a much-discussed subject—violence in the arts.

Man-as-Killer in Fiction and Film

The idea of Man-as-Killer has found support among novelists and film makers, people whose appeal is emotional rather than rational, and who are therefore considerably more influential than the scholars. William Golding's novel *Lord of the Flies,* a brilliant and terrifying story, has been read by countless young people on college campuses and in high school English classes. It concerns a group of English schoolboys cast away on a small island, and their struggle for leadership. Ralph, Piggy, and Simon, representing order, intelligence, and religion, are persecuted and crushed by the mob led by Jack, representing sadism, superstition, and lust for power. It is a strong and deeply depressing book. Golding has been quoted as saying that his purpose in writing it was "to trace the defects of society back to the defects of human nature." Whatever his purpose, his effect has been to persuade many thousands of students that human beings are intrinsically evil.

Golding is no scientist, and so he may perhaps be excused for not realizing that such behavior may be an expression not so much of human nature as of the background and education of the small group with which he is familiar, namely, British schoolboys. Not all children under similar circumstances behave as his fictional characters did. A similar episode, with quite another outcome,

From *The Nature of Human Aggression* by Ashley Montagu. Published by Oxford University Press, 1976. Reprinted by permission of the author.

is reported to have occurred some years ago in Melanesia. I give it here for what it may be considered to be worth.

3   In 1967 Dr. Alphonse van Schoote, a Belgian physician, while traveling among the islands, learned of a Melanesian group, perhaps an extended family, that had embarked upon what was evidently a routine voyage between islands. At some point they deposited six or seven children, ranging in age from two to twelve, on an atoll, planning to return shortly to pick them up, but a storm ensued which kept them away, not briefly but for some months. When the children were finally "rescued," it turned out that they had got along famously: they knew how to dig for water, evidently copious underground in the form of brackish water wells; they lived mainly on fish; they had no difficulty fashioning shelters, and in general they flourished, without any fighting or falling out or issues of leadership.

4   This account was given Mr. Bob Krauss, of the *Honolulu Advertiser,* by Dr. van Schoote when he was on a journalistic assignment in the Pacific. It points to the relativity of human nature rather than to its fixity. Native children readily adapt to the kind of situation in which these children found themselves; such conditions scarcely pose a challenge. One can, however, *imagine* English schoolboys, rendered "nasty" by traditions of infant depravity and the virtues of caning, making a sordid mess of such a situation. But it is *imagination,* of course, bred on Dickens and the exploits of Dr. Arnold of Rugby and all that, which makes it *obvious* that such wicked creatures should devour each other. "Boys!" said Mr. Jagger on meeting Pip. "I've seen a good many boys in my time, and I find them a bad lot!"

5   It is much more likely that conditioning rather than "the defects of human nature" were responsible for the anarchy among Golding's boys. Unfortunately, not many people have heard about those Melanesian children.

6   Anthony Burgess's novel *A Clockwork Orange* is another book in this genre, made into a chillingly violent—and popular—movie by Stanley Kubrick, celebrating rape, violence, sexual sadism, brutality, and "the eternal savagery of man." Mr. Kubrick said, in an interview, "I'm interested in the brutal and violent nature of man because it's a true picture of him." On another occasion Kubrick wrote, "I am convinced it is more optimistic to accept Ardrey's

view that we are born risen apes, not fallen angels, and the apes were armed killers besides." Later he said, "Man isn't a noble savage; he's an ignoble savage. He is irrational, brutal, weak, silly, unable to be objective about anything where his own interests are involved—that about sums it up. . . . Any attempt to create social institutions on a false view of the nature of man is probably doomed to failure."

The star of *A Clockwork Orange,* Malcolm McDowell, agreed with his director. In a letter to the *New York Times,* McDowell wrote: "People are basically bad, corrupt. I always sense that man has not progressed one inch, morally, since the Greeks. Liberals, they hate *Clockwork* because they're dreamers, and it shows them the realities, shows 'em not tomorrow but *now. Cringe,* don't they, when faced with the bloody truth."

Another film director who subscribes enthusiastically to Ardrey's view of Man-as-Killer is Sam Peckinpah, director of *The Wild Bunch* and *Straw Dogs.* This latter movie revels in multiple killing by a variety of hideous methods, double rape, and other refinements of calculated violence. "The myth of the noble savage is bull," declared Peckinpah as he handed out copies of Ardrey's books. "People are born to survive. They have instincts that go back millions of years. Unfortunately some of these instincts are based on violence in every human being. If it is not channeled and understood, it will break out in war or in madness." Mr. Peckinpah, one of the more talented of American film directors, is no scientist, and so perhaps he, too, like William Golding—and like Stanley Kubrick and Malcolm McDowell, for that matter—cannot be expected to weigh the evidence critically, or to recognize the lack of it, in the books he admires so much. And when he states, inaccurately, that all men are violent, or that men are "just a few steps up from the apes in the evolutionary scale," people believe him, and why not? They admire his movie-making, and they, like him, have only the sketchiest understanding of what constitutes valid scientific evidence, and they, like most of us, tend to confuse their own personal opinions with solid fact. It is a common failing to mistake our prejudices for the laws of nature.

These novelists and dramatists provide us, incidentally, with an example of another phenomenon common enough when we discuss a subject no one knows much about, and one that all serious searchers after truth need to guard themselves against constantly, the tendency to circular thinking: One starts with a conviction; one proceeds to illustrate that conviction in dramatic terms; the illustration is then taken as proof of the original conviction. William Golding, for instance, "in tracing the defects of society back to the defects of human nature," was really not "tracing" anything. He was clearly beginning with his conviction that both society and human nature are filled to overflowing with cruelty, sadism, and murder. He wrote a brilliant book to illustrate it. To many people, however, *Lord of the Flies* is not so much an illustration of Golding's profound pessimism as it is searing proof that human beings—even children!—are basically evil. In the face of his terrible story, it is in truth difficult to remember that such facts as we have on such a situation do not in the least support his conclusions.

10   No wonder, then, that a vast number of people today accept the statements, made by scholars with reputations and by novelists and dramatists with the ability to terrify, and especially when the statements are made by both at once, that human beings in the "right environments" are inescapably and inevitably killers.

Discussing Content and Form

1. In what ways does Montagu's opening sentence suggest that the essay will be developed by the use of examples?

2. If you are familiar with some of the examples in the essay, explain why they are or are not suitable for the writer's purposes.

3. Does the illustration of the Melanesian children prove that people are naturally cooperative any more than such fiction as Lord of the Flies *proves them "brutal and violent"? Why or why not?*

4. Montagu gives the opinions of several persons who believe that human beings are basically evil (pars. 6–8). How does he counteract this view with his statements in paragraph 9?

5. Robert Ardrey is the author of Territorial Imperative, *a book that pictures human beings as struggling not only for survival but also for control of their environment. Montagu disa-*

grees with Ardrey's theory and with similar theories that have been popularized in literature and film. To what extent does Montagu convince you that he is right? Explain.

Considering Special Techniques

1.   Montagu gives a story summary of Lord of the Flies *and outlines the details of the news story concerning the Melanesian children. With the subsequent examples he gives less detail. Why do you think he develops the earlier examples more fully than those that follow? Is the point of each example clear even if you have not read the novel or seen the film?*

2.   *What is the effect of placing the example of the Melanesian children between the illustrations of violence?*

3.   *Although Montagu usually draws his conclusions rapidly and keeps them brief, paragraphs 8, 9, and 10 form a rather lengthy concluding section. What is the purpose of having so long a conclusion? How does he use all the preceding examples in leading up to his closing argument?*

4.   *Words to learn and use:* sadism, intrinsically *(par. 1);* atoll, ensued, copious, brackish *(par. 3);* fixity, depravity, caning *(par. 4);* genre, ignoble *(par. 6).*

Generating Ideas

1.   *Write your own answer to the question "Are people innately violent?" Develop your answer by using several examples that are arranged in a coherent pattern and that lead to a logical conclusion.*

2.   *Montagu says that the actions of both the British schoolboys in* Lord of the Flies *and the Melanesian children may be "conditioned." Write a paper about the behavioral conditioning you underwent as a child. Were you and your friends conditioned to violence, for example? Or were you conditioned to cooperate and live harmoniously? In either case, what circumstances and people were the shaping forces?*

3.   *Montagu says that it "is a common failing to mistake our prejudices for the laws of nature." Write a paper using that sentence as a controlling idea.*

4.   *Choose one of these topics for a paper developed by examples:*
a.   *Aggression in sports*
b.   *Competition among students or among people in business*

c.   *The coverage of violence by the news media*
d.   *Violent heroes in current films*
Narrow the topic as you wish and choose a clear central idea to control your paper. For instance, you might advocate that aggression in sports provides necessary outlets; or you might show that violence in the news media is a more influential factor than the schools in conditioning students.

5
Tracing the Steps:
Process Analysis

The first chapter of this book is an explanation of a process. It briefly traces the three important steps to follow in producing a paper: observing to get ideas and materials, recording to preserve and to see relationships, and writing and rewriting to achieve the desired product. Explanations of other processes are similar to the procedure illustrated in that chapter—narrating or tracing from start to finish how something is done, how something is made, or how something occurred.

The process or operation may be mental or physical—for instance, explaining the steps to follow in solving a math problem or giving instructions for learning to water-ski. The subject might be a phenomenon of physical growth or an event in history—how a potato develops or how a labor union organized and achieved power. Instruction manuals and recipes explain "how to do something"; these are examples of what may be called the *direction-giving process.* Explaining a scientific process—a minute-by-minute account of the eruption of a geyser—and historical tracing—the steps taken in preparation for D-day—tell "how something happens or happened"; these are examples of what may be called the *information-giving process.*

Process explanation may be very simple, as it is in this short set of instructions:

> *Greens:* pick, wash, and boil in water with piece of fat meat until tender, cooking slowly. Or parboil them. Take out of water and put in frying pan with grease. Fry five minutes with a little salt. Pick more greens than you think you need, as they shrink. Serve with vinegar or dill pickles, or cook and season as you would spinach. When greens are older,

cook in two waters, throwing cooking water away.—*Foxfire 2*

At other times direction-giving can be very complex and
lengthy. The chapter in *Foxfire 2* on making a wagon
wheel runs to several pages and includes diagrams and
pictures. But the same principles of composition apply
in both cases: the order of steps must be clear, usually
starting at the beginning and proceeding chronologically;
and the information offered must be sufficient to make
the process clear to the intended audience. For instance,
if you do not know the meaning of *greens* or *parboil,* you
might not understand the recipe from *Foxfire 2.*

The same principles apply also to keeping the process
clear when you are giving information about a scientific
or historical event or change. The writer of this paragraph
traces the relationship of the bicycle to the growing inde-
pendence of women:

> The widening of the physical world for women which these
> changed conditions involve did not really begin before
> 1890. Some years earlier, as we have seen, games were in-
> troduced into the more advanced girls' schools, but it was
> not until the early nineties that the idea that grown-up
> women could move about freely was at all generally ac-
> cepted; and the emancipating agent in this reform was the
> bicycle. The women who first began to ride upon this queer
> machine were thought to be incredibly venturous, and most
> people also thought them shocking. In the very early days,
> indeed, when only men's bicycles were made, the enormity
> of riding at all was intensified by the fact that it had to
> be done in Bloomers, and the bold pioneers were freely
> hooted in the streets. After a time adaptations of the ma-
> chine were made, so that the voluminous skirts of the pe-
> riod could be heaped up and stowed away, and a perfectly
> ladylike appearance maintained. The prejudice did not at
> once diminish, but the achievement was considered worth
> the persecution, and women persevered. They found in it
> not only what was then thought to be the exquisite pleasure
> of rapid motion, but also very great practical convenience.
> They were no longer prisoners in their own houses; they
> could spin off, if they chose, as far as six or seven miles
> away; they could go to the nearest town to do their shop-
> ping, and they could visit their friends, and be no longer
> dependent for these joys upon the convenience of the rest
> of the family, but only upon their own muscles. It was a
> wonderful change, and one which was rapidly appreciated
> by all sorts of women who had no conscious sympathy with

the Women's Movement at all. No doubt it was this emanci-
pating tendency which caused the opposition to be so acute;
certainly it was the reason why a deliberate propaganda
in favour of the innovation made its appearance, and a
little flock of quaint pamphlets urging women to "conquer
the world on wheels" remains to bear witness to this vital
social change.—Ray Strachey (Mrs. Rachel Conn Strachey),
"The Cause"

Notice that the connecting phrases in the explanation
are, like those in narration, *time* phrases: "did not really
begin before 1890," "Some years earlier," "but it was not
until," "in the very early days," "After a time" are linking
phrases indicating an orderly time sequence. As in narration, the sequence of verbs also sets the time and must
be kept clear. But while these technical features are the
same for narration and process, the purpose of process
is less to tell a story than to trace and explain the events
which are the subject.

Another difference sometimes marks the process paper,
distinguishing it from the usual expository essay. The purpose in tracing or in giving directions does not require
that you have in mind a *thesis* or controlling idea. This
difference is important to remember because in writing
other kinds of essays, you often need to formulate a thesis.
If a writing assignment calls for tracing a process, it is
often more logical to formulate a very general purpose
statement and let that be a guide in building your paper.
Among the selections in this chapter, you will discover
some for which you probably cannot state a central meaning. Rather, the writers have fulfilled their purpose
merely by tracing or by giving directions. But all such
generalizations about writing apply only at times. The
essay by John Stewart Collis (p. 140), for instance, combines the observation of a natural process with a thesis.
Furthermore, in his essay and in others, you will find that
process, like the other ways of organizing writing, is not
necessarily used in isolation but is intermingled with
other methods of development.

Robert Hendrickson

Robert Hendrickson (b. 1933) is a free-lance writer who has written over a thousand articles, stories, and poems for literary quarterlies and general magazines. His writing shows careful research into everyday subjects that previously have not had much written about them. In *The Great American Chewing Gum Book,* he recounts the history of an industry and a habit, tracing gum chewing from the time when the Indians taught early New England settlers the uses for spruce gum to the rise of today's giant gum manufacturers. "Civilization's First Chewing Gum Maker," a selection from that book, traces the early and colorful development of the spruce gum industry.

Civilization's First Chewing Gum Maker

1

Origins of spruce gum manufacturing (par. 1)

The man who started America and all people-kind chewing gum on a grand scale was named John Curtis, a former seaman born in Bradford, Maine. In our best rags-to-riches tradition, he and his son John Bacon Curtis prepared the world's first commercial chewing gum in one of his wife's large pots on a Franklin stove in the small kitchen of their little Bangor home. It was the younger Curtis, a $5 a month swamper who cleared underbrush and blocked out roads through the woods, who first saw the possibilities for manufacturing spruce gum. His father, a cautious man, doubted that anyone would buy it and only after his family's prodding did he agree to make the first batch in the spring of 1848. From the beginning John B. handled the selling end of the business, while his father manned and managed the production line.

2

John B. Curtis' early career as a salesman (par. 2)

Sales were hard to come by at first. John B. walked the streets of Portland, Maine, two full days talking spruce gum before he convinced a storekeeper to stock the family product. The gum quickly sold itself, but business was slow for the first few years, hardly enough to support a family, and young Curtis went on the road as a peddler, selling his spruce gum, patent medicines and whatever else he could take on. "Give a man all you can for his money, while making a fair profit yourself" was his motto, and he drove his team and cart throughout New England practicing what he pitched. He was so successful ("I was on the road while the other fellow was in bed") that he made the transition from peddler to commercial traveler, journeying all over the country selling his gum, which he carried with him, and as the representative of Eastern business houses. Indeed, some historians think John B. Curtis may have been one of America's first drummers, and he certainly traveled the West in advance of the railroads, using steamboat, canal boat, stage, horse, Shank's mare—whatever transportation he could get. "Many times I walked beside the stage with a rail on my shoulder, ready to help pry it out of the mud," he once said. "I passed hundreds of nights camping out with only a blanket for a covering and the ground for a bed. Did object to the rattlesnakes sometimes. It didn't pay to have them get too familiar . . ."

All for the glory of gum. The efforts of the young optimistic Curtis, who could have served as a model for William Wrigley, Jr., in the future, introduced spruce gum to thousands of new customers. The product was made with great care. "State of Maine Pure Spruce Gum" wasn't sold fresh-picked, but was roughly refined first. Curtis and his son threw the raw gobs of gum, bark and all, into a big black kettle and boiled it into about the consistency of thick molasses, skimming the bark and other impurities as they rose to the surface. At this point, they may have added some lard or grease, or pitch and sap from other trees to the mix, and possibly even a little sugar (none of these would change the taste of spruce gum much, but would merely

3
Physical process of manufacturing spruce gum (par. 3)

increase the volume and make the mixture thicker). For "State of Maine *Pure* Spruce Gum," however, no adulterants at all were added. The mixture was simply stirred until it became thicker and then poured out on a slab, where, while still hot, it was rolled out in a sheet about a ¼-inch thick and then chopped into pinkish pieces a ½-inch wide and ¾-inch long. These in turn were dipped in cornstarch, wrapped in tissue paper and sold as "State of Maine Pure Spruce Gum," about 20 pieces to the wooden box.

4
Historical process of the growth of the Curtis business (par. 4)

At two chaws for a penny (later a penny apiece) Curtis' spruce gum became a resounding success and he couldn't turn out his gum fast enough. He and his son advertised for more raw gum, which they bought in great quantities from lumberjacks, trappers, farmers, and a new breed of woodsmen who devoted themselves entirely to gum gathering in season and brought big bags of gum down to Bangor. The little Curtis Company grew so successful that Curtis was able to move into Portland in 1850 to get closer to big city markets like Boston. There the younger Curtis invented a number of machines for making gum that formed the basis for the gummaking process in chewing gum plants everywhere. Other brands were added to the Curtis line: Yankee Spruce, American Flag, Trunk Spruce, and 200 Lump Spruce, the last a more natural-looking gum, though nearly all the brands were identical in flavor. One of these gums, C.C.C. (no one knows why it was so named, unless it simply meant Curtis Chewing Gum Company), was popular throughout America and the *Portland City Guide* notes that it "started the tireless wagging of stenographer's jaws throughout the world." Curtis made enough money to take on over 200 employees, who turned out nearly 1,800 boxes of spruce gum every day. Once he wrote a check for $35,000 worth (ten tons) of raw spruce gum—a record that has never been topped. In 1852 he erected the three-story Curtis Chewing Gum Factory, which, to quote the *Portland City Guide* again, was the first chewing gum factory in the world. Curtis & Son (the company kept its original name even after John Curtis died in 1869, aged 69) thrived until the early part of this century when it was acquired by the Sen-Sen Chiclet Company, which in turn merged with the American Chicle Company. The younger Curtis died in 1897, aged 70, a very wealthy man indeed.

Oddly enough, neither John Curtis nor his son ever patented their machines or their process for making spruce gum; they probably thought it was all too obvious. Hosts of imitations soon appeared on the market and they too sold well. Only in Maine, however, did the new firms rise up, mostly in the lower half of the state; other New Englanders appeared content just to gather their own spruce gum from the woods. Latecomers included the Maine Gum Company, the B. C. Oglivie Gum Company, Roudlett Brothers, Garceau and Thistle, The Happy Day Gum Company, and, naturally, the Hiawatha Gum Company.

5
The rise of competing gum manufacturers (par. 5)

One notable competitor was John Davis, who set up a small factory in Portland in 1850. Davis is said to have improved on his father's rudimentary attempts to prepare and market spruce gum and, but for a little luck, his father might have been the first man in history to manufacture chewing gum. Davis' business possibly survived until the late 1930's; at least a man by the name of Harry Davis was running the Eastern Gum Company at that time, employing some 20 gum gatherers, buying about 30,000 pounds of rough gum annually, and shipping his finished product out on the Monson-Maine Slate Company narrow gauge railroad, the only commercial line in New England. His was a fairly complex manufacturing operation, too, though on a much smaller scale than the Curtis firm's. But Davis found his market shrinking with each passing

6
Brief history of a rival company, whose decline parallels the shrinking popularity of spruce gum (par. 6)

year; a lot of work was required for very small profits. Indeed, there were very few spruce gum manufacturers remaining toward the beginning of World War II. Except for workers at the Shaker Colony at Sabbath Day Lake, Maine, and perhaps a small firm in Canada, Davis seems to be the only maker of spruce gum left in the world at the time. In fact, if another Mainer hadn't stepped in to fill his shoes when he retired, the art of spruce gum making might have been lost forever.

7

Popularity of spruce gum in the 19th century contrasted with its virtual nonexistence today (pars. 7–8)

Spruce gum offers a good example of how popular tastes change. So many people were chewing the gum in the nineteenth century that according to Maine Forest Service records, the annual harvest of raw gum was estimated at over 150 tons and valued at $300,000, furnishing employment to hundreds. And these are very conservative figures; other writers put the yearly crude gum yield at closer to 1,500 tons. Gum chewing spread rapidly across nineteenth century America, long before chicle came on the scene. "There are the spruce gum-chewers, all backlotters; and vulgar," an early sermonizer despaired. "The careful observer cannot fail to note the prevalency of spruce gum chewing, and gum is universally chewed down East," a Maine newspaper pointed out a century later.

8

Today, only one spruce gum manufacturer remains in America, or in the world for that matter. He is the genial Gerald F. Carr who lives in Portland, but does his gumming in Five Islands, Maine, which is near Bath. Carr, a Mainer from birth (60 years ago), is a railroad man "from way back," but has been making gum on the side since 1937, when he took over the C. A. McMahan Company owned by his wife's Canadian grandfather.

Discussing Content and Form

1. Is the focus of this selection on the chewing gum maker or on the development of the gum business? Explain.

2. *What qualities made John B. Curtis a good businessman? In what ways is his story the typical American success chronicle? What is meant by the statement that Curtis "could have served as a model for William Wrigley, Jr."?*

3. *Which details concerning the gum business surprised you? Compare the names given the early brands with those of today's chewing gum. Which do you think more colorful? Why?*

4. *In what sense does this selection present three interlocking processes? Explain how paragraph 3 presents a "process within the process" of the larger selection.*

5. *Which details help portray life as it was in late nineteenth-century America?*

Considering Special Techniques

1. *Point out several connectives that indicate the passing of time, for example, "From the beginning" (par. 1) and "At this point" (par. 3). Why are such connectives important in explaining a process?*

2. *Several of the informal words in this selection are now seldom used, although they are probably clear from the context. Explain* drummers *and* Shank's mare *(par. 2). In New England villages the better homes were often built around a green or square; what then would you take* backlotters *(par. 7) to mean? What is the stylistic effect of these and other words such as* gobs *(par. 3),* chaws *(par. 4), and* chewing *(par. 8)?*

3. *Explain the play on words in paragraph 2: "he drove his team and cart throughout New England practicing what he pitched."*

4. *Writers often let a character reveal himself with a few well-chosen quotations. What is the effect of quoting Curtis' motto and his description of his travels (par. 2)? What does his* understatement *(the minimizing or playing down of something serious) about the rattlesnakes reveal about Curtis' sense of humor: "It didn't pay to have them get too familiar" (par. 2)?*

5. *Although this selection is packed with factual detail, it is lively reading. In your opinion, what are some of the characteristics that make it lively?*

Generating Ideas

1. Trace the development of some venture in which you have been involved or about which you have a good deal of information, e.g., a small business, a club, a special project, a musical group, etc. Who had the original idea for the venture? How did it start? How long did you keep it going? What success or influence did it have? Make your paper factual but lively, and keep the explanations and steps clear.

2. Write a short history of someone you know who has been very successful in a career or some venture. Take into consideration the beginning of the endeavor and follow its progress step by step. (Do not, however, write a straight narration of the person's life.)

3. Explain how something is manufactured or made, using as your example the process explained in paragraph 3.

4. Several ideas or phrases in this selection might prompt papers that are organized by patterns other than process. Write a short paper explaining why the "rags-to-riches" tradition has such appeal for Americans. Or write a paper about your reaction to gum-chewing or about an unusual experience you may have had with chewing gum.

Jess Stearn

Jess Stearn was born in Syracuse, New York, and attended Syracuse University. After many years as a prize-winning reporter for the *New York Daily News* and as an editor for *Newsweek,* Stearn turned to writing about ESP and the world of psychic phenomena. Among the most popular of his many books are *Yoga, Youth, and Reincarnation* (1965), *Edgar Cayce: The Sleeping Prophet* (1967), *The Seekers* (1969), and *A Time for Astrology* (1971). The selection given here is a carefully structured set of instructions appended to his latest book, *The Power of Alpha-Thinking: Miracle of the Mind* (1976).

Do-It-Yourself Exercise to Alpha-Thinking

For the convenience of the reader who plans a do-it-yourself program the steps to Alpha-thinking are here reviewed: 1

Settle yourself comfortably, and take a deep breath, allowing the mind to drift leisurely. Relax the shoulders and neck, and, hopefully, the rest of the body will take a hint. Your conscious mind may be restless at first, but don't let that bother you. It is normal. Begin your first countdown, thinking of each numeral as a step. Always visualize, whatever the specific exercise. On the countdown from twenty-one, which can be ticked off silently or aloud, drift deeper and deeper with each number into the very core of your being. See that core as something substantial, however it comes to you. 2

On this countdown you may pause briefly at intervals of three . . . to scan your own muscles, skin, bones and nerves mentally. After reaching the count of one, continue to relax. At this deeper and more inward level, visually pick out a passive scene from nature that is meaningful to you, still keeping the eyes closed. Become calm, still, at peace, and see yourself within this scene from nature. Enjoy it. In my own case, I pictured the rolling waves breaking on the surf outside my Pacific window. Sit this way, eyes closed, body relaxed, for as long as you like, putting aside all conscious thinking as your imagination roams over this scene. 3

4   Again, take a deep breath, and still, with the eyes closed, move mentally through the colors of Alexander's rainbow. Each color should suggest a different and vivid sensation. As you continue to relax, getting ever more deeply into your subconscious levels, see first the color Red, visualizing an apple, if you will. See yourself biting into it. With the color Orange, visualize an orange, and consider the times you have been needlessly upset emotionally. Needlessly is the watchword. With Yellow, bask in the golden sunshine of your mind, and grow even calmer. With the soothing color Green, you visualize the forest and inner peace; with Blue, the azure sky and a feeling of love; with Purple, the mystical twilight; and, with Violet, a misty haze gradually merging into the endless sea. The student, if he feels more comfortable thereby, may run through the rainbow first and then go into the countdown, sandwiching the passive scene from nature between the two. In the beginning I found the countdown a more effective way of proceeding into my own levels.

5   Now mentally create a large screen some distance away. Make this screen as large as you like. Design it to your own tastes, for this is to be your Screen of the Mind. On this Screen of the Mind, which could resemble Cinerama's living color, visualize ten pictures in sequence, increasing your ability to visualize and imagine. Put a white light around the frame of what you see, and always visualize the problem or project in light.

6   You are now ready to visualize the elevator which will take you into your imaginary Workshop at the count of three. Or you can walk down, if you will, using twelve steps. Make the Workshop into what you want it to be visually. Preferably, it should be a large room, capable of containing everything you will require. In my own case, I installed a large oblong table, similar to the copydesk of a newspaper city room, a television set, a telephone, a walkie-talkie, chairs, tables and a comfortable couch for reclining. All these are optional and help stimulate your creative faculties.

7   Every Workshop has its raised platform and its Screen of the Mind at one end of the room. Whatever problems you wish to solve are projected like a motion picture onto the platform or the Screen of the Mind, where a radiant white light is put around them.

8   The student sits comfortably at his desk, which he may

take the count of twelve to get to, leisurely examining the furniture and decorations as he crosses the room to take his place. On either side of him, in equally comfortable chairs, he installs an imaginary assistant, whom he can pick deliberately, or who, at this point, may present himself through the now altered awareness of Alpha-thinking. Whenever in a quandary, the student can mentally turn to his assistants for help.

With practice, the beginner will find, as so many students have, that he can by-pass the preliminary stages—the rainbow and the countdowns—and go directly to his Workshop and the Screen of the Mind.

Some have found that with the circle technique, forming a circle with thumb and index finger, they immediately slip into the problem-solving stage of Alpha. Others surround themselves with the white light associated with the Screen of the Mind and are able to help themselves and others.

After a while in visualizing the colors of the rainbow or the Screen of the Mind I could very quickly get into my Alpha levels. However, visualization had to be practiced daily or the facility slackened off and vanished. Sometimes meditation was difficult and the mind wandered restlessly. On one such occasion, drawing on the experience of others, I immersed myself in an infinity of white light which gave off a loving, restorative quality. As I concentrated on this light, which diffused itself into a glowing nimbus of a cloud, I began to associate with it an infinite, all-knowing intelligence. My whole being blended with this radiance, as I was made aware of this infinite presence, this inner healer, expressed as beauty and love, wisdom and power. I was conscious of a new liberating force and felt a sudden rise and flow of energy. I felt myself regaining a center of awareness, an identifying strength which intuitively told me the right course for myself. The counsel and advice of others seemed superficial, even superfluous. The answer, as for us all, lay within the deeper layers of the mind and in our relation to the universal force about us. I now understood what that young Vietnam veteran had meant when he said: "For the first time in my life I realize that I have a companion who is part of me just as I am part of him, somebody who loves me just as I love him."

12   And I, too, like everybody else, was part of that universe
and had the same help. None of us was alone.

Discussing Content and Form

*1.   In the kind of exercise described in this selection, alpha,
the first letter of the Greek alphabet, is used as a label for "primary" or "deepest" thought. What does Stearn, an advocate
of this type of meditation, believe that one can achieve by sus-
pending disturbing surface thoughts and withdrawing into this
"alpha" level?*

*2.   If you or people you know have tried "Alpha-thinking" or
similar techniques, evaluate Stearn's directions.*
a.   How does he make the steps in the process clear?
*b.   Does he give sufficient help with the steps? Justify your an-
swer by referring to the selection.*

*3.   Where does Stearn first mention the importance of
visualizing? How many of the steps in the process require the
practitioner to exercise powers of visualizing? Point out various
words in the essay that in some way refer to seeing.*

*4.   Near the end of the selection, Stearn says that the process
becomes easier with practice (par. 9). What results or rewards
does he say come from this continued effort?*

Considering Special Techniques

*1.   What function does the first paragraph serve? Why is such
a statement a good introduction to the rest of the selection?*

*2.   The direction-giving process is often written in the second
person. How many paragraphs in the selection are written in
the second person? Where does Stearn shift to the more general
third person? Why do you think he drops the "you" at that
point?*
*a.   Sentences that begin with a verb whose subject is an under-
stood "you" are called imperative, for example, "Settle yourself comfortably, and take a deep breath . . . ." and "Begin
your first countdown . . . ." (par. 2). Find other sentences
of this type. What is the effect of using them?*
*b.   If every sentence in a "how-to" process were imperative,
its style would quickly become monotonous. Find sentences
interspersed in the direction paragraphs that break the imperative pattern.*

3. Point out words that clearly mark or outline the order of steps as these are presented in paragraphs 2–6.
*a. How many of the words indicate time (*first, now, *etc.)?*
b. How many provide a step-by-step pattern? Examine particularly the presentation of the colors of the rainbow in paragraph 4. What is gained by introducing each of the successive colors with the word with?

4. Words to learn and use: quandary *(par. 8);* restorative, nimbus, intuitively, superficial, superfluous *(par. 11).*

Generating Ideas

1. Write a paper in which you give instructions for a do-it-yourself program in a field you know well. Some suggestions:
a. Learning to drive, ski, or sail
b. Training for a sport or other physical activity
c. Maintaining a car, motorcycle, or bicycle
d. Acquiring skill in a craft
e. Taking and developing photographs
f. Raising, training, or showing a dog (cat, horse)
g. Improving your knowledge of an academic subject

2. Even though you may be skeptical about Alpha-thinking, try following the directions that Stearn gives and judge whether such a process leads to some form of relaxation. Write a paper giving your reactions.

3. Scientific observation requires the careful tracing of the process of an experiment. Choose a lab report that you have written recently for one of your science classes. Rewrite it, giving special attention to such devices as linking words, parallel structure of sentences to show repeated patterns, and introductory and concluding paragraphs that frame the steps you trace.

4. Explain the process by which you may have solved a problem that once seemed insoluble. Or write a paper in which you recount the steps that led you to a new and enlarged understanding of a situation, relationship, or idea.

John Stewart Collis

John Stewart Collis (b. 1900) is of Irish ancestry and was educated at Rugby and Oxford. He lives now in Ewell, Surrey. He has written biographies of George Bernard Shaw, Leo Tolstoy, and Christopher Columbus, but his best-known work is based on his observations of nature. Among the titles are *An Irishman's England* (1937), *The Triumph of the Tree* (1950), *The Moving Waters* (1955), and *The Worm Forgives the Plough* (1973), from which the following essay is taken. The lowly potato may seem an unlikely subject, but Collis proves that there is much to say—both serious and humorous—about the process of its growth.

The Potato

1   I am anxious to say a word about the potato. . . . We sing the flower, we sing the leaf: we seldom sing the seed, the root, the tuber. Indeed the potato enters literature with no very marked success. True, William Cobbett abused it, and Lord Byron made it interesting by rhyming it with Plato; but for the most part it enters politics more easily and has done more to divide England from Ireland than Cromwell himself.

2   Yet if we praise the potato we praise ourselves, for it is an extreme example of artificiality. "The earth, in order that she might urge us to labour, the supreme law of life," says Fabre, "has been but a harsh stepmother. For the nestling bird she provides abundant food; to us she offers only the fruit of the Bramble and the Blackthorn." Not everyone realizes this, he said. Some people even imagine that the grape is today just like that from which Noah obtained the juice that made him drunk; that the cauliflower, merely with the idea of being pleasant, has of its own accord evolved its creamy-white head; that turnips and carrots, being keenly interested in human affairs, have always of their own motion done their best for man; and that the potato, since the world was young, wishing to please us, has gone through its curious performance. The truth is far otherwise. They were all uneatable at first: it is we who have forced them to become what they now are. "In its native countries," says Fabre, "on the mountains of Chili and Peru, the Potato, in its wild state,

is a meagre tubercle, about the size of a Hazel-nut. Man extends the hospitality of his garden to this sorry weed; he plants it in nourishing soil, tends it, waters it, and makes it fruitful with the sweat of his brow. And there, from year to year, the Potato thrives and prospers; it gains in size and nourishing properties, finally becoming a farinaceous tuber the size of our two fists."

During my first year in the agricultural world I decided to have a good look at the potato and carefully watch its operations. I had never done this before. In fact I had little idea how potatoes actually arrive. With me it is always a question of either knowing a thing or not knowing it, of knowing it from A to Z or not at all; the man who knows a little about everything, from A to B, is incomprehensible to me. Thus I could approach the potato with the clear head of ignorance.

I took one in my hand and offered it my attention. It looked like a smooth stone; a shapeless shape; so dull in appearance that I found it hard to look at it without thinking of something else. I took a knife and cut it in two. It had white flesh extremely like an apple. But it had nothing in the middle, no seed-box, no seeds. How then can it produce more of itself? Well, the season had now come to put it down into the earth. So we planted them into the prepared field, at a distance of one foot from each other—plenty of space in which laboratory they could carry out any work they desired.

In about a fortnight's time I decided to dig up one and see if anything had happened. The first I came to had not changed in appearance at all. From the second, however, two white objects, about the length of a worm, were protruding. On a human face, I reflected, such protuberances would have seemed like some dreadful disease. One of them looked like a little white mouse trying to get out. I covered up these phenomena again and left them to it, wondering what they would do next.

After a few weeks I again visited this earthly laboratory to see how things were getting on. I found that the protuberances had become much longer and had curled round at their ends—now white snakes coming out of the humble solid. They had curly heads like purplish knots, and some of these knots had half opened into a series of green ears. And now there was another addition: at the place where these stems, as we may now call them, came out of the potato, a network had been set up, of string, as it were, connecting the outfit with the soil. These, the roots, went downwards seeking the darkness of the earth, while every stem rose up to seek the light. But as yet there was no indication where or how new potatoes could appear.

7   During these early weeks the surface of the field showed no sign that anything was going on underneath. Later the whole brown surface began to change into rows of green—the light-seeking stalks had risen into the air and unfurled their leaves. As the weeks passed, and the months, these little green bushes grew in size and complexity until in late July they were all flowering—and a very pretty field it then looked. As all flowers have fruit, so had these—potato fruits, of course. But not the ones we eat.

8   Even after the green rows had appeared above-board and I made a further examination below I still did not see where the crop of potatoes was going to come from. Eventually the problem cleared itself up. I found them forming at the end of the network of roots. A few of the roots began to swell at their extremity—first about the size of a bird's egg, then a baby's shoe, getting larger and larger until some of them were four times the size of the original potato planted in the ground. And here we come to the curious thing about potatoes. The substance which grows at the end of the root is not itself a root. It is a *branch.* It is not a root, the botanists say, because roots do not bear buds and do not bear leaves, while this, the potato, does have buds and does have leaves (in the shape of scales). It is a subterranean branch, swollen and misshapen, storing up food for its buds; and botanists, no longer having the courage to call it a branch, call it a tuber. So when we plant a potato we are not planting a seed, we are not planting a root; we are planting a branch from whose gateways, called "eyes," roots reach down and stalks reach up.

9   To complete the circle, what happens to the original potato? It conforms to the rule of eternal return by virtue of which the invisible becomes visible, and the visible takes on invisibility. It darkens, it softens, it becomes a squashy brown mash, and finally is seen no more. I used to enjoy taking it up in my hand when I saw it lying on the ground looking like an old leather purse. It had performed a remarkable act. Now its work was done. All the

virtue had gone out of it. It had given its life to the green stalks above and the tubers below. Here I seemed to see a familiar sight in nature; many things coming from one thing, much from little, even something out of nothing. This is what we seem to see. Yet it is not so. True, the original potato started the business going, sending down those roots and sending up those stalks; but they in their turn built the building. The earth is not a solid; it is chiefly gas. The air is not thin; it is massed with food. Those roots sucked gases from the earth, those leaves sucked gases from the sky, and the result was the visible, hard, concrete potato. When we eat a potato we eat the earth, and we eat the sky. It is the law of nature that all things are all things. That which does not appear to exist today is tomorrow hewn down and cast into the oven. Nature carries on by taking in her own washing. That is Nature's economy, contrary to political economy; so that he who cries "Wolf! Wolf!" is numbered amongst the infidels. "A mouse," said Walt Whitman, "is enough to stagger sextillions of infidels." Or a potato. What is an infidel? One who lacks faith. What creates faith? A miracle. How then can there be a faithless man found in the world? Because many men have cut off the nervous communication between the eye and the brain. In the madness of blindness they are at the mercy of intellectual nay-sayers, theorists, theologians, and other enemies of God. But it doesn't matter; in spite of them, faith is reborn whenever anyone chooses to take a good look at anything—even a potato.

Discussing Content and Form

1. Ostensibly, much of this essay is devoted to observing and tracing a physical process: the growth "operations" of the potato. But Collis also conveys a more general message through the recording of his observations.

a. How does paragraph 1 indicate that Collis is writing with a broader purpose than tracing physical growth?

b. Paragraph 9 is an explicit and fully developed philosophical statement. In which sentence (or sentences) is Collis' key idea or thesis most clearly presented?

c. Find other sentences that are in themselves memorable messages.

d. We are accustomed to comments on the miracles of nature. What special force is gained by observing these miracles in "even a potato"? How does Collis relate his message to Walt Whitman's statement about the mouse (par. 9)?

2.   *Collis says that the potato "enters literature with no very marked success" (par. 1). In what way is his essay an answer to writers who have ignored or "abused" the lowly or ugly in nature in favor of praising its more beautiful creations?*

3.   *The Irish potato famine (1846 and 1847) and the invasion of Ireland by the Puritan leader Oliver Cromwell in 1649 both caused great strife between Ireland and England. How does Collis' allusion to these events (par. 1) give another kind of significance to the potato?*

4.   *The quotations in paragraph 2 are from Jean Henri Fabre (1823–1911), a French naturalist who wrote a ten-volume work on insect life. What, according to Fabre and Collis, is man's relationship to nature? Is there a conflict between their view as it is expressed here and the belief that nature is better left alone? Explain.*

5.   *Discuss Collis' statement that he wants to know something from "A through Z" or not at all. You might compare Collis' methods of observation to those of Samuel Scudder in his study of the fish (p. 3). Construct an argument in favor of the opposite view: knowing "a little about everything, from A to B."*

Considering Special Techniques

1.   *Collis frequently uses the semicolon for a variety of stylistic effects. In order to see how he uses it to separate balanced elements, look at the fourth sentence in paragraph 2 (beginning "Some people even imagine . . . .") and at two sentences from paragraph 9: "The earth is not a solid; it is chiefly gas. The air is not thin; it is massed with food." Check a handbook of grammar for the rules governing the use of the semicolon, and explain why it is effective punctuation in these examples. What, for instance, would be the effect achieved by separating the various elements into shorter sentences?*

2.   *Notice how Collis uses the dash, often a troublesome mark of punctuation. (Note especially paragraph 7.) What effects does Collis achieve from such use of the dash?*

3.   *Paragraphs 4 through 8 trace the growth process of the potato. List the connecting words in these paragraphs, both those that link paragraphs and those that link sentences within the paragraphs. How many of these words are "time" words*

that indicate sequence? Which ones might indicate the presence of cause-and-effect relationships (see pp. 203–206)? Why are such links especially important in tracing a process?

4. *Collis employs a question-and-answer pattern both at the beginning of paragraph 9 and again near the end of the essay. What is the effect of this technique? Note also that the questions at the end of paragraph 9 are answered with phrases. What is the effect of these short answers?*

5. *The concluding phrase "—even a potato" serves as a reminder of the opening of the essay. Explain the force of the word* even *in this position.*

6. *Words to learn and use:* tubercle, farinaceous *(par. 2);* incomprehensible *(par. 3);* subterranean *(par. 8);* infidels *(par. 9).*

Generating Ideas

1. *Many writers and thinkers, such as Thoreau (p. 15) and Annie Dillard (p. 189), have responded to the profound beauty of nature with an affirmation and a sense of wonder about the eternal. Collis, on the other hand, arrives at the same belief from observing the lowly potato. Consider some phenomenon of nature that has seemed to you miraculous or wonderful and write a short paper explaining your reactions. If you can, trace the process by which you arrived at your conclusions.*

2. *If you are a gardener, write a paper tracing the physical process involved in either the growth of one plant or the growth of an entire garden. For instance, if you have observed a "spider plant," you might explain its "multiplication" process. Or you might write a "how-to" paper in which you give directions for cultivating a particular kind of plant or for planting a garden.*

3. *Do some research into Irish history and write a paper tracing the influence of the potato on the economy of Ireland. Or choose another foodstuff that has been economically or politically important to a nation and explain the process by which it became influential. For instance, you might look into the recent grain embargo. Your paper may, of course, involve both the tracing and the explanation of causes and results.*

4. *Many agricultural processes provide substance for interesting papers. Here are a few suggestions, some of which may lead to topics of your own devising:*

The process of reforestation (limit to one place, one type)
Protection of the fisheries
Checking erosion through contour plowing
Problems in waste disposal
The selective cutting of trees
Planned farming of the seas
The renewal of tired soils
Harvesting a specific crop

5.   Choose some industrial process as a subject for analysis. Here are a few titles that may serve as the basis for your paper:
"From Wheat into Flour: A Visit to a Modern Mill"
"The Modern Refinery—Oil for a Mechanized World"
"On the Set—Making a Movie"
"The Garment Factory—10,000 Blue Jeans a Day"
"A Visit to a Brewery"

Fletcher Pratt

Fletcher Pratt (1897–1956) was a novelist, historian, and specialist on military and naval history. He wrote more than fifty books on subjects ranging from science fiction to codes and ciphers. For several years, he was a member of the staff of the Bread Loaf Writer's Conference in Vermont. "How Champollion Deciphered the Rosetta Stone" (editor's title) is taken from Pratt's book *Secret and Urgent: The Story of Codes and Ciphers* (1939). The Rosetta Stone was discovered by members of Napoleon's Egyptian expedition in 1799 and later seized by the British as part of the spoils of war. Now in the British Museum, the Stone is inscribed in three languages: hieroglyphics, demotic characters, and Greek. Beginning his study of hieroglyphics at the age of eleven, Jean François Champollion announced his solution to the riddle of the hieroglyphics in 1822. His solution provided a key that subsequently unlocked many of the mysteries of the ancient world.

How Champollion Deciphered the Rosetta Stone

Scientific history is filled with the strangest repetitions, as though new ideas float into the world on some invisible medium and are caught through senses attuned by study in many places at once. The planet Uranus was discovered twice within a month; the periodic law which forms the basis of modern chemistry was propounded separately by two men who had never heard of each other and were working along different lines. Similarly, at about the time that Georg Friedrich Grotefend was painfully spelling out the names of forgotten kings, another archaeological cryptographer was using the same methods to work out the other great puzzle of antiquity—the Egyptian hieroglyphics.

He was Jean François Champollion, an infant prodigy, whose father had been an archaeologist before him and had talked shop over the dinner table so entertainingly that at the age of fifteen the boy was already publishing a learned essay on "The Giants of the Bible" which won the applause of the bewigged professors at the French Institute.

Champollion's problem in dealing with hieroglyphic was radically different from the one Grotefend of Göttingen had faced. The latter had before him various combinations of markings which were altogether meaningless except as the letters of an unknown language. Champollion was trying to read verbal sense into long strings of pictures which were considered by many very good scientists to have no more than a mystic religious sense, like the work of certain savage races which draw a picture of a deer when they feel hungry, expecting the gods to send them the real article in exchange for the pictured image.

4   Again, Niebuhr had identified forty-two different alphabetic signs, or letters in ancient Persian; but the scientists who had already held hieroglyphic under investigation for centuries had discovered over a hundred and sixty signs—far too many to constitute any alphabet, beside which they were unmistakably conventionalized pictures. Moreover Grotefend had plunged into a new field, where all thought was independent thought; Champollion entered a domain already strewn with the wreckage of hypotheses, where it would be fatally easy to accept the errors along with the logic of some previous failure.

5   Particularly since the discovery of the famous Rosetta Stone. That celebrated chunk of crockery had been found by the scientists who accompanied Napoleon's expedition to Egypt, and was surrendered to the English with the remains of that expedition. It bore an inscription in Greek, together with two other inscriptions, one in hieroglyphic and one in a third form known as Egyptian Demotic, then as unreadable as hieroglyphic. No great intelligence was required to make the supposition that all three inscriptions said essentially the same thing; but some of the best brains in Europe had spent years trying to resolve the hieroglyphic into an intelligible language, and even with the aid of the Greek texts it had proved impossible. The general conclusion was that the problem was insoluble.

6   For everything seemed to indicate that if the hieroglyphic were a language at all (and not a series of mystical pictures) it was that extremely rare thing, a purely syllabic tongue. For example, in the place where the word *king* appeared in the Greek text, the hieroglyphic had a picture of an extraordinarily tall man with a sword in his hand. This was a logical symbol for *king;* a whole word in one picture-letter. And if this were true, many of the other symbols stood for entire words or syllables; there would

be no clue from the interrelation of letters as to how the language had been pronounced, and it would be forever unreadable.

There was also another difficulty. The British scientists who first handled the Rosetta Stone had taken the obvious step of making parallel lists of Greek words and the hieroglyphics that supposedly represented them. To their dismay they discovered that Greek words which appeared more than once in the inscription were represented on these different appearances by wholly unrelated sets of hieroglyphics, and that the same hieroglyphics were sometimes used to represent different words of the Greek text. Even the names, through which Grotefend was even then breaking ancient Persian, were of no help in this case. The only personal name in the Greek text was that of King Ptolemy V; in the hieroglyphic it was represented by four symbols—too few to spell it out with letters, too many to spell it in syllables. There seemed no conclusion but that the hieroglyphics were purely symbolical; and they had been generally abandoned as such when Jean François Champollion, the boy wonder, entered the lists.

His first step was to count the total number of symbols in the Greek and hieroglyphic texts, a method which is now a commonplace of decipherment, but which Champollion seems to have been first to take in this science. The count revealed that there was something radically wrong with all previous efforts to solve hieroglyphic; for there were three times as many Egyptian as Greek letters. If the hieroglyphics were, then, either symbols for syllables or for ideas expressed as directly as the cave man's deer, the Egyptian inscription must be more than three times as long as the Greek. But the very basis of any deduction must be that the inscriptions say the same thing; and the nature of the Greek text (a hymn of praise to Ptolemy V by a corporation of priests) made it seem unreasonable that there could be any great difference. If the inscriptions were identical, then the hieroglyphics must, after all, be letter-symbols. There were too many of them for any other theory.

On the other hand an alphabet of 160 letters remained inadmissible. But since other scientists had allowed themselves to be hung up on the horns of this dilemma, Champollion neglected it and plunged ahead on the alphabetic theory, attacking the names as Grotefend had in Persian.

The name of Ptolemy was neatly enclosed in an outline, preceded by the symbol the English investigators had taken to represent the word for *king.* Now "Ptolemy" is a Greek word; Champollion made the reasonable deduction that in Egyptian it would have to be spelled phonetically. If the four symbols that stood for the name on the Rosetta Stone were letters, some letters in the name must have been omitted—which? The vowels, Champollion answered himself, remembering that Hebrew, which had a considerable Egyptian heritage, also omitted the vowels. The four symbols of the name were the letters pronounced *P, T, L,* and *M.*

10   At this point the investigator turned to some older hieroglyphic inscriptions to check his conclusions. He had at hand a couple whose origin in the reigns of Kings Rameses and Thutmoes were proved by portraits and other evidence. The symbol he had adopted as *M* appeared in both names, and the *T* twice, in the proper places, in the second name. Thus it checked and, checking, gave him values for *R* and *S;* and with six letters to work on the scientist-cryptographer began to work through all the Egyptian inscriptions containing known names, obtaining new letter values at every step.

11   Very rapidly as scientific processes go—that is, in a matter of a few years—he accumulated enough data from names to provide the correct symbols for every possible consonant sound. There remained many letters of the impossibly extended alphabet for which he had no values; letters which never appeared as part of a name. Of these Champollion formed a separate list.

12   Returning to the Rosetta Stone inscriptions, he noted that one of these unidentified symbols appeared before every noun in the hieroglyphic text, and a few of them appeared before verbs. Now one such symbol was the picture of a tall man that had preceded King Ptolemy's name. Later, where a temple was mentioned the word was preceded by a conventionalized picture of a building, and when the sun-god Ra's name appeared there was a conventionalized solar disc. Champollion therefore reasoned that such characters were "determinatives"—special signs placed in the text by the Egyptian writers to indicate the character of the object they were talking about.

13   He died at the age of thirty-four without having worked

out all the alphabet, and without having accounted for the remainder of the enormous surplus of letters, for even with the determinatives taken out, most of the words were far too long. It remained for later investigators to show that the Egyptians, in writing words, were never satisfied by expressing a sound in a single letter, but must repeat the same sound in three or four other ways to make certain the reader got the idea. It is as though one were to write the word "seen" as S-C-SC-EE-IE-EA-N. In a cryptological sense hieroglyphic was thus a substitution cipher with suppression of frequencies and the introduction of a prodigious number of nulls; and Champollion's great merit as a decipherer was that he held to the main issue without allowing these things to throw him off the track.

Discussing Content and Form

1. At first, the subject of this essay might seem rather obscure and scholarly. What features of Pratt's style indicate that he is writing to explain a complex subject for the ordinary reader?

2. What does the work of an "archaeological cryptographer" involve? How does this work differ from that of archaeology in general?

3. What does the information about Champollion's background as a prodigy add to the essay? For laymen who are unfamiliar with scholars of ancient languages and archaeology, Pratt's mention of the work of Grotefend and Niebuhr serves a purpose. Explain what is added to the selection by this information.

4. Pratt several times says that Champollion faced a special problem, but he explains the exact nature of that problem only gradually. In which paragraph is the problem most clearly stated? What exactly is the problem?

5. What is the purpose of paragraphs 8–13? How does Pratt clarify the process Champollion followed in deciphering the Rosetta Stone? In what sense was Champollion's work a "scientific process" (par. 11)?

6. Why do you think Pratt bothered to mention Champollion's death at age thirty-four?

Considering Special Techniques

1.   In tracing a process, the writer must be very conscious of his use of verb tense and sequence, as well as of the connecting words that link one step to the next. Notice some of the words Pratt uses to indicate connections in time: "His first step was to count . . . ." (par. 8); "The count revealed . . . ." (par. 8); "Champollion neglected it and plunged ahead . . . ." (par. 9); "At this point . . . ." (par. 10).

Another equally important type of connection is a word that indicates a cause-and-effect linkage. Note some of these, all from paragraph 8: "If the hieroglyphics were, then, either symbols . . . ."; "But the very basis of any deduction must be . . . ."; "If the inscriptions were identical, then . . . ."

Discuss how such connectives help the reader follow the logic of Champollion's thinking in the process of solving the riddle.

2.   Pratt several times uses verbs in the subjunctive *mood. Such verbs are usually found in Formal English to express improbable conditions or conditions contrary-to-fact. Note these partial sentences from paragraph 6; try to find others in the selection: "For everything seemed to indicate that if the hieroglyphic were a language at all . . . ."; "And if this were true, many of the other symbols . . . ." Why do you think Pratt chose to express the conditions here and elsewhere through the use of such verbs?*

3.   Comment on the use of these phrases: "that celebrated chunk of crockery" (par. 5); "hung up on the horns of this dilemma" (par. 9); "held to the main issue without allowing these things to throw him off the track" (par. 13). Do the phrases seem out of keeping with the more formal language of the rest of the selection? Why or why not?

4.   Refer to a dictionary for the derivation and meaning of the technical words in this essay. Some of them appear in different forms in various paragraphs: archaeological, cryptographer, hieroglyphics *(par. 1);* alphabetic, hypotheses *(par. 4);* syllabic *(par. 6);* decipherment *(par. 8);* phonetically *(par. 9). And check these additional words:* propounded *(par. 1);* conventionalized *(par. 4);* inscriptions, supposition, insoluble *(par. 5);* prodigious *(par. 13). In paragraphs 10 and 11, Pratt speaks of "letter values"; check the dictionary and explain the use of the word* values *in this sense.*

Generating Ideas

1.   If you have ever devised a private code or have learned a more conventional system, such as Morse code or the use of semaphores, write a paper about your experience. Approach your subject in a step-by-step fashion so that you approximate as nearly as possible the actual learning process.

2. Pratt speaks of the use of pictures as a way of communicating. After doing some research on the subject, write a paper tracing the discovery of one of these picture languages found on the walls of ancient caves. One good subject would be the discovery of prehistoric art in the caves of Dordogne in France.

3. C.B.-radio operators use colorful slang in communicating with one another. If you have any experience with a C.B., write a paper telling how you became acquainted with the special dialect.

4. Breakthroughs and advancements in medicine and science make good subjects for tracing a process. Here are some possibilities for such a paper:
The discovery of the first safe and effective anesthetic
The development of vaccines for immunization
The first studies of the circulatory system
The development of pasteurization
The discovery of the causes of yellow fever
Recent controversies over genetic experimentation and DNA

5. Write a paper in which you briefly trace the career of a prodigy such as Champollion. Your subject can either be from the distant past or be a contemporary figure. It can also be someone who has shown unusual and early achievement in non-intellectual or nonartistic activities.

6. Using one (or several) of the following books as references, write a report on the deciphering of other kinds of codes, either ancient or modern.
John Chadwick, The Decipherment of Linear B *(Cambridge University Press, 1958)*
Leonard Cottrell, Reading the Past: The Story of Deciphering Ancient Languages *(Thomas Crowell, 1971)*
Ladislas Farago, The Broken Seal: The Story of Operation Magil and the Pearl Harbor Disaster *(Random House, 1967)*
David Kahn, The Codebreakers: The Story of Secret Writing *(Macmillan, 1967)*
Ole Godfred Landsverk, Ancient Norse Messages on American Stones *(Norseman Press, Glendale, Calif., 1969)*
James Norman, Ancestral Voices, Decoding Ancient Languages *(Four Winds Press, 1975)*
Maurice Pope, The Story of Archaeological Decipherment from Egyptian Hieroglyphics to Linear B *(Scribners, 1975)*

6
Seeing Similarities and Differences:
Comparison and *Contrast*

"The drought today is like that of 1936, but this year's is even worse because of the lack of snow last winter." "The United States and Great Britain finance medical care differently." "Learning to cook and learning to play the piano were alike for me in that my mother taught me both, but they differed—I hated one and liked the other."

You constantly compare and contrast, finding likenesses and differences between two (or more) objects, persons, events, or ideas. Comparing (the one word is often used to cover both actions since there is usually no reason for comparing unless some contrast is involved) is often the basis for clarifying thought and making judgments, and for explaining choices and reaching conclusions. Whether you use comparison and contrast in speech or in writing, the same principles apply: you must use things that are logically comparable, and you must make the similarities and differences clear and comprehensible. The comparison should have a purpose. That is, it should be employed to sustain a thesis or lead to a point that you wish to make, and the choice and arrangement of the elements to be compared should fulfill that purpose.

Notice how this paragraph of comparison and contrast leads to a point:

> By comparison with the deep involvement of women in living, men appear to be only superficially engaged. Compare the love of a male for a female with the love of the female for the male. It is the difference between a rivulet and a great deep ocean. . . . Women love the human race; men behave as if they were, on the whole, hostile to it.

Men act as if they haven't been adequately loved, as if they had been frustrated and rendered hostile. Becoming aggressive, they say that aggressiveness is natural, and that women are inferior because they tend to be gentle and un-aggressive! But it is precisely in the capacity to love, in their cooperativeness rather than aggressiveness, that the superiority of women to men is demonstrated; for whether it be natural to be loving and cooperative or not, as far as the human species is concerned, its evolutionary destiny, its very survival, are more closely tied to the capacity for love and cooperation than to any other.—Ashley Montagu, *The Natural Superiority of Women*

Montagu uses the word *compare* in its broad sense, for he actually mentions only contrasts between the male and female capacities for love. His paragraph follows the *point-by-point* method of structuring comparison and contrast. That is, he treats the subjects or items that he is placing side by side according to their points of differ-ence, thus achieving a "ping-pong" effect. In the para-graph, note these *points* of comparison:

1. Females and males differ in their capacity for loving each other. (This view is further illustrated by another type of comparison, the analogy of rivulet to ocean. This device is explained more fully in Chapter 7.)
2. Female love for the human race contrasts with male hostility toward it.
3. Men's hostility and aggressiveness contrast with wom-en's gentleness and unaggressiveness.

After presenting the three points of difference in a back-and-forth pattern, Montagu generalizes that female love is superior and that the destiny of the "human species" is "closely tied to the capacity for love."

Here is an example of a second type of comparison:

Columbus was a discoverer and not an explorer. The cru-cial distinction between these two roles we can see in the origins of our English words. The etymology of the word "discover" is obvious. Its primary meaning is to uncover, or to disclose to view. The discoverer, then, is a *finder.* He shows us what he already knew was there. Columbus set out to "discover," to find, the westward oceanic route to Asia. Of course he knew the ocean, and he knew of Asia. He set out to find the way. The word "explore" has quite different connotations. Appropriately, too, it has a disputed etymology. Some say it comes from *ex* (out) and *plorare* (to cry out), on the analogy of "deplore." The better view appears to be that it comes from *ex* (out) and *plorare* (from *pluere,* to flow). Either etymology reminds us that the explorer is one who surprises (and so makes people cry out) or one who makes new knowledge flow out.—Daniel Boorstin, *The Exploring Spirit*

You will see at once that this paragraph has a different structure. After his initial sentence, which signals the fact that the paragraph contains contrasting elements, Boorstin explains the etymology of *discover.* Then, almost precisely mid-paragraph, he moves on to explain the contrasting etymology of *explore.* This method of organizing is called the *unit* system of comparison: the topics, rather than the points about them, become the basis for the structure.

It may be convenient to describe the point-by-point and the unit systems with outlines. Assume that the items to be compared are A and B, and that the points of likeness or difference are 1, 2, 3, and 4.

Point-by-Point
1. A/B
2. A/B
3. A/B
4. A/B

Unit
A.
    1
    2
    3
    4
B.
    1
    2
    3
    4

Actually many long comparison papers use both methods of organizing. This paragraph by Boorstin immediately follows the one contrasting the words *discoverer* and *explorer:*

The discoverer simply uncovers, but the explorer opens. The discoverer concludes a search; he is a finder. The explorer begins a search; he is a seeker. And he opens the way for other seekers. The discoverer is the expert at what is known to be there. The explorer is willing to take chances. He is the adventurer who risks *un*certain paths to the *un*known. Every age is inclined to give its laurels to the discoverers, those who finally arrive at the long-thought-inaccessible known destination. But posterity—the whole human community—owes its laurels to the happener-upon dark continents of the earth and of the mind. The courageous wanderer in worlds never known to be there is the explorer.

Here again is the ping-pong effect; the sentences bounce back and forth, clarifying the points of difference that lead to a conclusion. As a writer you must, of course, decide which of the methods of organization to use. While there are no hard-and-fast rules about which is better, these considerations should be kept in mind:

1. Choose the pattern that best suits your purpose, that allows you to support or to lead to the overall statement you will make on the basis of the comparison.
2. If points of difference or likeness should stand out, probably the point-by-point system is preferable. If the two topics themselves are of major interest, the unit method may be the better choice.
3. The point-by-point system may require more care in organization, but the unit system may become repetitive or tend to break the piece of writing into two nearly unrelated parts. With either structure, be coherent. Establish smooth relationships between all of the elements.

Just as comparison and contrast structures vary in purpose so they vary in complexity and length. When the items compared are more numerous or when both similarities and differences are considered, as is frequently the case in long papers, the structure is, of course, more complex. Notice how the writer of this paragraph brings together many items to show similarities and differences among various kinds of people.

On a recent morning, when I was running late because of an emergency, I noticed in my waiting room a backup of patients. Among them were an Irish nun and a bearded Hasidic rabbi, an affluent Wasp businessman and a young black man who lived in one of Harlem's poorer neighborhoods. Now, *there* was a diversity of cultures, right in that room; yet it would have been a mistake to assume that all of these people needed to be treated entirely differently. The Irish nun, raised in a convent, and the Orthodox rabbi, who grew up in Hungary, had a number of problems in common. Both, for instance, suffered from a marked obsession with perfectionism, and from obsessive doubts about their own characters and abilities. The white corporation executive and the black ghetto youth both had an inclination to deny their symptoms and to minimize the need for treatment; and I knew that if I didn't exercise proper care (or even if I did!), there was a higher-than-average risk that they would drop out of therapy prematurely. My last two patients that morning, as it happened, were both teen-age black girls from poor families—but oh, so different. One was from a rural Southern family; the other was a New York City native. One held rigidly puritanical views about sex, while the other was relaxed and easygoing in her sexual attitudes. They came from different universes in some respects; yet the fact that they were both black in today's United States did of course influence the development of both their personalities in a variety of ways.—Ari Kiev, "Is Psychiatry a White-Middle-Class Invention?" *Saturday Review*

The particulars of this comparison are the basis on which Kiev generalizes in his next paragraph: "In sum, then, one must be aware of both the similarities and the differences and always of the uniqueness of each individual." In the selections that follow, you will once again discover the interlocking relationships between the specific and the general, but in comparison and contrast the generalization involves two or more subjects, two or more sets of specifics, side by side.

From "Is Psychiatry a White-Middle-Class Invention?" by Ari Kiev from *Saturday Review,* February 21, 1976. Reprinted by permission of *Saturday Review.*

Russell Baker

Russell Baker (b. 1925) was educated at Johns Hopkins University and began his career in journalism with the *Baltimore Sun.* In 1954 he became a member of the Washington bureau of the *New York Times,* and out of that experience came his first two books: *Washington: City on the Potomac* (1958) and *An American in Washington* (1961). Since 1962 he has written the popular column "Observer" for the Sunday *Times* and contributed to almost every major magazine in the nation. His ironic and humorous commentaries are in the tradition of an earlier American newspaperman, Benjamin Franklin, who was inspiration for "Ben Was Swell, but He's Out." This essay, contrasting the values of Franklin's time with those of today, is included in the collection *All Things Considered* (1965). Baker followed the Franklin tradition again by calling another of his collections *Poor Russell's Almanac* (1972).

Ben Was Swell, but He's Out

Old saws are wearing out. Take the case of "The devil finds work for idle hands to do." As recently as fifteen years ago when a mother caught a son loafing around the pornography rack at the corner drugstore, she could take him by the ear and lead him home to wash the windows, with the perfectly satisfactory explanation that "The devil finds work for idle hands to do."

1
Initial general statement, followed by incident picturing "the way it was" (par. 1)

Nowadays, the world is different. With the march of automation, idleness is becoming the national occupation and sociologists will speak sternly to mothers who oppose it. Since ever-expanding idleness is the goal of the American economy, it is unpatriotic to mention it in the same breath with Beelzebub.

2
Contrasting view of the same adage today (par. 2)

The goal now is to rehabilitate idleness, and the first step in every rehabilitation program is a name change. During World War I, when Germany became the enemy, the Hunnish sauerkraut was restored to respectability by being renamed "liberty cabbage." In the same way, ugly satanic old idleness is now rechristened "leisure."

3
Expansion of the idea that yesterday's "idleness" is today's "leisure" (par. 3)

4
Contrasting meanings of the two terms (par. 4)

Leisure sounds ever so much more decent than idleness. It sounds like something that the uptown set might go in for enthusiastically. Idleness was an evil to be fought by placing such weapons as window-washing rags and lawnmowers in the hands of the indolent young. Leisure is merely another typical American problem to be solved by a nexus of committees, study groups and Congressional investigations.

5
Explanation of today's "creative leisure" (par. 5)

Now, if a boy loafs around the pornography rack, it is merely because he has a "leisure-time problem." The solution is not to put him to work—the machines have most of the jobs well in hand—but to encourage him to take up the oboe or start a bee colony. In this way, we say, he uses his leisure "creatively."

6
Further exploration of the idea of creative leisure (pars. 6–7)

The notion of creative leisure is mostly nonsense, of course. The sin that a boy may stumble into by keeping company with oboe players or going to bee-keepers' conventions is considerable, especially if his interest in oboes or bees is only a substitute for loafing around the drugstore.

7

The American economic system must, nevertheless, be justified. And so, if a boy follows the oboe path to sin, his parents are no longer permitted to blame it all on Satan; instead, the parents are indicted for failing to find a creative solution to the leisure-time problem.

8
Contrasting of second adage then and now (pars. 8–10)

There are many other pieces of ancient wisdom that have turned obsolete under the bizarre new American prosperity. Take "A penny saved is a penny earned." Sound enough in Franklin's day perhaps, but clearly subversive in 1965.

9

The first economic duty of every citizen today is to consume. To keep the economy booming we must consume with our cash, consume with our credit cards, consume with our charge accounts and then go to the bank to borrow the means to consume again.

10

It is obvious that if people began acting on the theory that "A penny saved is a penny earned," production would fall, unemployment would rise, salaries would be cut and the country would stagnate. Nowadays, the homily should read, "A penny spent is not good enough."

Then there is the collapse of "A stitch in time saves nine." To maintain even the present unsatisfactory level of employment, it is absolutely imperative that we never settle for the timely one-stitch job when a bit of dallying can make work for nine additional stitchers.

11
Application of same method to third adage (pars. 11–12)

As we have seen in too many industries, the nine stitchers thrown out of work either go on relief—which reduces the timely stitcher's take-home pay—or turn in desperation to braining the smug stitch-in-time takers for their entire pay envelopes. In this type of economy, the canny stitcher takes his stitch too late.

12

And, of course, there is old "Early to bed and early to rise makes a man healthy, wealthy and wise." Taken literally, this advice would now be disastrous.

13
Application to final adage (pars. 13–16)

In the first place, rising early would immediately raise the leisure-time problem to unmanageable proportions. The safest of all leisure-time activities is sleep, and the fellow who rolls out at cock's crow to work on his oboe is going to be thoroughly sated with leisure by breakfast time.

14

What's more, early rising tends to make a man reflect on the absurdity of his life. In this mood, he may very well realize that his way of life is insane and decide to change it by saving a penny, thereby triggering an economic catastrophe.

15

Very likely he will go to the office feeling energetic and healthy and, before he can stop himself, take a stitch in time, thus causing unemployment, raising his taxes and increasing crime. "Early to bed and early to rise" has had its day.

16

So, apparently, has Benjamin Franklin.

17
Conclusion (par. 17)

Discussing Content and Form

1.   How many "old saws" does Baker consider? How many of the adages are familiar to you?

2.   Baker first uses the word economy *in paragraph 2. Show that the relationship to the American economy is the "common denominator" that links all the sayings. On the basis of that link, what is the wider implication of the essay, the subject other than that stated in the first paragraph?*

3.   In what ways does Baker say that "ever-expanding idleness" is a sociological problem? An economic one?

4.   How many paragraphs are devoted to the first application of saying to practice? How many to each of the sayings that follow? Why does Baker devote more space to the first "old saw" than he does to subsequent ones?

5   Point out several terms Baker uses to refer to the devil. Explain what he means by saying that "parents are no longer permitted to blame . . . Satan" (par. 7). How are parents "indicted for failing to find a creative solution to the leisure-time problem"?

6.   Why is Baker's phrase "rehabilitate idleness" ironic? Why is the notion of "creative leisure" fundamentally ironic? Find other ironic phrases in the essay and explain the basis for their irony.

Considering Special Techniques

*1.   As illustrated in his use of various names for the devil, Baker achieves variety in his style by employing synonyms or using slight changes in diction (*name change *and* rechristened *in par. 3;* unpatriotic *in par. 2 and* subversive *in par. 8). Find other examples of synonomous words and phrases that Baker uses to lend variety to his style.*

2.   Baker occasionally repeats words to give special force to an idea. Note, for instance, the use of consume *in paragraph 9. Find other examples of such intentional repetition. Does the repetition ever lead to exaggeration? Explain.*

3.   Baker comments on the way we change words to make a disagreeable idea more pleasant and acceptable. Such changes (for example, the use of sanitation-worker *instead of* garbageman) *are called* euphemisms. *What are the implications of Baker's replacing* idleness *or* sin *with* leisure-time problem? *How does his point about changes in language reflect the overall pattern of contrasting "then" and "now"?*

4. *Baker makes references to Benjamin Franklin in the title and in the last sentence. How, then, does the entire essay relate to Franklin? In what ways does Baker use the title and the ending to make his point and to give the essay unity?*

5. *Some of the single sentences are miniature patterns of comparison or contrast. For instance, "Sound enough in Franklin's day perhaps, but clearly subversive in 1965" (par. 8) is such a sentence. Find other balanced sentences that present this pattern of "then" and "now."*

6. *Words to learn and use:* indolent, nexus *(par. 4);* indicted *(par. 7);* obsolete, bizarre *(par. 8);* homily *(par. 10);* imperative *(par. 11);* canny *(par. 12);* sated *(par. 14).*

Generating Ideas

1. *Write a comparison and contrast paper explaining the recreative, as opposed to the wasteful or foolish, use of leisure time. Or compare and contrast the ways you spend your leisure with the ways enjoyed by someone you know, perhaps someone from another generation. Here are some titles that may help you get started:*
"But I Thought It Would Be Fun"
"Play Today, Pay Tomorrow"
"Never Dull—Until I Got Tired"
"Our Games and Theirs"
"A New Name for an Old Game"
"Boring to Some—Delight for Others"
"Two Saturday Nights"

2. *Discuss Baker's idea that we are committed to idleness in order to boost the economy. Use any rhetorical method you wish.*

3. *Select several old sayings that you consider obsolete and write a paper comparing their original and their present-day applications. Or choose several other old sayings and show that they are as valid today as they once were. In developing the paper you might show how their application differs even though the "truth" still stands. For instance, "A stitch in time" referred to the literal stitching of a garment to prevent its unraveling. Today it has applications other than the literal.*

4. Is the work ethic obsolete as Baker suggests? Are we headed for trouble if we disregard it? Take any stand you wish as to the value of work and support your views with appropriate examples.

5. A famous cartoon by J. N. Darling ("Ding") pictures several successful leaders beside a boy idling on a street corner; the caption reads, "They didn't get that way hanging around the corner drugstore." Write a paper about various places where people "hang around" or loaf; if you can, draw some comparisons between such hangouts. Treat the subject seriously or satirically, as you wish.

William Zinsser

William Zinsser (b. 1922) was educated at Princeton and began his career in 1946 as a feature writer with the *New York Herald Tribune.* He served there as drama critic and editorial writer until 1959, when he left to do free-lance writing. *Seen Any Good Movies Lately?,* a collection of his reviews, was published in 1958; and his articles and essays have appeared in many periodicals. Other books include *Pop Goes America* (1966) and *The Lunacy Boom* (1970). *On Writing Well* (1976) grew out of a course in nonfiction writing that Zinsser teaches at Yale. The following essay, from that book, demonstrates the freshness of style and control of material that he encourages in his students.

The Transaction

Several years ago a school in Connecticut held "a day de-   1
voted to the arts," and I was asked if I would come and talk about writing as a vocation. When I arrived I found that a second speaker had been invited—Dr. Brock (as I'll call him), a surgeon who had recently begun to write and had sold some stories to national magazines. He was going to talk about writing as an avocation. That made us a panel, and we sat down to face a crowd of student newspaper editors and reporters, English teachers and parents, all eager to learn the secrets of our glamorous work.

Dr. Brock was dressed in a bright red jacket, looking   2
vaguely Bohemian, as authors are supposed to look, and the first question went to him. What was it like to be a writer?

He said it was tremendous fun. Coming home from an   3
arduous day at the hospital, he would go straight to his yellow pad and write his tensions away. The words just flowed. It was easy.

I then said that writing wasn't easy and it wasn't fun.   4
It was hard and lonely, and the words seldom just flowed.

Next Dr. Brock was asked if it was important to rewrite.   5
Absolutely not, he said. "Let it all hang out," and whatever form the sentences take will reflect the writer at his most natural.

I then said that rewriting is the essence of writing. I   6
pointed out that professional writers rewrite their sen-

---

tences repeatedly and then rewrite what they have rewritten. I mentioned that E. B. White and James Thurber were known to rewrite their pieces eight or nine times.

7   "What do you do on days when it isn't going well?" Dr. Brock was asked. He said he just stopped writing and put the work aside for a day when it would go better.

8   I then said that the professional writer must establish a daily schedule and stick to it. I said that writing is a craft, not an art, and that the man who runs away from his craft because he lacks inspiration is fooling himself. He is also going broke.

9   "What if you're feeling depressed or unhappy?" a student asked. "Won't that affect your writing?"

10   Probably it will, Dr. Brock replied. Go fishing. Take a walk.

11   Probably it won't, I said. If your job is to write every day, you learn to do it like any other job.

12   A student asked if we found it useful to circulate in the literary world. Dr. Brock said that he was greatly enjoying his new life as a man of letters, and he told several luxurious stories of being taken to lunch by his publisher and his agent at Manhattan restaurants where writers and editors gather. I said that professional writers are solitary drones who seldom see other writers.

13   "Do you put symbolism in your writing?" a student asked me.

14   "Not if I can help it," I replied. I have an unbroken record of missing the deeper meaning in any story, play or movie, and as for dance and mime I have never had even a remote notion of what is being conveyed.

15   "I *love* symbols!" Dr. Brock exclaimed, and he described with gusto the joys of weaving them through his work.

16   So the morning went, and it was a revelation to all of us. At the end Dr. Brock told me he was enormously interested in my answers—it had never occurred to him that writing could be hard. I told him I was just as interested in *his* answers—it had never occurred to me that writing could be easy. (Maybe I should take up surgery on the side.)

17   As for the students, anyone might think that we left them bewildered. But in fact we probably gave them a broader glimpse of the writing process than if only one of us had talked. For of course there isn't any "right" way

to do such intensely personal work. There are all kinds of writers and all kinds of methods, and any method that helps somebody to say what he wants to say is the right method for him.

Some people write by day, others by night. Some people need silence, others turn on the radio. Some write by hand, some by typewriter, some by talking into a tape recorder. Some people write their first draft in one long burst and then revise; others can't write the second paragraph until they have fiddled endlessly with the first. 18

But all of them are vulnerable and all of them are tense. They are driven by a compulsion to put some part of themselves on paper, and yet they don't just write what comes naturally. They sit down to commit an act of literature, and the self who emerges on paper is a far stiffer person than the one who sat down. The problem is to find the real man or woman behind all the tension. 19

For ultimately the product that any writer has to sell is not his subject, but who he is. I often find myself reading with interest about a topic that I never thought would interest me—some unusual scientific quest, for instance. What holds me is the enthusiasm of the writer for his field. How was he drawn into it? What emotional baggage did he bring along? How did it change his life? It is not necessary to want to spend a year alone at Walden Pond to become deeply involved with a man who did. 20

This is the personal transaction that is at the heart of good nonfiction writing. Out of it come two of the most important qualities that the writer should strive for: humanity and warmth. Good writing has an aliveness that keeps the reader reading from one paragraph to the next, and it's not a question of gimmicks to "personalize" the author. It's a question of using the English language in a way that will achieve the greatest strength and the least clutter. 21

Can such principles be taught? Maybe not. But most of them can be learned. 22

Discussing Content and Form

1. List the points of difference in the two attitudes toward writing that are presented in this selection. Judging from your experience, with which of the two do you agree?

2. *How significant is it that Brock talks "about writing as an avocation" (par. 1), while Zinsser speaks as one who writes as a vocation?*

3. *What is the main point that Zinsser wants to make by presenting the opposing views about writing? How can a student learn the best way to write when there is little agreement concerning the process?*

4. *Does Zinsser succeed in involving you in a "personal transaction" with this essay? If so, try to account for your reactions.*

5. *What does Zinsser mean by "the personal transaction that is at the heart of good nonfiction writing" (par. 21)? What does he consider the most important qualities in good writing, no matter how it is achieved? Compare the qualities of writing you admire to those Zinsser mentions.*

Considering Special Techniques

1. *The section of dialogue (pars. 2–15) is arranged in a point-by-point structure, with the "he said" and then the "I said" speeches tapping out the points in rapid order. Comment on the effectiveness of this arrangement. Why do you think Zinsser chose it over the unit pattern of presenting all of Brock's views first, then his own?*

2. *Examine paragraphs 18 and 19 as smaller units of comparison and contrast.*
a. *In paragraph 18, how do the sentences and the paragraph pattern present the point-by-point organization in miniature?*
b. *What is the function of paragraph 19? How does the writer change the sentence patterns in this paragraph to suggest likenesses rather than contrasts?*

3. *In paragraph 21, Zinsser says that "Good writing has an aliveness . . . ." Point out qualities in his style that you think contribute to liveliness. Do the short paragraphs have this effect? What is contributed by sentence openers such as "But" (pars. 17, 19, and 22), and "For" (par. 17), which you sometimes are told to reserve for mid-sentence connectives?*

4. *Zinsser refers to three writers represented elsewhere in this book: E. B. White and James Thurber (par. 6) and (by allusion)*

Henry David Thoreau (par. 20). From your reading of these writers, determine what techniques they use that might cause Zinsser to admire them.

Generating Ideas

1. Write an analysis of your writing process. You might trace the procedure you followed in producing your last paper, or you might explain your customary way of tackling a composition. From your preliminary analysis, you should become more aware of how you write, and such insights should help you arrive at some conclusions for your paper.

2. Try the dialogue method of presenting contrasting viewpoints. Here are some subjects that you might have two real or imaginary debaters differ about:

a. Pop versus classical music; country versus rock music

b. American versus imported cars; small versus large cars

c. The merits of a book and the merits of a film made from the book (Alex Haley's Roots *is an example.)*

d. Two similar resorts or amusement centers (for instance, Disneyland in California and Disneyworld in Florida)

e. The small town versus the city as a place to live; or inner city versus suburb

f. Winter versus summer vacations

g. Television versus radio as providers of good day-to-day news reporting

It may help in getting started to imagine the situation of the speakers. For instance, a student who drives a Volkswagen and his father who drives a large Buick might discuss the merits of their automobiles. Look back at Zinsser's first paragraph and notice how he sets the stage for the dialogue of differences that ensues.

3. Zinsser says that a "personal transaction . . . is at the heart of good nonfiction writing." Choose some piece of nonfiction (an article, essay, biography, etc.) that engaged you fully and discuss the personal transaction that you felt with its author. What did you know of the man behind the work? How did he impress you? Would you like to know him better or read more of his writing? These questions and those that Zinsser asks in paragraph 20 may help you get started.

4. Try setting up a comparison and contrast paper regarding the ways people study:

a. Studying with the radio on or off

b. Studying in the library or alone in a room

c. *Reviewing with others for a test or cramming alone*
d. *Studying late at night or early in the morning*
e. *Preparing for a next class or test right after the assignment is made or just before the time it is due*

Arrive at some conclusions for yourself or, if you wish, make the paper an "advice for others" essay similar to Zinsser's notions about writing.

Marya Mannes

Marya Mannes (b. 1905) was educated at private schools in New York City, and has lived in various European countries. In her autobiographical *Out of My Time* (1971) she tells the fascinating story of growing up as the child of artistic parents and of defining her role as a woman and as a writer. She has written novels, essays, satirical poems, and many articles. For some time she was a staff writer for the *Reporter,* and she has appeared widely as a lecturer and panelist.

Mannes has been described as a "questioner," and many of her essays and speeches question the myths and practices of government, business, and other institutions. "What's Wrong with Our Press?" was first delivered as a speech in 1960 to the Women's National Press Club, where Mannes appeared as a substitute for Eleanor Roosevelt. The speech, which is now part of the collection *But Will It Sell?* (1964), was printed by only a few newspapers and magazines at the time. But the comparison Mannes makes between television reporting and the news coverage by most newspapers is still a subject for discussion and controversy.

What's Wrong with Our Press?

Newspapers have two great advantages over television. 1 They can be used by men as barriers against their wives. It is still the only effective screen against the morning features of the loved one, and, as such, performs a unique human service. The second advantage is that you can't line a garbage pail with a television set—it's usually the other way around.

But here are some interesting statistics from a little, 2 and little known, survey by Mr. Roper called "The Public's Reaction to Television Following the Quiz Investigations." In it he asks everybody but me this question: Suppose you could continue to have only one of the following—radio, television, newspapers, or magazines—which would you prefer? Newspapers came in second: Forty-two per cent said if they could only have one, they would keep television. Thirty-two per cent said if they could only have one, they would keep newspapers.

Even so, newspaper people should be much happier 3 than the magazine people, because only four per cent said they needed magazines, as against nineteen per cent for radio.

But listen to this. Mr. Roper asked these same harried 4

people: "If you get conflicting or different reports of the same news story from radio, television, the magazines, and the newspapers, which of the four versions would you be most inclined to believe?" Thirty-two per cent believe newspapers as against thirty per cent who believe television. But then something really strange happens. When Mr. Roper asked his guinea pigs *which* of these media they would be *least* inclined to believe, the newspapers topped the list. In a big way, too. Twenty-four per cent don't believe newspapers as against nine per cent who don't believe television. And though I'm as leery of certain polls as anyone, this margin of credulity is too wide to be discounted.

5 The fact is that although network television still allots too little time to the vital service of informing the public, it does a better job in that little time than the nation's press as a whole. And when I speak of the nation's press as a whole, I am *not* speaking of the five or six splendid newspapers—and the one great newspaper—which serve the world as models of responsible public information. I am speaking of the local press which in hundreds of American communities is the *only* news available, aside from those recitals of ticker tape that pass for radio news, and which defaults on its obligations to the public.

6 Why do I think network TV does a better job of informing than these papers? Well, let's get the partisan bit over with. Television lives on advertising to an even greater extent than newspapers, and since advertising is big business, advertising is by nature Republican. Yet nowhere in network newscasts or network commentaries on current events have I encountered the intense partisanship, the often rabid bias that colors the editorial pages of the majority of newspapers in this country. Douglass Cater, in his book *The Fourth Branch of Government,* confines himself to only one pungent footnote on this subject. "I have deliberately avoided," he writes, "getting into the predominantly one-party nature of newspaper ownership. It is a fact of life." This particular fact of life is a shameful one: that newspapers whose duty it is to inform the American public give them only one side of the issues that affect them profoundly—the Republican side. This is shameful not only for Democrats—they have survived it before and will survive it again—but for the maturity of our people. Some of the same papers which loudly extol the virtues

of free enterprise and a free press are consistently failing to print the facts on which a people can form a balanced and independent opinion. That balanced and independent opinion is our only real security as a nation.

Now, very often, television coverage of news is superficial and inadequate. Very often the picture takes precedence over the point. But by and large the news reports and commentaries on CBS and NBC and ABC make every effort to present viewers with more than one aspect of an issue, either by letting opposing spokesmen have their say, or by outlining the positions held by both major parties on the subject involved.

Television also provides a wide range of opinion by setting up four or five experts and letting them knock each other down. What has the local press of this nature? Is it discharging its duty to diversity by printing snippets of opinion from unqualified readers? Is this exploring an issue?

Television may not have a Lippmann or a Reston, but then, what papers in America can claim an Eric Sevareid, a Walter Cronkite, a Huntley or a Brinkley, or—although he is invisible—an Edward Morgan?

Another thing. Among the leading commentators on television, you find no Pegler, no Winchell, no Fulton Lewis, Jr. Fortunately for the American public, television does not tolerate the kind of distortion of fact, the kind of partisan virulence and personal peeve, that many newspapers not only welcome but encourage. In its entertainment, television caters far too much to the lowest instincts of man, particularly the lust for violence and—at the opposite end of the spectrum—the urge to escape from reality into sedation. But there is one appetite it does not feed and which the partisan newspapers of the nation do: the appetite for hate—hate of whatever is different. I do not find on television the kind of editorials chronic in the New York tabloids as well as in many local papers across the country where the techniques of demagoguery prevail: Rouse the Rabble by Routing Reason.

A newspaper has the right—the duty even—to assume an attitude, to take a position. But it has an equally sacred right to explain that position in the light of the opposing one, to document that position, and to bolster it, not with emotion but with fact.

Here, of course, is where background information helps

the public to draw its conclusions. TV does a great deal of this in the form of documentaries, and you can of course say that they have the time and the money to do this and you haven't. Yet across this wide country, and with the exception of a handful of syndicated columns, I fail to find in any local paper any attempt, however minimal, to strengthen this muscle of digestion, without which news can neither nourish nor inform. It can only stuff. Between the opinions of the editor and the bare statements of the wire services there is nothing, nothing, that is, except a collection of snippets used as fillers between the ads and picked at random.

13   One of the greatest and most justified criticisms of television has been that in appealing to the largest audience possible, it neglects minority audiences and minority tastes. This is still largely true. But there is, perhaps, one program a day and many, of course, on Sunday which an intelligent man or woman can enjoy and derive interest from. In my trips east or west or north or south, I pick up the local paper to find this enjoyment or interest—in vain. Now, surely there's something wrong here. Many of these places I've visited—and I'm sure this is true of the whole country—have college communities where highly intelligent and talented people live, whether they are teachers or doctors or lawyers or musicians or scientists. What is there for them in the paper, usually the only paper, of their town? What features are provided for these people? What stimulation? How many times have I heard them say: "If you want to see what a really bad paper is like, read our sheet." When a local paper has a monopoly in a region, as most of them do, why is it necessary to aim at the lowest common denominator?

14   I believe that over a period of decades newspapers have become a habit rather than a function. They have held their franchise so long that change has become inadmissible. I do not know, in fact, of any medium that has changed as little in the last twenty years as the daily press. And this resistance to change is the end of growth—which, in turn, marks the end of usefulness.

15   Change means trouble, change means work, change means cost. It is easier to print wire services dispatches than have a reporter on the beat. It is easier to buy syndicated columns than find—and train—local talent. It is easier to let the ads dictate the format than develop a format

that elevates news above dogfood. It is easier to write editorial copy that appeals to emotion rather than reason. And in handling straight news, it is easier to assume the pious mantle of objectivity than to edit. To quote Eric Sevareid: "Our rigid formulae of so-called objectivity, beginning with the wire agency bulletins and reports—the warp and woof of what the papers print . . . our flat, one-dimensional handling of news, have given the lie the same prominence and impact that truth is given. They have elevated the influence of fools to that of wise men; the ignorant to the level of the learned; the evil to the level of the good." This featureless objectivity is nothing less than the editor's abdication of responsibility and is just as dangerous as the long and subtle processing of fact to fit a policy that characterizes certain weekly magazines. The one is dereliction; the other is deception. And both may provide a reason for the decline of public confidence in their press.

This is, to me, a tragedy. I am a printed-word woman myself, and I still think the word was not only in the beginning but will be in the end. No picture can ever be an adequate substitute. The word will prevail; that is, if you, who are its guardians, treat it with the respect it deserves. For if you degrade and cheapen the word too long, the people will turn to the picture. They are beginning to turn to the picture now. Not in New York, maybe, not in Washington, D.C., or St. Louis, or two or three other cities, but in hundreds of towns across the country. Oh, they will buy your papers—to hold up at breakfast or to line the trash can or to light a fire. But not to learn. And you may wake up one day to find you have lost the greatest power entrusted to men: to inform a free people. 16

Discussing Content and Form

1. The thesis of this essay, first written as a speech in 1960, involves the relative merits of television and newspaper coverage of the news. Where does Mannes first state the thesis directly? Do you think it applies just as well today?

2. List the points of difference that Mannes finds between press and television news coverage (beginning with paragraph 6). In your opinion, how many of these differences still exist?

3.   Point out elements of humor in the article. What is the purpose of opening with humorous contrasts (par. 1)? How would you characterize Mannes' humor?

4.   What is the purpose of reporting the results of the Roper survey (pars. 2–4)? How would you answer the questions in the survey?

5.   Identify the names Mannes mentions in paragraphs 9 and 10. Why does she object to the appeal of "Pegler . . . Winchell . . . Fulton Lewis, Jr."? What is meant by the "techniques of demagoguery" (par. 10)? If you find any of her critical comments unjustified, explain your position.

6.   Why does Mannes exclude the names of the "five or six splendid newspapers—and the one great newspaper" in this country (par. 5)? How would you evaluate the newspapers that you read regularly?

7.   Characterize the tone of this article. When it was first presented as a speech, very few newspapers and magazines printed it. Might the tone of the comments offend some groups other than the press? Explain.

Considering Special Techniques

1.   In order to show logical connections from point to point, a writer must choose appropriate words, phrases, and sentences. In the essay, note these examples of such connectives: "But listen to this" (par. 4); "The fact is that" (par. 5); "Why do I think network TV does a better job" (par. 6). Find other phrases and sentences that help you follow Mannes' points.

2.   Writers often use statistics to support generalizations. Comment on the statistical evidence that Mannes cites in paragraphs 2–4. Another device that lends weight to general statements is the "appeal to authority," a method Mannes uses in paragraph 15. What force does Mannes gain by citing Eric Sevareid?

3.   Analyze the Sevareid statement as an example of comparison and contrast.

4.   Writers often bring their essays "full circle" by repeating at the end a phrase or image that they used in the beginning sentence or paragraph. Discuss the effectiveness of Mannes' last three sentences. How do they provide a sense of unity?

5. *Comment on the metaphors in the following two phrases:
"I fail to find . . . any attempt . . . to strengthen the muscle
of digestion, without which news can neither nourish nor inform" (par. 12); "the wire agency bulletins and reports—the
warp and woof of what the papers print" (par. 15).*

6. *Words to learn and use:* credulity *(par. 4);* partisan, pungent
(par. 6); virulence, spectrum, sedation, tabloids *(par. 10);*
abdication, dereliction *(par. 15).*

Generating Ideas

1. *Write a paper comparing and contrasting the coverage offered by the newspaper and the television news shows with
which you are familiar.*

2. *Compare and contrast two or more reporter-commentators
from either television or the newspapers. In order to make your
points, you might analyze similarities and differences in styles
of presentation, in the choice of material that is covered, in
the special appeal that the reporters may have, etc.*

3. *Do you think there is a "decline of public confidence in
the press" as Mannes says in paragraph 15? Write a paper in
which you cite illustrations of what you consider responsible
or irresponsible journalism.*

4. *Mannes says that "by and large the news reports and commentaries on CBS and NBC and ABC make every effort to present viewers with more than one aspect of an issue" (par. 7).
Choose a documentary, news special, or interview program that
shows two sides of an issue and write a comparison and contrast
paper about the opinions presented. You may do this paper
as an exercise in following the pattern of the presentation; or
you may, of course, go further in examining the issues.*

5. *Use Mannes' statement "Change means trouble, change
means work, change means cost" (par. 15) as the key idea for
a paper on the subject of your choice.*

John Muir

John Muir (1838–1914) is sometimes called "The Father of the National Park System." He was born in Scotland, but his family soon migrated to Wisconsin, where they pioneered on a farm. Leaving the University of Wisconsin because of trouble with his eyes, Muir began his extensive travels to many of this country's wilderness areas, where he closely observed nature and wildlife. He became especially attracted to California's Yosemite region, which he wrote about in several books and which he helped establish as a national park in 1890.

Muir was a great admirer of Henry David Thoreau (see Chapter 1), although his writing style was shaped more by the English classics and the Bible. His best-known books include *My First Summer in the Sierra* (1911), *The Yosemite* (1912), *Stickeen* (a novel, 1909), and autobiographical and personal writings such as *Story of My Boyhood and Youth* (1913) and *Letters to a Friend* (1915). In "Shadow Lake," taken from *The Mountains of California* (1894), Muir contrasts the mountain region as he first saw it and as it later became. His message is still that of conservationists today.

Shadow Lake

1   The color-beauty about Shadow Lake during the Indian summer is much richer than one could hope to find in so young and so glacial a wilderness. Almost every leaf is tinted then, and the goldenrods are in bloom; but most of the color is given by the ripe grasses, willows, and aspens. At the foot of the lake you stand in a trembling aspen grove, every leaf painted like a butterfly, and away to right and left round the shores sweeps a curving ribbon of meadow, red and brown dotted with pale yellow, shading off here and there into hazy purple. The walls, too, are dashed with bits of bright color that gleam out on the neutral granite gray. But neither the walls, nor the margin meadow, nor yet the gay, fluttering grove in which you stand, nor the lake itself, flashing with spangles, can long hold your attention; for at the head of the lake there is a gorgeous mass of orange-yellow, belonging to the main aspen belt of the basin, which seems the very fountain whence all the color below it had flowed, and here your eye is filled and fixed. This glorious mass is about thirty feet high, and extends across the basin nearly from wall to wall. Rich bosses of willow flame in front of it, and from the base of these the brown meadow comes forward to the water's edge, the whole being relieved against the unyielding green of the coniferae, while thick sun-gold is poured over all.

During these blessed color-days no cloud darkens the 2
sky, the winds are gentle, and the landscape rests, hushed
everywhere, and indescribably impressive. A few ducks
are usually seen sailing on the lake, apparently more for
pleasure than anything else, and the ouzels at the head
of the rapids sing always; while robins, grosbeaks, and
the Douglas squirrels are busy in the groves, making delightful company, and intensifying the feeling of grateful
sequestration without ruffling the deep, hushed calm and
peace.

This autumnal mellowness usually lasts until the end 3
of November. Then come days of quite another kind. The
winter clouds grow, and bloom, and shed their starry crystals on every leaf and rock, and all the colors vanish like
a sunset. The deer gather and hasten down their well-
known trails, fearful of being snow-bound. Storm succeeds
storm, heaping snow on the cliffs and meadows, and bending the slender pines to the ground in wide arches, one
over the other, clustering and interlacing like lodged
wheat. Avalanches rush and boom from the shelving
heights, piling immense heaps upon the frozen lake, and
all the summer glory is buried and lost. Yet in the midst
of this hearty winter the sun shines warm at times, calling
the Douglas squirrel to frisk in the snowy pines and seek
out his hidden stores; and the weather is never so severe
as to drive away the grouse and little nut-hatches and
chickadees.

Toward May, the lake begins to open. The hot sun sends 4
down innumerable streams over the cliffs, streaking them
round and round with foam. The snow slowly vanishes,
and the meadows show tintings of green. Then spring
comes on apace; flowers and flies enrich the air and the
sod, and the deer come back to the upper groves like birds
to an old nest.

I first discovered this charming lake in the autumn of 5
1872, while on my way to the glaciers at the head of the
river. It was rejoicing then in its gayest colors, untrodden,
hidden in the glorious wildness like unmined gold. Year
after year I walked its shores without discovering any
other trace of humanity than the remains of an Indian
camp-fire, and the thigh-bones of a deer that had been
broken to get at the marrow. It lies out of the regular
ways of Indians, who love to hunt in more accessible fields
adjacent to trails. Their knowledge of deer-haunts had

probably enticed them here some hunger-time when they wished to make sure of a feast; for hunting in this lake-hollow is like hunting in a fenced park. I had told the beauty of Shadow Lake only to a few friends, fearing it might come to be trampled and "improved" like Yosemite. On my last visit, as I was sauntering along the shore on the strip of sand between the water and sod, reading the tracks of the wild animals that live here, I was startled by a human track, which I at once saw belonged to some shepherd; for each step was turned out 35° or 40° from the general course pursued, and was also run over in an uncertain sprawling fashion at the heel, while a row of round dots on the right indicated the staff that shepherds carry. None but a shepherd could make such a track, and after tracing it a few minutes I began to fear that he might be seeking pasturage; for what else could he be seeking? Returning from the glaciers shortly afterward, my worst fears were realized. A trail had been made down the mountain-side from the north, and all the gardens and meadows were destroyed by a horde of hoofed locusts, as if swept by a fire. The money-changers were in the temple.

Discussing Content and Form

1. Although this selection opens with four paragraphs of description, Muir has a broader message. State this purpose in your own words. At what point do you actually realize that purpose? How do the descriptive paragraphs contribute to the overall idea?

2. Muir's description provides verbal "paintings" of three seasons at Shadow Lake. Why did he omit the fourth season? Why is the amount of space given to the descriptions of winter and spring considerably less than that given to the description of autumn?

3. Point out the qualities that make Muir's description very exact.
a. How many words relate specifically to colors? How do these help you visualize the scene? Find other words that merely suggest color, e.g., "every leaf is tinted" (par. 1).
b. What is the effect of naming specific birds and animals?
c. Which words evoke impressions of sound?
d. In what way could Muir's writing be called scientific?

4. *While the first four paragraphs compare and contrast the three seasons, the final paragraph introduces a new pattern of comparison. What exactly is this pattern? Why do you think Muir uses it here?*

Considering Special Techniques

1. *Although Muir only implies a thesis, the meaning of his essay becomes clear by his use of* allusion *in the two final sentences. Even if you do not know the references, you probably get his point. In what ways has Muir prepared you for the concept of Shadow Lake as a region destroyed by a horde of locusts and as a temple full of money-changers? Check the following biblical references more fully. The plague of the locusts was sent upon the Egyptian Pharaoh as a sign that God demanded the release of the imprisoned people of Israel (Exod. 10:4–5). And the story of Christ's eviction of the money-changers is found in several of the Gospels: ". . . and Jesus went into the temple, and began to cast out them that sold and bought in the temple, and overthrew the tables of the money-changers" (Mark 11:15). What does the use of these allusions reveal about Muir's background and reading?*

2. *Muir's essay outlines easily, with the first four paragraphs of comparison preparing for the final pattern that leads to the meaning. The initial phrases in the first four paragraphs signal the comparison pattern: "The color beauty" (par. 1) prepares for "During these blessed color-days" (par. 2); "This autumnal mellowness usually lasts" and "Then come days" (par. 3); "Toward May" (par. 4). Which words or phrases mark the pattern or division in the final paragraph? Why are such links helpful in following the arrangement of the paragraph?*

3. *Why does Muir call the green of the coniferae "unyielding" (par. 1)? What is meant by a "feeling of grateful sequestration" (par. 2)?*

4. *Point out examples of* metaphor *(an implied comparison that says one thing in terms of another), e.g., "a curving ribbon of meadow" (par. 1). Find examples of stated comparisons or* similes, *e.g., "interlacing like lodged wheat" (par. 3). What do these figures of speech add to the quality of the description?*

5. *Muir uses many* cumulative sentences, *in which details are added to the main clause in order to enlarge and enrich the meaning, e.g., "Storm succeeds storm, heaping snow on the cliffs and meadows, and bending the slender pines to the ground in wide arches, one over the other, clustering and interlacing like*

lodged wheat" (par. 3). Find other examples of this cumulative pattern.

Generating Ideas

1.   Choose a scene that you once found particularly lovely but that has, like Shadow Lake, changed when you revisited it. Or choose a spot that was once attractive but that has since been made more beautiful. Write a short paper comparing either kind of place "then" and "now."

2.   Muir was one of the founders of our national park system; but many people now think that the development of our national parks has led to masses of careless visitors, to the overbuilding of highways, and to the eventual desecration of the areas. Write a paper in which you explain the two viewpoints— the pro and con of developing large park and recreation areas. You may take a definite stand or merely explain the differing views.

3.   Write a paper comparing the ways that a driver of a truck-camper and a hiker (or bicycler) might view a park or wilderness area. If you wish, assume the identity of both persons, using the "I" viewpoint to give the personal reactions of each.

4.   If you have seen an area that has been quarried or strip-mined, describe what it might have looked like "before" and how it looks "after." Or read about some of the conflicts that have occurred in the western United States over grazing rights and write a paper comparing the attitudes of conservationists and ranchers. Some titles like these may get you started:
"We Have to Have the Coal"
"Keep Out the Hoofed Locusts"
"Dams and the Damned—Water Rights and Industrial Change"

7
Discovering Likenesses: *Analogy*

"Compare the love of a male for a female with the love of the female for the male. It is the difference between a rivulet and a great deep ocean." These sentences from Ashley Montagu's paragraph about love (p. 154) involve another type of comparison known as analogy. In comparing the two kinds of love, Montagu draws an analogy between male love and a rivulet and between female love and an ocean, thus making the difference, as he perceives it, impressive. You may find this comparison vivid or helpful, or you may find it somewhat overdrawn; either way you react, the writer's purpose is the same: to illumine one thing by referring to it in terms of another. Donald Davidson, in his *American Composition and Rhetoric,* says that analogy "is . . . stating a possible or imagined likeness between two things" and that it "enables the reader to visualize and through visualization to understand."

Analogy is based on metaphor, and is sometimes referred to as extended metaphor. Metaphor too describes one thing in terms of another: "the tree of life," "a family tree," "the flower of love." We call some event "the final chapter." Or we say of someone who is pretending, "He's just playacting." But when we develop the metaphor further, not just to give a momentary picture but to clarify more fully, we use analogy as Shakespeare does in this famous passage from *As You Like It:*

All the world's a stage,
And all the men and women merely players,
They have their exits and their entrances;
And one man in his time plays many parts,
His acts being seven ages.

In these lines the idea that life is fleeting and that men and women play temporary scenes is clarified by means of analogy. The comparison is not employed in order to make apparent the similarities and differences between two objects or ideas, but rather to explain something new or difficult (often an abstract idea) by showing its likeness to something familiar (often something concrete). The purpose of analogy is to make one-half of the comparison clear by using the other half. If it is apt, if it rings true and is fresh, analogy makes the ideas memorable as well as clear. Notice how the following analogy helps you both visualize and understand the values the writer places on ancient literature:

> In these old books the stucco has long since crumbled away, and we read what was sculptured in the granite. They are rude and massive in their proportions, rather than smooth and delicate in their finish. The workers in stone polish only their chimney ornaments, but their pyramids are roughly done. There is a soberness in a rough aspect, as of unhewn granite, which addresses a depth in us, but a polished surface hits only the ball of the eye. The true finish is the work of time, and the use to which a thing is put. The elements are still polishing the pyramids. Art may varnish and gild, but it can do no more. A work of genius is rough-hewn from the first, because it anticipates the lapse of time, and has an ingrained polish, which still appears when fragments are broken off, an essential quality of its substance. Its beauty is at the same time its strength, and it breaks with a lustre.
>
> The great poem must have the stamp of greatness as well as its essence. The reader easily goes within the shallowest contemporary poetry, and informs it with all the life and promise of the day, as the pilgrim goes within the temple, and hears the faintest strains of the worshipers; but it will have to speak to posterity, traversing these deserts, through the ruins of its outmost walls, by the grandeur and beauty of its proportions.—Henry David Thoreau, *A Week on the Concord and Merrimack Rivers*

This analogy—describing great books as lasting architectural achievements, built of granite and growing increasingly beautiful with use and time—fulfills another requirement suggested by Donald Davidson: "Analogy is a resemblance that may be reasoned from, so that from the likeness in certain respects we may infer that other and deeper relations exist." Thoreau is defining, through his analogy, the qualities that he considers permanent in literature. And his words undoubtedly have made many readers "reason from" the analogy to speculate about these qualities.

Because analogy is memorable and thought-provoking, you will find it at the beginnings and at the ends of many essays. In both places the analogy serves a special purpose—to start the thinking and to continue it. Here is a striking analogy used as the opener for an article on the debate over genetic engineering:

> The rules of the game have not changed for upwards of three billion years: every living creature is dealt a genetic hand, the best stay in for another round. Five years ago in California a few biochemists learned how to stack the deck. They contrived a method for mixing, at will, genes from any two organisms on the planet. Genes cause a creature to be like its relatives and unlike anything else. They say, in a universal chemical language, "Wings, not feet; brown feathers, not blue; quack, not warble"; or "orange fruit, not yellow; pungent, not bland; round, not elongated."—William Bennett and Joel Gurin, "Science That Frightens Scientists," the *Atlantic*

Analogy may be subtle, a mere suggestion, allowing you as reader to fill in some of the comparison for yourself. Or it may be direct and obvious. Either way, it must seem suitable—all of the "parts" of the comparison as it is extended or developed must seem to fit. If they do not fit, the analogy becomes forced or strained. Two cautions: analogies that are obvious or overworked may seem trite— for instance, comparing a family of various uncles, aunts, and cousins to a branching tree. But sometimes trying for an unusual or fresh analogy leads to one that may seem farfetched or artificial. For instance, comparing a group of children to many kinds of wild flowers might become rather ridiculous and funny, rather than apt or effective. Somewhere between the extremes of the obvious or hackneyed and the artificial or strained lies the happy analogy that rings true.

Sydney J. Harris

Sydney J. Harris (b. 1917) came to the United States from England when he was five years old. He attended public schools in Chicago and the University of Chicago before starting his career with various newspapers in that city. Since 1941 he has been identified with the *Chicago Daily News* and with the syndicated column "Strictly Personal." Harris has had numerous awards and honorary degrees, and he has published several collections of his columns as well as other popular books. Best known are *Strictly Personal* (1953), *Last Things First* (1961), *For the Time Being* (1972), *Winners and Losers* (1973), and *The Best of Harris* (1975). In his columns Harris comments on every facet of American life, from the misuse of language to foreign relations. In "War Is Cancer of Mankind," he provides a new way of looking at an age-old problem.

War Is Cancer of Mankind

1

Introductory statement (par. 1)

We say that the aim of life is self-preservation, if not for the individual, at least for the species. Granted that every organism seeks this end, does every organism know what is best for its self-preservation?

2

First part—the "base"—of the analogy: the destruction of the body by cancer cells (pars. 2–5)

Consider cancer cells and non-cancer cells in the human body. The normal cells are aimed at reproducing and functioning in a way that is beneficial to the body. Cancer cells, on the other hand, spread in a way that threatens and ultimately destroys the whole body.

3

Normal cells work harmoniously, because they "know," in a sense, that their preservation depends upon the health of the body they inhabit. While they are organisms in themselves, they also act as part of a substructure, directed at the good of the whole body.

4

We might say, metaphorically, that cancer cells do not know enough about self-preservation; they are, biologically, more ignorant than normal cells. The aim of cancer cells is to spread throughout the body, to conquer all the normal cells—and when they reach their aim, the body is dead. *And so are the cancer cells.*

For cancer cells destroy not only all rival cells, in their ruthless biological warfare, but also destroy the larger organization—the body itself—signing their own suicide warrant.

5

The same is true of war, especially in the modern world. War is the *social cancer* of mankind. It is a pernicious form of ignorance, for it destroys not only its "enemies," but also the whole superstructure of which it is a part—and thus eventually it defeats itself.

6
Analogy between cancer and war established (par. 6)

Nations live in a state of anarchy, not in a state of law. And, like cancer cells, nations do not know that their ultimate self-interest lies in preserving the health and harmony of the whole body (that is, the community of man), for if that body is mortally wounded, then no nation can survive and flourish.

7
Elaboration of the analogy, followed by a call for the preservation of the species (par. 7–9)

If the aim of life is self-preservation—for the species as well as for the individual—we must tame or eradicate the cancer cells of war in the social organism. And this can be done only when nations begin to recognize that what may seem to be "in the national interest" cannot be opposed to the common interest of mankind, or both the nation and mankind will die in this "conquest."

8

The life of every organism depends upon the viability of the system of which it is a member. The cancer cells cannot exist without the body to inhabit, and they must be exterminated if they cannot be re-educated to behave like normal cells. At present, their very success dooms them to failure—just as a victorious war in the atomic age would be an unqualified disaster for the dying winner.

9

Discussing Content and Form

1. *Analogies often provide fresh insights into commonly held ideas and beliefs. You probably already agree with Harris that war must be eradicated, but does the analogy reinforce the idea for you? Why or why not?*

2.   This essay falls neatly into two main parts, a division that is clearly marked by the transitional paragraph (6) which states the analogy. Assuming that analogy is extended metaphor (Harris actually uses the word metaphorically *in paragraph 4), then the means or base of the analogy may be labeled a "vehicle." The extension of meaning is called the "tenor." What special advantage is there in giving the vehicle first and then developing the tenor thereafter?*

3.   What does Harris say are the factors contributing to the social cancer of war? What does he say must be done to eradicate it? How does prevention of war as social cancer relate to what is known about the causes, prevention, and treatment of cancer as a disease?

Considering Special Techniques

1.   How does the fact that Harris is journalist, writing a daily newspaper column, account for the very short paragraphs into which he breaks the essay? Check the paragraphs in two or three other essays in this text and draw some conclusions about paragraph length and about variety in lengths.

2.   Point out several words or phrases by which Harris seems to exhort the reader into thinking about the cancer of war.

3.   Why do you think that Harris does not use the personal "I" in the essay?

4.   Point out several words or phrases used in connection with cancer to suggest the dread generally associated with the disease.

5.   Check the meaning of viability *(par. 9), a word that has become widely used in the last decade or so. Harris, a stickler for the correct use of language, sometimes objects to the loose and wide application of such words to situations where they do not fit. After you check the word, decide whether or not Harris is using it precisely.*

Generating Ideas

1.   Choose some other social cancer—some danger to the human community—and write a paper calling attention to its potential destructiveness. If you can, use an analogy.

2.   Use the analogy of some other disease in explaining a danger to a community or state. For instance, you might choose some social trait that is like a rash or allergy.

Annie Dillard

Annie Dillard (b. 1945) lives on a farm in the Roanoke Valley of Virginia. Her Pulitzer Prize-winning book, *Pilgrim at Tinker Creek* (1974), is a deeply appreciative record of her observations of that region. "Hidden Pennies" (editor's title) is taken from "Sight into Insight," an essay adapted from that book for publication in *Harper's* magazine, to which Dillard is a contributing editor. In the selection Dillard expresses her responses to nature, which she sees as something to be treasured. She is also the author of a collection of poems, *Tickets for a Prayer Wheel* (1975), and she writes a column for *Living Wilderness,* the quarterly publication of the Wilderness Society.

Hidden Pennies

When I was six or seven years old, growing up in Pittsburgh, I used to take a precious penny of my own and hide it for someone else to find. It was a curious compulsion; sadly, I've never been seized by it since. For some reason I always "hid" the penny along the same stretch of sidewalk up the street. I'd cradle it at the roots of a maple, say, or in a hole left by a chipped-off piece of sidewalk. Then I'd take a piece of chalk and, starting at either end of the block, draw huge arrows leading up to the penny from both directions. After I learned to write I labeled the arrows "SURPRISE AHEAD" or "MONEY THIS WAY." I was greatly excited, during all this arrow-drawing, at the thought of the first lucky passerby who would receive in this way, regardless of merit, a free gift from the universe. But I never lurked about. I'd go straight home and not give the matter another thought, until, some months later, I would be gripped by the impulse to hide another penny.

There are lots of things to see, unwrapped gifts and free surprises. The world is fairly studded and strewn with pennies cast broadside from a generous hand. But—and this is the point—who gets excited by a mere penny? If you follow one arrow, if you crouch motionless on a bank to watch a tremulous ripple thrill on the water, and are rewarded by the sight of a muskrat kit paddling from its den, will you count that sight a chip of copper only, and go your rueful way? It is very dire poverty indeed for a man to be so malnourished and fatigued that he won't stoop to pick up a penny. But if you cultivate a healthy poverty and simplicity, so that finding a penny will make your day, then, since the world is in fact planted in pennies, you have with your poverty bought a lifetime of days. What you see is what you get.

3   Unfortunately, nature is very much a now-you-see-it, now-you-don't affair. A fish flashes, then dissolves in the water before my eyes like so much salt. Deer apparently ascend bodily into heaven; the brightest oriole fades into leaves. These disappearances stun me into stillness and concentration; they say of nature that it conceals with a grand nonchalance, and they say of vision that it is a deliberate gift, the revelation of a dancer who for my eyes only flings away her seven veils.

4   For nature does reveal as well as conceal: now-you-don't-see-it, now-you-do. For a week this September migrating red-winged blackbirds were feeding heavily down by Tinker Creek at the back of the house. One day I went out to investigate the racket; I walked up to a tree, an Osage orange, and a hundred birds flew away. They simply materialized out of the tree. I saw a tree, then a whisk of color, then a tree again. I walked closer and another hundred blackbirds took flight. Not a branch, not a twig budged: the birds were apparently weightless as well as invisible. Or, it was as if the leaves of the Osage orange had been freed from a spell in the form of red-winged blackbirds; they flew from the tree, caught my eye in the sky, and vanished. When I looked again at the tree, the leaves had reassembled as if nothing had happened. Finally I walked directly to the trunk of the tree and a final hundred, the real diehards, appeared, spread, and vanished. How could so many hide in the tree without my seeing them? The Osage orange, unruffled, looked just as it had looked from the house, when three hundred red-winged blackbirds cried from its crown. I looked upstream where they flew, and they were gone. Searching, I couldn't spot one. I wandered upstream to force them to play their hand, but they'd crossed the creek and scattered. One show to a customer. These appearances catch at my throat; they are the free gifts, the bright coppers at the roots of trees.

Discussing Content and Form

*1.   The thesis of the selection is stated clearly in the first two
sentences of paragraph 2. Find restatements of the same generalization. Why does Dillard restate the generalization throughout
the four paragraphs?*

2.   List several specific details that illustrate the thesis.
*a.   How many of these details are linked to the "penny" by
the suggestion of color?*
*b.   How many of the details illustrate the quality of "flashing"
or suddenness of appearance?*

*3.   Dillard uses several symbolic or figurative phrases; discuss
the meaning of these:*
*a.   "The world is fairly studded and strewn with pennies cast
broadside from a generous hand." (par. 2)*
*b.   "But if you cultivate a healthy poverty and simplicity . . .
finding a penny will make your day." (par. 2)*

*4.   How can poverty buy "a lifetime of days" (par. 2)? What
is ironic about making great purchases with small coins?*

*5.   What impression do you get of Dillard from this selection?
Which words or details give you that impression?*

Considering Special Techniques

*1.   Point out several examples of the repetition of words or ideas
in the selection, e.g., "gift" and "gifts." How does such repetition aid in achieving coherence?*

*2.   What special value has the opening narrative as an atten-
tion-getter? What does the incident make you feel about the
writer?*

*3.   Why does Dillard close by reiterating the image of the
"coppers at the roots of trees"? Does the ending help you visualize and understand her meaning?*

*4.   Compare the word order in the first sentence of paragraph
3 with that in the first sentence of paragraph 4. Explain the
differences in structure.*

*5.   What is meant by nature's "grand nonchalance" (par. 3)?
Check the allusion in the last line of that paragraph: "a dancer
who . . . flings away her seven veils." Does it help to know the*

allusion, or is the image sufficiently clear without that knowl-edge? Explain.

6. Dillard's prose is poetic in ways other than the use of analogy.
a. Point out examples of the use of sensory words to produce vivid pictures.
b. Point out at least two examples of alliteration (the repetition of initial consonant sounds).

7. Words to learn and use: compulsion *(par. 1);* tremulous, rue-ful *(par. 2);* nonchalance *(par. 3);* diehards *(par. 4).*

Generating Ideas

1. You undoubtedly have found "hidden pennies," gifts of beauty or magic provided by nature. Write a paper that con-veys some glimpses of beauty that you have experienced, those you have found either in nature or in your more everyday existence.

2. J. B. Priestley, an English essayist and novelist, has written a collection of essays entitled Delight. *Each essay is a bit of praise, commemorating some delightful happening or discov-ery. Look up Priestley's volume and write about a delight or delights that you have experienced. If you can employ an anal-ogy, all the better.*

3. Write a paper in which you use an analogy comparing the idea of retrieving lost memories with one of the following situa-tions or objects.
a. A photograph album of family memories, places visited or past friendships
b. A trunk in the attic as a storehouse for tradition
c. A jewel box in which old treasures are stored
d. A cabinet of curios as a place for unexplainable occurrences
e. A cupboard of broken dishes or a box of glass bits represent-ing lost glories or unrealized hopes
f. An old notebook of forgotten or neglected ideas
g. An art gallery of grotesque portraits or a wax museum of strange figures out of the past
h. A stamp collection representing forgotten but important events in shaping a nation or culture

Barry Lopez

Barry Lopez (b. 1945) is a free-lance writer and photographer who lives at the edge of the Willamette Forest in Oregon. He has published articles and pictures in *National Wildlife, American Forests, Audubon* magazine, and many other periodicals devoted to nature and conservation. His first book, *Desert Notes: Reflections in the Eye of a Raven,* was published in 1975. A photo-story, "Fire Camp," in *American Forests* for August 1975 portrays the tensions and struggles of men who fight forest fires. In "My Horse," which first appeared in the *North American Review,* Lopez describes his attachment to his truck and provides a colorful glimpse into the life of a modern-day vagabond.

My Horse

It is curious that Indian warriors on the northern plains in the nineteenth century, who were almost entirely dependent on the horse for mobility and status, never gave their horses names. If you borrowed a man's horse and went off raiding for other horses, however, or if you lost your mount in battle and then jumped on mine and counted coup on an enemy—well, those horses would have to be shared with the man whose horse you borrowed, and that coup would be mine, not yours. Because even if I gave him no name, he was my horse.

If you were a Crow warrior and I a young Teton Sioux out after a warrior's identity and we came over a small hill somewhere in the Montana prairie and surprised each other, I could tell a lot about you by looking at your horse.

Your horse might have feathers tied in his mane, or in his tail, or a medicine bag tied around his neck. If I knew enough about the Crow, and had looked at you closely, I might make some sense of the decoration, even guess who you were if you were well-known. If you had painted your horse I could tell even more, because we both decorated our horses with signs that meant the same things. Your white handprints high on his flanks would tell me you had killed an enemy in a hand-to-hand fight. Small horizontal lines stacked on your horse's foreleg, or across his nose, would tell me how many times you had counted coup. Horse hoof marks on your horse's rump, or three-sided boxes, would tell me how many times you had stolen horses. If there was a bright red square on your horse's neck I would know you were leading a war party and that there were probably others out there in the coulees behind you.

4   You might be painted all over as blue as the sky and covered with white dots, with your horse painted the same way. Maybe hailstorms were your power—or if I chased you a hailstorm might come down and hide you. There might be lightning bolts on the horse's legs and flanks, and I would wonder if you had lightning power, or a slow horse. There might be white circles around your horse's eyes to help him see better.

5   Or you might be like Crazy Horse, with no decoration, no marks on your horse to tell me anything, only a small lightning bolt on your cheek, a piece of turquoise tied behind your ear.

6   You might have scalps dangling from your rein.

7   I could tell something about you by your horse. All this would come to me in a few seconds. I might decide this was my moment and shout my war cry—*Hoka hey!* Or I might decide you were like the grizzly bear: I would raise my weapon to you in salute and go my way, to see you again when I was older.

8   I do not own a horse. I am attached to a truck, however, and I have come to think of it in a similar way. It has no name; it never occurred to me to give it a name. It has litte decoration; neither of us is partial to decoration. I have a piece of turquoise in the truck because I had heard once that some of the southwestern tribes tied a small piece of turquoise in a horse's hock to keep him from stumbling. I like the idea. I also hang sage in the truck when I go on a long trip. But inside, the truck doesn't look much different from others that look just like it on the outside. I like it that way. Because I like my privacy.

9   For two years in Wyoming I worked on a ranch wrangling horses. The horse I rode when I had to have a good horse was a quarter horse and his name was Coke High. The name came with him. At first I thought he'd been named for the soft drink. I'd known stranger names given to horses by whites. Years later I wondered if some deviate Wyoming cowboy wise to cocaine had not named him. Now I think he was probably named after a rancher, an historical figure of the region. I never asked the people

who owned him for fear of spoiling the spirit of my inquiry.

We were running over a hundred horses on this ranch. 10
They all had names. After a few weeks I knew all the horses and the names too. You had to. No one knew how to talk about the animals or put them in order or tell the wranglers what to do unless they were using the names— Princess, Big Red, Shoshone, Clay.

My truck is named Dodge. The name came with it. I 11
don't know if it was named after the town or the verb or the man who invented it. I like it for a name. Perfectly anonymous, like Rex for a dog, or Old Paint. You can't tell anything with a name like that.

The truck is a van. I call it a truck because it's not a 12
car and because "van" is a suburban sort of consumer word, like "oxford loafer," and I don't like the sound of it. On the outside it looks like any other Dodge Sportsman 300. It's a dirty tan color. There are a few body dents, but it's never been in a wreck. I tore the antenna off against a tree on a pinched mountain road. A boy in Midland, Texas, rocked one of my rear view mirrors off. A logging truck in Oregon squeeze-fired a piece of debris off the road and shattered my windshield. The oil pan and gas tank are pug-faced from high-centering on bad roads. (I remember a horse I rode for a while named Targhee whose hocks were scarred from tangles in barbed wire when he was a colt and who spooked a lot in high grass, but these were not like "dents." They were more like bad tires.)

I like to travel. I go mostly in the winter and mostly 13
on two-lane roads. I've driven the truck from Key West to Vancouver, British Columbia, and from Yuma to Long Island over the past four years. I used to ride Coke High only about five miles every morning when we were rounding up horses. Hard miles of twisting and turning. About six hundred miles a year. Then I'd turn him out and ride another horse for the rest of the day. That's what was nice about having a remuda. You could do all you had to do and not take it all out on your best horse. Three car family.

My truck came with a lot of seats in it and I've never 14
really known what to do with them. Sometimes I put the seats in and go somewhere with a lot of people, but most of the time I leave them out. I like riding around with

that empty cavern of space behind my head. I know it's something with a history to it, that there's truth in it, because I always rode a horse the same way—with empty saddle bags. In case I found something. The possibility of finding something is half the reason for being on the road.

15   The value of anything comes to me in its use. If I am not using something it is of no value to me and I give it away. I wasn't always that way. I used to keep everything I owned—just in case. I feel good about the truck because it gets used. A lot. To haul hay and firewood and lumber and rocks and garbage and animals. Other people have used it to haul furniture and freezers and dirt and recycled newspapers. And to move from one house to another. When I lend it for things like that I don't look to get anything back but some gas (if we're going to be friends). But if you go way out in the country to a dump and pick up the things you can still find out there (once a load of cedar shingles we sold for $175 to an architect) I expect you to leave some of those things around my place when you come back—if I need them.

16   When I think back, maybe the nicest thing I ever put in that truck was timber wolves. It was a long night's drive from Oregon up into British Columbia. We were all very quiet about it; it was like moving clouds across the desert.

17   Sometimes something won't fit in the truck and I think about improving it—building a different door system, for example. I am forever going to add better gauges on the dash and a pair of driving lamps and a sunroof, but I never get around to doing any of it. I remember I wanted to improve Coke High once too, especially the way he bolted like a greyhound through patches of cottonwood on a river flat. But all I could do with him was to try to rein him out of it. Or hug his back.

18   Sometimes, road-stoned in a blur of country like southwestern Wyoming or North Dakota, I talk to the truck. It's like wandering on the high plains under a summer sun, on plains where, George Catlin wrote, you were "out of sight of land." I say what I am thinking out loud, or point at things along the road. It's a crazy, sun-stroked sort of activity, a sure sign it's time to pull over, to go

for a walk, to make a fire and have some tea, to lie in the shade of the truck.

I've always wanted to pat the truck. It's basic to the   19
relationship. But it never works.

I remember when I was on the ranch, just at sunrise,   20
after I'd saddled Coke High, I'd be huddled down in my
jacket smoking a cigarette and looking down into the valley, along the river where the other horses had spent the
night. I'd turn to Coke and run my hand down his neck
and slap-pat him on the shoulder to say I was coming
up. It made a bond, an agreement we started the day with.

I've thought about that a lot with the truck, because   21
we've gone out together at sunrise on so many mornings.
I've even fumbled around trying to do it. But metal won't
give.

The truck's personality is mostly an expression of two   22
ideas: "with-you" and "alone." When Coke High was
"with-you" he and I were the same animal. We could have
cut a rooster out of a flock of chickens, we were so in
tune. It's the same with the truck: rolling through Ken-
tucky on a hilly two-lane road, three in the morning under
a full moon and no traffic. Picture it. You roll like water.

There are other times when you are with each other   23
but there's no connection at all. Coke got that way when
he was bored and we'd fight each other about which way
to go around a tree. When the truck gets like that—
"alone"—it's because it feels its Detroit fat-ass design
dragging at its heart and making a fool out of it.

I can think back over more than a hundred nights I've   24
slept in the truck, sat in it with a lamp burning, bundled
up in a parka, reading a book. It was always comfortable.
A good place to wait out a storm. Like sleeping inside a
buffalo.

The truck will go past 100,000 miles soon. I'll rebuild   25
the engine and put a different transmission in it. I can
tell from magazine advertisements that I'll never get another one like it. Because every year they take more of
the heart out of them. One thing that makes a farmer
or a rancher go sour is a truck that isn't worth a shit.
The reason you see so many old pickups in ranch country
is because these are the only ones with any heart. You
can count on them. The weekend rancher runs around

in a new pickup with too much engine and not enough transmission and with the wrong sort of tires because he can afford anything, even the worst. A lot ot them have names for their pickups too.

26   My truck has broken down, in out of the way places at the worst of times. I've walked away and screamed the foulness out of my system and gotten the tools out. I had to fix a water pump in a blizzard in the Panamint Mountains in California once. It took all day with the Coleman stove burning under the engine block to keep my hands from freezing. We drifted into Beatty, Nevada, that night with it jury-rigged together with—I swear—baling wire, and we were melting snow as we went and pouring it in to compensate for the leaks.

27   There is a dent next to the door on the driver's side I put there one sweltering night in Miami. I had gone to the airport to meet my wife, whom I hadn't seen in a month. My hands were so swollen with poison ivy blisters I had to drive with my wrists. I had shut the door and was locking it when the window fell off its runners and slid down inside the door. I couldn't leave the truck unlocked because I had too much inside I didn't want to lose. So I just kicked the truck a blow in the side and went to work on the window. I hate to admit kicking the truck. It's like kicking a dog, which I've never done.

28   Coke High and I had an accident once. We hit a badger hole at a full gallop. I landed on my back and blacked out. When I came to, Coke High was about a hundred yards away. He stayed a hundred yards away for six miles, all the way back to the ranch.

29   I want to tell you about carrying those wolves, because it was a fine thing. There were ten of them. We had four in the truck with us in crates and six in a trailer. It was a five hundred mile trip. We went at night for the cool air and because there wouldn't be as much traffic. I could feel from the way the truck rolled along that its heart was in the trip. It liked the wolves inside it, the sweet odor that came from the crates. I could feel that same tireless wolf-lope developing in its wheels; it was like you might never have to stop for gas, ever again.

30   The truck gets very self-focused when it works like this; its heart is strong and it's good to be around it. It's good to be *with* it. You get the same feeling when you pull

someone out of a ditch. Coke High and I pulled a Volkswagen out of the mud once, but Coke didn't like doing it very much. Speed, not strength, was his center. When the guy who owned the car thanked us and tried to pat Coke, the horse snorted and swung away, trying to preserve his distance, which is something a horse spends a lot of time on.

So does the truck. 31

Being distant lets the truck get its heart up. The truck 32 has been cold and alone in Montana at 38 below zero. It's climbed horrible, eroded roads in Idaho. It's been burdened beyond overloading, and made it anyway. I've asked it to do these things because they build heart, and without heart all you have is a machine. You have nothing. I don't think people in Detroit know anything at all about heart. That's why everything they build dies so young.

One time in Arizona the truck and I came through one 33 of the worst storms I've ever been in, an outrageous, angry blizzard. But we went down the road, right through it. You couldn't explain our getting through by the sort of tires I had on the truck, or the fact that I had chains on, or was a good driver, or had a lot of weight over my drive wheels or a good engine, because it was more than this. It was a contest between the truck and the blizzard—and the truck wouldn't quit. I could have gone to sleep and the truck would have just torn a road down Interstate 40 on its own. It scared the hell out of me; but it gave me heart, too.

We came off the Mogollon Rim that night and out of 34 the storm and headed south for Phoenix. I pulled off the road to sleep for a few hours, but before I did I got out of the truck. It was raining. Warm rain. I tied a short piece of red avalanche cord into the grill. I left it there for a long time, like an eagle feather on a horse's tail. It flapped and spun in the wind. I could hear it ticking against the grill when I drove.

When I have to leave that truck I will just raise up my 35 left arm—*Hoka hey!*—and walk away.

Discussing Content and Form

1. Many people have thought of a car as possessing a personality and other human characteristics. What is your reaction to Lopez' comparison of his truck to a horse? Discuss the effectiveness of the analogy.

2. What special effect is produced by describing the Indian horses before mentioning the truck? What would be lost if the introductory paragraphs revealed the eventual purpose of the essay?

3. Lopez compares the truck to his own horse only after stating the analogy clearly. What is the essential difference in the way Lopez uses the two parts of the comparison—that to the Indian horses and that to his own horse?

4. Comment on the exactness and the vividness of the details. Do any of them seem superfluous? Why or why not?

5. Which details provide some insights into Lopez as a person? For instance, what is revealed by his statement, "I go mostly in winter and mostly on two-lane roads" (par. 13)? By the kinds of cargo that he carries in the truck? By his acting as his own repairman? Point out other statements by Lopez that reveal his philosophy or life-style.

6. What does the writer mean when he says that his truck has "heart" (par. 25)? Why do some vehicles, such as the trucks of the weekend ranchers who "can afford anything, even the worst," lack heart as Lopez defines it?

7. Lopez only once (par. 18) refers to an authority or another writer—George Catlin (1796–1872), an American artist and writer who lived with Indians in the Midwest and in Central and South America. Which details in the essay might be derived from knowing the works of an artist-writer such as Catlin?

Considering Special Techniques

1. In a sentence or two, try to characterize the style of this essay. Then consider these specific questions:
a. What elements help make the essay easy or smooth reading?
b. What elements contribute to a sense of informality? Could you label the style "conversational"? Why or why not?

2. In the first few paragraphs, Lopez poses some "possibilities," e.g., "If you borrowed a man's horse" (par. 1); "If you were a Crow warrior and I a young Teton Sioux" (par. 2). How does the use of such hypothetical situations involve the reader in the essay?

3.   What is the effect of the single-sentence paragraph (6): "You might have scalps dangling from your rein"?

4.   What is the effect of introducing the Indian war cry "Hoka hey" at the end of the imaginative description in par. 7? Why (or why not) does this cry then make an effective ending (par. 35)? Why is it advantageous for a writer to anticipate what he will use as an ending?

5.   Lopez' style is marked by the use of specific and vivid details. Examine several of these. Consider, for instance, what is gained by his use of place names. What would be lost if he said in paragraph 13, "I like to travel widely and have seen much of the country in the last few years"?

6.   Consider the following sentence fragments that Lopez uses and draw some conclusions about their effectiveness:
a.   "I like it that way. Because I like my privacy." (par. 8)
b.   "You could do all you had to do and not take it all out on your best horse. Three car family." (par. 13)
c.   ". . . I always rode a horse the same way—with empty saddlebags. In case I found something." (par. 14)
Find still other fragments and speculate about the writer's reasons for using them where he does.

7.   Lopez uses some words that are peculiar to a locale or a type of work. What is the effect of these technical or slang words: high-centering, spooked *(par. 12);* remuda *(par. 13);* road-stoned *(par. 18)?*

Generating Ideas

1.   Choose an object (car, bicycle, boat, piece of sports equipment, cabin, musical instrument, art object, heirloom, etc.) or an animal to which you have had a particular attachment. Use an analogy to explain that association, to clarify its meaning.

2.   Lopez includes in his essay several memorable ideas, bits of philosophy summarized in quotable form. Use one of these (or another of your choice) as starter for a paper:
a.   "The possibility of finding something is half the reason for being on the road." (par. 14)
b.   "The value of something comes to me in its use." (par. 15)
c.   "The weekend rancher runs around in a new pickup . . . because he can afford anything, even the worst." (par. 25) (You may adapt this to fit other occupations, of course.)

d. *"I don't think people in Detroit know anything at all about heart. That's why everything they build dies so young." (par. 32)*

3. *Define "heart" as you might find it in things other than a truck or a horse; be sure to illustrate with one or more examples.*

4. *We often hear that America is built on waste, that we do not cherish objects that have lost their initial value. Using Lopez' feeling for his truck as well as other examples, prove that this philosophy is changing.*

3
Analyzing Reasons and Results: *Cause* and *Effect*

One of the first questions we ask as children is "why?" "Why does it snow?" "Why did that team win the game?" We probe for causes, wanting this action or that thought explained. And we also want to know about effects: "Will connecting these wires make the motor work?" "Will putting in more money help win the election?"

A great deal of writing in your academic work requires the analysis of causes and effects. You may be asked in a history class to explain the reasons why the United States Senate failed to support President Wilson's dream of the League of Nations; you may be required in sociology to analyze the effects of a bussing policy in the city schools; or in biology you may have to report on the cause-effect relationships between certain substances and the diseased respiratory systems of a group of rats. Similarly, in the business or professional world, you may be asked to issue a bulletin on the causes of a rise in coffee prices; or you may have to report on your search for causal relationships between asbestos and lung disease.

Whatever the subject or investigative task, writing based on cause-effect analysis requires careful observation and research. Analysis must be precise and well-founded in facts; often it requires experiment and proof. The "why" questions must get at fundamental causes, the true ones, and not stop with the merely superficial. Faulty analysis of causes results in false or careless inferences, in relating effects to causes that are inaccurate or only partial. For instance, from seeing one accident involving a Volkswagen you cannot infer that all small cars are dangerous. If a quarterback is injured, the team will not necessarily lose. The driver may have been at fault; the effect might be to make the team play harder. If writing based on cause-effect analysis is to be clear and convincing, it must show the logical relationships between the causes and the effects under discussion.

In the following paragraph the key phrase "two simple reasons" immediately points to the writer's purpose and his method of analyzing the causes of suburban sprawl, which he has described previously:

> Suburbia got that way for two simple reasons: first, because the developers who built it are, fundamentally, no different from manufacturers of any other mass-produced product: they standardize the product, package it, arrange for rapid distribution and easy financing, and sell it off the shelf as fast as they can. And, second, because the federal government, through FHA and other agencies set up to cope with the serious housing shortages that arose after World War II, has imposed a bureaucratic strait jacket on the design of most new houses, on the placement of these houses on individual lots, on landscaping, on street-planning, and on just about everything else that gives Suburbia its "wasteland" appearance. As Senator Harrison Williams, of New Jersey, put it recently: "The Federal Government, directly and indirectly, through the laws it writes, the programs it enacts and the regulations it issues, has contributed more than its share to the ugliness of our landscape."—Peter Blake, *God's Own Junkyard*

Cause-effect analysis, like other methods of exposition, may extend beyond the paragraph and become a dominant method for a longer unit. The complexity of the form increases, of course, in dealing with interrelated forces or ideas. But the presentation of causes and effects must always be based on the careful examination of evidence and must show clearly all inner connections.

Here is another paragraph that shows causes and effects. Again, the first sentence signals the writer's purpose and method:

> There have been a great many forces that have helped to shape the American household and the buildings that have kept it dry and warm and in some cases embellished it. The process of our domestication (some people might call it our becoming civilized, others our being tamed) has in some respects been slowed and in others hastened by our inability to stay put either physically or socially. Our mobil-

ity has revealed itself in our tastes in architecture, in our manners in the living room, and in the uses and characters of our parlors and dining rooms and kitchens. So, of course, has the wastefulness in which a nation overly rich in natural resources can indulge. So, too, has the inventiveness that has made our houses into museums of gadgets which replace servants that we have been, at least theoretically, rather embarrassed as good democrats to employ. Our beliefs in equality and our flouting of them have shaped our houses as surely as have our plentiful forests, our fascination with technology, and the surges of immigration of inexpensive labor from countries less fortunate than our own.—Russell Lynes, *The Domesticated Americans*

In writing to explain causes and effects, certain words serve as keys to the content and provide convenient links. The two sample paragraphs contain words such as "because" and "reasons," and phrases such as "has contributed" and "forces that . . . shape." A paragraph concerning effects might have phrases such as "several results" or "possible effects are . . . ." But both causes and effects can be stated without the use of such clues. In this selection almost every sentence indicates an interlocking cause-effect relationship:

As the world daily grows larger, more complex, and more impersonal, man, more than ever, seeks the security of things. To fill in the void both around and within himself, man craves possessions to give his life an identifiable and pleasing shape. Paradoxically, however, by investing inanimate objects with power and significance, the individual, like Lear, often diminishes himself. By seeking—whatever the cost—to be possessor, man often becomes, in turn, possessed. Or, as Ralph Waldo Emerson once lamented, "Things are in the saddle / And ride mankind."—Cynthia Golomb Dettelback, *In the Driver's Seat: the Automobile in American Literature and Popular Culture*

Here are four effects of the impersonal world on the modern individual: the search for security, the possession of objects, the diminishment of the self, and the possession by objects. The paragraph forms a kind of chain link, with each sentence providing the link to the next, for example: the "complex" and "impersonal" world causes "man" [to seek] "the security of things"; the desire "to fill in the void" [causes craving for] "possessions."

As in other methods of developing paragraphs and essays, the material should be narrowed and focused. The causes should truly fit the effect being analyzed. A paper based on cause-effect analysis avoids oversimplifications and mere suppositions. It contains well-reasoned inferences supported by concrete evidence. And it contains words and phrases that clearly and logically connect one idea to the next.

Russell Lynes

Russell Lynes (b. 1910) was educated at Yale and has held positions in publishing and served on the boards of many educational funds and museums. He has written extensively about American culture and art and the social forces that shape the national tastes, subjects on which he has also lectured widely. His best-known books include *Highbrow, Lowbrow, Middlebrow* (1949), *The Tastemakers* (1954), *The Domesticated Americans* (1963), and *Confessions of a Dilettante* (1963). In "The Movers," from *The Domesticated Americans,* he comments on American mobility and the effect it has on national life. Lynes' detached and intelligent observations always have the capacity to provoke further thought.

The Movers

On a winter afternoon in 1842, Charles Dickens, who had a marked talent for setting the teeth of Americans on edge, took a train from Boston, a city of which he had generally approved, to Worcester, a matter of fifty odd miles. There was a quality about the landscape that he saw from the windows of the train that surprised and amused him. "All the buildings," he wrote in his *American Notes,* "looked as if they had been built and painted that morning and could be taken down on Monday with very little trouble." Dickens, of course, was used to stone houses in the English landscape, houses that looked as though they were as permanent as the hills about them. A New England village where "every house is the whitest of white" and where "the clean cardboard colonnades had no more perspective than a bridge on a Chinese tea cup" made him wonder if Americans ever intended to settle down. Not only did the houses look impermanent; they looked unprivate. ". . . those slightly built wooden dwellings," he noted, "behind which the sun was setting with a brilliant lustre, could be so looked through and through, that the idea of any inhabitant

1
Introduction: Dickens' observation of American buildings (par. 1)

From pp. 5–7 in *The Domesticated Americans* by Russell Lynes. Copyright © 1957, 1963 by Russell Lynes. Reprinted by permission of Harper & Row, Publishers, Inc.

being able to hide himself from the public gaze, or have any secrets from the public eye, was not entertainable for a moment."

2
Reasons why Americans built as they did (par. 2)

One of the reasons why Mr. Dickens got under the skin of so many Americans was that his observations were so frequently and so uncomfortably accurate. It was easy enough to explain, of course, that Americans built of wood rather than of stone because wood was so cheap and so available, but that did not explain either the disregard for privacy or why, as Dickens noted of the suburbs around Boston, American houses looked to be "sprinkled and dropped about in all directions, without seeming to have any root at all in the ground." Indeed, it appeared to him as though "the whole affair could be taken up piecemeal like a child's toy, and crammed into a little box." It was something more than white clapboards that gave America a here-today-gone-tomorrow look. It was more than just the newness of the houses and the fresh white paint, the meadows, "rank, and rough, and wild." It was something in the American character that, though Dickens did not define it, he seemed to discern: a restlessness, an urge to move on, a sense of there being unlimited space to be used or wasted, an unwillingness, in spite of all protestations to the contrary, to put down permanent roots.

3
Examples of metaphors for moving that are part of our national heritage (par. 3)

The truth of the matter is that ours is a society as mobile as wheels, ambition, almost unlimited expanses of land, and an itch to sample the grass in the next pasture can make us. To move is as natural to the American as maintaining roots is to the European. Our restlessness and mobility are in our metaphors. In England a man *stands* for Parliament; in America he *runs* for the Senate. The American prides himself on his "get up and go." We think of progress as "covering ground" and we admire the man who "makes it under his own steam." The bright young man of promise is "a young man who's going places." The failure in our society is the man (or the institution, for that matter) who "stands still." The most famous exhortation in the American vernacular is "Go west, young man." We sing: "Where do we go from here, boys? Where do we go from here?" and "Don't Fence Me In," "How You Gonna Keep 'em Down on the Farm?" and "It's a Long, Long Trail."

There is more truth than humor for the American in the aphorism "Home is where you hang your hat." It is part of our mythology, rather than of our history or of our longest memories, that the American homestead is the symbol of family continuity and stability and the stronghold of democratic institutions. We associate the homestead with the virtues of family unity and solidarity, the sacrifices that the family makes for its members, the peace and reassurance of the hearth, and the sharing of pleasures and tragedies. No legend, no nostalgia, is without some basis in fact, but enduring homesteads have been few in our history compared with the vast number of transitory homes, pickings-up and puttings-down, homes that were expected to be only stepping stones to something better. Our romanticized notion of the homestead reflects actuality about as accurately as a cheerful Currier and Ives print reflects nineteenth-century life on a farm. Americans are nomadic.

4
Refutation of the myth of the American homestead (par. 4)

It is not possible to understand the relationship between the American and his house, which he is more likely to regard as a piece of equipment than as an institution, without considering the conflict that has been in progress for more than a century and a half between foot-loose Americans and those who have tried to get them to settle down and put permanent roots into the community. Some of the pressures that have kept us moving have been practical ones, some have been romantic. Sometimes our motives have been greed, sometimes escape, sometimes hope,

5
Reasons why Americans keep moving (par. 5)

sometimes despair, and sometimes merely the restlessness of boredom or loneliness. We have moved in order to avoid the snapping of an economic trap sprung by a failing industry or worn-out soil; we have moved because someone a long way off needed our skills and because nobody at home any longer did. We have moved because the character of neighborhoods changed and we no longer felt at home in them. We have moved because of divorce or because our children had been fledged. We have moved because of our social aspirations or because of our loss or gain in financial status. We have moved for the fun of it, because we got tired of the view from the terrace, because of another child in the family, or because we wanted a house with a picture window. We have moved for no reason at all, except for the sake of moving.

Discussing Content and Form

1.   Summarize Dickens' description of the American scene. Is it still accurate? Explain.

2.   One of the assumptions underlying Dickens' and Lynes' observations is that our houses reflect the character of the people who live in them. Do both writers build a strong enough case for this assumption? Explain.

3.   Lynes gives examples of several metaphors that express American restlessness. Identify other popular metaphors that show the opposite tendency—a love of home and stability. Consider, for example, such song lines as "Over the river and through the woods, to Grandmother's house we go."

4.   How many separate reasons for moving does Lynes give in paragraph 5?

5.   What is the effect of his conclusion that "We have moved for no reason at all, except for the sake of moving"? In what way does that statement relate to his assertions about the American character?

Considering Special Techniques

1.   Notice the development in paragraph 5, the section that deals most clearly with why Americans move.
a.   Find several words that signal the fact that the structure is a list of reasons.
b.   How does the structure of several of the sentences reflect the logical relationship between cause and effect?

2.   In what ways is the use of Dickens' observations an effective opener? Does it serve to do anything besides catch interest? Explain.

3.   There are some subtle internal links between paragraphs in this selection.
a.   What relationships exist between the images in the Dickens description (par. 1) and the images of the homestead (par. 4)?
b.   Explain why Lynes refers to the nineteenth-century prints by Currier and Ives (par. 4).

4.   Words to learn and use: protestations *(par. 2);* aphorisms, transitory, nomadic *(par. 4);* aspirations *(par. 5).*

Generating Ideas

1.   The noted historian Frederick Jackson Turner advanced the theory that the American character was shaped by the presence of a frontier, and that American life and character would change when the frontier vanished. Consider Turner's theory (look up more about it if you can) and write an essay on the vanishing American dream or the necessary changes in the pioneer spirit.

2.   Huckleberry Finn, at the end of Mark Twain's novel that bears his name, turns his back on society and says that he is "going to strike out for the territory ahead of the rest." Write a paper explaining the reasons why you or some person or persons you know want to strike out for new territories.

3.   Communities are sometimes classified as traditional or mobile, depending on whether they are places where families stay put or where there is constant migration in and out. Write a paper in which you analyze the community where you have lived most of your life. Into which type does it fall? What are the reasons for its stability or its constant change? How does

*the nature of the community affect attitudes and values, educa-
tion, and social life? If you have lived in both types of communities, you might show why one differs from the other.*

4. *Use one of these topics to develop a paper by cause-effect:*
a. *Why do people look for roots? Analyze some reasons for such
things as visits to ancestral homes or countries, the collection and preservation of family heirlooms, the craze for antiques, or research into genealogy.*
b. *Cities and villages all over the country are devoting increasing amounts of money and interest to developing historical
societies. And every year thousands of tourists visit restored
villages such as Williamsburg in Virginia, Sturbridge in
Massachusetts, and Greenfield Village outside Detroit. Account for this interest in the past. Does it lie in a need to
identify more strongly with our heritage or does it stem
from mere curiosity?*

5. *Some people sentimentalize their childhood homes while
others reject them. Account for one or the other of these ways
of looking back by citing examples from your reading or from
life.*

6. *Lynes finds metaphors for transiency, but in American folk
arts there are some metaphors which represent an attempt
to achieve permanence. Discuss the reasons behind some of these
efforts to perpetuate the past: photograph albums, patch-
work quilts or braided rugs made from family clothing, collections of memorabilia.*

Alvin Toffler

Alvin Toffler (b. 1928) is well known as a writer on education and sociology. He grew up in New York City and was educated at New York University. After serving as Washington correspondent for various magazines and newspapers, he was associate editor of *Fortune* from 1959 to 1961. Toffler has also held many positions in educational fields, and was for a time on the faculty of The New School for Social Research. Among his numerous books are *The Culture Consumers* (1964), *Future Shock* (1970), *The Futurists* (1970), *Learning for Tomorrow* (1974), and *The Eco-Spasm Report* (1975). "A Superabundance of Selves" comes from *Future Shock*. Like the highly popular book, the selection challenges readers to speculate about the possible results of present social trends.

A Superabundance of Selves

To be "between styles" or "between subcults" is a life-crisis, and the people of the future spend more time in this condition, searching for styles, than do the people of the past or present. Altering his identity as he goes, super-industrial man traces a private trajectory through a world of colliding subcults. This is the social mobility of the future: not simply movement from one economic class to another, but from one tribal grouping to another. Restless movement from subcult to ephemeral subcult describes the arc of his life.

There are plenty of reasons for this restlessness. It is not merely that the individual's psychological needs change more often than in the past; the subcults also change. For these and other reasons, as subcult membership becomes ever more unstable, the search for a personal style will become increasingly intense, even frenetic in the decades to come. Again and again, we shall find ourselves bitter or bored, vaguely dissatisfied with "the way things are"—upset, in other words, with our present style. At that moment, we begin once more to search for a new principle around which to organize our choices. We arrive again at the moment of super-decision.

At this moment, if anyone studied our behavior closely, he would find a sharp increase in what might be called the Transience Index. The rate of turnover of things, places, people, organizational and informational relationships spurts upward. We get rid of that silk dress or tie, the old Tiffany lamp, that horror of a claw-footed Victorian end table—all those symbols of our links with the subcult of the past. We begin, bit by bit, to replace them with new items emblematic of our new identification. The same process occurs in our social lives—the through-put of people speeds up. We begin to reject ideas we have held (or to explain them or rationalize them in new ways). We are suddenly free of all the constraints that our subcult or style imposed on us. A Transience Index would prove a sensitive indicator of those moments in our lives when we are most free—but, at the same time, most lost.

4 It is in this interval that we exhibit the wild oscillation engineers call "searching behavior." We are most vulnerable now to the messages of new subcults, to the claims and counterclaims that rend the air. We lean this way and that. A powerful new friend, a new fad or idea, a new political movement, some new hero rising from the depths of the mass media—all these strike us with particular force at such a moment. We are more "open," more uncertain, more ready for someone or some group to tell us what to do, how to behave.

5 Decisions—even little ones—come harder. This is not accidental. To cope with the press of daily life we need more information about far more trivial matters than when we were locked into a firm life style. And so we feel anxious, pressured, alone, and we move on. We choose or allow ourselves to be sucked into a new subcult. We put on a new style.

6 As we rush toward super-industrialism, therefore, we find people adopting and discarding life styles at a rate that would have staggered the members of any previous generation. For the life style itself has become a throwaway item.

7 This is no small or easy matter. It accounts for the much lamented "loss of commitment" that is so characteristic of our time. As people shift from subcult to subcult, from style to style, they are conditioned to guard themselves against the inevitable pain of disaffiliation. They learn to armor themselves against the sweet sorrow of parting. The extremely devout Catholic who throws over his religion and plunges into the life of a New Left activist, then throws himself into some other cause or movement or subcult, cannot go on doing so forever. He becomes, to

adapt Graham Greene's term, a "burnt out case." He learns from past disappointment never to lay too much of his old self on the line.

And so, even when he seemingly adopts a subcult or style, he withholds some part of himself. He conforms to the group's demands and revels in the belongingness that it gives him. But this belongingness is never the same as it once was, and secretly he remains ready to defect at a moment's notice. What this means is that even when he seems most firmly plugged in to his group or tribe, he listens, in the dark of night, to the short-wave signals of competing tribes.

In this sense, his membership in the group is shallow. He remains constantly in a posture of non-commitment, and without strong commitment to the values and styles of some group he lacks the explicit set of criteria that he needs to pick his way through the burgeoning jungle of overchoice.

The super-industrial revolution, consequently, forces the whole problem of overchoice to a qualitatively new level. It forces us now to make choices not merely among lamps and lampshades, but among lives, not among life style *components,* but among whole life *styles.*

This intensification of the problem of overchoice presses us toward orgies of self-examination, soul-searching and introversion. It confronts us with that most popular of contemporary illnesses, the "identity crisis." Never before have masses of men faced a more complex set of choices. The hunt for identity arises not out of the supposed choicelessness of "mass society," but precisely from the plenitude and complexity of our choices.

Each time we make a style choice, a super-decision, each time we link up with some particular subcultural group or groups, we make some change in our self-image. We become, in some sense, a different person, and we perceive ourselves as different. Our old friends, those who knew us in some previous incarnation, raise their eyebrows. They have a harder and harder time recognizing us, and, in fact, we experience increasing difficulty in identifying with, or even sympathizing with, our own past selves.

The hippie becomes the straight-arrow executive, the executive becomes the skydiver without noting the exact steps of transition. In the process, he discards not only the externals of his style, but many of his underlying attitudes as well. And one day the question hits him like a splash of cold water in a sleep-sodden face: "What remains?" What is there of "self" or "personality" in the sense of a continuous, durable internal structure? For some, the answer is very little. For they are no longer dealing in "self" but in what might be called "serial selves."

14   The Super-industrial Revolution thus requires a basic change in man's conception of himself, a new theory of personality that takes into account the discontinuities in men's lives, as well as the continuities.

15   The Super-industrial Revolution also demands a new conception of freedom—a recognition that freedom, pressed to its ultimate, negates itself. Society's leap to a new level of differentiation necessarily brings with it new opportunities for individuation, and the new technology, the new temporary organizational forms, cry out for a new breed of man. This is why, despite "backlash" and temporary reversals, the line of social advance carries us toward a wider tolerance, a more easy acceptance of more and more diverse human types.

16   The sudden popularity of the slogan "do your thing" is a reflection of this historic movement. For the more fragmented or differentiated the society, the greater the number of varied life styles it promotes. And the more socially accepted life style models put forth by the society, the closer that society approaches a condition in which, in fact, each man does his own, unique thing.

17   Thus, despite all the anti-technological rhetoric of the Elluls and Fromms, the Mumfords and Marcuses, it is precisely the super-industrial society, the most advanced technological society ever, that extends the range of freedom. The people of the future enjoy greater opportunities for self-realization than any previous group in history.

18   The new society offers few roots in the sense of truly enduring relationships. But it does offer more varied life niches, more freedom to move in and out of these niches, and more opportunity to create one's own niche, than all earlier societies put together. It also offers the supreme exhilaration of riding change, cresting it, changing and growing with it—a process infinitely more exciting than riding the surf, wrestling steers, playing "knock hubcaps" on an eight-lane speedway, or the pursuit of pharmaceuti-

cal kicks. It presents the individual with a contest that requires self-mastery and high intelligence. For the individual who comes armed with these, and who makes the necessary effort to understand the fast-emerging super-industrial social structure, for the person who finds the "right" life pace, the "right" sequence of subcults to join and life style models to emulate, the triumph is exquisite.

Undeniably, these grand words do not apply to the majority of men. Most people of the past and present remain imprisoned in life niches they have neither made nor have much hope, under present conditions, of ever escaping. For most human beings, the options remain excruciatingly few. [19]

This imprisonment must—and will—be broken. Yet it will not be broken by tirades against technology. It will not be broken by calls for a return to passivity, mysticism and irrationality. It will not be broken by "feeling" or "intuiting" our way into the future while derogating empirical study, analysis, and rational effort. Rather than lashing out, Luddite-fashion, against the machine, those who genuinely wish to break the prison-hold of the past and present would do well to hasten the controlled—selective—arrival of tomorrow's technologies. To accomplish this, however, intuition and "mystical insights" are hardly enough. It will take exact scientific knowledge, expertly applied to the crucial, most sensitive points of social control. [20]

Nor does it help to offer the principle of the maximization of choice as the key to freedom. We must consider the possibility, suggested here, that choice may become overchoice, and freedom unfreedom. [21]

Discussing Content and Form

1. Toffler, like Lynes, deals with restlessness, but Toffler is concerned with social mobility rather than with geographical mobility. Discuss his statement that "Restless movement from subcult to ephemeral subcult describes the arc of . . . life" for people in the future. In what ways is such rapid social change already a part of life?

2. Toffler deals with results or effects more than he does with causes. While he says that there are "plenty of reasons" for social instability, he attributes it to one overriding cause from

*which the others spring. What is that basic cause for shifting
life styles?*

3. *Discuss Toffler's assertion that "life style itself has become
a throw-away item" (par. 6). How does he account for the
"loss of commitment" and the "pain of disaffiliation"? Do you
agree that we learn from "disappointment never to lay too
much of [ourselves] on the line" (par. 7)? Why or why not?*

4. *Why does Toffler say that for "most human beings, the
options remain excruciatingly few" (par. 19)? Why does he reject
the "tirades against technology" represented by "calls for
a return to passivity, mysticism and irrationality" (par. 20)?
Discuss instances of these forms of reaction to the "super-industrial revolution."*

5. *Why is it ironic that in having too many choices, too much
freedom, the individual then loses that very freedom? Have you
known people who tried various life styles and found in the
end that this freedom led only to discontinuity? Explain.*

Considering Special Techniques

1. *Toffler's essay furnishes excellent examples of careful linking devices that help organize his complex ideas. Examine the
opening sentences of each paragraph, noting how certain
phrases and words provide a careful sequence or interconnec-
tion between ideas. Here is a start for your analysis:*
a. *"restlessness" (par. 2) echoes "Restless" from par. 1.*
b. *"At this moment" (par. 3) links to "at the moment" in par.
2.*
c. *"It is in this interval" (par. 4) provides a sequential link
to the ideas at the end of par. 3.*

2. *Choose one of Toffler's paragraphs and analyze the ways
in which the sentences are joined by connecting words or
phrases, by the repetition or echoes of ideas, and by the repetition of sentence patterns. (A particularly good example of the
repetition of sentence patterns is found in paragraph 5.)*

3. *Toffler uses several words and phrases that are jargon taken
from the social sciences and business, e.g.,* maximization *(par.
21). Find other words and phrases in the essay that you consider
jargon. Are they offensive or effective here? Explain.*

4. *Find examples of clichés that Toffler uses (e.g., "the press
of daily life") and comment on possible reasons for employing
them in the essay.*

5. *Words to learn and use:* trajectory, ephemeral *(par. 1);* frenetic *(par. 2);* emblematic *(par. 3);* oscillation *(par. 4);* disaffiliation *(par. 7);* burgeoning *(par. 9);* qualitatively, components *(par. 10);* intensification, introversion, plenitude *(par. 11);* incarnation *(par. 12);* individuation *(par. 15);* exhilaration, emulate *(par. 18);* excruciatingly *(par. 19);* tirades, derogating, empirical, intuition *(par. 20);* maximization *(par. 21).*

Generating Ideas

1. *If you have undergone an "identity crisis," explain the causes for that experience. Or you might explain the causes and effects of your search for a set of principles by which to live.*

2. *When a person adopts a subcult or style, Toffler says, he may still withhold himself even though he conforms outwardly. Support this view with evidence from your experiences or from those of people you know. What makes people hesitant about commitment? In what ways is this care about choices good and in what ways is it bad? You might crystallize your discussion with a title like one of these:*
"Trying the New—With Caution"
"Maybe Yes, Maybe No"
"Even the Elephant Tests the Bridge"
"Hang Your Clothes on a Hickory Limb, but
  Don't Go Near the Water"

3. *Toffler discusses what he calls a "Transience Index" (par. 3), a means of judging the rate at which "things, places, people, organizational and informational relationships" are discarded. Write an essay in which you explain why you discard some things (even friends), and show what effects those losses have on you and your life.*

4. *The process of maturing inevitably brings a struggle between "belongingness" and "individuality." Write a paper in which you consider the reasons for your reactions to the "short-wave signals of competing tribes" (par. 8) that influenced you as you were growing up.*

Ruth Gay

Ruth Gay is the author of *Jews in America: A Short History* (1965). She
has also published many articles in *Commentary, Midstream, Horizon,*
and the *American Scholar,* some of them in collaboration with her husband, Peter Gay, a professor of history at Yale University. Her interest
in the history and the sociological implications of food, the subject of
the following selection, led her to do research on the subject in Europe
and America. "Fear of Food" appeared in slightly longer form in the
American Scholar.

Fear of Food

1   Supermarket shelves, the great barometer of what America eats, all seem to be colored brown now. Instant cereals,
white flours, refined sugars appear solemnly packaged in
their tan sacks to persuade us that there has been hardly
any intervention between the manure that nourished
them and the recycled paper that wraps them. What is
this flight into the natural, the coarse, all about? Dr. Reu-
ben, who told us all we ever wanted to know about sex,
now tells us what we need to know about our health—
or, more properly, about our digestion. And here, too, we
learn that we have been too refined, our food too delicate,
our palates too exquisite. With him, we are back to seeing
man as a machine, and the machine, it seems, requires
a certain amount of grit to keep functioning. This theory,
based on a study by a pair of English investigators, is
obviously an idea whose time has come. It was first
presented in the popular press in the winter of 1974 in
England. By the spring of 1975 it was getting a lot of attention in the German newspapers and feature stories in the
women's magazines. By last summer, it was in full bloom
in the United States.

2   These days, then, when Americans talk about food, they
are not talking about something good to eat. They are talking about their health, or the stress of modern life, or
about the world's surviving. A great fear has overwhelmed
us in the last decade, as we have begun to contemplate
not only the atom, but also ineradicable pollution,

Reprinted from the *American Scholar,* Volume 45, Number 3, Summer 1976. Copyright © 1976 by the United Chapters of Phi Beta Kappa. By permission of the
publishers.

indestructible poison gases, harmful chemicals irretrievably soaked into the food chain. . . .

Although there does seem to be a reasonable connection between our perception of the poisoned food chain and our worry about what we eat, our newest crisis actually revives a very old pattern in Western life, a pattern in which food and medicine, food and magic have been inextricably mixed. It is an ancient tradition that potions for magic and potions for healing come out of the same caldron. Who does not have in his family some form of a story much cherished in mine? Our version took place at the turn of the century in the Ukraine when my great-aunt, then a child, lay ill of smallpox. Her case was so severe that she was expected to die and had been removed to a little hut away from the main house. At this point an old peasant woman came by and peeped in the window. Seeing the plight of the child, she hurried away and returned with a bowl of sour milk, which she fed her spoonful by spoonful. From that moment on, the child began to mend, and, as they say in old German fairy tales, if she hasn't died, she is still alive to this day.

There is much that is suggestive in this story. The old peasant woman, for example: is she not the prototype of the witch, the dangerous guardian of dangerous secrets, controlling health and sickness at her whim? And the sour milk is itself a dish most susceptible to magic, easily curdled by malign influences or evil presences. Yet sour milk was also a staple in the Ukraine, being one of the commonest ways of preserving milk—halfway between a drink and cheese—in a time before refrigeration. Whether the story is asserting the magical power of sour milk as a potion brewed by the knowing old woman or pointing out its inherent goodness as a primal food remains ambiguous, and properly so. The best stories, after all, always leave an echo of uncertainty in the air.

It is hard to remember that the science of nutrition is barely half a century old, so that many of our attitudes were formed, and are still propagated, by people who grew up with the helpless analogies or pragmatic conclusions available to medicine around the turn of the century. The English had learned something about scurvy and citrus fruit, about "fever" and quinine. Digitalis seemed to help certain heart conditions. But why or how these simple medicines worked no one understood.

6   The combination of our helplessness and our need for certainty, however, led us for decades to rely on principles whose origin we would now blush to acknowledge. I recently heard someone say that she had discovered why she had a certain kind of rash. A friend had pointed out to her the resemblance between her spots and tomato seeds. Her remedy, therefore, was to avoid eating tomatoes. Did she know that she was reasoning by the old medieval doctrine of Signatures?

7   According to this fascinating science, as expounded by Paracelsus in the sixteenth century, fruits and vegetables carry certain signs that reveal their properties for good or evil. "Behold the *Satyrion* root," he wrote; "is it not formed like the male privy parts? No one can deny this. Accordingly magic discovered it and revealed that it can restore a man's virility and passion. And then we have the thistle; do not its leaves prickle like needles? Thanks to this sign, the art of magic discovered that there is no better herb against internal prickling." Jerusalem artichokes that grew as stumpy, deformed-looking roots were thought, as late as the nineteenth century, to induce leprosy, because, as Paracelsus would say, were they not like the misshapen fingers of the late stages of leprosy? Similarly, the beloved port wine tonic so gravely prescribed by physicians to improve the blood of pale Victorian young ladies had no more relation to blood than artichokes had to leprosy. But the principle of analogy is persuasive and not easily shakable.

8   In the fields of food and drink we are still most vulnerable to the claims of superstition. The pseudo-scientific reasoning that introduces so many food fads comes dressed in the impressive language of medicine, and instantly quenches every spark of skepticism still feebly alive within us by satisfying our conscious need for "scientific" proof while feeding our simple credulity. Although we learned long ago to abandon magical thinking in connection with weather, crops, the care of animals, and other natural phenomena, it still has us in its grip when we think of diet. Our latest thinking about food, based on fear, is proportionately retrograde—willing to accept, indeed seeking out, the consolations of magic, the mute

practice of peasants, and the quaint devices of folklore. Books on the saving properties of "honegar" (a mixture of honey and vinegar), of blackstrap molasses, of sprouting mung beans, succeed one another in unending succession. The *Foxfire* book of homely know-how has gone into a third volume in response to popular interest, just as the earlier *Whole Earth Catalogue* was the guide for all seekers of the true way. The dividing line between recipes for natural foods and other natural remedies, for illness, for making a garden, for building a house, has grown steadily fainter. The Department of Agriculture pamphlets that were once sought after for the best scientific solutions to problems in domestic economy are being supplanted in popularity by books reviving traditional methods of cultivation and cures, the more ancient and more bizarre the better. "Chicken shit," I heard one cosmopolite in New Hampshire say, "isn't that what you're supposed to put on cuts?"

With our sophisticated imaginations we endow all these stratagems with the patina of ancient wisdom, of lost truths, and we flee from the modern world, condemning packaged white bread with a passion we reserve for few other evils. We hardly notice, in this flight from reason, the disappearance of smallpox, or that we no longer expect a "cholera season," or that the eight million people who live in the squalor called New York are drinking safe water. 9

The unexamined residue of literal magic—the heritage of the Signature, or vaguer memories of aphrodisiacs— is augmented by the history of manners and social usage that has created a mystical hierarchy of foods, each with its own special and instantly identifiable attributes. It was in recognition of the power of this symbolism that the West German government recently barred a cigarette company from continuing a false advertisement. What was striking about it was that, although wordless, the meaning of the ad was unmistakable: in the foreground lay a package of cigarettes, in the background a loaf of crusty bread, an earthenware milk jug, and a picturesque cluster of wheat stalks, all bathed in a golden light. In any part of the Western world, the message was instantly decipherable: whatever is natural, elemental, is therefore wholesome. What could be purer and more innocent in our imaginations than bread and milk? With bread such 10 a universal symbol, it is no wonder that so much feeling is again centering on it.

11   Much of the history of Europe could be written using the fine wheaten loaf as a barometer. For a long time, sumptuary laws forbade it to all but members of noble households. Like the Cadillac to the slum dweller today, it came to stand for all kinds of things that had nothing to do with its function. The peasant's black bread may have been ultimately more nutritious, but to him it was the sign of poverty and servitude, as white bread was the sign of wealth and freedom. The oldest prejudice of mankind has probably been in favor of wheat to the denigration of all other grains. While bread was not the first food of man, it has been a staple since Neolithic times, and has been the main, and sometimes the only, food for all but the tiny percentage of the privileged. What is visible from the earliest times is that all grains are not equal, and even in Egyptian wall paintings the priests are offering the gods beautiful cone-shaped loaves made of wheat flour, while the fellahin are eating millet.

12   We can endorse the prejudices of our ancestors, of course, by agreeing that fine wheaten bread is obviously "better" than bread made of rye or oats or millet or spelt or chestnuts. But the objective merits of wheat bread—its lightness, delicate flavor, rich texture—are all less significant to the imagination than its having been for so long an unattainable luxury. In England even the symbolic status of the brown-bread bakers was inferior to that of white-bread bakers. The arms granted to them in 1622, a quarter of a century after the white-bread bakers, are similar in most details, but are instantly perceptible as lesser by the lack of supporting festoons and a motto. During the nineteenth century, the brown-bread bakers began to find allies in various groups that had discovered the evils of white bread. "A Physician" in 1846 pointed out that the nourishing "ingredients are removed by the miller in his efforts to please the public so that fine flour, instead of being better than meal is the least nourishing. . . . It seems desirable that the poor be brought to inquire whether they do not purchase at too dear a rate the privilege of indulging in the use of it." All this was written under the old, relatively primitive conditions when grain was still stone-ground.

13   When the new roller mills were introduced in the 1870s,

making the production of white flour cheaper and less nutritious than ever, one of the big brown-bread baking companies in London attempted to defend its product by inviting a "distinguished gathering of physicians, medical officers and representatives of the press" to view a newly installed set of steam ovens. At the luncheon that followed, the vice-chairman of the firm laid at the door of white bread "the sickly, stunted and ricketty children which infest the courts and alleys of all large towns where the poor congregate." Indeed, the chemicals used to produce the much-longed-for "nice white loaf," he concluded, produced in actuality nothing more than "whited sepulchers."

But neither the revelations of the brown-bread bakers 14 nor the reasoning of the Bread Reform League had any effect. "Why," one of its members asked in 1888, "in our craze for white bread, should we raise so many feeble, nervous, undersized children upon an impoverished flour, because it looks white and light . . . ? White bread alone will not sustain life. Dogs fed on white bread died at the end of forty days, whilst those fed on wheat bread alone throve and flourished." Quite deaf to these pleas, the English working-class poor knew what they wanted and, as soon as they could, bought their white, wheaten loaf— although by the time they could afford it, they were getting the proverbial stone for bread. The fine white loaf, and the tea with canned, skimmed milk that became the basis of the working-class English diet, was nutritionally so valueless that, as George Orwell once said, it did no more than cheat hunger three times a day. Ironically enough, by the nineteenth century, when wheat was produced in sufficient quantity to supply the demand of all those who wanted it, bread consumption had begun to fall everywhere.

In our search now for whole wheat bread and coarse 15 pumpernickel, we have turned one of the oldest ideals of Europe upside down. One historian of diet, Günther Wiegelmann, has pointed out that when new technology and changes in fashion make traditional ingredients scarce, they are suddenly revived as delicacies by the middle classes. Honey, for example, for centuries man's only sweetener, came back as a delicacy in the nineteenth century after sugar had long since driven it out. Buckwheat groats, bean soups, and now dark bread are restored out of the same impulses that brought back Morris dancing in England and societies for the preservation of local costume in Germany. Perhaps we should read some of the labels on the brown paper sacks. One of the biggest distributors of whole wheat flour notes (in small print, to be sure) that it has added malted barley. Someone there knows that customers will accept the newly desired brown loaf more readily if it is made tastier by the addition of malt. Despite our new aims, we are still buying the package rather than the contents, as we have for so long been in the habit of doing.

16   In America, unlike Europe, bread has been less than central to our diet, which makes the passionate search for the home-baked loaf all the more remarkable. It is one phenomenon that cannot be laid at the door of the wave of nostalgia that seems to be overtaking every other area of life. Requiring both time and real effort, baking appears as an active attempt to build up something original. Bread bakers are not looking for shortcuts and scorn the easy no-knead breads. The whole point of the exercise is to go back as far in the bread-making chain as possible. Some serious bakers even buy their wheat in the grain and grind it at home. Sourdough starters and homemade yeasts are commonplace. In an epoch that has been devoted to the development of convenience foods, this change must be seen as an attempt to regain control of what is eaten by manufacturing it at home.

17   In other areas as well, the primitive is reasserting itself. No one will be surprised to learn that seventy million Americans are overweight, and most of them at one time or another are on a diet. Some are impelled by vanity, but many are dieting for their lives, fearing fats, salt, sugar, carbohydrates, all those villains that bring on heart attacks and untimely death. Here mythology again offers sweet reassurances: in the Bulgarian peasants who live forever on yogurt, in the remote Mongol tribe that reaches a shapely and vigorous old age on a diet of cornmeal and cheese. In short, the ancient urban yearning for a largely imaginary pastoral, an idea already old when put into verse by Vergil, has reasserted itself in the headlong flight from refinement to soups, stews, and breads—the coarser, the better.

Discussing Content and Form

1. Gay analyzes the causes and effects of several of our beliefs about food:

a. What forces or changes in these beliefs have caused the recent desire for foods that are "colored brown" rather than for the white bread that was once popular?

b. How does Gay show that the new preoccupation with health foods is related to folk customs and superstition?

c. What social forces caused the popularity of the light wheat loaf in the first place? Why does Gay say that "Much of the history of Europe could be written using the fine wheaten loaf as a barometer" (par. 11)?

2. Point out recent news stories that confirm what Gay is saying about today's mass-produced food. You might cite stories about mislabeling, factory recall of food products, various kinds of diet fads, new (real or imagined) connections between foods and diseases. Which of the recent scares seem well-founded?

3. Gay says that in our passionate denunciation of white bread we hardly notice the eradication of several diseases and the availability of safe drinking water (par. 9). What are the implications of her assertions?

4. This essay combines historical tracing with the analysis of causes. Explain how the two methods of development are interrelated. Find sentences that combine historical tracing and causal analysis—for instance, "Like the Cadillac to the slum dweller today, it [white bread] came to stand for all kinds of things . . . ." (par. 11); or "Our latest thinking about food, based on fear, is proportionally retrograde . . . ." (par. 8).

Considering Special Techniques

1. Discuss the effectiveness of the narrative illustration that Gay uses in paragraphs 3 and 4. Why does she say that "The best stories . . . always leave an echo of uncertainty in the air"?

2. The description of undernourished British children (par. 13) concludes with a quote that they were "whited sepulchers." Look up the meaning of the phrase and explain the play on words the speaker makes in this twisted use of the image.

3. Even when writing is factual rather than personal, a writer leaves an individual stamp upon the work. Cite evidence from this essay to show that Gay is at the same time very scholarly and knowledgeable and very much aware of current trends.

4.   *Most references to persons or specific events are clear from the context of this essay. Discuss Gay's economical way of explaining enough about specific references to make them clear. For instance, see paragraph 15: "One historian of diet, Günther Wiegelmann, has . . . ."*

5.   *Words to learn and use:* ineradicable, irretrievably *(par. 2);* inextricably, potions, caldron *(par. 3);* prototype, primal *(par. 4);* propagated, pragmatic *(par. 5);* expounded, virility *(par. 6);* vulnerable, credulity, retrograde, bizarre *(par. 8);* stratagems, patina*(par. 9);* aphrodisiacs, augmented, hierarchy, decipherable *(par. 10);* denigration, fellahin, millet *(par. 11).*

Generating Ideas

1.   *Write a paper analyzing the causes for your choice of diet. What influences your eating habits? What are the discernible effects of the diet? Consider descriptive titles such as these:*
"Fears, Fussing, and Food—A Fine Fettle!"
"Considering Little But Taste—Some Grim Results"
"Packaged Foods and Poor Nutrition"
"Health Foods—Fact and Fancies"
"Why I Am a Vegetarian"
"Mother Made Me Eat It—Now I Like It" (or "Now I Won't")
"Learning to Like What Is Good for You"

2.   *Why do fads, such as certain diets, catch on so quickly and then just as quickly disappear? Analyze the causes and results of some fad among your group of friends.*

3.   *Write a paper accounting for the recent popularity of various books with an emphasis on folklore and simple living: the* Foxfire *series, the* Whole Earth Catalogue, *Euell Gibbons'* Stalking the Wild Asparagus, *or others that you know.*

4.   *Gay demonstrates that social factors cause us to want things not easily available—for instance, she finds that white bread was a universal symbol of success because it was for so long an unattainable luxury (pars. 10–12). Write a paper in which you analyze the causes of your (or other people's) attempts to acquire some status symbol.*

5.   *Analyze the causes, as you see them, for the recent rapid rise in "eating out." Whether you use a serious or a humorous approach, be careful to keep the tone consistent.*

George Orwell

George Orwell (1903–1950), whose real name was Eric Blair, is one of this century's best-known satirists and essayists. Born in India, educated at Eton, he served for a time with the Imperial Police in Burma and fought in the Spanish Civil War. All these experiences provided material for his writing. In *Animal Farm* (1945), a satirical fable, Orwell pointed out the shortcomings of a communistic state. In *Nineteen Eighty-Four* (1949), he envisioned the horrors of a future totalitarian society. Uncannily, many of his predictions have been fulfilled. The British writer V. S. Pritchett called him "the conscience of his generation." Orwell himself said that he "wanted to make political writing into an art," and his essay "Why I Write" analyzes some of the reasons for his becoming a writer.

Why I Write

From a very early age, perhaps the age of five or six, I knew that when I grew up I should be a writer. Between the ages of about seventeen and twenty-four I tried to abandon this idea, but I did so with the consciousness that I was outraging my true nature and that sooner or later I should have to settle down and write books.

I was the middle child of three, but there was a gap of five years on either side, and I barely saw my father before I was eight. For this and other reasons I was somewhat lonely, and I soon developed disagreeable mannerisms which made me unpopular throughout my schooldays. I had the lonely child's habit of making up stories and holding conversations with imaginary persons, and I think from the very start my literary ambitions were mixed up with the feeling of being isolated and undervalued. I knew that I had a facility with words and a power of facing unpleasant facts, and I felt that this created a sort of private world in which I could get my own back for my failure in everyday life. Nevertheless the volume of serious—*i.e.* seriously intended—writing which I produced all through my childhood and boyhood would not amount to half a dozen pages. I wrote my first poem at the age of four or five, my mother taking it down to dictation. I cannot remember anything about it except that it was about a tiger and the tiger had "chair-like teeth"—a good enough phrase, but I fancy the poem was a plagiarism of Blake's "Tiger, Tiger." At eleven, when the war of 1914–18 broke out, I wrote a patriotic poem which was printed in the local newspaper, as was another, two years later, on the death of Kitchener. From time to time, when I was a bit older, I wrote bad and usually unfinished "nature poems" in the Georgian style. I also, about twice, attempted a short story which was a ghastly failure. That was the total of the would-be serious work that I actually set down on paper during all those years.

3   However, throughout this time I did in a sense engage in literary activities. To begin with there was the made-to-order stuff which I produced quickly, easily and without much pleasure to myself. Apart from school work, I wrote *vers d'occasion,* semi-comic poems which I could turn out at what now seems to me astonishing speed—at fourteen I wrote a whole rhyming play, in imitation of Aristophanes, in about a week—and helped to edit school magazines, both printed and in manuscript. These magazines were the most pitiful burlesque stuff that you could image, and I took far less trouble with them than I now would with the cheapest journalism. But side by side with all this, for fifteen years or more, I was carrying out a literary exercise of a quite different kind: this was the making up of a continuous "story" about myself, a sort of diary existing only in the mind. I believe this is a common habit of children and adolescents. As a very small child I used to imagine that I was, say, Robin Hood, and picture myself as the hero of thrilling adventures, but quite soon my "story" ceased to be narcissistic in a crude way and became more and more a mere description of what I was doing and the things I saw. For minutes at a time this kind of thing would be running through my head: "He pushed the door open and entered the room. A yellow beam of sunlight, filtering through the muslin curtains, slanted on to the table, where a matchbox, half open, lay beside the inkpot. With his right hand in his pocket he moved across to the window. Down in the street a tortoise-shell cat was chasing a dead leaf," etc., etc. This habit continued till I was about twenty-five, right through my non-literary years. Although I had to search, and did search, for the right words, I seemed to be making this descriptive effort almost against my will, under a kind of compulsion from outside. The "story" must, I suppose,

have reflected the styles of the various writers I admired at different ages, but so far as I remember it always had the same meticulous descriptive quality.

When I was about sixteen I suddenly discovered the 4 joy of mere words, *i.e.* the sounds and associations of words. The lines from *Paradise Lost*—

> "So hee with difficulty and labour hard
> Moved on: with difficulty and labour hee,"

which do not now seem to me so very wonderful, sent shivers down my backbone; and the spelling "hee" for "he" was an added pleasure. As for the need to describe things, I knew all about it already. So it is clear what kind of books I wanted to write, in so far as I could be said to want to write books at that time. I wanted to write enormous naturalistic novels with unhappy endings, full of detailed descriptions and arresting similes, and also full of purple passages in which words were used partly for the sake of their sound. And in fact my first completed novel, *Burmese Days,* which I wrote when I was thirty but projected much earlier, is rather that kind of book.

I give all this background information because I do not 5 think one can assess a writer's motives without knowing something of his early development. His subject matter will be determined by the age he lives in—at least this is true in tumultuous, revolutionary ages like our own— but before he ever begins to write he will have acquired an emotional attitude from which he will never completely escape. It is his job, no doubt, to discipline his temperament and avoid getting stuck at some immature stage, or in some perverse mood: but if he escapes from his early influences altogether, he will have killed his impulse to write. Putting aside the need to earn a living, I think there are four great motives for writing, at any rate for writing prose. They exist in different degrees in every writer, and in any one writer the proportions will vary from time to time, according to the atmosphere in which he is living. They are:

(1) Sheer egoism. Desire to seem clever, to be talked 6 about, to be remembered after death, to get your own back on grown-ups who snubbed you in childhood, etc., etc. It is humbug to pretend that this is not a motive, and a strong one. Writers share this characteristic with scientists, art-

ists, politicians, lawyers, soldiers, successful business-men—in short, with the whole top crust of humanity. The great mass of human beings are not acutely selfish. After the age of about thirty they abandon individual ambi-tion—in many cases, indeed, they almost abandon the sense of being individuals at all—and live chiefly for oth-ers, or are simply smothered under drudgery. But there is also the minority of gifted, wilful people who are deter-mined to live their own lives to the end, and writers belong in this class. Serious writers, I should say, are on the whole more vain and self-centered than journalists, though less interested in money.

7   (2) Aesthetic enthusiasm. Perception of beauty in the external world, or, on the other hand, in words and their right arrangement. Pleasure in the impact of one sound on another, in the firmness of good prose or the rhythm of a good story. Desire to share an experience which one feels is valuable and ought not to be missed. The aesthetic motive is very feeble in a lot of writers, but even a pamphleteer or a writer of textbooks will have pet words and phrases which appeal to him for nonutilitarian rea-sons; or he may feel strongly about typography, width of margins, etc. Above the level of a railway guide, no book is quite free from aesthetic considerations.

8   (3) Historical impulse. Desire to see things as they are, to find out true facts and store them up for the use of posterity.

9   (4) Political purpose—using the word "political" in the widest possible sense. Desire to push the world in a certain direction, to alter other people's idea of the kind of society that they should strive after. Once again, no book is genu-inely free from political bias. The opinion that art should have nothing to do with politics is itself a political attitude.

10   It can be seen how these various impulses must war against one another, and how they must fluctuate from person to person and from time to time. By nature—taking your "nature" to be the state you have attained when you are first adult—I am a person in whom the first three mo-tives would outweigh the fourth. In a peaceful age I might have written ornate or merely descriptive books, and might have remained almost unaware of my political loy-alties. As it is I have been forced into becoming a sort of pamphleteer. First I spent five years in an unsuitable profession (the Indian Imperial Police, in Burma), and

then I underwent poverty and the sense of failure. This increased my natural hatred of authority and made me for the first time fully aware of the existence of the working classes, and the job in Burma had given me some understanding of the nature of imperialism: but these experiences were not enough to give me an accurate political orientation. Then came Hitler, the Spanish civil war, etc. By the end of 1935 I had still failed to reach a firm decision. I remember a little poem that I wrote at that date, expressing my dilemma:

"A happy vicar I might have been
Two hundred years ago,
To preach upon eternal doom
And watch my walnuts grow;

But born, alas, in an evil time,
I missed that pleasant haven,
For the hair has grown on my upper lip
And the clergy are all clean-shaven.

And later still the times were good,
We were so easy to please,
We rocked our troubled thoughts to sleep
On the bosoms of the trees.

All ignorant we dared to own
The joys we now dissemble;
The greenfinch on the apple bough
Could make my enemies tremble.

But girls' bellies and apricots,
Roach in a shaded stream,
Horses, ducks in flight at dawn,
All these are a dream.

It is forbidden to dream again;
We maim our joys or hide them;
Horses are made of chromium steel
And little fat men shall ride them.

I am the worm who never turned,
The eunuch without a harem;
Between the priest and the commissar
I walk like Eugene Aram;

And the commissar is telling my fortune
While the radio plays,
But the priest has promised an Austin Seven,
For Duggie always pays.

I dreamed I dwelt in marble halls,
And woke to find it true;
I wasn't born for an age like this;
Was Smith? Was Jones? Were you?"

The Spanish war and other events in 1936–7 turned the
scale and thereafter I knew where I stood. Every line of
serious work that I have written since 1936 has been written, directly or indirectly, *against* totalitarianism and *for*
democratic socialism, as I understand it. It seems to me
nonsense, in a period like our own, to think that one can
avoid writing of such subjects. Everyone writes of them
in one guise or another. It is simply a question of which
side one takes and what approach one follows. And the
more one is conscious of one's political bias, the more
chance one has of acting politically without sacrificing
one's aesthetic and intellectual integrity.

11   What I have most wanted to do throughout the past ten
years is to make political writing into an art. My starting
point is always a feeling of partisanship, a sense of injus-
tice. When I sit down to write a book, I do not say to myself,
"I am going to produce a work of art." I write it because
there is some lie that I want to expose, some fact to which
I want to draw attention, and my initial concern is to get
a hearing. But I could not do the work of writing a book,
or even a long magazine article, if it were not also an
aesthetic experience. Anyone who cares to examine my
work will see that even when it is downright propaganda
it contains much that a full-time politician would consider
irrelevant. I am not able, and I do not want, completely
to abandon the world-view that I acquired in childhood.
So long as I remain alive and well I shall continue to
feel strongly about prose style, to love the surface of the
earth, and to take a pleasure in solid objects and scraps
of useless information. It is no use trying to suppress that
side of myself. The job is to reconcile my ingrained likes
and dislikes with the essentially public, non-individual
activities that this age forces on all of us.

12   It is not easy. It raises problems of construction and

of language, and it raises in a new way the problem of truthfulness. Let me give just one example of the cruder kind of difficulty that arises. My book about the Spanish civil war, *Homage to Catalonia,* is, of course, a frankly political book, but in the main it is written with a certain detachment and regard for form. I did try very hard in it to tell the whole truth without violating my literary instincts. But among other things it contains a long chapter, full of newspaper quotations and the like, defending the Trotskyists who were accused of plotting with Franco. Clearly such a chapter, which after a year or two would lose its interest for any ordinary reader, must ruin the book. A critic whom I respect read me a lecture about it. "Why did you put in all that stuff?" he said. "You've turned what might have been a good book into journalism." What he said was true, but I could not have done otherwise. I happened to know, what very few people in England had been allowed to know, that innocent men were being falsely accused. If I had not been angry about that I should never have written the book.

In one form or another this problem comes up again. 13
The problem of language is subtler and would take too long to discuss. I will only say that of late years I have tried to write less picturesquely and more exactly. In any case I find that by the time you have perfected any style of writing, you have always outgrown it. *Animal Farm* was the first book in which I tried, with full consciousness of what I was doing, to fuse political purpose and artistic purpose into one whole. I have not written a novel for seven years, but I hope to write another fairly soon. It is bound to be a failure, every book is a failure, but I do know with some clarity what kind of book I want to write.

Looking back through the last page or two, I see that 14
I have made it appear as though my motives in writing were wholly public-spirited. I don't want to leave that as the final impression. All writers are vain, selfish and lazy, and at the very bottom of their motives there lies a mystery. Writing a book is a horrible, exhausting struggle, like a long bout of some painful illness. One would never undertake such a thing if one were not driven on by some demon whom one can neither resist nor understand. For all one knows that demon is simply the same instinct that makes a baby squall for attention. And yet it is also true that one can write nothing readable unless one constantly

struggles to efface one's own personality. Good prose is like a window pane. I cannot say with certainty which of my motives are the strongest, but I know which of them deserve to be followed. And looking back through my work, I see that it is invariably where I lacked a *political* purpose that I wrote lifeless books and was betrayed into purple passages, sentences without meaning, decorative adjectives and humbug generally.

Discussing Content and Form

1. What childhood influences led Orwell to become a writer? What do you think his early education and practice contributed? Why does he say this "background information" is important?

2. How much of the development of writing talent does Orwell say is caused by mere chance? Discuss Orwell's statements (par. 5) that both subject matter and the writer's attitude are determined by external forces.

3. Orwell says that there are four "great motives" that lead one to write. Why do you think he first puts aside "the need to earn a living"? Find examples of essays in this text that may have been written because of one or another of the motives Orwell suggests.

4. What caused Orwell to write for political purposes? From your knowledge of the historical events he mentions, explain how the age he lived in influenced his choice of subject matter.

5. What was happening to Orwell at the time when he wrote the verse in paragraph 10? Relate his experience to the "identity crisis" or search for styles that Alvin Toffler in "A Superabundance of Selves" says confronts the modern individual. In what way is Orwell's exposure of his verse an act of courage?

6. What does Orwell mean by aesthetic and intellectual integrity? Even though he says that he writes "because there is some lie . . . to expose, some fact to which [he wants] to draw attention" (par. 11), he is also vitally concerned with his writing style. Discuss his goal of reconciling political purpose and artistic purpose (par. 14). If you have read Animal Farm or others of his works, decide whether you think he attains that lofty ideal.

*7. In the final paragraph Orwell says, "One would never under-
take [to write a book] if one were not driven by some demon
whom one can neither resist nor understand." How does this
statement bear out what he says of his nature and the shaping
forces of his childhood?*

Considering Special Techniques

*1. Divide the essay into four distinct parts, four major sections
of an "outline."*
a. How does each section build toward the next?
*b. In what ways are the transitions skillfully provided by the
organization of the material itself?*
*c. What is the relationship between the beginning and the end?
(See question 7 above.)*

*2. Orwell several times expresses his interest in language, his
love of words for their own sake.*
*a. Find examples in his style to show that he is carefully
artistic in his choice of language. Consider particularly his
economy of expression.*
*b. He twice refers to "purple passages," defining these in
paragraph 4. Why does he object to them? Why were they
such a temptation for him as a writer?*

*3. Words to learn and use: vers d'occasion, burlesque, narcis-
sistic, meticulous (par. 3); tumultuous (par. 5); aesthetic,
pamphleteer, typography (par. 7); partisanship, ingrained (par.
11); picturesquely (par. 13).*

Generating Ideas

*1. Analyze the shaping influences in your childhood and envi-
ronment in order to explain some attitude or interest. If you
think these influences combine with "nature," explain that
combination as Orwell does. You might use his title by substitut-
ing a word of your own: "Why I . . ."*

*2. Consider some profession, area of work, or life-style and ex-
plain the motives that influence one to choose it. You do not,
of course, have to put "aside the need to earn a living."*

*3. Write a paper in which you use one of the following topics
related to language.*
*a. If you have developed an interest in language, analyze the
causes that seem to you to have brought it about.*
b. If you have ever felt that your vocabulary is limited, exam-

     ine the effects of this weakness and suggest reasons for over-coming it.

c. *Explain some ways that teachers might arouse an interest in words and to increase students' command of the language.*

4. *Write a paper analyzing the effects of political language on language in general. You will probably need to narrow the subject to the role of language in the career of a particular politician or in a single situation or campaign.*

9
Making Meanings Clear:
Definition

"There's glory for you!" says Humpty Dumpty to Alice in Lewis Carroll's *Through the Looking Glass,* and Alice says, "I don't know what you mean by 'glory.'" "Of course you don't—till I tell you. I meant 'there's a nice knock-down argument for you!'" "But 'glory' doesn't mean 'a nice knock-down argument,'" objects Alice.

Alice's and Humpty's disagreement over a definition results from a situation in which a word means one thing to one person and something else to the other. All of us ask for definitions, and we all have to give them. And many of the problems arise over the words most difficult to define—abstract ones like *glory, love, democracy,* and the like.

It is fairly easy to make concrete words clear, those whose meaning can be demonstrated by reference to actual objects and experiences. You ask the service-station attendant, "What do you mean, trouble with the generator?" He points to the mechanism, explains its function, and describes the trouble.

For most words, whether abstract or concrete, you check a dictionary. Friends tell you that they have been sailing in a sloop. A dictionary tells you a sloop is a "single-masted, fore-and-aft-rigged sailing boat with a short standing bowsprit or none at all." You may have to look up *bowsprit,* too. You will understand more clearly if you look at pictures of a sloop and compare it to other sailing vessels such as a ketch or a schooner, noting the differences in the masts and sails the three carry. And you will know that you, your friends, and others who use the term *sloop* will be talking about the same thing.

Synonyms often help to clarify meanings. If you look

up *lucrative,* you find that a dictionary gives only synonyms in explanation: "Producing wealth, profitable." Here there is only one meaning. Across the page you see *lukewarm,* with two: "1) mildly warm; tepid. 2) lacking in enthusiasm; indifferent." And if you were confronted with the word in a piece of writing, you would then determine the more appropriate meaning from the context.

Misunderstandings may arise unless the context is established, and this is particularly true when words, unlike those we have been considering, do not have clear and precise referents, but are abstract, like *glory,* or *love,* or *democracy.* Such words are used to explain unfamiliar objects, to generalize about unshared experiences, to present new concepts. An abstract word has a general area of meaning within which different definitions are possible. For instance, a teacher might say, "She is a creative student," meaning that she brings insight and imagination to her work. But someone might limit *creative* to the more restricted and literal notion of creative *doing.* He would then need some illustrations to enlarge the word's circle of meaning to include creative *thinking.*

In a formal, or logical, definition, the writer draws a circle of meaning, and invites the reader to share in understanding the extent and limits of the term defined. Such a definition first places the term in a class, sometimes called the *genus,* and then gives the characteristics, or *differentia,* which distinguish it from other items in the same class:

term	*genus*	*differentia*
sloop	sailing boat	single-masted
		fore-and-aft-rigged
		short standing bowsprit
		or no bowsprit

Logical definition is particularly well-suited for factual or scientific terms. In writing exposition it is often helpful to see the parts of the logical definition and relate them to your wider purpose. Suppose, for instance, you are writing a paper on the history of several kinds of sailing vessels. Your introductory paragraphs might incorporate logical definitions of *sloop, ketch,* and *schooner* before you begin to trace their development. (You will find an expanded logical definition in the selection "Ethology" in this chapter.)

Notice how logical definition is used in this opening paragraph of an essay that examines the nature of a university:

> If I were asked to describe as briefly and popularly as I could, what a University was, I should draw my answer from its ancient designation of a *Studium Generale,* or "School of Universal Learning." This description implies the assemblage of strangers from all parts in one spot— *from all parts;* else, how will you find professors and students for every department of knowledge? and *in one spot;* else, how can there be any school at all? Accordingly, in its simple and rudimental form, it is a school of knowledge of every kind, consisting of teachers and learners from every quarter. Many things are requisite to complete and satisfy the idea embodied in this description; but such as this a University seems to be in its essence, a place for the communication and circulation of thought, by means of personal intercourse, through a wide extent of country.— John Henry Newman, "What Is a University?"

Newman places the university in a wider class: "School of Universal Learning." He then examines what this designation means in terms of particular characteristics, picking up the idea of universality and the central location implied by the word *school.* The rest of the essay extends the definition by explaining, among other things, how a university functions.

Another kind of definition is the one based on a word's etymology. An etymological definition traces the derivation of a word back to its original meaning in order to shed light on its present meaning. *Democracy,* for example, is better understood when one knows that it is derived from *demos,* the Greek word for "common people." But it should be remembered that the meanings of many other words have changed radically over a period of time. *Romantic,* for instance, is now used in ways totally unrelated to its original meaning. (You will find a useful etymological definition in "Ethology," p. 245.)

Writing definition, obviously, involves other methods of development. Definitions can be supported by giving illustrations, by clarifying the unfamiliar through the familiar. Comparison may be used to explain how one term resembles or differs from another. For instance, to explain the meaning of the word *antique* one might first establish criteria such as age and authenticity, then cite examples fulfilling them, and then contrast genuine antiques with reproductions or with items that are merely old. Another method is to trace origins or causes to explain the nature of something like *naturalism* in literature or the *dada* movement in art. How did the trend start? What influenced it? What effect did it have on later writers and artists?

Just as definition can involve other methods of development, definition itself is essential to almost every other kind of exposition. In writing essay answers, in giving a report or speech, in writing a research paper, you are expected to define your terms. Definition may be the whole or a part; it may be the central purpose or a step toward another goal; it may be as short as a single sentence or as long as a series of paragraphs of examples, comparisons, causes; it may be instructional and informative, personal and philosophical. Above all, it must be clear.

In the following informal definition, the writer uses several methods of development to suggest a core meaning from which a logical definition may be derived:

> The metaphor is something more than an amusing literary device; it is a continual play of wit, an illuminating *double entendre,* a nimble magic, in which writer and reader conspire to escape reality. Perhaps "escape" is the wrong word—the play of metaphor acts to enrich reality, even to heighten it. The average reader enjoys its intensification so much that he cannot help employing it. "My heart leaps," he says, knowing quite well that it contracts and expands quietly within the pericardium. Or, he declares still more mendaciously, but earnestly, "my heart stood still." Even while he scorns poetry, the ordinary man helps himself to its properties and symbols; his daily life is unthinkable without metaphor. Having slept "like a log," he gets up in the morning "fresh as a daisy" or "fit as a fiddle"; he "wolfs down" breakfast, "hungry as a bear," with his wife, who has a "tongue like vinegar," but "a heart of gold." He gets into his car, which "eats up the miles," steps on the gas, and, as it "purrs" along through the "hum" of traffic, he reaches his office where he is "as busy as a one-armed paper hanger with hives." Life, for the average man, is not "a bed of roses," his competitor is "sly as a fox" and his own clerks are "slow as molasses in January." But

From "The Metaphor" by Louis Untermeyer, published in *Good Housekeeping*. Reprinted by permission of Louis Untermeyer.

"the day's grind" is finally done, and though it is "raining cats and dogs," he arrives home "happy as a lark."—Louis Untermeyer, "The Metaphor"

Writing definition, of course, involves a knowledge of the reader it is intended for. Untermeyer clarifies the meaning of *metaphor* by the use of examples taken from everyday speech and life. But if he were explaining the term for a scholarly audience, he would probably put his explanation in more formal language and would describe how metaphor operates in literature, as the writer of this definition does:

> *Metaphor:* An implied analogy which imaginatively identifies one object with another and ascribes to the first one or more of the qualities of the second or invests the first with emotional or imaginative qualities associated with the second. It is one of the tropes; that is, one of the principal devices by which poetic "turns" on the meaning of words are achieved. I. A. Richards' distinction between the *tenor* and the *vehicle* of a metaphor has been widely accepted and is very useful. The *tenor* is the idea being expressed or the subject of the comparison; the *vehicle* is the image by which this idea is conveyed or the subject communicated.—C. Hugh Holman, *A Handbook to Literature*

It is not surprising that the examples that follow this definition come from literary works rather than from everyday life. Complex or simple, the definition must suit the purpose and audience for which it is written. The following selections employ various methods of defining terms and ideas that vary in complexity, but all of the writers present their subjects clearly and logically.

Sally Carrighar

Sally Carrighar was born in Cleveland, Ohio, and attended Vassar College. After serving as a scriptwriter for films and radio, she became a free-lance writer in 1937. Her first books, *One Day on Beetle Rock* (1944) and *One Day at Teton Marsh* (1947), reflect her love of the American West. In the 1950s she spent some time in Alaska, and from that experience wrote *Icebound Summer* (1952) and *Wild Voice of the North* (1959). Her autobiography, *Home to the Wilderness* (1973), is a poignant account of her unhappy childhood and her search for a satisfying vocation. The clear and careful definition in "Ethology" (editor's title) is taken from *Wild Heritage* (1965), perhaps her best-known book. Its thesis is that we learn about ourselves from observing the behavior of animals in their natural surroundings.

Ethology

1

Introduction of the concept of ethology (par. 1)

By . . . the 1920's and 1930's, there was a new generation of biologists and many were ready to listen. While some of them have preferred to do their work in laboratories, others have gone out of doors, to make a real science of animal observation. They call themselves, these co-operating indoor and outdoor men, ethologists, and it is largely due to their efforts that we now have a reliable body of knowledge about our animal forebears.

2

Analysis of ethology according to its *genus* (biological science) and its *differentia* (par. 2)

For laymen ethology is probably the most interesting of the biological sciences for the very reason that it concerns animals in their normal activities and therefore, if we wish, we can assess the possible dangers and advantages in our own behavioral roots. Ethology also is interesting methodologically because it combines in new ways very scrupulous field observations with experimentation in laboratories.

3

Enumeration of problems and solutions that characterize ethology (pars. 3–4)

The field workers have had some handicaps in winning respect for themselves. For a long time they were considered as little better than amateur animal-watchers—certainly not scientists, since their facts were not gained by experimental procedures: they could not conform to the hard-and-fast rule that a problem set up and solved by one scientist must be tested by other scientists, under identical conditions and reaching identical results. Of course many situations in the lives of animals simply cannot be rehearsed and controlled in this way. The fall flocking of wild free birds can't be, or the homing of animals over long distances, or even details of spontaneous family relationships. Since these never can be reproduced in a laboratory, are they then not worth knowing about?

The ethologists who choose field work have got themselves out of this impasse by greatly refining the techniques of observing. At the start of a project all the animals to be studied are live-trapped, marked individually, and released. Motion pictures, often in color, provide permanent records of their subsequent activities. Recording of the animals' voices by electrical sound equipment is considered essential, and the most meticulous notes are kept of all that occurs. With this material other biologists, far from the scene, later can verify the reports. Moreover, two field observers often go out together, checking each other's observations right there in the field.

Ethology, the word, is derived from the Greek *ethos,* meaning the characteristic traits or features which distinguish a group—any particular group of people or, in biology, a group of animals such as a species. Ethologists have the intention, as William H. Thorpe explains, of studying "the whole sequence of acts which constitute an animal's behavior." In abridged dictionaries ethology is sometimes defined simply as "the objective study of animal behavior," and ethologists do emphasize their wish to eliminate myths.

5
Etymology and dictionary definitions of the word *ethology* (par. 5)

Perhaps the most original aspect of ethology is the way that field observation is combined with experimentation in laboratories. Although the flocking of birds cannot be studied

6
Presentation of its most distinguishing feature (par. 6)

indoors, many other significant actions of animals that are seen only infrequently in the field, or seen only as hints, may be followed up later with indoor tests. Likewise investigations made first in laboratories can be checked by observations of animals ranging free in their normal environments.

7

Examples of etho-
logical field work
(pars. 7–8)

Suppose that a field man, watching marked individuals, notes that an infant animal, *a,* is nursed by a female, *B,* known not to be its mother. Later he sees other instances of such maternal generosity. Is this willingness on the female's part a case of inherited behavior, or has it been picked up as one of the social customs of the species; that is, is it *learned?* Does it mean that all the adult females of this species feel some responsibility for the young, and if so, is such a tendency innate, or could behavior like that be acquired?

8

Elephant mothers are among those which give milk to offspring not their own. A group of elephants cannot very well be confined in a laboratory; but if the field worker is concerned with a species of smaller animals, he can bring newborn young into captivity, raise them and mate them there, and then note the behavior of the new mothers. Since they never have seen other females nursing young, their actions will be innate, inherited. And if it does turn out that one of these females will nurse any young that come to her, it will further have to be determined whether she recognizes her own. That question too can be answered in the laboratory; it is an easy problem for an experimental psychologist. By such techniques it has been found, for example, that in the species of small brown bats called *Myotis myotis* the mothers do know their own young and likewise will nurse any hungry infant regardless of blood relationship. This maternal behavior could have been observed in a colony of animals kept for generations indoors, but since the habitat there is artificial, the only way to know whether the behav-

ior is normal to the species was to observe it
first in animals living free in their natural
world. Only by such a combination of laboratory and field work can instincts and acquired
characteristics be distinguished. The value of
knowledge like that is so great that the wonder
is why such cooperation had not developed
much earlier.

Discussing Content and Form

*1. Carrighar uses conventional methods of definition to ex-
plain the work of the ethologist. Discuss the value of her method
in making the subject clear. How does each step in the definition contribute to an easy understanding of this special area
of biological science?*

*2. Show how Carrighar successfully answers the question she
asks in paragraph 3: "Since these [facts about animal life] never
can be reproduced in a laboratory, are they then not worth
knowing about?"*

*3. The writer says that the work of the ethologist is interesting
to laymen. What in the selection serves to make the subject
interesting to the reader?*

*4. Find phrases and statements that show how the observations
of ethologists have special implications for human life.*

*5. Why is it important that a newly developed scientific
field affirm both its usefulness and its objectivity as a science?
Where does Carrighar establish the fact that ethology has accomplished this?*

Considering Special Techniques

*1. Why do you think Carrighar places the etymological defini-
tion where she does? What is gained by giving the derivation
as well as referring to the more limited statement from the
abridged dictionary?*

*2. The principal problem in writing scientific articles for the
general public is achieving clarity. What features of Carrighar's
style make this selection both clear and easy to read?*
*a. Note the details that clarify the methods used by the etholo-
gist (par. 4). What would be lost if the writer had said merely,
"the ethologists developed better scientific techniques"?*

b. *What point is made clear through the details concerning flocking birds (pars. 3 and 6) and elephant mothers (par. 8)?*

c. *Why do you think the writer does not use more scientific terminology? Point out places where careful use of restatement helps make an idea clearer: for instance, "that is, is it learned?" (par. 7).*

3. *Carrighar several times poses questions that a reader might ask and that serve as links or introductions in her chain of ideas. The question at the end of paragraph 3, for instance, leads logically to the next paragraph. Find other such linking questions.*

4. *Words to learn and use:* scrupulous *(par. 2);* impasse, meticulous *(par. 4);* innate *(par. 7).*

Generating Ideas

1. *Choose one of the following branches of science or technology as the subject for an explanatory paper that requires definition as part of its development:*

seismology	*thermodynamics*	*meteorology*
genetics	*oceanography*	*limnology*
paleontology	*(human) oncology*	*aerospace studies*
radiology	*anesthesiology*	
cartography	*geophysics*	

2. *Many words from the sciences and technology have interesting derivations, some of them from Greek and Latin. Write an extended definition of one of these words; include one or several examples to show how the word is used. Here are some suggestions:*

cellular	*laser*	*chronometer*
radioisotopes	*microwave*	*aerolite*
neurosis	*algorithms*	*computer language*
psychochemistry	*biofeedback*	*systemic*
phoneme	*astronaut (cosmonaut)*	*hydrofoil*

3. *Do some reading and write a report about the work of a particular scientist or group of scientists who study animal behavior. For instance, some interesting research has been done by ethologists who band butterflies to study their patterns of migration.*

4. *Write a paper about some human trait such as intelligence over which exists the "inherited" versus "learned" controversy. You may need to look up some factual material to support your conclusions.*

Robert Pirsig

Robert Pirsig (b. 1928), a former college teacher and technical writer, says that he started "about 7000" writing projects in the four years he took to produce *Zen and the Art of Motorcycle Maintenance*. Published in 1974, it became an extraordinarily popular success. Pirsig's account of a motorcycle journey his narrator takes with his son combines elements of fiction and autobiography with philosophical musings. Each day the narrator presents a "Chautauqua," a lecture in which he not only gives instructions in motorcycle maintenance but also teaches values and attitudes. "Gumption" (editor's title), one of the Chautauquas, defines a quality needed for accomplishing important tasks, from maintaining a motorcycle to writing a book.

Gumption

I like the word "gumption" because it's so homely and so forlorn and so out of style it looks as if it needs a friend and isn't likely to reject anyone who comes along. It's an old Scottish word, once used a lot by pioneers, but which, like "kin," seems to have all but dropped out of use. I like it also because it describes exactly what happens to someone who connects with Quality. He gets filled with gumption.

The Greeks called it *enthousiasmos,* the root of "enthusiasm," which means literally "filled with *theos,"* or God, or Quality. See how that fits?

A person filled with gumption doesn't sit around dissipating and stewing about things. He's at the front of the train of his own awareness, watching to see what's up the track and meeting it when it comes. That's gumption. . . .

The gumption-filling process occurs when one is quiet long enough to see and hear and feel the real universe, not just one's own stale opinions about it. But it's nothing exotic. That's why I like the word.

You see it often in people who return from long, quiet fishing trips. Often they're a little defensive about having put so much time to "no account" because there's no intellectual justification for what they've been doing. But the returned fisherman usually has a peculiar abundance of gumption, usually for the very same things he was sick to death of a few weeks before. He hasn't been wasting time. It's only our limited cultural viewpoint that makes it seem so.

6   If you're going to repair a motorcycle, an adequate supply of gumption is the first and most important tool. If you haven't got that you might as well gather up all the other tools and put them away, because they won't do you any good.

7   Gumption is the psychic gasoline that keeps the whole thing going. If you haven't got it there's no way the motorcycle can possibly be fixed. But if you *have* got it and know how to keep it there's absolutely no way in this whole world that motorcycle can *keep* from getting fixed. It's bound to happen. Therefore the thing that must be monitored at all times and preserved before anything else is the gumption.

8   This paramount importance of gumption solves a problem of format of this Chautauqua. The problem has been how to get off the generalities. If the Chautauqua gets into the actual details of fixing one individual machine the chances are overwhelming that it won't be your make and model and the information will be not only useless but dangerous, since information that fixes one model can sometimes wreck another. For detailed information of an objective sort, a separate shop manual for the specific make and model of machine must be used. In addition, a general shop manual such as *Audel's Automotive Guide* fills in the gaps.

9   But there's another kind of detail that no shop manual goes into but that is common to all machines and can be given here. This is the detail of the Quality relationship, the gumption relationship, between the machine and the mechanic, which is just as intricate as the machine itself. Throughout the process of fixing the machine things always come up, low-quality things, from a dusted knuckle to an accidentally ruined "irreplaceable" assembly. These drain off gumption, destroy enthusiasm and leave you so discouraged you want to forget the whole business. I call these things "gumption traps."

10   There are hundreds of different kinds of gumption traps, maybe thousands, maybe millions. I have no way of knowing how many I don't know. I know it *seems* as though I've stumbled into every kind of gumption trap imaginable. What keeps me from thinking I've hit them all is

that with every job I discover more. Motorcycle maintenance gets frustrating. Angering. Infuriating. That's what
makes it interesting . . . .

What I have in mind now is a catalog of "Gumption   11
Traps I Have Known." I want to start a whole new academic field, gumptionology, in which these traps are
sorted, classified, structured into hierarchies and interrelated for the edification of future generations and the ben-
efit of all mankind.

Gumptionology 101—An examination of affective, cog-   12
nitive and psychomotor blocks in the perception of Qual-
ity relationships—3 cr, VII, MWF. I'd like to see that in
a college catalog somewhere.

In traditional maintenance gumption is considered   13
something you're born with or have acquired as a result
of good upbringing. It's a fixed commodity. From the lack
of information about how one acquires this gumption one
might assume that a person without any gumption is a
hopeless case.

In nondualistic maintenance gumption isn't a fixed   14
commodity. It's variable, a reservoir of good spirits that
can be added to or subtracted from. Since it's a result of
the perception of Quality, a gumption trap, consequently,
can be defined as anything that causes one to lose sight
of Quality, and thus lose one's enthusiasm for what one
is doing. As one might guess from a definition as broad
as this, the field is enormous and only a beginning sketch
can be attempted here.

As far as I can see there are two main types of gumption   15
traps. The first type is those in which you're thrown off
the Quality track by conditions that arise from external
circumstances, and I call these "setbacks." The second
type is traps in which you're thrown off the Quality track
by conditions that are primarily within yourself. These
I don't have any generic name for—"hang-ups," I
suppose . . . .

Discussing Content and Form

1. Pirsig explains the word gumption *by describing the actions
of people who possess the attribute and by relating it to a synonym,* enthusiasm. *List some other possible synonyms. What*

do you think Pirsig means when he says that "someone who connects with Quality" is filled with gumption (par. 1)?

2. Where does Pirsig describe what gumption is *not*? Why is the negative definition effective here?

3. What examples of gumption does the selection give? Why is it "the first and most important tool" in the maintenance job? Explain how this statement might relate to all fields of work.

4. In paragraph 8, why does the narrator find it a problem "to get off generalities"? Explain how gumption helps him solve this problem.

5. What are "gumption traps"? Why are they particularly likely to occur in any sort of maintenance work?

6. In the proposal for "Gumptionology 101," Pirsig classifies the traps as "affective, cognitive, and psychomotor blocks." After checking the meanings of these words, explain how deterrents to good work can be of these three kinds.

7. Why does the "traditionalist" believe gumption is "a fixed commodity" (par. 13)? What then is the "nondualistic" view (par. 14)? To which attitude do you subscribe—that gumption is fixed or that it is attainable?

8. How do you think Pirsig would answer someone who says, "I can't do it because I wasn't born smart or brought up right"?

Considering Special Techniques

1. The tone of this selection is at once informal and serious, personal and philosophical. Find words and phrases that contribute to this mixed tone. Paragraph 5, for example, contains the informal "no account" and "sick to death," along with more formal phrases such as "intellectual justification" and "limited cultural viewpoint." Which of the two types seem to dominate the selection?

2. A definition often involves a word's etymology, but Pirsig uses this technique differently by tracing the derivation of a synonym rather than that of the word being defined. Why do you think he gives the derivation of enthusiasm, *but not of* gumption (par. 2)? (Check the derivation of gumption.)

3. Discuss how the following metaphors help clarify Pirsig's definition:
a. "He's at the front of the train of his own awareness,

watching to see what's up the track and meeting it when
it comes." *(par. 3)*
b.   ". . . gumption is the first and most important tool." *(par.
6)*
c.   "Gumption is the psychic gasoline that keeps the whole
thing going." *(par. 7)*
d.   "It's variable, a reservoir of good spirits that can be added
to or subtracted from." *(par. 14)*

4.   *What is the purpose of capitalizing the word* Quality?

5.   *Connotations—the overtones of meaning, rather than the
literal meaning or denotation—surrounding a word are very
important in conveying emotions or arousing responses from
readers. What connotations do you think* gumption *has for most
people? In associating* gumption *with* kin *(par. 1), how does
Pirsig suggest the connotations of both words?*

6.   *In the following phrases, analyze the connotations of the
italicized words; then substitute some synonyms for them and
comment on any changes in meaning that result:*
a.   "it's nothing exotic" *(par. 4). What is the effect of substitut-
ing* flashy *or* unusual?
b.   "paramount *importance" (par. 8). Try* first *or* chief *instead.*
c.   "I've stumbled *into every kind of gumption trap" (par. 10).
Substitute* fallen *or* experienced.
Do the same thing with other examples in the selection.

7.   *Read paragraph 10 aloud. How do the sentence structure
and arrangement of sentences give the effect that the writer
is talking or thinking aloud?*

Generating Ideas

1.   *Use Pirsig's catalogue description for a new college course
in* Gumptionology 101 *as a model for a projected course that
you would like to see taught. Create your own course description
and then explain what you would put into the syllabus and
the method you would use to teach the course.*

2.   *Do you believe that perseverance is inborn or determined
by early training and thus cannot be acquired in later life?
Or do you believe that the individual can develop a personal
reservoir of strength that might be called gumption? Write a
paper that discusses these two views, using specifics from your
experiences or from those of other people to support your stand.*

3.   *Choose a desirable or undesirable character trait and write
a definition of it. Here are some suggestions:*

common sense	nobility	poise
persistence	integrity	egoism
gregariousness	courage	self-assurance
aspiration	generosity	abrasiveness
sense of humor	imagination	shyness
taste (bad or good)	modesty (immodesty)	good breeding
ambition	self-control	humility

4. *Define* Quality *and explain how you think it is possible to "connect" with it. You might consider whether it too may be a word that is "out of style [and] looks as if it needs a friend" (par. 1).*

5. *Slang phrases or labels often require definition. Choose some term currently used to describe an action or person and explain it to someone who is unfamiliar with it. Here are a few examples:*
a. *"He's kooky—by that I mean . . . ."*
b. *"When I say something is weird, I just mean . . . ."*
c. *"That's far-out—really far-out . . . ."*
d. *"When someone is off the wall, he's . . . ."*
Occasionally a word takes on so many meanings, covers so much, that it becomes almost meaningless, for example, fantastic *and* terrific. *Write a paper about such words; you may define them, classify them, or trace their popularity and decline.*

Laurie Lee

Laurie Lee (b. 1914) is a poet and essayist who lives in London. During World War II, he was a documentary film maker and publications editor for the British Ministry of Information. For six years following the war, he served as a film scriptwriter. In addition to several collections of poems, he has written two autobiographical accounts, *Cider with Rosie* (1959) and *As I Walked Out One Midsummer Morning* (1969), and a volume of personal reflections, *I Can't Stay Long* (1975). All of these have a congenial tone and lively style that are evident in "Charm," an essay taken from the latter book.

Charm

Charm is the ultimate weapon, the supreme seduction, against which there are few defences. If you've got it, you need almost nothing else, neither money, looks, nor pedigree. It's a gift, only given to give away, and the more used the more there is. It is also a climate of behaviour set for perpetual summer and thermostatically controlled by taste and tact.

True charm is an aura, an invisible musk in the air; if you see it working, the spell is broken. At its worst, it is the charm of the charity duchess, like being struck in the face with a bunch of tulips; at its best, it is a smooth and painless injection which raises the blood to a genial fever. Most powerful of all, it is obsessive, direct, person-to-person, forsaking all others. Never attempt to ask for whom the charm-bells ring; if they toll for anyone, they must toll for you.

As to the ingredients of charm, there is no fixed formula; they vary intuitively between man and woman. A whole range of mysteries goes into the cauldron, but the magic remains the same. In some cases, perhaps, the hand of the charmer is lighter, more discreet, less overwhelming, but the experience it offers must be absolute—one cannot be "almost" or "partly" charmed.

Charm in a woman is probably more exacting than in a man, requiring a wider array of subtleties. It is a light in the face, a receptive stance, an air of exclusive welcome, an almost impossibly sustained note of satisfaction in one's company, and regret without fuss at parting. A

woman with charm finds no man dull, doesn't have to
pretend to ignore his dullness; indeed, in her presence
he becomes not just a different person but the person he
most wants to be. Such a woman gives life to his deep-
held fantasies and suddenly makes them possible, not so
much by flattering him as adding the necessary conviction
to his long suspicion that he is king.

5   Of those women who have most successfully charmed
me in the past, I remember chiefly their eyes and voices.
That swimming way of looking, as though they were
crushing wine, their tone of voice, and their silences. The
magic of that look showed no distraction, nor any wish
to be with anyone else. Their voices were furred with comfort, like plumped-up cushions, intimate and enveloping.
Then the listening eyes, supreme charm in a woman, be-
traying no concern with any other world than this, warmly
wrapping one round with total attention and turning one's
lightest words to gold. Looking back, I don't pretend that
I was in any way responsible; theirs was a charm to charm
all men, and must have continued to exist, like the flower
in the desert, when there was nobody there to see it.

6   A woman's charm needn't always cater to such extremes
of indulgence—though no man will complain if it does.
At the least, she spreads round her that particular glow
of well-being for which any man will want to seek her
out, and by making full use of her nature, celebrates the
fact of his maleness and so gives him an extra shot of
life. Her charm lies also in the air of timeless maternalism, that calm and pacifying presence, which can dispel
a man's moments of frustration and anger and salvage
his failures of will.

7   Charm in a man, I supppose, is his ability to capture
the complicity of a woman by a single-minded acknowledgment of her uniqueness. Here again it is a question
of being totally absorbed, of forgetting that anyone else
exists—but *really* forgetting, for nothing more fatally betrays than the suggestion of a wandering eye. Silent devotion is fine, but seldom enough; it is what a man says
that counts, the bold declarations, the flights of fancy, the
uncovering of secret virtues. Praise can be a jewel, but
the gift must be personal, the only one of its kind in the
world; while flattery itself will never be thought excessive
so long as there's no suspicion that it's been said before.

8   A man's charm strikes deepest when a woman's imagi-

nation is engaged, with herself as the starting point; when she is made a part of some divine extravaganza, or mystic debauch, in which she feels herself both the inspirer and ravished victim. A man is charmed through his eyes, a woman by what she hears, so no man need be too anxious about his age. As wizened Voltaire once said: "Give me a few minutes to talk away my face and I can seduce the Queen of France."

No man, even so, will wish to talk a woman to death; there is also room for the confessional priest, a role of unstinted patience and dedication to the cause, together with a modest suspension of judgment. "You may have sinned, but you couldn't help it, you were made for love. . . . You have been wronged, you have suffered too much. . . ." If man has this quality, it is as much a solace to a woman as his power to dilate her with praise and passion. 9

But charm, after all, isn't exclusively sexual, it comes in a variety of cooler flavours. Most children have it— till they are told they have it—and so do old people with nothing to lose; animals, too, of course, and a few outdoor insects, and certain sea-creatures if they can claim to be mammals—seals, whales, and dolphins, but not egg-laying fish (you never saw a fish in a circus). With children and smaller animals it is often in the shape of the head and in the chaste unaccusing stare; with young girls and ponies, a certain stumbling awkwardness, a leggy inability to control their bodies. The sullen narcissism of adolescents, product of over-anxiety, can also offer a ponderous kind of charm. But all these are passive, and appeal to the emotions simply by capturing one's protective instinct. 10

Real charm is dynamic, an enveloping spell which mysteriously enslaves the senses. It is an inner light, fed on reservoirs of benevolence which well up like a thermal spring. It is unconscious, often nothing but the wish to please, and cannot be turned on and off at will. Which would seem to cancel the claims of some of the notorious charmers of the past—Casanova, Lawrence of Arabia, Rubirosa—whose talent, we suspect, wasn't charm at all so much as a compulsive need to seduce. Others, more recent, had larger successes through being less specific in their targets—Nehru, for instance, and Yehudi Menuhin, Churchill, and the early Beatles. As for the women—Cleopatra, Mata Hari, Madame du Barry—each one endowed with superb physical equipment; were they charmers, 11 too?—in a sense they must have been, though they laid much calculated waste behind them.

12   You recognize charm by the feeling you get in its presence. You know who has it. But can you get it, too? Properly, you can't, because it's a quickness of spirit, an originality of touch you have to be born with. Or it's something that grows naturally out of another quality, like the simple desire to make people happy. Certainly, charm is not a question of learning palpable tricks, like wrinkling your nose, or having a laugh in your voice, or gaily tossing your hair out of your dancing eyes and twisting your mouth into succulent love-knots. Such signs, to the nervous, are ominous warnings which may well send him streaking for cover. On the other hand, there is an antenna, a built-in awareness of others, which most people have, and which care can nourish.

13   But in a study of charm, what else does one look for? Apart from the ability to listen—rarest of all human virtues and most difficult to sustain without vagueness— apart from warmth, sensitivity, and the power to please, what else is there visible? A generosity, I suppose, which makes no demands, a transaction which strikes no bargains, which doesn't hold itself back till you've filled up a test-card making it clear that you're worth the trouble. Charm can't withhold, but spends itself willingly on young and old alike, on the poor, the ugly, the dim, the boring, on the last fat man in the corner. It reveals itself also in a sense of ease, in casual but perfect manners, and often in a physical grace which springs less from an accident of youth than from a confident serenity of mind. Any person with this is more than just a popular fellow, he is also a social healer.

14   Charm, in the abstract, has something of the quality of music: radiance, balance, and harmony. One encounters it unexpectedly in odd corners of life with a shock of brief, inexplicable ravishment: in a massed flight of birds, a string of running horses, an arrangement of clouds on the sea; wooded islands, Tanagra figures, old balconies in Spain, the line of a sports car holding a corner, in the writings of Proust and Jane Austen, the paintings of Renoir and Fragonard, the poetry of Herrick, the sound of lute and guitar. . . . Thickets of leaves can have it, bare arms interlocking, suds of rain racing under a bridge, and

such simplicities as waking after a sleep of nightmares to see sunlight bouncing off the ceiling. The effect of these, like many others, is to restore one's place in the world; to reassure, as it were, one's relationship with things, and to bring order to the wilderness.

But charm, in the end, is flesh and blood, a most potent act of behaviour, the laying down of a carpet by one person for another to give his existence a moment of honour. Much is deployed in the weaponry of human dealings: stealth, aggression, blackmail, lust, the urge to possess, devour, and destroy. Charm is the rarest, least used, and most invincible of powers, which can capture with a single glance. It is close to love in that it moves without force, bearing gifts like the growth of daylight. It snares completely, but is never punitive, it disarms by being itself disarmed, strikes without wounds, wins wars without casualties—though not, of course, without victims. He who would fall in the battle, let him fall to charm, and he will never be humbled, or know the taste of defeat. 15

In the armoury of man, charm is the enchanted dart, light and subtle as a hummingbird. But it is deceptive in one thing—like a sense of humour, if you think you've got it, you probably haven't. 16

Discussing Content and Form

1. Does Lee say that charm is one thing or many things? Explain why a definition of such a quality as charm is of necessity very complex.

2. Art and literary critics disagree over whether a quality such as "meaning" resides in the work of art or exists only in the viewer's or reader's response. Does Lee think charm is entirely in the charmer? Explain. Find statements that indicate the importance of the respondent, the one who is being charmed.

3. This essay has a clear plan; make a gloss or outline of the essay by paragraphs and then group together those paragraphs which constitute each major section.

4. Why does Lee say that "one cannot be 'almost' or 'partly' charmed"?

5. Discuss the differences Lee sees between charm in a woman and in a man. Why do you think he remembers "eyes and voices" in the women who have charmed him? What are "listening eyes" (par. 5)?

6.   What role does Lee say physical features play in female and male charm? How much of charm is sexual? Find phrases to support your answers. Discuss the statement, "A man is charmed through his eyes, a woman by what she hears, so no man need be too anxious about his age" (par. 8).

7.   Lee mentions other kinds of charm in paragraph 10. What is the significance of this addition?

8.   What is Lee's answer to the crucial question of whether charm can be acquired (par. 12)?

9.   What is gained by discussing "charm in the abstract" (par. 14)? Why, after that section, does Lee say, "But charm, in the end, is flesh and blood" (par. 15)?

Considering Special Techniques

1.   Lee uses many images in developing his definition.
a.   Note the unifying imagery of charm as a "weapon." Compare the images in the first sentence of the essay with those in the last two paragraphs. How many words in the concluding section carry the "weapon" image?
b.   Discuss the following images and find others which have "picture-making power."
"It [charm] is also a climate of behaviour set for perpetual summer and thermostatically controlled by taste and tact." (par. 1)
"That swimming way of looking, as though they were crushing wine . . . ." (par. 5)
"Their voices were furred with comfort, like plumped-up cushions . . . ." (par. 5)
"the line of a sports car holding a corner . . . ." (par. 14)

2.   In defining charm, the essayist offers several seeming contradictions. What makes statements like the following provocative? In what way are they paradoxical?
a.   "It's a gift, only given to give away, and the more used the more there is." (par. 1)
b.   "if you see it working, the spell is broken." (par. 2)
c.   "one cannot be 'almost' or 'partly' charmed." (par. 2)
d.   "Most children have it—till they are told they have it . . . ." (par. 10)

3. *In paragraphs 11, 13, and 14, Lee presents examples of various kinds. Discuss the way these paragraphs develop through the use of examples.*

4. *Explain if you can the literary allusion Lee uses in paragraph 2: "Never attempt to ask for whom the charm-bells ring; if they toll for anyone, they must toll for you." What is the relationship of the allusion to Lee's statement that by recognizing that someone possesses charm, we admit to being charmed?*

5. *Words to learn and use:* seduction *(par. 1);* genial *(par. 2);* maternalism *(par. 6);* extravaganza, wizened *(par. 8);* unstinted, solace *(par. 9);* narcissism *(par. 10);* thermal, compulsive *(par. 11);* palpable, ominous *(par. 12);* inexplicable, ravishment *(par. 14);* deployed, invincible, punitive *(par. 15).*

Generating Ideas

1. *During the next few days, jot down questions that you hear which necessitate an answer in the form of a definition, for example, "How do you define success, anyhow? Not the way I define it, I'll bet!" Or pose some questions for yourself and write paragraph-length answers for at least two of them.*

2. *Everyone has experienced charm, sometimes to the point of being obsessed with another person or with some object or place. Consider someone or something that has exerted power over you and write a definition using that experience as part of the extended development.*

3. *Choose a popular term that expresses extreme attraction of one person for another (e.g.,* charisma, sex appeal, machismo, spark*) and write a paper that defines the term and then explains (seriously or humorously) the course of its influence in a particular situation. For example, you may choose* charisma *and show how the word applies (or fails to apply) to a specific politician or movie star.*

4. *In his play* What Every Woman Knows, *Sir James Barrie provides this description of female charm: "If you have it, you don't need to have anything else; and if you don't have it, it doesn't much matter what else you have. Some women, the few, have charm for all; and most have charm for one. But some have charm for none."*
a. *Write a descriptive paper in which you portray someone (real or imaginary) who has either "charm for all" or "charm*

*for none." Show the difference the abundance or the defi-
ciency makes in the life of your character.*

b. *Check a book of quotations to find some other definition
or comment about charm; then use that quotation as a
starter for a paper written in the form of your choice.*

5. *Choose a term that you have come to understand from
the work in one of your academic courses and write an explanatory paper defining it for a fellow student. Here are a few suggestions from several fields:*

a. *literature:* imagery, sonnet, blank verse, parody, allegory,
satire, dénouement.

b. *economics or business:* negative income tax, GNP, bull market or bear market, inflation, pump-priming, monopoly, supply and demand.

c. *health sciences:* immunology, pathology, syndrome, genes,
aphasia, neurosis, virus.

d. *art:* gouache painting, tempera, perspective, chiaroscuro,
etching, cubism, impressionism.

e. *music:* sonata, coloratura, clef, woodwind, symphony,
minuet, staccato.

6. *There has been a great deal of recent legal controversy over
such terms as* censorship *and* pornography. *Do some careful
research and write a paper in which you define one of these
terms or some other that must be interpreted legally:* obscenity,
invasion of privacy, civil rights, pollution. *Or write a paper defining some term used as a label for a crime:* misdemeanor,
felony, fraud, larceny (petty *or* grand), rape, arson.

Aldo Leopold

Aldo Leopold (1887–1948), a leading conservationist, began his career with the United States Forest Service in 1909. He later became Associate Director of the Federal Forest Products Laboratory in Madison, Wisconsin; and he was an adviser on conservation to the United Nations when he died while fighting a grass fire near his Wisconsin farm. The author of two books and numerous articles on game management and forestry, Leopold collected several of his essays, which he called his "delights and dilemmas," into *Sand County Almanac* (1949), from which "A Man's Leisure Time" is taken. His superb nature writing is often compared to that of Thoreau and John Muir; and Leopold's words from the introduction to that book express a philosophy all three held in common: "We abuse the land because we regard it as a commodity belonging to us. When we see land as a community to which we belong, we may begin to use it with love and respect."

A Man's Leisure Time

The text of this sermon is taken from the gospel according to Ariosto. I do not know the chapter and verse, but this is what he says: "How miserable are the idle hours of the ignorant man!" 1

There are not many texts that I am able to accept as gospel truths, but this is one of them. I am willing to rise up and declare my belief that this text is literally true; true forward, true backward, true even before breakfast. The man who cannot enjoy his leisure is ignorant, though his degrees exhaust the alphabet, and the man who does enjoy his leisure is to some extent educated, though he has never seen the inside of a school. 2

I cannot easily imagine a greater fallacy than for one who has several hobbies to speak on the subject to those who may have none. For this implies prescription of avocation by one person for another, which is the antithesis of whatever virtue may inhere in having any at all. You do not annex a hobby, the hobby annexes you. To prescribe a hobby would be dangerously akin to prescribing a wife—with about the same probability of a happy outcome. 3

Let it be understood, then, that this is merely an exchange of reflections among those already obsessed—for better or for worse—with the need of doing something 4

queer. Let others listen if they will, and profit by our behavior if they can.

5   What is a hobby anyway? Where is the line of demarcation between hobbies and ordinary normal pursuits? I
have been unable to answer this question to my own satisfaction. At first blush I am tempted to conclude that a
satisfactory hobby must be in large degree useless, ineffi-
cient, laborious, or irrelevant. Certainly many of our most
satisfying avocations today consist of making something
by hand which machines can usually make more quickly
and cheaply, and sometimes better. Nevertheless I must
in fairness admit that in a different age the mere fashioning of a machine might have been an excellent hobby.
Galileo, I fancy, derived a real and personal satisfaction
when he set the ecclesiastical world on its ear by embody-
ing in a new catapult some natural law that St. Peter had
inadvertently omitted to catalogue. Today the invention
of a new machine, however noteworthy to industry, would,
as a hobby, be trite stuff. Perhaps we have here the real
inwardness of our question: A hobby is a defiance of the
contemporary. It is an assertion of those permanent values
which the momentary eddies of social evolution have con-
travened or overlooked. If this is true, then we may also
say that every hobbyist is inherently a radical, and that
his tribe is inherently a minority.

6   This, however, is serious; becoming serious is a grievous
fault in hobbyists. It is an axiom that no hobby should
either seek or need rational justification. To wish to do
it is reason enough. To find reasons why it is useful or
beneficial converts it at once from an avocation into an
industry—lowers it at once to the ignominious category
of an "exercise" undertaken for health, power, or profit.
Lifting dumbbells is not a hobby. It is a confession of subservience, not an assertion of liberty.

7   When I was a boy, there was an old German merchant
who lived in a little cottage in our town. On Sundays he
used to go out and knock chips off the limestone ledges
along the Mississippi, and he had a great tonnage of these
chips, all labeled and catalogued. The chips contained
little fossil stems of some defunct water creatures called
crinoids. The townspeople regarded this gentle old fellow
as just a little bit abnormal, but harmless. One day the
newspaper reported the arrival of certain titled strangers.

It was whispered that these visitors were great scientists. Some of them were from foreign lands, and some among the world's leading paleontologists. They came to visit the harmless old man and to hear his pronouncements on crinoids, and they accepted these pronouncements as law. When the old German died, the town awoke to the fact that he was a world authority on his subject, a creator of knowledge, a maker of scientific history. He was a great man—a man beside whom the local captains of industry were mere bushwhackers. His collection went to a national museum, and his name is known in all the nations of the earth.

I knew a bank president who adventured in roses. Roses 8 made him a happy man and a better bank president. I know a wheel manufacturer who adventures in tomatoes. He knows all about them, and, whether as a result or as a cause, he also knows all about wheels. I know a taxi driver who romances in sweet corn. Get him wound up once and you will be surprised how much he knows, and hardly less at how much there is to be known.

The most glamorous hobby I know of today is the revival 9 of falconry. It has a few addicts in America, and perhaps a dozen in England—a minority indeed. For two and a half cents one can buy and shoot a cartridge that will kill the heron whose capture by hawking requires months or years of laborious training of both the hawk and the hawker. The cartridge, as a lethal agent, is a perfect product of industrial chemistry. One can write a formula for its lethal reaction. The hawk, as a lethal agent, is the perfect flower of that still utterly mysterious alchemy— evolution. No living man can, or possibly ever will, understand the instinct of predation that we share with our raptorial servant. No man-made machine can, or ever will, synthesize that perfect co-ordination of eye, muscle, and pinion as he stoops to his kill. The heron, if bagged, is inedible and hence useless (although the old falconers seem to have eaten him, just as a Boy Scout smokes and eats a flea-bitten summer cottontail that has fallen victim to his sling, club, or bow). Moreover the hawk, at the slightest error in technique of handling, may either "go tame" like *Homo sapiens* or fly away into the blue. All in all, falconry is the perfect hobby.

To make and shoot the longbow is another. There is a 10 subversive belief among laymen that in the hands of an expert the bow is an efficient weapon. Each fall, less than a hundred Wisconsin experts register to hunt deer with the broadheaded arrow. One out of the hundred may get a buck, and he is surprised. One out of five riflemen gets his buck. As an archer, therefore, and on the basis of our record, I indignantly deny the allegation of efficiency. I admit only this: that making archery tackle is an effective alibi for being late at the office, or failing to carry out the ashcan on Thursdays.

11   One cannot make a gun—at least I can't. But I can make a bow, and some of them will shoot. And this reminds me that perhaps our definition ought to be amended. A good hobby, in these times, is one that entails either making something or making the tools to make it with, and then using it to accomplish some needless thing. When we have passed out of the present age, a good hobby will be the reverse of all these. I come again to the defiance of the contemporary.

12   A good hobby must also be a gamble. When I look at a rough, heavy, lumpy, splintery stave of *bois d'arc,* and envision the perfect gleaming weapon that will one day emerge from its graceless innards, and when I picture that bow, drawn in a perfect arc, ready—in a split second— to cleave the sky with its shining javelin, I must envision also the probability that it may—in a split second—burst into impotent splinters, while I face another laborious month of evenings at the bench. The possible debacle is, in short, an essential element in all hobbies, and stands in bold contradistinction to the humdrum certainty that the endless belt will eventuate in a Ford.

13   A good hobby may be a solitary revolt against the common-place, or it may be the joint conspiracy of a congenial group. That group may, on occasion, be the family. In either event it is a rebellion, and if a hopeless one, all the better. I cannot imagine a worse jumble than to have the whole body politic suddenly "adopt" all the foolish ideas that smolder in happy discontent beneath the conventional surface of society. There is no such danger. Non-conformity is the highest evolutionary attainment of social animals, and will grow no faster than other new functions. Science is just beginning to discover what incredible regimentation prevails among the "free" savages and the freer mammals and birds. A hobby is perhaps creation's first denial of the "peck-order" that burdens

the gregarious universe, and of which the majority of mankind is still a part.

Discussing Content and Form

1.   In what sense would you call this essay a sermon? Why does Leopold think the person who enjoys leisure is "to some extent educated, though he has never seen the inside of a school"? Explain how the second paragraph reinterprets the indirect quote from the Italian poet Ludovico Ariosto (1474–1533)?

2.   Why does the writer consider it foolish to prescribe a hobby or avocation? To what extent can you accept the idea that a hobby is "doing something queer" (par. 4)?

3.   The actual process of definition begins with the query, "What is a hobby anyway?" (par. 5). How do the characteristics set forth in paragraphs 5 and 6 develop the idea that a hobby is a queer pursuit and the hobbyist himself abnormal?

4.   Writers use examples to clarify their points and to support their ideas. Discuss the examples Leopold presents in paragraphs 7 and 8. How do the hobbyists illustrate a defiance of the ordinary? In what ways do their avocations seem irrational?

5.   Why does Leopold consider falconry and the sport of making and shooting the longbow good hobbies (par. 9–10)? How well do they fit the requirements he sets forth in paragraphs 5 and 6?

6.   Paragraphs 11 to 13 further define a "good hobby." How do the characteristics here differ from the general definition given in paragraphs 5 and 6? Why do you think the writer separated the general definition from the paragraphs containing the more explicit requirements and the specific examples?

7.   Discuss the statement that "Nonconformity is the highest evolutionary attainment of social animals" (par. 13). In what ways does a hobby enable a person to deny the "peck-order"?

Considering Special Techniques

1.   The tone of Leopold's essay is ironic, often playful, in spite of the fact that he seriously advocates pursuing a hobby. Consider some of the elements that contribute to this lightness of tone:

a. *What is the effect of announcing that the essay is a ser-
    mon? Of opening with a text? (It may help to know that
    Ariosto's romantic poem* Orlando Furioso *is a somewhat sa-
    tiric story of a mad medieval knight. What is ironic about
    referring to such a source as a "gospel"?)*

b. *Many words and phrases contribute to the essay's light tone,
    e.g., "true forward, true backward, true even before break-
    fast" (par. 2) and "To prescribe a hobby would be danger-
    ously akin to prescribing a wife" (par. 3). Find and discuss
    other twists of expression and plays on words in the essay.*

c. *What is the effect of Leopold's statement that a man whose
    "degrees exhaust the alphabet is ignorant if he does not enjoy
    leisure" (par. 2)? Of admitting that "making archery tackle
    is an effective alibi for being late at the office, or failing to
    carry out the ashcan on Thursdays" (par. 10)? Find still other
    points that evidence a definite but restrained humor.*

d. *Find examples of language that carries out the sermonizing
    or preaching effect suggested by the opening paragraphs:
    for instance, "Let others listen . . . and profit" (par. 4) and
    "an axiom" and "a confession of subservience" (par. 6). Some
    of the vocabulary in the essay might be labeled as* lofty.
    What does this vocabulary contribute to the tone?

e. *Study the choice of verbs in paragraph 8. Explain in particu-
    lar the effect of* adventured *in describing the actions of
    the banker and the manufacturer, and of* romances *in refer-
    ence to the taxi driver.*

2. *It may at first appear that Leopold does not follow the patterns of logical definition: he does not explicitly place* hobby
*in a larger class. But examine the first few paragraphs again.
What is the connection between the way one enjoys leisure
and the word which is to be defined? See also the sentence that
shows that the hobby is being differentiated from other similar
items in a "class": "Where is the line of demarcation between
hobbies and ordinary normal pursuits?" (par. 5). In what ways
are the four adjectives in the following sentence—"useless, inef-
ficient, laborious, or irrelevant"—used as differentia?*

3. *What is ironic about Leopold's statement in paragraph 9
that training a hawk may lead to its going tame "like* Homo
sapiens" *(Latin for "knowing man" or "wise man")? The French
bois d'arc (par. 12) means "wood for (or of) the bow," the wood
from which a bow is fashioned. What is the effect of juxtapos-
ing the two possible outcomes for the wood—the creation of a
perfect bow or one that will "burst into impotent splinters"?*

4. *Words to learn and use:* antithesis *(par. 3);* catapult, contra-
vened, inherently *(par. 5);* ignominious, subservience *(par. 6);*

fossil, defunct, crinoids, paleontologists *(par. 7);* lethal, alchemy, raptorial, synthesize, pinion *(par. 9);* allegation *(par. 10);* contradistinction *(par. 12).*

Generating Ideas

1.   Have you ever been annexed *by a hobby? Explain the process by which you became involved in it and its outcomes for you. Do any of Leopold's requirements fit: i.e., was it useless? a gamble? out of the ordinary?*

2.   We hear a great deal about "educating for leisure." Write a paper in which you advocate better education in the use of free time. You may assume either a serious or a humorous tone.

3.   Tell the story of someone you know who adventured in an avocation that won eventual recognition. Or recount the experiences of someone who turned a hobby into a business: "from avocation to vocation."

4.   Leopold declares that "exercise undertaken for health, power, or profit" is not a hobby, but subservience. At present we see many instances of persons who spend a great deal of time in such exercise. Write an essay explaining why you think such practices represent "subservience" or why they may be "liberating."

5.   Many people spend their leisure in the same way: watching television. Write a paper in which you explain how this national pastime violates almost every requisite Leopold sets down for a hobby.

10
Sorting It Out: *Classification* and *Division*

In everyday life we sift, sort, arrange, and group items and ideas in order to arrive at patterns and meanings. A traveler, for instance, may arrange slides of a trip in various ways, depending upon the purpose for showing them. At times the slides may tell a story, tracing the sequence of a trip in an arrangement similar to that of a narrative or a process paper. But at other times, slides might be grouped according to their subjects—cathedral pictures, for example, divided from those of mountain scenery or the seashore. Such a classification makes it possible to convey certain impressions or conclusions that would not be immediately apparent from a sequential or random arrangement.

Classification systems are necessary in all types of thought and in all types of work. Scientists constantly divide and classify. The medical researcher isolates various kinds of drugs, separating them into groups in order to study such things as potential curative effects or possible reactions each group might cause. Or an agricultural-biologist studies classes of plants, determining which grow best in certain soils.

Writers often devise a classification system as one of the structural patterns for transferring thoughts into expository writing. The method actually begins by comparing the facts, items, or ideas that are to be considered. From the comparison it is possible to identify a common characteristic or characteristics among the items. This characteristic, or commonality, furnishes a principle by which the items can be divided into groups and conveniently labeled, thus making it possible to get a handle on the subject.

The writer of this paragraph uses one principle to divide his subject:

> But what is a virus? Nobody knows. The term is difficult to define. We can say that most of the infectious diseases may be roughly classified under three headings according to the nature of the causal parasite: (1) the protozoal diseases, such as malaria and amoebic dysentery, which are caused by the invasion of microscopic animals; (2) the bacterial diseases, such as tuberculosis, meningitis, and the thousand and one infections which are spread by cocci, bacilli, spirilla, and other microscopic plants; and (3) the virus diseases, whose agent is neither like any of the little animals we know nor yet like any of the little plants, but appears to be of an entirely different order of organization. A few years ago the viruses were commonly known as the filter-passers, but this term ceased to be significant when it was found that certain bacteria could also pass through the fine pores of a porcelain filter and that some of these bacteria are as small as some of the viruses; i.e. the virus of smallpox.—George W. Gray, "The Problem of Influenza," *Harper's*

Gray classifies infectious diseases according to "the nature of the causal parasite," and labels the classes protozoal, bacterial, and virus. These labels serve as markers for the divisions in the paragraph. The number of items in a class may vary, of course, from only one or two to many.

Not all classification is this simple or directly announced, but no matter how complex the material or numerous the items, the grouping should be governed by one principle. Even when that principle is not named specifically, the reader should be able to see the relationships between items in a group. All the items should fit within the group where they are placed; that is, they should have the characteristics identified for that group. If there is overlapping or blurring, that group itself will need to be identified as one where items merge or fuse. This paragraph about the forms and variations of snow crystals reveals a more subtle handling of classification:

> In a single snowfall lasting an hour and a half several types of snow may fall from the sky. For ten or fifteen minutes the clouds may send down nothing but curtains

of stellar crystals. Then the stars will become mixed with a few plates and a goodly quantity of asymmetrical crystals. Toward the end of the storm, most of the snow may be slender needles, mingled with brief showers of bouncing gravel. If you have the patience and an explorer's wardrobe—complete with warm long underwear—for making an extensive census of visitors from a January storm, you may be rewarded with the acquaintance of a few spatial dendrites and capped columns that managed to slip into the snow.—Corydon Bell, *The Wonder of Snow*

Although Bell says that he will treat "several types of snow," he does not announce the basis for his classification nor does he use numbers to designate his classes. Instead he employs transitional words and phrases to achieve a smooth coherence among his items.

There are several points to remember about a piece of writing that is structured around classification and division:

1.   There should be a logical purpose for the system chosen. For instance, one way to divide various enjoyable novels is to group them according to the elements that make them pleasurable reading. Perhaps one group appeals because of its colorful characters; another because of the suspense or mystery in the plots; and a third because of its powerful and haunting themes.

2.   The principle of classification should be consistent. In the classification of novels according to their appeal, for example, it would be inconsistent to include a group of novels that have been made into movies, or a class labeled "Novels written before 1900." To be sure, some of the enjoyable novels may have been made into movies, and that fact may be mentioned; but introducing this class violates the consistency and logic of the system and the outline of the paper.

3.   The classification system should not be too rigid. One class may require more extensive development than another. In his famous *Screwtape Letters,* C. S. Lewis divides "the causes of human laughter into Joy, Fun, the Joke Proper, and Flippancy." His analyses of Joy, Fun, and Flippancy each require only a single paragraph, but the Joke Proper takes two, considerably longer, paragraphs. The system chosen should not be confining, but should provide the freedom to emphasize and expand any of the groups.

In the essays that follow, both dividing and classifying are used to handle numerous specifics. Like other patterns of development, classification is a method of conveying in an orderly and clear way the materials selected from close observation.

Robert Heilbroner

Robert Heilbroner (b. 1919) is an economist, author, and lecturer. At present, he is Norman Thomas Professor of Economics at the New School for Social Research in New York City, the school from which he earned his doctorate. Writing not only for fellow scholars but also for the general public, he has published many articles on various aspects of the economy. Heilbroner's books include *The Future as History* (1960), *A Primer of Government Spending: Between Capitalism and Socialism* (1970), and *An Inquiry into the Human Prospect* (1974). "Middle-Class Myths, Middle-Class Realities" shatters some misconceptions about the American class structure and makes some long-term predictions about the nation's economic future. In it, the classification system established in the first half forms the basis for the development of Heilbroner's subsequent ideas.

Middle-Class Myths, Middle-Class Realities

Introduction: examines the notion that America is based on a large, economically troubled, middle class (pars. 1–3)

1

Some years ago, in a moment of serious levity, I wrote that there were only two nations in the world that refused to admit to the presence of an upper class—the United States and the Soviet Union. (I suppose I should have included China.) It is still next to impossible for an American to admit that he or she is "upper-class," and almost as difficult to confess to being "working-class." But when it comes to the middle class, we are the most class-conscious nation on earth. A recent survey by Yankelovich, Skelly & White, one of the most sophisticated pollsters in the country, has come up with this profile, based partly on the judgment of the poll-taker (occupation, neighborhood) and partly on the feelings of the interviewee:

	Percent
Lower class	18
Middle class	61
Prosperous upper middle class	21

2

Are Americans in fact a one-class society?

Perhaps they are from the point of view of political orientation, or morality, or simply self-image. The Yankelovich poll is certainly not wrong when it tells us that 82 percent of Americans *think* of themselves as "middle-class." That does not mean, however, that Americans see themselves clearly. We are great ones for playing up regional differences, but equally avid on playing down economic ones. The banker goes out of his way to talk baseball to the gas station attendant. The richer we are, the more we insist that we are just like everybody else (except that we pay more taxes).

In a word, a cloud of myth obscures the realities of American class structure. For example, it says that the middle class is by far the largest group in our society. Is it?

3

Nothing explodes myths like facts. My facts appear in the United States *Statistical Abstract,* 1975. You will not find a category called the Middle Class anywhere in the *Statistical Abstract.* Neither will you find an economic group called the Rich or one called the Working Class. But there *is* a useful category described as "125 percent of Low Income Level," which is economic jargon for the Poor. That figure establishes an income of $6298 for a nonfarm family of four in 1974. If you round out to $6500 for convenience' sake, 11 million families—one fifth of all the families in the nation—fell into this group.

4
First classification: the "poor," and their relation to the middle class (pars. 4–6)

A great divide separates the poor from the economic middle class, but the poor nonetheless affect middle-class prosperity in two ways. First, many of the amenities of middle-class existence are made possible because the bottom group includes large numbers of working poor. Here are the nation's bellhops, porters, washroom attendants, shoeshine boys, hotel maids, parking lot attendants, restaurant kitchen help. It would be too much to say that the middle class lives off the low-cost

5

services of the working poor. It is not too much to say that it enjoys them.

6   Second, the poor are the class that the economic middle class pays for. The poor are major beneficiaries of the taxes paid by the nation—almost a third of their income comes from public assistance. The middle class is not, to be sure, the only class that supports the nonworking poor. It shares that burden with the rich and the working class. It shares as well the mixed attitudes of pity, contempt, hatred, and fear with which upper- and working-class America regards the bottom group.

7   Identifying the poor is statistically easy. It is not so easy to identify the working class. One way would be to add up all the families who have what we call "working-class" occupations—bricklayers, factory operatives, and so on. There are, very roughly, 25 million such blue-collar workers. The trouble is, some are not married (hence not "families"); a considerable number are low earners (hence already included in the working poor); a few are working-class by trade but certainly not by income (skilled craftsmen).

Second classification: the "working class" (pars. 7–10)

8   Therefore we will count up the working class by an easier method. We will simply include in it every family that earns more than a near-poverty income of $6500 and less than an income of $15,000. Forty percent of all families in the nation have incomes in this range.

9   The working class affects the economic middle class in a way that is different from what the poor does. The middle class feels that it is bled by the poor, but that it is challenged by the workingman. When a middle-class engineer making $20,000 reads about a building trades worker who pulls down $8.00 an hour, he feels pressured. He complains that "unions are pushing the country into bankruptcy."

10   Well, maybe unions are pushing some parts of the country, especially the cities, into bank-

ruptcy, but the hard facts of income distribution nonetheless draw a clear line between working-class incomes and middle- or upper-class ones. Average *annual* earnings for male craft workers, the aristocracy of the working class, were just over $8000 in 1969—perhaps they are up to $10,000 today. Most working-class families who make it up to the $15,000 level do so because they have two earners in the family. But realities are often less important than perceptions. And there is no doubt that the middle class feels the union man breathing down its neck.

With the bottom three fifths of the nation tagged—one fifth poor, two fifths working class—we are almost ready to examine the true economic middle class. But first we must take a look at the rich.

11
Third classification: the "rich," further subdivided into the wealthy and the "upper class" (pars. 11–14)

Where do riches begin? A realistic answer is probably around $100,000 a year, that magic six-figure number attached to major corporate responsibility. We can only guess how many $100,000 families there are. In 1972, slightly over one million taxpayers filed returns showing incomes of $50,000 or more. The number with $100,000 incomes was certainly less than half that number, probably fewer than 200,000. A separate estimate of taxable estates tells us that there are 250,000 households worth $1 million or more. There is obviously a lot of overlap between the two groups, but even if there were no overlap at all, only 450,000 families—less than one percent—would be rich.

12

Under the rich is a much larger group that we shall call the upper class. This is the top 5 percent of the nation, numbering some 2,750,000 families. In 1974 a family made it into this upper class with an income of $32,000. Coincidentally, there are about the same number of families with estates ranging from $200,000 to $1 million.

13

These numbers have a certain shock effect.

14

It takes much more money to be rich, and much less money to be upper class, than we think. Lots of families who picture themselves as middle class—families with incomes derived from modest positions in business or professional work—discover that they are actually upper class by economic standards. Indeed, what really separates upper class from middle class, at the $30,000 to $40,000 range, is not so much income as wealth. The successful middle-class family enters the upper-class income range during its peak earning years, and then slips back to middle-class levels on its retirement income. The true upper-class family stays there after retirement, because it has dividends and interest to supplement its retirement pay.

15

Fourth classification: the boundaries of the "middle class" defined (pars. 15–17)

All these investigations finally bring us to our target. The economic middle class is what is left, after we count up the working class and the poor, and after we exclude the upper class and the rich. It is by no means a small class—by our calculations it includes 35 percent of all the families in the nation. Its income ranges from $15,000, where the working class stops, to $32,000, where the upper class begins.

16

What occupations, what characteristics, mark this group? There is no simple answer to the question. Some professions—doctors, lawyers, airline pilots—are virtually all middle-class or higher. So are some broad occupational groups—managers and proprietors. But the category is more inclusive than that. In 1974, the average white couple, where both husband and wife worked, made $16,500. That was enough to put it just over the middle-class boundary.

17

Nonetheless, large as it is, the middle class is only about half as large as it appears in the Yankelovich survey, based on the standards of occupation or residence or self-perception. In addition, note that the upper class, defined as the top 5 percent of incomes, is only a quarter as large as the "prosperous upper middle class" of the survey. Hence the first great myth explodes. Eighty-two percent of Americans may *think* of themselves as middle-class or higher, but more than half of these families are kidding themselves.

One thing emerges very clearly from this look at the economic realities. The economic middle class is a lot less rich (as well as a lot less large) than most people think. This delusion lends support to a second general myth about the middle class. It is that the middle class has been caught in a ferocious squeeze between rising prices and rising taxes.

18
Transition that reemphasizes the inaccuracy of the first myth and introduces the second (par. 18)

Let us begin with inflation. Consumer prices have doubled since 1950, and have risen by two thirds since 1965. Hasn't this inevitably taken its toll of middle-class well-being? The answer is that it hasn't, because middle-class incomes have risen even faster than prices. In 1974, it required an income of $15,000 to enter the top 40 percent of families, where the middle class is found. Back in 1950, however, to get into the top 40 percent required an income of only $3822. An extraordinary fact, but true. In those days the poor included all families with incomes of less than $1661, and the upper class—the top 5 percent—began at a family income of only $8666. If we doubled those 1950 amounts, we would keep everyone approximately abreast of inflation. But actual incomes have far more than doubled. That marginal upper-class family of 1950 has not doubled its $8666 income, but has quadrupled it.

19
Examination of the effect of inflation on the middle class (pars. 19–24)

Thus, in "real" terms—that is, with full allowance for inflation—the middle class has fared very well. Then why does the middle class *feel* squeezed by rising prices?

20

Three answers suggest themselves. One is that the psychological costs of inflation are

21

greater than its economic gains. Once every year or so, we get ahead of the inflationary spiral, when salaries are raised, promotions are won, year-end profits are shared. On that day there is a real sense of moving ahead, an acute moment of economic triumph. But the triumph is followed by 364 days of irritation as shopping bills rise. The small defeats of 364 experiences of inflation may actually amount to less than the victory on Getting Ahead Day, but the sense of loss far outweighs the memory of gain.

22   Second, there is the problem of property. Another testimony to the actual economic strength of the middle class is that the number of property owners with estates ranging from $60,000 to $200,000 rose from 2.3 million in 1958 to over 10 million in 1972. This is an enormous gain in the number of modestly propertied families. It is also an enormous increase in the number of households who watch with impotent alarm as their savings accounts melt, their life insurance policies lose value, their bonds deteriorate in purchasing power, and their stocks go nowhere (from 1965 until the present boom, stocks have essentially moved sideways, with no net gain at all).

23   Last, there is the fact that the two years of inflation and recession since 1974 *have* ground down on the economic middle class along with everyone else. The process of staying ahead of inflation has depended on economic growth. For almost two years, until very recently, our economic growth has been negligible or even negative. Probably the burden of recession has hurt families in the working-class income brackets more severely than those in middle and upper brackets, but better-off families have also felt its impact, either in reduced incomes or in frozen ones, or even in unemployment.

24   Thus it is understandable that we believe in the myth of a killing inflationary experience for the middle class. Inflation is psycho-

logically painful, hell on property, fierce when it is accompanied by recession. Nonetheless, inflation over the last twenty-five years has been more than matched by growth, in both income and property. Over this period, the middle class has not been killed—in fact, it has done extremely well.

The same surprising conclusion awaits us when we take a look at taxation. Is the middle class suffering under a growing burden of taxation? It thinks it is. There is a great rumble of tax revolt. Politicians are falling all over themselves to promise tax relief to the middle class. Yet, once again, realities differ from perceptions.

25
Analysis of the actual effect of taxes on the middle class (pars. 25–30)

Let's begin with federal tax rates. Everyone assumes they are much higher, because everyone is paying more money to the federal government. But tax rates are *not* higher, except for Social Security taxes. From 1954 to 1963, a married couple with two dependents making a taxable income of $20,000 paid $3800 to the government. By 1975 that tax liability had dropped to $2740. The tax rate on $20,000 has actually *fallen* from 19 percent in 1954–1963 to less than 14 percent today.

26

Of course state and local taxes have gone up. One cannot say how much, because they vary from locality to locality. State and local taxes from all sources, property, sales, and income, have roughly quadrupled over the last twenty years. Yet it seems doubtful that the *total* tax bill has risen on a given family income.

27

That brings us to the second complication. Family incomes are not "given." They have risen sharply over the period. As a consequence, families have moved into higher tax brackets. Take a successful young couple with two infants in 1955, earning $10,000—enough to put it into the upper class (the top 5 percent) in that year. In 1955 our couple paid a federal

28

income tax of $1372 plus a few hundred dollars in state and local taxes.

29 Now suppose that our couple prospered along with everyone else over the next twenty years. Its $10,000 income would today be about $35,000. At this level its federal taxes (still assuming two dependents) would be a little over $7000, and we will estimate very generously that it paid an additional $2000 in state and local income taxes. Thus it has left only $26,000 of its $35,000 income, and this $26,000 has to be cut in half to allow for the doubling of prices between 1950 and 1975.

30 Such a family may indeed feel burdened by taxation. Nine thousand dollars of taxes, where it used to pay $1500! The fact remains, however, that its income, *after* taxes and *after* allowing for inflation, is still about 50 percent higher today than its post-tax income of twenty years ago.

31
Transition and introduction to the final myth (par. 31)

All this presents a picture of the middle class very different from that to which we are accustomed. In fact it brings us to the last of our myths—the belief that the middle class is indestructible. The middle class, for all its anxieties and trials, has triumphed over adversity. It would not be difficult to project a future in which the middle class will go on forever, gaining economic strength and security.

32
Projection that the middle class will cease to prosper because of class conflict (pars. 32–37)

Alas, I fear this too is a myth. The success of the middle class has been based on the process of economic growth. It is the steady expansion of output that has enabled the middle class to pay higher taxes and higher prices and still enjoy a higher real income. But growth is a process whose days are numbered, partly because of a shortage of resources, partly because of pollution dangers. Probably within our lifetime, certainly within that of our children, growth will have to be throttled back (as is already the case in Japan). When it does, the fate of the middle class may be decided.

For then we will finally have to face the problem that the myth of a one-class society has obscured. It is the problem of what to do about the working class, not to mention the poor, who have the temerity to ask for "more," and to be discontented even after they get more. This is an attitude that the middle and upper classes celebrate in themselves, but deplore in others. It is, however, an attitude they can tolerate as long as *everyone* gets more, because growth sheds its benefits on all classes. 33

What happens when growth slows down? There is only one possible answer. The working class must come into conflict with the middle class. Of course it will also come into conflict with the upper class and the rich. But the top 5 percent get only 15 percent of all income. Even if we took all its surplus income and gave it to the working class, this would not be enough to bring the working class to parity with the middle class. And this still leaves us with the lower class, condemned to live on 5 percent of the nation's income. 34

Thus, when growth slows down, we must expect a struggle of redistribution on a vast scale—a confrontation not just between a few rich and many poor, but between a relatively better-off upper third of the nation and a relatively less well-off, slightly larger working class. And fighting against both will be the bottom 20 percent—the group with the most to gain, the least to lose. 35

This struggle will not be confined to the United States. Although social and political differences are very great throughout the Western world, income structures are much alike. By and large, the middle classes of Europe and Japan have prospered during the last twenty years, thanks to the curative powers of growth. They too must face the prospect of a struggle for position when growth begins to peter out, ten or twenty years from now. In England, the victim of twenty years of slug- 36 gish growth, the contest is already joined. In Japan, reduced by energy scarcities and pollution damage from the fastest to one of the slowest growing industrial nations, the contest soon may surface. In the more fortunate nations, one of which is the United States, it is still a decade or two away.

37   Can the middle class survive this challenge? It is difficult to be hopeful in the face of the reluctance with which any class surrenders one inch of economic territory. I expect that in many nations the outcome will be the rise of authoritarian governments, some seeking to protect the income advantages of middle or upper groups, some trying to impose an egalitarian economic order on all. Certainly if an end to growth should come rapidly, authoritarian regimes of the Right or Left would seem very probable.

38
Suggested solution
to the problem (par.
38)

But we still have a breathing spell, perhaps even a whole generation if we are lucky. Hence there is time to try for another solution. This is the resolution of the problem by the gradual fashioning of a genuine social contract, a widely shared consensus as to what constitutes a "fair" distribution of income. Such a distribution would probably not be equal, although it would not tolerate extremes of either wealth or poverty. It would be, in fact, the realization of the myth of the one—"middle"—class society.

Discussing Content and Form

1. State the thesis or central message Heilbroner gives in his analysis of classes. What myths does he explode with the factual information he presents?

2. Why does the subject of this essay lend itself to development by classification and division? Does it necessitate this method? Why or why not?
a. What is the basic principle or system for the divisions in the article? Find places where this principle is stated directly.

b. *Why does Heilbroner further divide the broad groups "upper, middle, and lower"?*
c. *Which lines of division are hard to identify? In what way does the writer prepare for the blurring of these lines?*

3. *Discuss Heilbroner's assertion that an economic conflict between the upper and middle groups and the nation's working-classes and poor is inevitable (par. 35). What evidence does he give that this struggle will not be confined to the United States?*

4. *What political outcome does Heilbroner think likely as economic growth slows? Discuss the solution he offers.*

Considering Special Techniques

1. *Analyze some of the techniques Heilbroner uses in this tightly organized blend of facts, opinions, and speculations.*
a. *What kinds of characteristics does he analyze in his delineation of each class?*
b. *Compare the arrangement of the statistics (income, kind of work, etc.) for each class. If the arrangement or data differ, account for the variation.*
c. *Discuss the effectiveness of the introductory or transition sentences that open each major section (introduce each "class").*

2. *Note Heilbroner's use of questions as a way of getting the reader to follow his thoughts.*
a. *After saying that Americans believe "the middle class is by far the largest group in our society," (par. 3) he asks, bluntly, "Is it?" How does this blunt query prepare for much of the development to come?*
b. *How does the question at the end of paragraph 20 ("Then why does the middle class* feel *squeezed by rising prices?") prepare for what is to come?*

3. *The structure of the essay is clearly marked by transition words and phrases, by echoes, and by repeated ideas. Go through one of Heilbroner's major divisions and underline the lead sentence in each paragraph. Discuss the way these leads act as predictors and as links in his chain of ideas. Paragraphs 25 to 30 provide a good block for this exercise.*

4. *Comment on your reaction to the numerous statistics in the essay. If you find such material cumbersome or boring, explain why you feel as you do. What conclusions can you draw about the appropriateness or necessity for the statistics?*

5. *Why does Heilbroner, who is writing as an authority in a specialized field, use such phrases as "more than half of these families are kidding themselves" (par. 17) and "the middle class has been caught in a ferocious squeeze" (par. 18)?*

6. *Words to learn and use:* avid *(par. 3);* amenities *(par. 5);* beneficiaries *(par. 6);* ferocious *(par. 18);* deteriorate *(par. 22);* negligible *(par. 23);* indestructible *(par. 31);* temerity *(par. 33);* parity *(par. 34);* curative *(par. 36);* reluctance, authoritarian *(par. 37);* consensus *(par. 38).*

Generating Ideas

1. *From one of your other courses, choose a question that requires an answer based on classification and create an outline of its structure. For instance, you might find a question like this in biology or environmental studies: "Controversy among farmers often arises over the control of various kinds of predators; discuss some suggested methods of dealing with this problem and determine which are most acceptable." Or in sociology you might be asked to discuss various types of welfare services and suggest better ways to deliver them. In constructing your outline, be aware that classification is not an end in itself, but is used to set forth some conclusion or proposal.*

2. *Use the statement, "Nothing explodes myths like facts" (par. 4), as the basis for a paper in which you offer a well-structured argument to show why a popularly held belief is unfounded. You may use classification to group reasons or facts, but your method of development should, of course, be determined by the nature of your subject.*

3. *Select several examples of inflation as it affects you and classify them by some principle—for instance, inflation in clothing, in transportation costs, in school expenses. Use statistical evidence to support the point you wish to make.*

4. *Write a paper about taxation in which you employ a classification system suitable to your purpose. Even though this is a serious subject, you might treat it humorously.*

5. *Heilbroner mentions some of the problems that accompany a slowing economic growth (par. 36). Do a little research (by reading or interview) and write an essay about these problems as they affect your community or state.*

Shana Alexander

Shana Alexander (b. 1925), after graduating from Vassar College in 1945 and working as a writer and editor for various publications, served as a staff writer and columnist for *Life* magazine from 1954 to 1964. She was also a contributing editor for *Newsweek* and has made frequent appearances on radio and television, most notably as part of the "Point-Counterpoint" feature of the CBS show "60 Minutes." Out of her observations of the contemporary social scene have come three books: *The Feminine Eye* (1970), *Shana Alexander's State-by-State Guide to Women's Rights* (1975), and *Woman Talking* (1976), a collection of several of her articles, including "The Fine Art of Marital Fighting." Presented here in a slightly shortened version, the essay is a model of classification as well as a tongue-in-cheek account of various ways to handle marital strife.

The Fine Art of Marital Fighting

In the morning, his secretary quits; in the afternoon, his archrival at the office gets a promotion; when he gets home that evening he finds out his wife has put a dent in the new car. He drinks four martinis before dinner, and then calls his wife a lousy cook. She says how can he tell with all that gin in him, and he says she is getting as mean tempered as her stupid mother, and she says at least her mother wasn't stupid enough to marry a phony slob, by which time he is bellowing like an enraged moose, she is shrieking and hurling dishes, the baby is screaming, the dogs are yapping, the neighbors are pounding on the walls, and the cops are on their way. Suddenly a car screeches to the curb and a little man with a tape recorder under his arm hops out and dashes inside.

This scene is a recurrent dream of George R. Bach, Ph.D., a Los Angeles clinical psychologist and West Coast chairman of the American Academy of Psychotherapy. For him, it is not a nightmare but a rosy fantasy of things to come. His great ambition is to set up a Los Angeles Municipal Fight Center which any embattled husband or wife, regardless of race, creed, or hour of the night, could telephone and get a fair hearing. Trained marriage counselors would man the switchboards, referee the disputes, tape-record the hubub for analysis by dawn's early light, and if necessary, dispatch a mobile referee on a house call.

3   It is Bach's dream to become that referee. He studies human aggression, and he loves his work. Over the last twenty-five years, he has professionally analyzed 23,000 marital fights, including, he figures, at least 2,500 of his own. Gifted marital gladiators in action thrill him as the sunset does the poet.

4   Unfortunately, his clinical practice yields so few sunsets that Bach feels the future of American family life is gravely threatened. He recently told a startled audience of newsmen and psychiatrists at the annual meeting of the Ortho-Psychiatric Association that a primary aim of psychotherapy and marriage counseling should be "to teach couples to have more, shorter, *more constructive* fights." Along with a growing number of his colleagues, he says, he has come to believe that proper training in "the fine art of marital fighting" would not only improve domestic tranquillity, it could reduce divorces by up to 90 per cent.

5   What dismays the doctor is not bloodshed per se; it is the native cowardice and abysmal crudity of American domestic fighting style. Most husbands and wives, he has found, will avail themselves of any sneaky excuse to avoid a fight in the first place. But if cornered, they begin clobbering away at one another like dull-witted Neanderthals. They are clumsy, weak-kneed, afflicted with poor aim, rotten timing, and no notion of counterpunching. What's more, they fight dirty. Their favorite weapons are the low blow and the rock-filled glove.

6   The cause of the shoddy, low estate of the marital fight game is a misunderstanding of aggression itself, says the fight doctor. "Research has established that people always dream, and *my* research has established that people are always to some degree angry. But today they are ashamed of this anger. To express hostile feelings toward a loved one is considered impolite, just as the expression of sexual feelings was considered impolite before Freud."

7   What Freud did for sex, Bach, in his own modest way, would like to do for anger, which is almost as basic a human impulse. "We must remove the shame from aggression," he exhorts in a soft, singsong German accent much like Peter Lorre's. "Don't repress your aggressions—program them!"

When primitive man lived in the jungle, surrounded 8
by real, lethal enemies, the aggressive impulse is what
kept him alive. For modern man, the problem gets complicated because he usually encounters only what the psychologist calls "intimate enemies"—wives, husbands,
sweethearts, children, parents, friends, and others whom
he sometimes would like to kill, but toward whom he
nonetheless feels basic, underlying goodwill.

When he gets mad at one of these people, modern man 9
tends to go to pieces. His jungle rage embarrasses, betrays,
even terrifies him. "He forgets that real intimacy *demands*
that there be fighting," Bach says. He fails to realize that
"nonfighting is only appropriate between strangers—people who have nothing worth fighting about. When two
people begin to really *care* about each other, they become
emotionally vulnerable—and the battles start."

Listening to Bach enumerate the many destructive, 10
"bad" fight styles is rather like strolling through a vast
Stillman's gym of domestic discord. Over there, lolling
about on the canvas, watching TV, walking out, sitting
in a trancelike state, drinking beer, doing their nails, even
falling asleep, are the "Withdrawal-Evaders," people who
will not fight. These people, Bach says, are very sick. After
counseling thousands of them, he is convinced that "falling asleep causes more divorces than any other single
act."

And over *there,* viciously flailing, kicking, and throwing 11
knives at one another, shouting obnoxious abuse, hitting
below the belt, deliberately provoking anger, exchanging
meaningless insults (You stink! *You* doublestink!)—simply
needling or battering one another for the hell of it—are
people indulging in "open noxious attack." They are the
"Professional Ego-Smashers," and they are almost as
sick—but not quite—as the first bunch.

An interesting subgroup here are the "Chain-Reactors," 12
specialists in what Bach once characterized as "throwing
in the kitchen sink from left field." A chain-reacting husband opens up by remarking, "Well, I see you burned the
toast again this morning." When his wife begins to make
new toast, he continues, "And another thing . . . that no-
good brother of yours hasn't had a job for two years." This
sort of fight, says Bach, "usually pyramids to a Valhalla-
type of total attack."

The third group of people are all smiling blandly and 13

saying, "Yes, dear." But each one drags after him a huge gunnysack. These people are the "Pseudo-Accommodators," the ones who pretend to go along with the partner's point of view for the sake of momentary peace, but who never really mean it. The gunnysacks are full of grievances, reservations, doubts, secret contempt. Eventually the overloaded sacks burst open, making an awful mess.

14   The fourth group are "Carom Fighters," a sinister lot. They use noxious attack not directly against the partner but against some person, idea, activity, value, or object which the partner loves or stands for. They are a whiz at spoiling a good mood or wrecking a party, and when they *really* get mad, they can be extremely dangerous. Bach once made a study of one hundred intimate murders and discovered that two-thirds of the killers did not kill their partner, but instead destroyed someone whom the partner loved.

15   Even more destructive are the "Double Binders," people who set up warm expectations but make no attempt to fulfill them or, worse, deliver a rebuke instead of the promised reward. This nasty technique is known to some psychologists as the "mew phenomenon": "Kitty mews for milk. The mother cat mews back warmly to intimate that kitty should come and get it. But when the kitten nuzzles up for a drink, he gets slashed in the face with a sharp claw instead." In human terms, a wife says, for example, "I have nothing to wear." Her husband says, "Buy yourself a new dress—you deserve it." But when she comes home wearing the prize, he says, "What's that thing supposed to be, a paper bag with sleeves?"—adding, "Boy, do you look fat!"

16   The most irritating bad fighters, according to Bach, are the "Character Analysts," a pompous lot of stuffed shirts who love to explain to the mate what his or her real, subconscious, or hidden feelings are. This accomplishes nothing except to infuriate the mate by putting him on the defensive for being himself. This style of fighting is common among lawyers, members of the professional classes, and especially, psychotherapists. It is presumptuous, highly alienating, and never in the least useful except in those rare partnerships in which husband and wife are equally addicted to a sick, sick game which Bach calls "Psychoanalytic Archaeology—the earlier, the farther back, the deeper, the better!"

In a far corner of Bach's marital gym are the "Gimmes," overdemanding fighters who specialize in "overloading the system." They always want more; nothing is ever enough. New car, new house, more money, more love, more understanding—no matter what the specific demand, the partner never can satisfy it. It is a bottomless well.

Across from them are found the "Withholders," stingily restraining affection, approval, recognition, material things, privileges—anything which could be provided with reasonable effort or concern and which would give pleasure or make life easier for the partner.

In a dark, scary back corner are the "Underminers," who deliberately arouse or intensify emotional insecurities, reinforce moods of anxiety or depression, try to keep the partner on edge, threaten disaster, or continually harp on something the partner dreads. They may even wish it to happen.

The last group are the "Benedict Arnolds," who not only fail to defend their partners against destructive, dangerous, and unfair situations, forces, people, and attacks but actually encourage such assaults from outsiders.

Husbands and wives who come to Psychologist Bach for help invariably can identify themselves from the categories he lists. If they do not recognize themselves, at least they recognize their mate. Either way, most are desperate to know what can be done. Somewhere, they feel, there must be another, sunnier, marital gym, a vast Olympic Games perhaps, populated with nothing but agile, happy, bobbing, weaving, superbly muscled, and incredibly sportsmanlike gladiators.

Discussing Content and Form

1. What is the effect of treating marital fights as a sport, setting them in a "marital gym" and calling the psychotherapist a "referee"? Does Alexander treat the subject satirically or merely lightly? Explain.

2. A workable classification system must follow a single principle, and each item must fit into one of the classes or groups.
a. What is the principle by which Alexander classifies her marital fighters? Explain why this system is successful for her purpose.

b. *How many classes or groups of marital fighters does she actually name? Why does she make the group in paragraph 12 a subgroup, rather than another major division?*

3. *What are "intimate enemies" (par. 8)? Why, in Alexander's opinion, is it more difficult to handle aggressions with people who are closely related, even loved? What do you think of the statement that "real intimacy demands that there be fighting" (par. 9)?*

4. *Do you think that it would be possible for most husbands and wives to identify themselves from the categories listed here? Would other kinds of fights also fit some of the categories? Explain.*

Considering Special Techniques

1. *One notable feature of the essay is Alexander's ability to re-create scenes in a way that makes them come alive.*
a. *Which details make the fighters and their fights especially vivid?*
b. *What does the use of dialogue contribute? Note especially the imaginary exchange between a husband and wife in paragraph 15.*
c. *Find several examples of colorful metaphors or similes: e.g., "like an enraged moose" (par. 1) and "marital gladiators" (par. 3). Analyze the analogy, or extended metaphor, explaining the "mew phenomenon" in paragraph 15.*

2. *Each of the various groups of fighters is clearly designated by an introductory phrase, starting with "Over there, lolling about on the canvas" in paragraph 10. Make a list of these phrases and examine their similarities and differences.*

3. *Alexander's lively style is achieved partly by sentences which pile up parallel elements in rapid-fire succession; for example:*
a. *". . . he is bellowing like an enraged moose, she is shrieking and hurling dishes, the baby is screaming, the dogs are yapping, the neighbors are pounding on the walls, and the cops are on their way." (par. 1)*
b. *"They are clumsy, weak-kneed, afflicted with poor aim, rotten timing, and no notion of counterpunching." (par. 5)*
Find several other sentences that contain the same pattern.

4. *How would you characterize the level of language in this selection?*

Generating Ideas

1. Write a paper in which you extend some of the Bach-Alexander classifications to fighting in general. For instance, are there children who are "Gimmes"? Parents who are "Double Binders"? Do you have friends who are "Pseudo-Accommodators"?

2. Write a paper classifying human relationships in some way; before starting, work out a list of your groupings. One method might classify human ties as those we are born to, those we choose, and those forced on us by circumstance. You may, of course, limit the area of relationships to be classified.

3. One purpose of classification and division is to make the whole group of which the classes are a part more readily understood. Choose one subject from the list below and divide it into several classes, making sure that your technique leads to a generalization about the subject:

a. Types of academic courses
b. Career choices
c. Various purposes for reading
d. Kinds of reading material
e. Ways in which the public is kept informed about current events: e.g., governmental agencies, the media, public relations organizations
f. Types of neighborhoods/shopping facilities/recreational services in your city or area
g. Methods of travel/transportation
h. Current favorites in music, musicians, films, television shows, etc.

4. Make a point about one of these subjects by using classification and division as part of the development: kinds of restaurants; advertisements; heroes or heroines in fiction; types of parents; entertainers; television personalities.

5. Adapt one of these thesis sentences as the basis for a classification paper:

a. "The tactics for getting good grades fall into several distinct patterns."
b. "Part of my education has been achieved through observation of the ways of getting ahead."
c. "Among my fellow workers I saw several methods of fooling the boss."
d. "Coaches (basketball, football, etc.) may be classified as parents, bosses, or very good friends."

James Thurber

James Thurber (1894–1961) grew up in Columbus, Ohio, and graduated from Ohio State University. After a start as a newspaperman, he began his lifelong career with the *New Yorker* as a writer and cartoonist, an association he commemorated in his book *The Years with Ross* (1959). Many of his articles have been collected in *The Thurber Album* (1952) and *Thurber Country* (1953), and his other books include *My Life and Hard Times* (1933), *Fables for Our Times* (1940), and *My World and Welcome to It!* (1942). All of his work displays a humorous and gently mocking view of the human condition. "A Discussion of Feminine Types," in a slightly longer form, first appeared in *Is Sex Necessary?* (1929), a book to which E. B. White (p. 86) also contributed. In the essay Thurber treats what has become a delicate subject with characteristically affectionate humor.

A Discussion of Feminine Types

1   In speaking of the weaker sex in this book, the authors usually confine themselves to the generalization "Woman," "women," and "the female." For the larger discussions of sex, these comprehensive terms suffice. Yet no examination of the pitiable problem of Man and Woman would be complete without some effort to define a few of the more important types of the female. One cannot say, "Oh, well, you know how women are," and let it go at that. Many truths apply, and many foibles are common, to the whole sex, but the varieties of the female of the species are as manifold as the varieties of the flower called the cineraria.

2   Successfully to deal with a woman, a man must know what type she is. There have been several methods of classification, none of which I hold thoroughly satisfactory, neither the glandular categories—the gonoid, thyroid, etc.—nor the astrological—Sagittarius, Virgo, Pisces, and so on. One must be pretty expert to tell a good gonoid when he sees one. Personally, I know but very little about them, nor if I had a vast knowledge would I know what to do with it. It is even more difficult, and just as unimportant, to arrive at a zodiacal classification, because that is altogether dependent upon determining the year the woman was born, and because, even if you should ascertain her date of birth, the pishtosh of analysis and predic-

tion which derives therefrom is a lot of mediæval guess-work. Or so it seems to me, and to Zaner, Blifil, Gorley, Peschkar, Rittenhouse, and Matthiessen.

Of much greater importance is a classification of females by actions. It comes out finally, the nature of a woman, in what she does—her little bag of tricks, as one might say. 3

A type of which one hears a great deal but which has never been very ably or scientifically analyzed, for the guidance of men, is the Quiet Type. How often one hears the warning, "Look out for the Quiet Type." Let us see if we should look out for it, and why. 4

The element of menace in the Quiet Type is commonly considered very great. Yet if one asks a man who professes knowledge of the type, why one should look out for it, one gets but a vague answer. "Just look out, that's all," he usually says. When I began my researches I was, in spite of myself, somewhat inhibited by an involuntary subscription to this legendary fear. I found it difficult to fight off a baseless alarm in the presence of a lady of subdued manner. Believing, however, that the best defense is an offense, I determined to carry the war, as it were, into the enemy's country. The first Quiet Type, or Q.T., that I isolated was a young woman whom I encountered at a Sunday tea party. She sat a little apart from the rest of the group in a great glazed chintz, I believe it was, chair. Her hands rested quietly on the chair arms. She kept her chin rather down than up, and had a way of lifting her gaze slowly, without disturbing the set of her chin. She moved but twice, once to put by a cup of tea and once to push back a stray lock from her forehead. I stole glances at her from time to time, trying to make them appear ingenuous and friendly rather than bold or suggestive, an achievement rendered somewhat troublesome by an unfortunate involuntary winking of the left eyelid to which I am unhappily subject. 5

I noted that her eyes, which were brown, had a demure light in them. She was dressed simply and was quite pretty. She spoke but once or twice, and then only when spoken to. In a chance shifting of the guests to an adjacent room to examine, I believe, some water colors, I was left quite alone with her. Steeling myself for an ordeal to which I am unused—or was at the time—I moved directly to her side and grasped her hand. "Hallo, baby! Some fun— 6

hah?" I said—a method of attack which I had devised
in advance. She was obviously shocked, and instantly rose
from her chair and followed the others into the next room.
I never saw her again, nor have I been invited to that
little home since. Now for some conclusions.

7   Patently, this particular Q.T., probably due to an individual variation, was not immediately dangerous in the
sense that she would seize an opportunity, such as I offered
her, to break up the home of, or at least commit some
indiscretion with, a man who was obviously—I believe I
may say—a dependable family man with the average off-
hand attractions. Dr. White has criticized my methodology
in this particular case, a criticism which I may say now,
in all good humor, since the danger is past, once threatened to interpose insuperable obstacles, of a temperamen-
tal nature, in the way of this collaboration. It was his
feeling that I might just as well have removed one of the
type's shoes as approach her the way I did. I cannot hold
with him there. Neither, I am gratified to say, can Zaner,
but in fairness to White it is only just to add that Tithridge
can.

8   However, the next Q.T. that I encountered I placed under observation more gradually. I used to see her riding
on a Fifth Avenue bus, always at a certain hour. I took
to riding on this bus also, and discreetly managed to sit
next her on several occasions. She eventually noticed that
I appeared to be cultivating her and eyed me quite can-
didly, with a look I could not at once decipher. I could
now, but at that time I couldn't. I resolved to put the matter
to her quite frankly, to tell her, in fine, that I was studying
her type and that I wished to place her under closer observation. Therefore, one evening, I doffed my hat and began.

9   "Madam," I said, "I would greatly appreciate making
a leisurely examination of you, at your convenience." She
struck me with the palm of her open hand, got up from
her seat, and descended at the next even-numbered
street—Thirty-sixth, I believe it was.

10   I may as well admit here and now that personally I
enjoyed at no time any great success with Q.T.'s. I think
one may go as far as to say that any scientific examination
of the Quiet Type, as such, is out of the question. I know
of no psychologist who has ever got one alone long enough
to get anywhere. (Tithridge has averred that he began
too late in life; Zaner that he does not concur in the major

premise.) The Quiet Type is not amenable to the advances of scientific men when the advances are of a scientific nature, and also when they are of any other nature. Indeed, it is one of the unfortunate handicaps to psychological experimentation that many types of women do not lend themselves readily to purposeful study. As one woman said to me, "It all seems so mapped out, kind of. . . ."

In my very failures I made, I believe, certain significant findings in regard to the Quiet Type. It is not dangerous to men, but to a particular man. Apparently it lies in wait for some one individual and gets him. Being got by this special type, or even being laid in wait for, would seem to me in some cases not without its pleasurable compensations. Wherein, exactly, the menace lies, I have no means of knowing. I have my moments when I think I see what it is, but I have other moments when I think I don't. 11

The Buttonhole-twister Type is much easier to come at. A girl of this persuasion works quite openly. She has the curious habit of insinuating a finger, usually the little finger of the right hand, unless she be left-handed, into the lapel buttonhole of a gentleman, and twisting it. Usually, she picks out a man who is taller than herself and usually she gets him quite publicly, in parks, on street corners, and the like. Often, while twisting, she will place the toe of her right shoe on the ground, with the heel elevated, and will swing the heel slowly through an arc of about thirty or thirty-five degrees, back and forth. This manifestation is generally accompanied by a wistful, faraway look on the woman's face, and she but rarely gazes straight at the man. She invariably goes in for negative statements during the course of her small writhings, such as "It is not," "I am not," "I don't believe you do," and the like. This type is demonstrative in her affections and never lies in wait with any subtlety. She is likely to be restless and discontented with the married state, largely because she will want to go somewhere that her husband does not want to go, or will not believe he has been to the places that he says he just came from. It is well to avoid this type. 12

A charming but altogether dangerous type is the "Don't, dear" Type. By assuming a middle of the road, this way and that way, attitude toward a gentleman's advances, 13 she will at once allure and repulse him. The man will thus be twice allured. He calls on her, and they sit in the porch swing, let us say. When he slips his arm around her, she will say in a low tone, "Don't, dear." No matter what he does, she will say, "Don't, dear." This type is a homemaker. Unless the man wants a home made for him within a very short time, it is better for him to observe the "don't" rather than the "dear," and depart. The type is common in the Middle West, particularly in university towns, or was some few years ago, at any rate. Any effort to classify modern university types would be difficult and confusing. They change from year to year, and vary with the region. I am told that one type has actually been known to get the man of her choice down and sit, as it were, side-saddle of him. I would not give even this brief mention, in passing, to college types of the female, were they not important because they so frequently divert a man from his career and tie him down before he has a chance to begin working, or even to say anything.

14   The rest of the types of American women, such as the Outdoors, the Clinging Vine, and so on and so on, are too generally known to need any special comment here. If a man does not know one when he sees it, or cannot tell one from another, of these more common types, there is little that can be done for him. No man should contemplate marriage, or even mingle with women, unless he has a certain measure of intuition about these more obvious types. For example, if a man could not tell instantly that a woman was the sort that would keep him playing tennis, or riding horseback, all afternoon, and then expect him to ride back and forth all night on the ferry, no amount of description of the Outdoors Type would be of any avail.

15   There is, however, one phenomenal modern type, a product of these strange post-war years, which will bear a brief analysis. This is the type represented by the girl who gets right down to a discussion of sex on the occasion of her first meeting with a man, but then goes on to betray a great deal of alarm and aversion to the married state. This is the "I-can't-go-through-with-it" Type. Many American virgins fall within this classification. Likewise it contains women who have had some strange and bitter experience about which they do a great deal of hinting but which they never clearly explain. If involved with, or even

merely presented to, a woman of this type, no man in his right mind will do anything except reach for his hat. Science does not know what is the matter with these women, or whether anything is the matter. A lot of reasons have been advanced for girls acting in this incredible, dismayed manner—eleven reasons in all, I believe—but no one really knows very much about it. It may be their mothers' teaching, it may have been some early childhood experience, such as getting caught under a gate, or suffering a severe jolting up by being let fall when a boy jumped off the other end of a teeter-totter, or it may simply be a whim. We do not know. One thing is sure, they are never the Quiet Type. They talk your arm off.

Discussing Content and Form

1. *The selection was first published in 1929, certainly with the intention of amusing the reader. Do changes in time and audience make it less humorous today? Explain.*

2. *How many classes or types of women does Thurber identify? What is his principle of classification?*

3. *If a method of classification is to be comprehensive, all of the subjects under consideration should fall into one of the classes. How does Thurber protect his system from the charge that he omits some women? Can all women be classified on the basis of Thurber's system? Why or why not?*

4. *Why does Thurber consider other methods of classification and reject them (par. 2)?*

5. *Make a list of Thurber's classes and discuss the order in which he presents them.*
    a. *Why does he give the most space to the Quiet Type?*
    b. *Why do you think he places the "I-can't-go-through-with-it" Type last?*
    c. *Analyze Thurber's use of transitions between his various types. Although he includes numerous details about each type, what transitions keep the essay moving coherently? Comment on the effect of these signals on the logic and the clarity of the selection.*

6. *Point out examples of Thurber's laughter at himself. What does this self-deprecation contribute to the tone of the essay?*

Considering Special Techniques

1. Classification is frequently part of scientific writing. Point out several methods that Thurber uses to give the impression that his study is based on scientific investigation.
a. What is the effect of the citation to authorities "Zaner, Blifil, Gorley, Peschkar, Rittenhouse, and Matthiessen" (par. 2)? Do these people need to be "real"? Why or why not? "Dr. White" (par. 7) is Thurber's collaborator on the book from which the selection comes. What special humor is achieved through recounting their differences?
b. In which incidents does Thurber attempt to give the appearance that he is a scientific observer? Could some of the humor in the essay be directed at scientists as well as at the man-woman relationship? Explain.

2. Thurber frequently uses lofty and elevated expressions to convey some rather simple ideas. For example, his statement, "I was . . . somewhat inhibited by an involuntary subscription to this legendary fear" (par. 5), basically means that he was afraid. Find examples of other such expressions and show how they contribute to the overall humorous effect of the selection.

3. Words to learn and use: foibles *(par. 1);* gonoid, thyroid, astrological *(par. 2);* zodiacal *(par. 3);* patently, insuperable, collaboration *(par. 7);* amenable *(par. 10).*

Generating Ideas

1. Write a paper based on a classification of "modern university types" (par. 13), including both females and males. Choose your own system for classifying.

2. Classify politicians or voters by using some system other than the customary broad classes of liberal *and* conservative.

3. Choose some large group of persons to classify according to a system that is inclusive and clear, then write a humorous paper describing the characteristics of each group. Here are some suggestions: students, professors or teachers, parents, sales clerks, automobile drivers, heroes, popular singers, policemen, sports personalities. For example, you might classify automobile drivers by a system based on their attitudes toward bikers and pedestrians.

4. Thurber's reaction to the behavior of the Quiet Type might be called "fresh" or "forward." Think of other types of approaches to this kind of person and write a humorous essay

*of classification in which you give various examples of the
"come-on" or "put-down."*

5. *Some words and incidents in Thurber's essay serve to date
it. Write a critical reaction to that "datedness," showing why
you find this characteristic appealing or objectionable. Be sure
to use specifics from the essay to support your opinion. For
instance, the porch swing (par. 13), once common in American
homes, is now largely obsolete.*

William Safire

William Safire (b. 1929) began his career as a reporter for the *New York Herald Tribune* Syndicate. He has been Washington columnist for the *New York Times* since 1973, and he has written numerous articles and essays on the American political scene. His book *Before the Fall* (1975) is an insider's account of the day-to-day operation of the Nixon administration before the Watergate scandal. Safire's interest in words and how they are used is evident in *The New Language of Politics* (1972), as it is in "Vogue Words Are Trific, Right?" The essay, which Safire calls his "first annual vogue-word watch," classifies the current crop of fad words and phrases in order to show the fickleness of American speech habits.

Vogue Words Are Trific, Right?

1   Vogue words are bits of language that slip into American speech, are disseminated far and wide by television talk shows, and make a person appear with-it. Many of the words run a flulike course and disappear, leaving memories of semantic headaches and fevered articulation. Others, like "détente," are formally banished by Presidential fiat. Here is my first annual vogue-word watch, compiled with the help of a few lexicographical colleagues around the country.

Vogues from All Over

2   Is a word merely for the nonce, or worth including in a dictionary? Some stalwart vogues seem to be establishing themselves as permanent features of the language. Among businessmen, "net net" has already faded, but *bottom line* (the "final accounting" or "essence") is spreading. Among youthful linguists, "way to go" has faded, "no way" is borderline, but the familiar *into*—as "he's into slang"—is putting down roots, and lexicographer David Guralnik thinks it may get into non-nonce status.

3   "Getting it together," picked up by lemminglike copywriters for commercials, has been dropped by the coiners who originate these phrases; "mellow," which went the opposite route, is also on the wane, as is "laid back," which might originally have had a sexual connotation but more

---

likely springs from reclining seats on motorcycles. "Heavy," a 40's word for "villain," became a 60's word for "depressing" but is sinking. *Off the wall,* on the other hand—which comes from the squash court and means "unexpected" or "veering crazily"—shows signs of life.

"That bums me out" has already given way to "that cracks me up," and the jazzman's "suss it out" (figure it out) doesn't seem to figure. The disgusted "yecchy," with its comic-strip origins, fades, but the equally disgusted *gross* (ugly, objectionable, and sometimes used admiringly) shows staying power. (To many, a "gross national product" is a derogation of the country's goods.)

Televisionese

The use of the phrase *has learned* to mean "found out" has been growing. "CBS has learned" does three things: *(1)* removes the need for *sourcing* (a journalism vogue word for identifying the person responsible for a story), *(2)* gives the impression of being the first to know and to tell the viewer and *(3)* plugs the network. The report is given as a certainty—much more solid than "reliable sources say"—but conceals, or covers up, the fact that nobody is willing to stand behind the message except the medium.

Private person is the *sine qua non* of soap operas and daytime talk shows. Nobody is an introvert any more; hermits no longer exist; damnable publicity-shunners have drifted from the scene—today, anybody who will not grant an interview is a "very private person."

Bleep has become a usable word-substitute, from the sound made when a word is excised from a tape. Columnist Herb Caen has popularized this as a euphemism, lexicographer Peter Tamony reports—as in: "That's no bull-bleep."

Testimony Talk

From the land of "to the best of my knowledge," comes the verb of perjury-avoiding fuzziness: *indicate.* Under cross-examination, nobody ever "said" or "told me" or even "suggested"—rather, they "indicated." To indicate, which used to mean "to point to," as "he indicated they went thataway," has now become a cover-up word for "he may have told me this, at least that's the impression I got, but if he says no, then maybe I was mistaken." The use of "indicate" indicates guilt.

9   *Cover-up* was originally used to describe a specific obstruction of justice. Now this compound word is used to describe a compounded felony. Of the recent vogue words, "cover-up," still too young to lose its hyphen, also stands a good chance of making it into the dictionaries, just after the entry for *cover story,* a C.I.A.-ism whose cover appears to have been blown.

Adjectival Jive

10   Long ago, it was "hep," then it changed to "hip," then, in the 60's, "cool" took hold; now, perhaps from a sanguine view of cool, comes *cold-blooded,* to convey in-group approval.

11   If a woman is "sexy" she is over 30 and not to be trusted. The replacement is *foxy,* a "counter word" with plenty of connotation but no denotation. (While *lady* has been replaced by "woman" or "person" in liberated dicourse, it has taken over the place formerly held by "girl friend." "She's my lady," claims the former "fella," now the *dude.*)

12   Turning a noun into an adjective is the vogue among fun couples, but the vogue word fades fast: "dynamite" (sometimes pronounced "dyn-o-*mite,*" as on the "Good Times" television show), was last year's favorite modifier, as in "Those are dynamite boots," which is being replaced by *killer,* as in "That's a killer whip."

Camp Following

13   "Camp" means "so banal as to be perversely sophisticated." It began as "establishing a camp," which was what the veterans of the Civil War called their reunions, then became a word to define any meeting of an insiders' group, and was taken up by homosexuals to mean the daring use in public of previously private ways.

14   The fashionable-by-being-unfashionable idea has several modern off-shoots, not synonymous but related: *kinky, funky* and *glitzy.*

15   "Kinky," from the Scandinavian "kink," or curl, bend or twist, became popularized in the United States as "kinky hair," and was applied in the past decade to young fashion, as "off-beat, deliberately bizarre." The word has moved to the sexy, or foxy, world, and now tumbles out

of its pornucopia: "Kinky" means perverse or twisted, usually cruel, sex, and the word has held on long enough to
merit serious lexicographic attention.

"Funky" has traveled a happier road. Originally a jazz 16
term referring to the smell of cigar smoke, the word bot-
tomed out in meaning as "old cigars, old and decrepit
surroundings, just plain old." (Louis Armstrong often referred to "Funky Butt Hall, where I first heard Buddy Bol-
den play.") Later, as "old" became desirable, "funky"
gained its current meaning of "nostalgic," or sweetly
memorable, if cornball. (Some of those old cigars were
Havanas.)

"Glitzy," often used to describe *"kitsch"* (which is un- 17
conscious in its tastelessness) comes directly from the German *"glitzen,"* and means "sparkling," or dazzlingly
meretricious.

In sum, "kinky" has curled away from "funky" in mean- 18
ing, leaving funkiness next to glitziness, though that may
be a glitzening generality.

Right?

Where funkiness is next to glitziness, trendiness is surely 19
next to godliness, and nowhere is that better illustrated
than in the interrogative reassurance.

In the early 70's, the grunted "y'know?" studded the 20
speech of every teen-ager. Put it this way: "I was walking—
y'know?—down the street—y'know?—and I ran into this
splivvy dude, y'know?" Youth responds quickly to ridicule
(adults move slowly, which is why "viable" and "meaningful" linger on) and when others began saying "No, I don't
know," "y'know?" began its disappearance.

However, the need for constant verbal reassurance re- 21
mained. Many people believe they are not being listened
to, or believe their listeners do not believe in them as a
source of communication. Thus, *right* has emerged, not
as something that makes might, but as a word that makes
a speaker feel secure, and usually as part of a historical
present tense: "Now I'm taking this walk—right?—down
the street—right?—minding my own business—right?"

Trific

Finally, the adjective-as-encouragement-to-continue. In 22
some discourses, encouragement is direct: "keep talking"

became "I dig" which became "lay it on me" and now crosses its transcendental t's with *keep it flowing.*

23   In most current speech, however, a single adjective is preferred. In the 30's, this was "fine-'n-dandy." In the 50's, "super" made the grade; in the 60's "fantastic" became a word used not to express amazement, but understanding; and in the early 70's, "beautiful"—usually murmured, head nodding as if in mutual meditation—became the most frequently used word of approval and reassurance. "I found a fish, y'know?" "Beautiful."

24   Today, the adjective-as-encouragement has become *terrific,* sometimes pronounced with two syllables, "trific." The root meaning—as that which causes one to "wriggle in fear"—changed to "tremble with enthusiasm"; after a brief vogue in the early 60's, "terrific" has returned with a rush. "I found a fish—right?" "Trific." Often, the word is repeated, just as "beautiful" used to be: "Now we're sitting around here at The Times—right? and we get this idea—right? for a piece on the way people talk today—right?" "Trific, trific. . . ."

Discussing Content and Form

1.   Where does Safire make a statement defining the area that he will treat in his classification? Why is it logical to limit the area as he does?

2.   A writer usually classifies a subject according to a single system or principle. Can you find a single system in this essay? Is one necessary? Explain why or why not. What determines the major *divisions?*

3.   Explain any principles of classification that you find used within the subdivisions. For instance, how much of the essay classifies vogue words that are adjectives?

4.   How much of the treatment within the subdivisions is devoted to tracing the history of certain vogue words? How much to comparing former ones to present favorites? How much to defining their meaning? Draw some conclusions about Safire's blending of these various expository methods.

5.   Which of the words or phrases Safire mentions are familiar to you? Which have you heard in the past but now consider out of date? Point out any that have changed meanings or to which you assign meanings different from those given in the essay.

6.   What is Safire's purpose? Is he objecting to the use of vogue words or satirizing the practice? Explain.

Considering Special Techniques

1.   How would you characterize the tone of this selection?

2.   Look carefully at the sentences and phrases with which Safire weaves his numerous examples together. What conclusions can you draw about his word choice apart from the examples of vogue words? Note, for instance, the opening sentence: "Vogue words are bits of language that slip into American speech, are disseminated far and wide by television talk shows, and make a person appear with-it."

3.   Safire comments on the practice of "turning a noun into an adjective" (par. 12). Later he explains "funky" (par. 16) and "glitzy" (par. 17); and at the beginning of paragraph 19, he turns these adjectives into nouns: "Where funkiness is next to glitziness . . . ." Point out other examples from the essay of words which shift from one part of speech to another. Think also of some examples that are not included in the selection.

4.   Explain these words and phrases: "semantic headaches" (par. 1); "lexicographical colleagues" (par. 1) and "lexicographer" (par. 2); "nonce" and "non-nonce status" (par. 2). What is the play on words in the phrase "tumbles out of its pornucopia" (par. 15)? What irony is involved in the phrase "interrogative reassurance" (par. 19)? Who is being reassured? How does the interrogative reassurance differ from the "adjective-as-encouragement-to-continue" (pars. 22–24)?

Generating Ideas

1.   Do a "vogue-word watch" of your own and classify the words you hear in conversation, on television, or see in print during the next few days. Although you will include some of the same words that Safire cites, you will undoubtedly have others as well.

2.   Write an essay about speech habits such as the constant use of "y'know" and "I mean." You might attempt to classify such filler words, or you might just give examples and discuss the effect that such habits have on the flow of speech or ease of listening.

3. Although laments about the decline of language are not new, several recent books have given the subject considerable attention. Read one of these, or part of one, and write a paper explaining how the ideas you find there apply to your own speech habits: Edwin Newman, Strictly Speaking *(1974) and* A Civil Tongue *(1976); Neil Postman and Charles Weingartner,* Language in America *(1970); Herman Estrin,* The American Language of the 70's *(1974).*

4. Browse through a copy of the Barnhart Dictionary of the New English Since 1963 *(1973) and select a number of words you can use for a classification paper. Be sure to limit your area of classification and to follow a single principle of organization. For instance, if your principle is "new words that interest me," you might classify them according to the various reasons for your special interest.*

5. Today we hear a great deal about sexist language. Write a paper in which you classify words that seem to you offensive because of their intended sex bias. Two recent books that might be useful here are Casey Miller's and Kate Swift's Words and Women *(1976), and Mary Ritchie Key's* Male-Female Language *(1975).*

6. There has been a great deal of critical talk about political language, bureaucratic jargon, or "double-speak." After doing some research, write a paper classifying a few of the terms from political talk that seem to you to conceal rather than to reveal the issues. As a way of getting started, you might check George Orwell's well-known essay, "Politics and the English Language."

11
Making a Telling Point:
Argument and *Persuasion*

"My firm opinion is . . . ." "There is plenty of proof . . . ." "You must believe that . . . ." In writing as in speech we constantly state propositions, take stands on issues or actions, and back up views with argument in order to persuade someone to agree. The writers of many of the essays in this text have not only given information but they have also expressed opinions; and in the process of explaining their subjects they have tried by various methods, subtle or obvious, to win agreement. Thus expository writing often has an argumentative edge, for a writer may explain and persuade simultaneously. The writer whose primary purpose is to persuade makes use of the expository techniques—arranging examples, comparing one thing to another, defining terms, tracing cause-effect relationships, and so on. But in persuasive writing, there are other methods used by the persuader that are worthy of special examination.

Consider some of the persuasive writing that occurs in daily life. One advertiser points out that a small car provides better gas mileage, while another hints that a large one gives its owner status. A political candidate hands out pamphlets explaining his proposals for cutting property taxes or building a downtown parking area. An editorialist denounces the city council for failing to extend bus service to the suburbs, or criticizes a President's cabinet appointments.

In every case the success of the persuasion depends on how well the writer reaches the intended audience. One of the writer's first requirements is to assess the interests and opinions of the reader, and then to decide on the kind of tone to employ in presenting the subject. Overdoing—

"the hard sell"—may offend; belittling—"talking down"—may insult; emotional appeals—"loaded language"—may be detected and assumed false, even in a good cause. It is usually safest to regard the reader as an intelligent thinker who will best respond to well-considered proof and careful logic. And it is usually best to assume an attitude of mutual concern, writing as one who shares rather than browbeats or badgers.

A classic failure in persuading is exemplified by Dr. Stockman, the main character of Henrik Ibsen's play *An Enemy of the People.* Dr. Stockman is a medical officer who discovers that the baths from which his town makes a living are polluted and that the people who visit the town are in danger of being infected from the waters. Envisioning himself as a savior with a message for which he feels certain he will win acclaim, Stockman rashly misjudges his audience and offends them with his arrogance. Even though he is completely right in what he says, he fails to win their support.

Although tone is important, good persuasion ultimately rests firmly on sound knowledge, on a command of the facts on all sides of an issue. Sufficient information, whether gathered by direct observation or by up-to-date research, is essential not only for building a convincing case but also for anticipating and refuting possible counterarguments.

Persuasive writing uses two principal methods: (1) logical argument, and (2) appeal to the emotions. Satiric persuasion is sometimes considered a third method, but satire usually combines the other two. In "A Modest Proposal" (p. 345), Jonathan Swift uses both logic and emotion, so that the difference is one of tone rather than of method. In persuasion as in exposition, the methods overlap, and most persuasion involves both logical argument and emotional appeal.

Because it is very prevalent and familiar in everyday life, it may be easier to consider emotional persuasion first. Arousing a reader's emotions depends largely upon choosing words with strong connotations to elicit a desired response. The use of such language colors almost every controversial issue. Environmentalists, for example, call industrialists "polluters" or "profiteering destroyers of national wildlife," while industry labels some conservation groups "obstructionists who are destroying our national economy." Repetition, especially of such strong words and of rhythmic sentence patterns, also helps move an audience or reader. The charged language and the rhythmic sentences of this passage first stirred readers during the American Revolution:

> These are the times that try men's souls. The summer soldier and the sunshine patriot will in this crisis, shrink from the service of his country; but he that stands it NOW, deserves the love and thanks of man and woman. Tyranny, like hell, is not easily conquered; yet we have this consolation with us, that the harder the conflict, the more glorious the triumph. What we obtain too cheap, we esteem too lightly; 'tis dearness only that gives everything its value. Heaven knows how to put a proper price upon its goods; and it would be strange indeed, if so celestial an article as FREEDOM should not be highly rated. Britain, with an army to enforce her tyranny, has declared that she has a right (*not only to* TAX) but "to BIND *us in* ALL CASES WHATSOEVER," and if being *bound in that manner,* is not slavery, then is there not such a thing as slavery upon earth. Even the expression is impious, for so unlimited a power can belong only to God.—Tom Paine, *The Crisis*

While such appeals can be sincere and moving, and can be effective in achieving immediate goals, they can also be dangerous and inaccurate. There is nothing inherently good or bad about appealing to the emotions, yet conscientious writers and wary readers must recognize the method and judge for themselves.

Logical argument proceeds by two chief avenues of reasoning—*induction* and *deduction.* Although the two are separated here for the purpose of examination, they function together in most pieces of persuasive writing. Inductive reasoning involves considering a number of particulars (facts, examples, observed phenomena) to arrive at a general conclusion. For example, if seven students you know get failing or D grades in Physics 101, you conclude that the course is difficult. Or if several bicycle owners mention that they find the Motobecane great for touring, you may decide to buy that make of bicycle. The scientist constantly employs induction. For instance, Samuel Scudder in Chapter 1 tells how his teacher expected him to observe a preserved fish and to reach conclusions about it; and Sally Carrighar in Chapter 9 explains how the ethologist observes animal behavior to arrive at generalized conclusions.

If the induction is sound, the particulars lead logically to the generalization by an *inductive leap,* or step in the thinking process. If the particulars are too few or are not representative, the reasoning will be illogical and will lead to a *hasty generalization.* From witnessing one accident involving a Triumph, you cannot logically conclude that sports cars are unsafe, nor can you assume that because a French restaurant in your neighborhood closes, your town does not appreciate continental cuisine. Such hasty generalizations will not convince a thinking reader.

Put simply, deductive reasoning is characterized by the application of the general to the specific, by moving from a general statement to further instances, similar cases, or comparable situations. The logician refers to this type of reasoning as a *syllogism,* and reducing an argument to syllogistic form is a test of the logic behind it. Follow the reasoning behind these syllogisms:

Major premise:	Students learn little in large classes.
Minor premise:	Classes in this school are large.
Conclusion:	Students in this school learn little.

Major premise:	Drivers who have accidents pay higher insurance rates.
Minor premise:	Tom recently had two accidents.
Conclusion:	Tom's insurance rate will increase.

If an argument is to hold up, to appear logical, the premises must be valid. Further induction, achieved by gathering additional evidence, may be necessary to validate the premises. In this way, the two types of logical reasoning work together. For instance, the first syllogism above may be considered too broad and the major premise may seem invalid. But if it were supported by data gathered from tests given in large classes and in smaller ones, the premise would be valid and the logic convincing.

Notice how evidence from history serves as the basis for an inductive leap to the conclusion in this paragraph:

> If anything conclusive could be inferred from experience, without psychological analysis, it would be that the things which women are not allowed to do are the very ones for which they are peculiarly qualified; since their vocation for government has made its way, and become conspicuous, through the very few opportunities which have been given;

while in the lines of distinction which apparently were freely open to them, they have by no means so eminently distinguished themselves. We know how small a number of reigning queens history presents, in comparison with that of kings. Of this smaller number a far larger proportion have shown talents for rule; though many of them have occupied the throne in difficult periods. It is remarkable, too, that they have, in a greater number of instances, been distinguished by merits the most opposite to the imaginary and conventional character of women: they have been as much remarked for the firmness and vigour of their rule, as for its intelligence. When, to queens and empresses, we add regents, and viceroys of provinces, the list of women who have been eminent rulers of mankind swells to a great length. This fact is so undeniable, that someone, long ago, tried to retort the argument, and turned the admitted truth into an additional insult, by saying that queens are better than kings, because under kings women govern, but under queens, men.—John Stuart Mill, *The Subjection of Women*

From Mill's "experience" of knowing about "a greater number of instances" in which women have ruled well in difficult times, he concludes that women are "peculiarly qualified" to govern. He might, of course, have named particular women who distinguished themselves as rulers, thereby making statements that were less abstract and more concrete, but the pattern of reasoning would remain the same. In contrast, this paragraph follows a deductive pattern:

I shall not go back to the remote annals of antiquity to trace the history of women; it is sufficient to allow, that she has always been either a slave or a despot, and to remark, that each of these situations equally retards the progress of reason. The grand source of female folly and vice has ever appeared to me to arise from narrowness of mind; and the very constitution of civil governments has put almost insuperable obstacles in the way to prevent the cultivation of the female understanding; yet virtue can be built on no other foundation! The same obstacles are thrown in the way of the rich, and the same consequences ensue.—Mary Wollstonecraft, *Observations on the State of Degradation to Which Woman Is Reduced by Various Causes*

The reasoning in this paragraph might be represented by a syllogism:

Slavery and despotism equally retard the progress of reason.

Women have always been either slaves or despots.

Therefore, women have been prevented from cultivating their powers of reason.

Effective persuasive writing involves several stages of development: first, a thoughtful presentation of the writer's self, a careful analysis of the intended audience, and a considered choice of tone provide the foundation. Second, a thorough knowledge of particulars (the basis for induction) and sound deductive logic establish the reasonableness of the argument. Finally, a judicious use of emotional appeals helps move the reader. Although the same methods may be utilized to persuade for wrong causes as for right ones, the ethical sense of the persuader and the intelligent appraisal by the reader should, ideally at least, guard against persuasion for wrong purposes.

Howard Temin

Howard Temin (b. 1935) is Professor of Oncology at the University of Wisconsin-Madison. He was awarded the 1975 Nobel Prize in Medicine for his research into the genetic basis of cancer. Temin's work at McArdle Laboratories continues to point the way for further research into the causes and cures for cancer. He has consistently spoken for the elimination of cancer-producing agents from the environment, as he does in the following selection. "A Warning to Smokers" was first presented as a speech to a Senate subcommittee, one of several Temin has delivered in his support of increased governmental regulation of research funding.

A Warning to Smokers

My point of view is that of a cancer researcher who has been working for the last 20 years with RNA viruses that cause cancer in chickens.

1
Statement of position as researcher (establishes speaker) (par. 1)

Since the early years of this century, it has been known that viruses cause cancer in chickens. In more recent years viruses have been shown to cause cancer not only in chickens, but also in mice, cats, and even in some primates. Therefore, it was a reasonable hypothesis that viruses might cause cancer in humans and that, if a human cancer virus existed, it could be prevented by a vaccine as so many other virus diseases have been prevented.

2
Summary of earlier hypothesis about possible cause and cure of cancer (provides background) (pars. 2–4)

Experiments performed in recent years have led to an understanding of much of the genetic basis of how viruses cause cancer in animals, namely, by adding their genetic information to the DNA, that is, the genetic material, of the cell. With this understanding and the tools of molecular biology, it has been possible to look for viruses potentially preventable by vaccines that might cause human cancer. Unfortunately, I think we can now

3

Dr. Howard Temin's address to the U.S. Congress on the effects of smoking as it appeared in "Editor's Notebook," *Wisconsin State Journal*, March 3, 1976. Reprinted by permission.

conclude that most human cancer is not caused by such viruses.

4

Scientifically this conclusion is an advance, for science progresses by disproving hypotheses. But, in terms of preventive medicine, I believe this conclusion ends the hope for a vaccine that would prevent cancer caused by viruses.

5

Transition (par. 5)

Must we, therefore, give up hope of preventing cancer?

6

Presentation of currently accepted hypothesis and call for action (par. 6)

No. For in recent years, the hypothesis that chemicals and radiation probably cause cancer by mutation of the cell genome has been strongly supported. Furthermore, epidemiological evidence has shown that the incidence of human cancer is not the same in all parts of the world and in all population groups, but that the incidence of human cancer varies from country to country, region to region, and population group to population group depending on the nature of the environment. Therefore, there must be environmental features that play a determining role in the formation of human cancer. One of the most clearly established of these environmental features is smoking, especially cigaret smoking. Cigaret smokers not only have a much greater probability of developing lung cancer than do otherwise similar nonsmokers, but the smokers have a greater probability of dying from a number of other diseases. Therefore, our best present hope of preventing cancer does not appear to lie in a vaccine against viruses, but in removing or reducing the levels of chemical carcinogens from the environment.

7

Expression of main point: cigaret smoking is the greatest source of carcinogens (states proposition) (par. 7)

The single most important source of these carcinogens and the one which should be most easily removable is tobacco, probably especially the tars from tobacco. The American Cancer Society estimates that the life expectancy of a man of 25 who continually smokes 2 packs of cigarets a day is 8 years less than that of a 25-year-old nonsmoker. Stopping cigaret smoking would have the greatest effect on increasing life expectancy, but, if that is not possible, reducing the level of tar from tobacco would at least serve to reduce the cancer risk of smokers. Therefore, if a tax based on the level of tar and nicotine in cigarets decreased the amount of exposure to tar, it would help to prevent some of the cancers which otherwise would be caused by smoking.

However, further research is still needed on cancer and other diseases both to help prevent those diseases that are not caused by smoking and to help cure those diseases that cannot be prevented. For example, we need to develop better therapies for cancer based upon an understanding of the differences in biochemistry and control of cell multiplication between cancer cells and normal cells. Comparison of virus-transformed cells and normal cells is one of the best systems to find such differences.

8
Call for better methods of cancer prevention (makes proposals) (pars. 8–9)

However, we must try even harder to prevent cancer before it starts, since so far it has been difficult to find many biochemical differences between cancer cells and normal cells that can be exploited in therapy. For prevention, we must devise better methods of testing for factors in the environment, including chemicals from industrial processes and possibly food additives, that can cause cancer, and after we find these factors we must try to remove them. In addition, we must try to understand more of the mechanisms by which chemicals and radiation cause cancer in the hope that such knowledge will make it easier for us to recognize these carcinogens and perhaps to devise means to prevent their action. However, when, as in the case of smoking, we find that a carcinogen exists, we must act to prevent it from entering the environment.

9

From the point of view of a scientist engaged in cancer research, it is paradoxical that the U.S. people, through Congress spend hundreds of millions of dollars a year for re-

10
Statement that government should take stronger stand on smoking (par. 10)

search to prevent and cure human cancer. But when we can say how to prevent much human cancer, namely, stop cigaret smoking, little or nothing is done to prevent this cancer. In fact, I believe the U.S. government even subsidizes the growing of tobacco. As I said at the Nobel festival banquet in Stockholm, I am outraged that this one major method available to prevent much human cancer, namely the cessation of cigaret smoking, is not more widely adopted.

11

Call for care in government research funding (par. 11)

I should also like to comment on a possible large increase in funding for biomedical and other health-related research. At present the U.S. system of support of biomedical research and the results of this biomedical research are the best in the world. Therefore, we must be careful before undertaking drastic changes in the way we fund biomedical research, and we should especially be careful to ensure that quality is stressed in all biomedical research. An excellent way to insure this quality is the system of peer review of grants used at NIH. Furthermore, although at a particular time we might wish to work on a particular problem in biomedical research or solve some health-related problems, if techniques and theoretical knowledge are not advanced enough to supply a proper foundation for the research, it may not be possible to approach such problems. Nature yields her secrets slowly, and only when a proper foundation of previous knowledge exists. Therefore, I wonder about the advisability of trying to spend rapidly much larger sums of money in this area. I suggest that a large and rapid increase in money is not warranted. More important is a mechanism for assurance of continuing support of good basic biomedical research and a good peer review system.

12

Recapitulation of previous views (par. 12)

In conclusion, I feel that the support previously extended to cancer research by the U.S. people through the Congress indicates a concern with preventing this disease. Research indicates that the best present method available to prevent much cancer is to decrease smoking. I, therefore, support Congressional action to decrease smoking.

Discussing Content and Form

1. Speakers and writers often establish their credentials—their "right to speak" on a subject—before beginning their main presentation, a convention that Temin follows in his first paragraph. What effect does his position as a scientist have on the tone, form, and content of the selection? What further personal qualifications does he mention after that paragraph?

2. Why do you think Temin dismisses the idea that cancer is caused by viruses before stating his own position?

3. Make a list of all the facts Temin presents in the order in which he presents them. Are his opinions and recommendations based logically on his facts? Explain.

4. Explain the statement, "science progresses by disproving hypotheses" (par. 4).

5. Is Temin's essay persuasive enough to convince you that cigaret smoking is a cause of cancer? If you are a smoker, is it persuasive enough to convince you to quit smoking? Why or why not?

Considering Special Techniques

1. Speakers and writers of persuasion must be especially sensitive to the audience they are addressing. How does the fact that this is a statement to a Senate subcommittee affect the tone, the form, and the content?

2. What is the effect of the single question paragraph (par. 5)? What is the effect of answering with the single word "No" (par. 6)?

3. Does Temin's use of scientific terms (DNA, cell genome, carcinogens, etc.) interfere with your understanding? Why or why not?

4. Restate paragraphs 6 and 7 in the form of syllogisms, and discuss the logic of Temin's deductive arguments.

5. *Examine some of the phrases and words that Temin uses to indicate logical connections between ideas: e.g., "With this understanding" and "we can now conclude" (par. 3); and in paragraph 6 he uses "Furthermore" once and "Therefore" twice. Why are such links especially important in Temin's argument?*

Generating Ideas

1. *Write a persuasive paper using the material in Temin's report and designing it for the popular audience of a magazine such as* Reader's Digest.

2. *Write a persuasive paper in which you present your view that no-smoking areas in public buildings should (or should not) be strictly enforced. Direct the paper to a specific audience, for example, an alderman or city council.*

3. *Make a study of the amount of money the U.S. government has spent on subsidizing the tobacco industry over the last few years and write a paper in which you suggest how this money could have been used for such purposes as health-related research. Or, write a paper in which you show the political reasons behind the tobacco subsidy.*

4. *Write a paper using the following sentence from the selection as a thesis statement: "Nature yields her secrets slowly, and only when a proper foundation of previous knowledge exists." Support your statements by citing examples.*

5. *In the* New Yorker, *December 13, 1976, and December 20, 1976, Paul Brodeur in "A Reporter at Large," discusses the biological effects of long-term, low-level microwave radiation on radar technicians and microwave workers. Read these articles and write a paper in which you present Brodeur's information, his conclusions and recommendations, and your opinion of the validity of his arguments. Also give your reactions to the government policy followed in the situations Brodeur presents.*

Robert Coles

Robert Coles (b. 1929) is a psychiatrist, social commentator, and author. After receiving his medical degree from Columbia University, he served on the staffs of several hospitals; he is now research psychiatrist with Harvard University Health Services. Coles, who has written for numerous magazines and is contributing editor for the *New Republic,* has published many books on mental health and the problems of youth. Among them are *Children of Crisis* (three volumes, 1968–71), *Dead End School* (1968), *Uprooted Children* (1970), *The Wages of Neglect* (1972), and *The Buses Roll* (1974). "On the Meaning of Work" employs several methods of persuasion to carry Coles' point that emphasizing industrial production at the expense of human dignity is dehumanizing and destructive.

On the Meaning of Work

In early December of 1934 a serious and scholarly young French lady, about to turn twenty-six, took a job in a factory at the outskirts of Paris. Day after day she operated a drill, used a power press, and turned a crank handle. From doing so Simone Weil became tired and sad, but she persisted—and all the while kept a "factory journal." In time she moved to another factory, there to pack cartons under distinctly unfavorable circumstances. She felt cramped, pushed, and in general badly used, even as her co-workers did; eventually she was fired. Still undaunted, she found employment in the well-known Renault works, the pride of industrial France. She lived in a world of machines and shop stewards and intense heat and long working days. She saw men and women hurt and insulted, men and women grow weak and bitter and weary. She also saw men and women struggle hard to find what joy and humor they could amid those long stretches of dangerous and exhausting work. Enraged, at a loss to know what she thought and believed to be true, she kept at her job. She also kept asking her co-workers to share their thoughts with her.

Simone Weil was a moral philosopher, a theologian, some would say. She had no interest in studying factory life sociologically or analyzing the psychological "adjustment" of workers to their jobs. Nor was she trying to see how "the other half" lives for one or another reason. She had in mind no shocking news stories as she worked week after week, month after month. She was not out to prove that the modern worker is "exploited" or on the verge of joining some "revolution"—or alternatively, happy beyond anyone's comprehension but his own. Though her mind was capable of constructing its fair share of abstractions, she sensed the danger of doing so. An intellectual, she profoundly distrusted, even scorned, the dozens and dozens of writers and scholars and theorists who wrote with assurance about the workingman and his lot. Instead she wanted to place herself in the very midst of what interested her, there to learn from concrete experience— and only later would she stop and ask herself what she *believed,* what she had to *say,* about subjects like "the effect of work on the worker," subjects that she well knew a mind like hers was tempted to seize and probe and dissect without the slightest exposure to a Renault factory building, let alone those who work inside it.

3   Eventually she would carry her experiences to the countryside; she learned to pick crops, plow the land, tend animals, and in general live the life of a peasant—to the point that she unnerved her hosts. She was no snob, no condescending "observer" bent on picking up a few facts, establishing a reputation of sorts, then hurrying off so as to cash in on the time spent "out there." The people with whom she stayed (at Bourges, about 100 miles due south of Paris) later remarked upon their guest's ability to cut through the barriers that naturally went to separate her from them—"and put herself at our level."

4   In fact Simone Weil wanted to do more than "understand" others, or make them feel that she was stooping ever so gracefully. She saw factory workers and field hands as her brothers and sisters, out of a deep and certainly religious need to do so, a longing she described (for herself and for the rest of us) in *The Need for Roots,* written toward the end of her short yet intense life. (She died in 1943 at the age of thirty-three.) In the book she emphasizes that we need desperately—indeed die spiritually if we do not have—a community, one whose life, whose values and customs and traditions, whose *sanction,* a person doesn't so much think about as take for granted. If that is not very original and surprising, Miss Weil's notion of

what a "community" is, or ought to be, goes much further; she sees us as always wanting to be in touch with others, not only our immediate families or more distant kin or our neighbors but those we work with, with whom we spend well over half our waking hours. For her, economists and political scientists (not to mention politicians), as well as psychologists and sociologists, all too often fail to grasp the true rhythms in life. True, they point out how much money we have or don't have, how much power one or another "class" has; or else they emphasize the lusts and rages we feel and try to express or subdue. Meanwhile, all over the world millions and millions of men and women (yes, and children) mark their lives by working, resting from work as best they can, and going back to work—until they die. And for Simone Weil it is with such day-to-day experiences that one who wants to comprehend man's nature and society's purposes ought to start.

Though she got on well with her fellow workers in several factories and on a farm, and though she held off at all times from extending cheap pity to those men and women, or condescension masked as moral outrage, or contempt dressed up as radical theory, she had to set down what she saw and heard. That is to say, she had to list the various kinds of suffering she saw among France's workers:

> We must change the system concerning concentration of attention during working hours, the types of stimulants which make for the overcoming of laziness or exhaustion—and which at present are merely fear and extra pay—the type of obedience necessary, the far too small amount of initiative, skill and thought demanded of workmen, their present exclusion from any imaginative share in the work of the enterprise as a whole, their sometimes total ignorance of the value, social utility, and destination of the things they manufacture, and the complete divorce between working life and family life. The list could well be extended.

She went on to do so; she extended her list and spelled out how life goes for millions of workmen in what she called "our industrial prisons"—where (she well knew) men are glad to be, rather than go hungry or be idle. But she was not primarily a social critic; perhaps more than anything else she was a visionary, hence easily written off as impractical—but uncannily able to say things starkly and prophetically and with apparent naïveté, which more cautious and "realistic" men only in time would come to see as indeed significant. So she noted how frightened and sullen her co-workers became, how drained they felt by the end of the day, how tempted they were to make minor mistakes, slow down, even at times cause considerable damage to the plant in which they worked or to the products they were turning out. Why is it so, she asked—why must men (in both America and Russia—that is, under capitalism and Communism alike) work in such huge, cold, impersonal places, and feel so fortunate (such is their vulnerability, their fear, their insecurity) for having even that kind of opportunity? The answer, no doubt, is that efficiency demands it; in a modern industrial nation mass production has to take place in large factories. Yet, in the France of the 1930s, Miss Weil saw what we in America are now beginning to notice and worry about: the dangers which a cult of efficiency and productivity, unqualified by ethical if not spiritual considerations, can present us with. She saw how much her worker friends needed one another, how hard they tried to enjoy one another's company, notwithstanding all the factory rules and regulations. She saw how tempted they were to stay off the job, to feign illness or offer some other excuse that enabled them to take at least this day off. She saw how greedy and thoughtless an industrial empire can become: land, water, air, raw materials, the lives of people—everything is grist for those modern mills of ours, which in turn are defended as necessary for our "advanced civilization," while all the while we cough and hold our noses and our ears and see about us an increasingly bleak and contaminated land, and feel upset as well, at a loss, and more than a little angry. The words and phrases are familiar, indeed have become clichés: absenteeism, ecological disaster, alienation, dehumanization, the loss of a sense of community.

7   Simone Weil sensed in her intuitive way that something was wrong, that a new order of attention must be given to the ordinary working man—whether he wears a blue collar or a white one—to his need for fellowship and dignity as well as money, to his struggle for meaning as well as possessions.

Working people with whom I have talked make quite   8
clear the ways they feel cornered, trapped, lonely, pushed
around at work, and, as Simone Weil kept on emphasizing,
confused by a sense of meaninglessness. These feelings,
I have noticed, often take the form of questions—and I
will take the liberty of paraphrasing some of them that
I have heard: What am I doing that *really matters?* What
is the point to it all—not life, as some philosophers say,
but the specific, tangible things I do or make? What would
I do if I had a real choice—something which I doubt I
ever will have? Is there some other, some better way to
work? Might we not break up these large factories and
offices, work closer to our homes, closer to one another
as workers—and work together on something that is not
a fragment of this, a minor part of that, but is whole and
significant and recognizable as important in our lives?

If those were "romantic" inquiries for a much-troubled   9
and fussy and brilliant French religious philosopher and
political essayist in the 1930s, they may not be altogether
impractical for us today. The workers I have heard may
not speak as Simone Weil did; but like her they are able
to be obsessed by the riddles and frustrations that life
presents—and like her, they can spot trouble when it is
in front of them, literally in the air, the dangerously contaminated air. As never before, our industrial societies
are now being forced to look inward, so to speak, to become
aware of the implications of our policies, among them
those followed by the thousands of businesses which employ millions of workers. No doubt in the 1930s a skeptic
could easily have made light of Simone Weil's concern
that the French landscape outside various giant factories
was in several ways being defaced. No doubt today what
she (and over the decades many, many workers) wanted
done inside those factories can still seem impractical. But
that word "impractical" is one that history has taught
us to think twice about. One generation's impracticality
has a way of becoming another's urgent necessity.

Discussing Content and Form

*1. How would you state the theme of the essay? Is it a plea
for a reform of working conditions or a protest against technology? Is it a plea for something broader than that? Explain.*

2. Explain why you think the writer chose to use the story of Simone Weil for all but the last two paragraphs of his essay. What special persuasive appeal does the narrative illustration have?

3. It may at first seem that Coles does not state his own conclusions about working people until the beginning of paragraph 8. Look again at paragraphs 6 and 7; at what point does Coles begin to move from the story of Simone Weil to his own interpretation and thesis?

4. Discuss Coles' concluding statement and give examples to illustrate its truth: "One generation's impracticality has a way of becoming another's urgent necessity."

5. What elements in the essay show that Coles has a medical background?

Considering Special Techniques

1. Like other persuasive writers, Coles carefully selects details in order to contribute forcefully to his point. Which of the details from Simone Weil's life—her "actions" as he reports them—have strong emotional appeal? What is the special effect of showing what she was "not out to prove" (par. 2)?

2. Coles uses a considerable amount of language for its emotional value. For instance, he calls Weil a "moral philosopher, a theologian, some would say" (par. 2) and a "visionary" who could "say things . . . prophetically" (par. 6). He speaks of the ways workers feel "cornered, trapped, lonely, pushed around" (par. 8). Find other words and phrases that are strongly emotive. Do you find the emotion excessive or effective? Is it justified in this context? Explain.

3. Examine some of Coles' long and rhythmic sentences. He often piles up details or descriptive words coordinately, *using* and *several times in one sentence. Notice, for instance, these sentences from paragraph 1: "She lived in a world of machines and shop stewards and intense heat and long working days. She saw men and women hurt and insulted, men and women grow weak and bitter and weary." What rhythmic effect is contributed by the extensive use of coordination here? What does the rhythmic pattern contribute to the style generally?*

4. One of the favorite devices of persuaders is the balanced sentence, in which several phrases or clauses of equal value are placed together in order to achieve a rhythmic effect. The follow-

*ing sentence, from paragraph 6, is arranged according to its
parallel or balanced elements:*
"So she noted

    (2)   how frightened and sullen her co-workers became,

    (2)   how drained they felt by the end of the day,

    (2)   how tempted they were

      (3)   to make minor mistakes

      (3)   [to] slow down

      (3)   even at times [to] cause considerable damage

        (4)   to the plant in which they worked

        (4)   or to the products they were turning out."

*Find other sentences in which balanced elements accumulate,
and discuss the effect of the rhythm produced by this device.*

5. *What is the effect of the series of questions in paragraph
8? Why are these arranged in the order that they are?*

6. *Words to learn and use:* undaunted *(par. 1);* theorists *(par.
2);* condescension *(par. 5);* uncannily, prophetically, naïveté, absenteeism, alienation, dehumanization *(par. 6). Explain these
phrases as they are used in the essay: "true rhythms in life"
(par. 4); "a visionary" (par. 6); "ecological disaster" (par. 6).*

Generating Ideas

1. *Write a paper in which you weigh the advantages and disadvantages of our "advanced civilization" and suggest a solution to the "dangers which a cult of efficiency and productivity, unqualified by ethical if not spiritual considerations, can present us with" (par. 6). Do you favor a return to a simpler way of life? Is this possible with our increased population?*

2. *Write a paper in which you argue for a particular solution to the frustration of working people who feel "cornered, trapped, lonely, pushed around at work." For instance, you might assert that the solution lies in a broad liberal education that would compensate individuals for their lack of feeling of accomplishment in their work. Or you might argue for the four-day work week or for "shared jobs" as ways of providing more freedom.*

Lewis Thomas

Lewis Thomas (b. 1913) earned his M.D. at Harvard, and has been dean of the medical schools at New York University–Bellevue and at Yale. President of Memorial Sloan-Kettering Cancer Center in New York since 1972, he is recognized nationally for his medical research. As a writer, Thomas has contributed to many scientific journals. *The Lives of a Cell* (1974), his first book, won a National Book Award in 1975. "Death in the Open," like the other chapters from the book, is an essay complete in itself. Here Thomas, in a style that may at first seem only mildly persuasive, gives a new perspective to society's attitudes toward death.

Death in the Open

1   Most of the dead animals you see on highways near the cities are dogs, a few cats. Out in the countryside, the forms and coloring of the dead are strange; these are the wild creatures. Seen from a car window they appear as fragments, evoking memories of woodchucks, badgers, skunks, voles, snakes, sometimes the mysterious wreckage of a deer.

2   It is always a queer shock, part a sudden upwelling of grief, part unaccountable amazement. It is simply astounding to see an animal dead on a highway. The outrage is more than just the location; it is the impropriety of such visible death, anywhere. You do not expect to see dead animals in the open. It is the nature of animals to die alone, off somewhere, hidden. It is wrong to see them lying out on the highway; it is wrong to see them anywhere.

3   Everything in the world dies, but we only know about it as a kind of abstraction. If you stand in a meadow, at the edge of a hillside, and look around carefully, almost everything you can catch sight of is in the process of dying, and most things will be dead long before you are. If it were not for the constant renewal and replacement going on before your eyes, the whole place would turn to stone and sand under your feet.

4   There are some creatures that do not seem to die at all; they simply vanish totally into their own progeny. Sin-

gle cells do this. The cell becomes two, then four, and so on, and after a while the last trace is gone. It cannot be seen as death; barring mutation, the descendants are simply the first cell, living all over again. The cycles of the slime mold have episodes that seem as conclusive as death, but the withered slug, with its stalk and fruiting body, is plainly the transient tissue of a developing animal; the free-swimming amebocytes use this organ collectively in order to produce more of themselves.

There are said to be a billion billion insects on the earth at any moment, most of them with very short life expectancies by our standards. Someone has estimated that there are 25 million assorted insects hanging in the air over every temperate square mile, in a column extending upward for thousands of feet, drifting through the layers of the atmosphere like plankton. They are dying steadily, some by being eaten, some just dropping in their tracks, tons of them around the earth, disintegrating as they die, invisibly.

Who ever sees dead birds, in anything like the huge numbers stipulated by the certainty of the death of all birds? A dead bird is an incongruity, more startling than an unexpected live bird, sure evidence to the human mind that something has gone wrong. Birds do their dying off somewhere, behind things, under things, never on the wing.

Animals seem to have an instinct for performing death alone, hidden. Even the largest, most conspicuous ones find ways to conceal themselves in time. If an elephant missteps and dies in an open place, the herd will not leave him there; the others will pick him up and carry the body from place to place, finally putting it down in some inexplicably suitable location. When elephants encounter the skeleton of an elephant out in the open, they methodically take up each of the bones and distribute them, in a ponderous ceremony, over neighboring acres.

It is a natural marvel. All of the life of the earth dies, all of the time, in the same volume as the new life that dazzles us each morning, each spring. All we see of this is the odd stump, the fly struggling on the porch floor of the summer house in October, the fragment on the highway. I have lived all my life with an embarrassment of squirrels in my backyard, they are all over the place, all year long, and I have never seen, anywhere, a dead squirrel.

9   I suppose it is just as well. If the earth were otherwise, and all the dying were done in the open, with the dead there to be looked at, we would never have it out of our minds. We can forget about it much of the time, or think of it as an accident to be avoided, somehow. But it does make the process of dying seem more exceptional than it really is, and harder to engage in at the times when we must ourselves engage.

10   In our way, we conform as best we can to the rest of nature. The obituary pages tell us of the news that we are dying away, while the birth announcements in finer print, off at the side of the page, inform us of our replacements, but we get no grasp from this of the enormity of scale. There are 3 billion of us on the earth, and all 3 billion must be dead, on a schedule, within this lifetime. The vast mortality, involving something over 50 million of us each year, takes place in relative secrecy. We can only really know of the deaths in our households, or among our friends. These, detached in our minds from all the rest, we take to be unnatural events, anomalies, outrages. We speak of our own dead in low voices; struck down, we say, as though visible death can only occur for cause, by disease or violence, avoidably. We send off for flowers, grieve, make ceremonies, scatter bones, unaware of the rest of the 3 billion on the same schedule. All of that immense mass of flesh and bone and consciousness will disappear by absorption into the earth, without recognition by the transient survivors.

11   Less than a half century from now, our replacements will have more than doubled the numbers. It is hard to see how we can continue to keep the secret, with such multitudes doing the dying. We will have to give up the notion that death is catastrophe, or detestable, or avoidable, or even strange. We will need to learn more about the cycling of life in the rest of the system, and about our connection to the process. Everything that comes alive seems to be in trade for something that dies, cell for cell. There might be some comfort in the recognition of synchrony, in the formation that we all go down together, in the best of company.

Discussing Content and Form

1. This essay moves from a series of particulars to a general conclusion. What seems to be the writer's purpose? State the thesis of the essay in your own words.

2. Explain the following statement and relate it to the essay as a whole: "In our way, we conform as best we can to the rest of nature" (par. 10). How does Thomas say we conform?

3. How do you explain the fact that animals conceal their dying? How does their dying compare with that of human beings? Why does Thomas say that we regard death as unnatural?

4. Explain the conclusion that "There might be some comfort in the recognition of synchrony . . ." (par. 11).

5. Which details in the essay reveal that the writer is a scientist? Is he writing for an audience of scientists or for people in general? Explain.

Considering Special Techniques

1. This essay offers an example of the inductive *pattern, moving as it does from specific examples to a general conclusion. Why does Thomas offer such a wide range of examples from the world of nature? What is the effect of these?*

2. Writers sometimes use a catalogue *technique, accumulating specifics to achieve a particular effect. Notice the list in this sentence: "Seen from a car window they appear as fragments, evoking memories of woodchucks, badgers, skunks, voles, snakes, sometimes the mysterious wreckage of a deer" (par.1). Point out other sentences that follow this pattern.*

3. Thomas uses many cumulative *sentences in which modifiers of various kinds are added after the main clause. Point out several sentences that follow this pattern and examine their effect on the style of the essay. Here are two examples:*
"It is the nature of animals to die alone, off somewhere, hidden" (par. 2).
"They are dying steadily, some by being eaten, some just dropping in their tracks, tons of them around the earth, disintegrating as they die, invisibly" (par. 5).

4. Thomas' reasoning involves the use of a very "strict" analogy: that is, he draws conclusions or points out similarities

*between two examples that may be said to be from the same
"class"—animal and human. Do you find the analogy between
animal and human dying in any way offensive? Why do you
think Thomas delayed the application to humanity until
paragraph 9?*

5. *Words to learn and use:* impropriety *(par. 2);* progeny, mutation, amebocytes *(par. 4);* plankton *(par. 5);* incongruity *(par.
6);* inexplicably *(par. 7);* enormity, anomalies *(par. 10);*
synchrony *(par. 11).*

Generating Ideas

1. *Thomas suggests that we should find "comfort in the recognition of synchrony," in the realization that death is part of a
natural process. Defend or attack his belief in an essay of your
own.*

2. *A great deal has been written recently about customs concerning death and dying. Write a persuasive paper defending
or attacking those customs you may be familiar with.*

3. *Use one of these lines from Thomas as the key idea for a
paper:*
*"Everything in the world dies, but we only know about it as a
kind of abstraction" (par. 3).*
*"We will need to learn more about the cycling of life in the
rest of the system, and about our connection to the process"
(par. 11). (This sentence could be applied to characteristics or
events other than death.)*

4. *Read at least two of these well-known poems and write a
paper presenting the poets' attitudes toward death: John Donne,
"Death Be Not Proud"; Emily Dickinson, "Because I Could Not
Stop for Death"; John Crowe Ransom, "Janet Waking"; Dylan
Thomas, "Do Not Go Gentle into That Good Night." Or read
William Cullen Bryant's "Thanatopis" and write a paper com-
paring the "comfort" expressed there to that suggested by Lewis
Thomas.*

Shirley Chisholm

Shirley Chisholm (b. 1924) attained national prominence in 1968 when she was elected to the U.S. House of Representatives from her home state of New York. After earning degrees from Brooklyn College and Columbia University, she became an influential educational consultant and authority on child welfare. Her autobiographical *Unbought and Unbossed* (1970) records the conflicts and struggles of her early political life, a theme she has continued in *The Good Fight* (1973). In "I'd Rather Be Black Than Female," she sets forth a proposition that is explained by the essay's title.

I'd Rather Be Black Than Female

Being the first black woman elected to Congress has made me some kind of phenomenon. There are nine other blacks in Congress; there are ten other women. I was the first to overcome both handicaps at once. Of the two handicaps, being black is much less of a drawback than being female. 1

If I said that being black is a greater handicap than being a woman, probably no one would question me. Why? Because "we all know" there is prejudice against black people in America. That there is prejudice against women is an idea that still strikes nearly all men—and, I am afraid, most women—as bizarre. 2

Prejudice against blacks was invisible to most white Americans for many years. When blacks finally started to "mention" it, with sit-ins, boycotts, and freedom rides, Americans were incredulous. "Who, us?" they asked in injured tones. *"We're* prejudiced?" It was the start of a long, painful reeducation for white America. It will take years for whites—including those who think of themselves as liberals—to discover and eliminate the racist attitudes they all actually have. 3

How much harder will it be to eliminate the prejudice against women? I am sure it will be a longer struggle. Part of the problem is that women in America are much more brainwashed and content with their roles as second-class citizens than blacks ever were. 4

Let me explain. I have been active in politics for more 5

---

than twenty years. For all but the last six, I have done the work—all the tedious details that make the difference between victory and defeat on election day—while men reaped the rewards, which is almost invariably the lot of women in politics.

6   It is still women—about three million volunteers—who do most of this work in the American political world. The best any of them can hope for is the honor of being district or county vice-chairman, a kind of separate-but-equal position with which a woman is rewarded for years of faithful envelope stuffing and card-party organizing. In such a job, she gets a number of free trips to state and sometimes national meetings and conventions, where her role is supposed to be to vote the way her male chairman votes.

7   When I tried to break out of that role in 1963 and run for the New York State Assembly seat from Brooklyn's Bedford-Stuyvesant, the resistance was bitter. From the start of that campaign, I faced undisguised hostility because of my sex.

8   But it was four years later, when I ran for Congress, that the question of my sex became a major issue. Among members of my own party, closed meetings were held to discuss ways of stopping me.

9   My opponent, the famous civil-rights leader James Farmer, tried to project a black, masculine image; he toured the neighborhood with sound trucks filled with young men wearing Afro haircuts, dashikis, and beards. While the television crews ignored me, they were not aware of a very important statistic, which both I and my campaign manager, Wesley MacD. Holder, knew. In my district there are 2.5 women for every man registered to vote. And those women are organized—in PTAs, church societies, card clubs, and other social and service groups. I went to them and asked their help. Mr. Farmer still doesn't quite know what hit him.

10   When a bright young woman graduate starts looking for a job, why is the first question always: "Can you type?" A history of prejudice lies behind that question. Why are women thought of as secretaries, not administrators? Librarians and teachers, but not doctors and lawyers? Because they are thought of as different and inferior. The happy homemaker and the contented darky are both stereotypes produced by prejudice.

11   Women have not even reached the level of tokenism

that blacks are reaching. No women sit on the Supreme Court. Only two have held Cabinet rank, and none do at present. Only two women hold ambassadorial rank. But women predominate in the lower-paying, menial, unrewarding, dead-end jobs, and when they do reach better positions, they are invariably paid less than a man gets for the same job.

If that is not prejudice, what would you call it? 12

A few years ago, I was talking with a political leader 13 about a promising young woman as a candidate. "Why invest time and effort to build the girl up?" he asked me. "You know she'll only drop out of the game to have a couple of kids just about the time we're ready to run her for mayor."

Plenty of people have said similar things about me. 14 Plenty of others have advised me, every time I tried to take another upward step, that I should go back to teaching, a woman's vocation, and leave politics to the men. I love teaching, and I am ready to go back to it as soon as I am convinced that this country no longer needs a woman's contribution.

When there are no children going to bed hungry in this 15 rich nation, I may be ready to go back to teaching. When there is a good school for every child, I may be ready. When we do not spend our wealth on hardware to murder people, when we no longer tolerate prejudice against minorities, and when the laws against unfair housing and unfair employment practices are enforced instead of evaded, then there may be nothing more for me to do in politics.

But until that happens—and we all know it will not be 16 this year or next—what we need is more women in politics, because we have a very special contribution to make. I hope that the example of my success will convince other women to get into politics—and not just to stuff envelopes, but to run for office.

It is women who can bring empathy, tolerance, insight, 17 patience, and persistence to government—the qualities we naturally have or have had to develop because of our suppression by men. The women of a nation mold its morals, its religion, and its politics by the lives they live. At present, our country needs women's idealism and determination, perhaps more in politics than anywhere else.

Discussing Content and Form

1.   Chisholm's title and thesis statement in paragraph 1 ("being black is much less of a drawback than being female") indicate that the essay centers on the problem of prejudice. How do the final paragraphs widen the initial thesis?

2.   Does the essay convince you that prejudice against women is stronger than prejudice against blacks? Why or why not?

3.   Why, according to Chisholm, do people fail to recognize the prejudice against women? On what basis does she say that the struggle for women will be even longer than that for blacks?

4.   What roles does Chisholm contend politicians have assigned to women? How do the examples from paragraphs 10 and 11 develop the general statement that "Women have not even reached the level of tokenism that blacks are reaching"?

5.   Chisholm says that we stereotype women, expecting them to be secretaries, not leaders; teachers, not politicians. Does the essay itself contain any material that could be considered stereotyping?

6.   What special contributions does Chisholm say that women can bring to politics? In what way does her own career show that she stands for the qualities that she says women can contribute (par. 17)?

Considering Special Techniques

1.   How much of the essay's persuasive power derives from Chisholm's personal history? What is the effect of the dates, names, and specific instances that Chisholm cites from her experience in politics, especially of the narrative incident in paragraph 9?

2.   How much of paragraph 11 is given to factual evidence? (You may wish to check to see which of these facts could now be changed, and just how much change is involved.) How much of the paragraph is judgment or generalization? What persuasive power is given the generalization by association with the facts in the paragraph?

3.   Analyze the pattern of the three sentences in paragraph 15. What is the effect of repeating that pattern? What is the effect of placing the longest of the sentences last?

4. Discuss the persuasive effect of these phrases and words:
"brainwashed and content" and "second-class citizens" (par.
4); "tedious details" and "men reaped the rewards" (par. 5);
"faithful envelope stuffing and card-party organizing" (par. 6);
"undisguised hostility" (par. 7); "lower-paying, menial, unre-
warding, dead-end jobs" (par. 11); "she'll only drop out . . .
to have a couple of kids" (par. 13). How would you characterize
the tone of the language in the essay?

Generating Ideas

1. Chisholm says that "Prejudice against blacks was invisible"
for many years (par. 3). Write a paper in which you analyze
what exactly invisible prejudice is, using specific examples to
prove your point.

2. Write a persuasive paper showing that prejudice plays a
dangerous role in our political choices (for instance, voting for
or against someone because of race, sex, religion, or some
personal characteristic). Use logical and suitable methods to
carry your argument.

3. Choose a thesis and write a paper on one of these ideas sug-
gested by Chisholm's essay:
a. The images politicians choose to project (see par. 9)
b. Women's power through organization (par. 9)
c. Tokenism (par. 11)
d. Investing time and training in young women (par. 13)
e. Need for women in politics (par. 16)

Neil Postman

Neil Postman is on the faculty of New York University, and is a writer on semantics and education. Perhaps his best-known book is *Teaching as a Subversive Activity* (1969), which he wrote with Charles Weingartner, a collaboration that has also produced *Linguistics: A Revolution in Teaching* (1966), *Language in America* (1970), and *The Soft Revolution* (1971). He has also written *Crazy Talk, Stupid Talk* (1976), from which "The Communication Panacea" is taken. In the essay he uses both logical and emotional persuasion to argue against what he considers the current preoccupation with the need to communicate.

The Communication Panacea

1   In the search for the Holy Grail of complete harmony, liberation, and integrity, which it is the duty of all true Americans to conduct, adventurers have stumbled upon a road sign which appears promising. It says, in bold letters, "All problems arise through lack of communication." Under it, in smaller print, it says: "Say what is on your mind. Express your feelings honestly. This way lies the answer." A dangerous road, it seems to me. It is just as true to say, This way lies disaster.

2   I would not go so far as Oliver Goldsmith, who observed that the principal function of language is to *conceal* our thoughts. But I do think that concealment is one of the important functions of language, and on no account should it be dismissed categorically. . . . Semantic environments have legitimate and necessary purposes of their own which do not always coincide with the particular and pressing needs of every individual within them. One of the main purposes of many of our semantic environments, for example, is to help us maintain a minimum level of civility in conducting our affairs. Civility requires not that we deny our feelings, only that we keep them to ourselves when they are not relevant to the situation at hand. Contrary to what many people believe, Freud does not teach us that we are "better off" when we express our deepest feelings. He teaches exactly the opposite: that civilization is impossible without inhibition. Silence, reticence, restraint, and, yes, even dishonesty can be great

virtues, in certain circumstances. They are, for example, frequently necessary in order for people to work together harmoniously. To learn how to say no is important in achieving personal goals, but to learn how to say yes when you want to say no is at the core of civilized behavior. There is no dishonesty in a baboon cage, and yet, for all that, it holds only baboons.

Now there are, to be sure, many situations in which trouble develops because some people are unaware of what other people are thinking and feeling. "If I'd only *known* that!" the refrain goes, when it is too late. But there are just as many situations which would get worse, not better, if everyone knew exactly what everyone else was thinking. I have in mind, for example, a conflict over school busing that occurred some time ago in New York City but has been replicated many times in different places. Whites against blacks. The whites maintained that they did not want their children to go to other neighborhoods. They wanted them close at hand, so that the children could walk home for lunch and enjoy all the benefits of a "neighborhood school." The blacks maintained that the schools their children attended were run-down and had inadequate facilities. They wanted their children to have the benefits of a good educational plant. It was most fortunate, I think, that these two groups were not reduced to "sharing with each other" their real feelings about the matter. For the whites' part, much of it amounted to, "I don't want to live, eat, or do anything else with niggers. Period." For the blacks' part, some of it, at least, included, "You honky bastards have had your own way at my expense for so long that I couldn't care less what happens to you or your children." Had these people communicated such feelings to each other, it is more than likely that there could have been no resolution to this problem. (This seems to have been the case in Boston.) As it was, the issue could be dealt with *as if* such hatred did not exist, and therefore, a reasonable political compromise was reached.

It is true enough, incidentally, that in this dispute and others like it, the charge of racism was made. But the word *racism,* for all its ominous overtones, is a euphemism. It conceals more than it reveals. What Americans call a *racist* public remark is something like "The Jews own the banks" or "The blacks are lazy." Such remarks are bad enough. But they are honorifics when compared to the "true" feelings that underlie them.

I must stress that the "school problem" did not arise in the first place through lack of communication. It arose because of certain historical, sociological, economic, and political facts which could not be made to disappear through the "miracle of communication." Sometimes, the less people know about other people, the better off everyone is. In fact, political language at its best can be viewed as an attempt to find solutions to problems by circumventing the authentic hostile feelings of concerned parties.

In our personal lives, surely each of us must have ample evidence by now that the capacity of words to exacerbate, wound, and destroy is at least as great as their capacity to clarify, heal, and organize. There is no good reason, for example, for parents always to be honest with their children (or their children always to be honest with them). The goal of parenthood is not to be honest, but to raise children to be loving, generous, confident, and competent human beings. Where full and open revelation helps to further that end, it is "good." Where it would defeat it, it is stupid talk. Similarly, there is no good reason why your boss always needs to know what you are thinking. It might, in the first place, scare him out of his wits and you out of a job. Then, too, many of the problems you and he have do not arise from lack of communication, but from the nature of the employer-employee relationship, which sometimes means that the less money you make, the more he does. This is a "problem" for a labor organizer, not a communication specialist.

Some large American corporations have, of late, taken the line that "improved communication" between employees and management will solve important problems. But very often this amounts to a kind of pacification program, designed to direct attention away from fundamental economic relationships. It is also worth noting that a number of such corporations have ceased to hold "communication seminars" in which executives were encouraged to express their "true" feelings. What happened, apparently, is that some of them decided they hated their jobs (or each other) and quit. Whether this is "good" or not depends on your point of view. The corporations don't think it's so good, and probably the families of the men don't either.

The main point I want to make is that "authentic com-   8
munication" is a two-edged sword. In some circumstances,
it helps. In others, it defeats. This is a simple enough idea,
and sensible people have always understood it. I am stress-
ing it here only because there has grown up in America
something amounting to a holy crusade in the cause of
Communication. One of the terms blazoned on its banners
is the phrase *real* (or *authentic*) feelings. Another is the
motto "Get in touch with your feelings!" From what I have
been able to observe, this mostly means expressing anger
and hostility. When is the last time someone said to you,
"Let me be *lovingly* frank"? The expression of warmth
and gentleness is usually considered to be a facade, masking what you are really thinking. To be certified as authentically in touch with your feelings, you more or less have
to be nasty. Like all crusades, the Communication Crusade
has the magical power to endow the most barbarous behavior with a purity of motive that excuses and obscures
just about all its consequences. No human relationship
is so tender, apparently, that it cannot be "purified" by
sacrificing one or another of its participants on the altar
of "Truth." Or, to paraphrase a widely known remark on
another subject, "Brutality in the cause of honesty needs
no defense." The point is that getting in touch with your
feelings often amounts to losing touch with the feelings
of others. Or at least losing touch with the purposes for
which people have come together.

A final word on the matter of "honesty." As I have said   9
before, human purposes are exceedingly complex—multi-
leveled and multilayered. This means that, in any given
situation, one does not have *an* "honest feeling," but a
whole complex of different feelings. And, more often than
not, some of these feelings are in conflict. If anger predominates at one instant, this does not mean it is more
"authentic" than the love or sorrow or concern with which
it is mingled. And the expression of the anger, alone, is
no less "dishonest" than any other partial representation
of what one is feeling. By *dishonesty,* then, I do not merely
mean saying the opposite of what you believe to be true.
Sometimes it is necessary to do even this in the interests
of what you construe to be a worthwhile purpose. But
more often, dishonesty takes the form of your simply not
saying *all* that you are thinking about or feeling in a given
situation. And, since our motives and feelings are never

all that clear, to our own eyes in any case, most of us are "dishonest" in this sense most of the time. To be aware of this fact and to temper one's talk in the light of it is a sign of what we might call "intelligence." Other words for it are discretion and tact.

10   The relevant point is that communication is most sensibly viewed as a means through which desirable ends may be achieved. As an end in itself, it is disappointing, even meaningless. And it certainly does not make a very good deity.

Discussing Content and Form

1.   What are Postman's objections to the belief that "All problems arise through lack of communication"? To what extent does he convince you that "civilization is impossible without inhibition"? Would you describe his position as moderate or extreme? Explain.

2.   Discuss the illustrations of the New York City and Boston conflicts over busing as "evidence" that open communication is harmful (par. 3).

3.   Although Postman deplores racist remarks, he worries that the full expression of "true" feelings might be even more harmful. What in the essay convinces you to accept this point? Where does Postman refute a possible opposing view? Explain.

4.   What function does the writer assign to "political language at its best" (par. 5)? Is this function usually thought of in connection with political language? Defend your answer.

5.   What basis does Postman offer for his statement that an "expression of warmth and gentleness is usually considered" a "facade" and that "To be certified as authentically in touch . . . you have to be nasty" (par. 8)? With what group does he mean that this is true?

6.   Explain the phrase "semantic environments" (par. 2). Apply Postman's idea that "the purpose of many of our semantic environments . . . is to help us maintain a minimum level of civility" (par. 2) to your circle of friends or to your neighbors at home.

7.   Postman is cautious not to make a sweeping generalization even though he makes a strong statement in his essay. Note such phrases as "I would not go so far . . . ." (par. 2) and "Now there are, to be sure, many situations in which trouble develops because some people are unaware of what other people are thinking and feeling" (par. 3). What does acknowledging exceptions contribute to the strength of the argument? What does this feature contribute to the impression the writer gives of himself? Discuss the importance of the writer's presentation of himself in a persuasive essay such as this.

8. In what sense is this essay an appeal for good manners?

Considering Special Techniques

1. Beginning with the "Holy Grail" in the first sentence, find several examples of language used to suggest the "religious" fervor of those who advocate communication as a panacea. What is the effect of repeating these words and images?

2. Argument by analogy has both advantages and dangers. Abraham Lincoln's analogy of the Union as a "house divided" was extremely effective as a stylistic device, but historians differ about its logic. What is your reaction to these analogies that Postman uses?
a. "adventurers have stumbled upon a road sign . . . . A dangerous road, it seems to me" (par. 1).
b. "There is no dishonesty in a baboon cage, and yet, for all that, it holds only baboons" (par. 2).

3. Why does Postman use quotation marks around such words and phrases as these: the "true" feelings that underlie them (par. 4); "school problems " (par. 5); "miracle of communication" (par. 5); Whether this is "good" (par. 7); A final word on the matter of "honesty" (par. 9)? If you think the quotation marks are unnecessary, explain your reasons for thinking so. What is the difference between using the quotation marks in these instances and the italics for the words conceal (par. 2) and real and authentic (par. 8)? You may point out other examples of both methods of punctuation as you consider the reasons for the writer's choice.

4. Why are balanced sentences such as the following easy to remember?
a. "Civility requires not that we deny our feelings, only that we keep them to ourselves . . ." (par. 2).
b. ". . . to learn how to say yes when you want to say no is at the core of civilized behavior" (par. 2).
c. "Sometimes, the less people know about other people, the better off everyone is" (par. 5).

*What does their memorability contribute to the persuasion?
Find other sentences in which the phrasing makes for easy
retention.*

*5.   Point out instances of Postman's use of irony or mild sar-
casm. Here is one example: "The corporations don't think
it's so good, and probably the families of the men don't either"
(par. 7). Would you call such use of irony emotional or logical persuasion? Why?*

6.   Words to learn and use: categorically, semantic, civility, inhibition *(par. 2);* honorifics *(par. 4);* circumventing *(par. 5);*
exacerbate *(par. 6);* facade, barbarous *(par. 8);* predominates,
construe *(par. 9).*

Generating Ideas

*1.   Write a paper about experiences you have had with people
who practice "lovingly frank" communication. Or write
about an experience in which you communicated exactly what
was on your mind.*

*2.   Think of other personal and social panaceas that people
sometimes advocate: for instance, jogging or a particular diet
as a preventative for almost every physical problem; more
(or less) education as a universal cure-all; or a four-day work
week as the answer to employee discontent. Write a paper refuting the belief in such a panacea.*

*3.   It has been estimated that about twelve trillion words a year
are uttered by people in the world. Write a persuasive paper
about some aspect of talk. These titles may give you some help:
"More Talk Would Help"; "Let's Have More Action and Less
Talk"; "Talking Is a Way to Stall."*

*4.   Write an essay using one of these lines from Postman as
your key idea:
"Civilization is impossible without inhibition" (par. 2).
"Sometimes the less people know about other people, the better
off everyone is" (par. 5).*

*5.   What are your opinions about greeting cards that contain
"humorous" insults? Are they amusing or are they ways to cloak
hidden hostilities? Are they an escape valve? Are they merely
a reaction against overly sentimental cards? Is it better to send
or receive such a card than none at all? Write a persuasive
paper condemning or defending the practice of sending such
cards.*

Jonathan Swift

Jonathan Swift (1667–1745), one of the greatest satirists in English literature, was the son of English parents residing in Ireland. Ordained as
an Anglican clergyman, he eventually became Dean of St. Patrick's,
Dublin, in 1713. During this time he began to write poetry, as well as
religious and political satire, most notably *The Battle of the Books* (1704)
and *A Tale of the Tub* (1704). In 1726 he published his best-known work,
Gulliver's Travels. "A Modest Proposal" (1729), one of a series of pamphlets he wrote on the English oppression of the Irish, is one of the
most bitter and outrageous satires in our language.

A Modest Proposal

For Preventing the Children of Poor People in Ireland from Being a Burden to Their Parents or Country, and for Making Them Beneficial to the Public

It is a melancholy object to those who walk through this
great town or travel in the country, when they see the
streets, the roads, and cabin doors, crowded with beggars
of the female-sex, followed by three, four, or six children,
all in rags and importuning every passenger for an alms.
These mothers, instead of being able to work for their
honest livelihood, are forced to employ all their time in
strolling to beg sustenance for their helpless infants, who,
as they grow up, either turn thieves for want of work,
or leave their dear native country to fight for the Pretender
in Spain, or sell themselves to the Barbadoes.

I think it is agreed by all parties that this prodigious
number of children in the arms, or on the backs, or at
the heels of their mothers, and frequently of their fathers,
is in the present deplorable state of the kingdom a very
great additional grievance; and therefore whoever could
find out a fair, cheap, and easy method of making these
children sound, useful members of the commonwealth
would deserve so well of the public as to have his statue
set up for a preserver of the nation.

But my intention is very far from being confined to provide only for the children of professed beggars; it is of a
much greater extent, and shall take in the whole number
of infants at a certain age who are born of parents in
effect as little able to support them as those who demand
our charity in the streets.

4   As to my own part, having turned my thoughts for many years upon this important subject, and maturely weighed the several schemes of other projectors, I have always found them grossly mistaken in their computation. It is true, a child just dropped from its dam may be supported by her milk for a solar year, with little other nourishment; at most not above the value of two shillings, which the mother may certainly get, or the value in scraps, by her lawful occupation of begging; and it is exactly at one year old that I propose to provide for them in such a manner as instead of being a charge upon their parents or the parish, or wanting food and raiment for the rest of their lives, they shall on the contrary contribute to the feeding, and partly to the clothing, of many thousands.

5   There is likewise another great advantage in my scheme, that it will prevent those voluntary abortions, and that horrid practice of women murdering their bastard children, alas, too frequent among us, sacrificing the poor innocent babes, I doubt, more to avoid the expense than the shame, which would move tears and pity in the most savage and inhuman breast.

6   The number of souls in this kingdom being usually reckoned one million and a half, of these I calculate there may be about two hundred thousand couple whose wives are breeders; from which number I subtract thirty thousand couples who are able to maintain their own children, although I apprehend there cannot be so many under the present distresses of the kingdom; but this being granted, there will remain an hundred and seventy thousand breeders. I again subtract fifty thousand for those women who miscarry, or whose children die by accident or disease within the year. There only remain an hundred and twenty thousand children of poor parents annually born. The question therefore is, how this number shall be reared and provided for, which, as I have already said, under the present situation of affairs, is utterly impossible by all the methods hitherto proposed. For we can neither employ them in handicraft or agriculture; we neither build houses (I mean in the country) nor cultivate land. They can very seldom pick up a livelihood by stealing till they arrive at six years old, except where they are of towardly parts; although I confess they learn the rudiments much earlier, during which time they can however

be looked upon only as probationers, as I have been informed by a principal gentleman in the county of Cavan, who protested to me that he never knew above one or two instances under the age of six, even in a part of the kingdom so renowned for the quickest proficiency in that art.

I am assured by our merchants that a boy or a girl before 7
twelve years old is no salable commodity; and even when they come to this age they will not yield above three pounds, or three pounds and half a crown at most on the Exchange; which cannot turn to account either to the parents or the kingdom, the charge of nutriment and rags having been at least four times that value.

I shall now therefore humbly propose my own thoughts, 8
which I hope will not be liable to the least objection.

I have been assured by a very knowing American of 9
my acquaintance in London, that a young healthy child well nursed is at a year old a most delicious, nourishing, and wholesome food, whether stewed, roasted, baked, or boiled; and I make no doubt that it will equally serve in a fricassee or a ragout.

I do therefore humbly offer it to public consideration 10
that of the hundred and twenty thousand children, already computed, twenty thousand may be reserved for breed, whereof only one fourth part to be males, which is more than we allow to sheep, black cattle, or swine; and my reason is that these children are seldom the fruits of marriage, a circumstance not much regarded by our savages, therefore one male will be sufficient to serve four females. That the remaining hundred thousand may at a year old be offered in sale to the persons of quality and fortune through the kingdom, always advising the mother to let them suck plentifully in the last month, so as to render them plump and fat for a good table. A child will make two dishes at an entertainment for friends; and when the family dines alone, the fore or hind quarter will make a reasonable dish, and seasoned with a little pepper or salt will be very good boiled on the fourth day, especially in winter.

I have reckoned upon a medium that a child just born 11
will weigh twelve pounds, and in a solar year if tolerably nursed increaseth to twenty-eight pounds.

I grant this food will be somewhat dear, and therefore 12

very proper for landlords, who, as they have already devoured most of the parents, seem to have the best title to the children.

13 Infant's flesh will be in season throughout the year, but more plentiful in March, and a little before and after. For we are told by a grave author, an eminent French physician, that fish being a prolific diet, there are more children born in Roman Catholic countries about nine months after Lent than at any other season; therefore, reckoning a year after Lent, the markets will be more glutted than usual, because the number of popish infants is at least three to one in this kingdom; and therefore it will have one other collateral advantage, by lessening the number of Papists among us.

14 I have already computed the charge of nursing a beggar's child (in which list I reckon all cottagers, laborers, and four fifths of the farmers) to be about two shillings per annum, rags included; and I believe no gentleman would repine to give ten shillings for the carcass of a good fat child, which, as I have said, will make four dishes of excellent nutritive meat, when he hath only some particular friend or his own family to dine with him. Thus the squire will learn to be a good landlord, and grow popular among the tenants; the mother will have eight shillings net profit, and be fit for work till she produces another child.

15 Those who are more thrifty (as I must confess the times require) may flay the carcass; the skin of which artificially dressed will make admirable gloves for ladies, and summer boots for fine gentlemen.

16 As to our city of Dublin, shambles may be appointed for this purpose in the most convenient parts of it, and butchers we may be assured will not be wanting; although I rather recommend buying the children alive, and dressing them hot from the knife as we do roasting pigs.

17 A very worthy person, a true lover of his country, and whose virtues I highly esteem, was lately pleased in discoursing on this matter to offer a refinement upon my scheme. He said that many gentlemen of this kingdom, having of late destroyed their deer, he conceived that the want of venison might be well supplied by the bodies of young lads and maidens, not exceeding fourteen years of age nor under twelve, so great a number of both sexes in every county being now ready to starve for want of

work and service; and these to be disposed of by their parents, if alive, or otherwise by their nearest relations. But with due deference to so excellent a friend and so deserving a patriot, I cannot be altogether in his sentiments; for as to the males, my American acquaintance assured me from frequent experience that their flesh was generally tough and lean, like that of our schoolboys, by continual exercise, and their taste disagreeable; and to fatten them would not answer the charge. Then as to the females, it would, I think with humble submission, be a loss to the public, because they soon would become breeders themselves: and besides, it is not improbable that some scrupulous people might be apt to censure such a practice (although indeed very unjustly) as a little bordering upon cruelty; which, I confess, hath always been with me the strongest objection against any project, how well soever intended.

But in order to justify my friend, he confessed that this 18 expedient was put into his head by the famous Psalmanazar, a native of the island Formosa, who came from thence to London above twenty years ago, and in conversation told my friend that in his country when any young person happened to be put to death, the executioner sold the carcass to persons of quality as a prime dainty; and that in his time the body of a plump girl of fifteen, who was crucified for an attempt to poison the emperor, was sold to his Imperial Majesty's prime minister of state, and other great mandarins of the court, in joints from the gibbet, at four hundred crowns. Neither indeed can I deny that if the same use were made of several plump young girls in this town, who without one single groat to their fortunes cannot stir abroad without a chair, and appear at the playhouse and assemblies in foreign fineries which they never will pay for, the kingdom would not be the worse.

Some persons of a desponding spirit are in great concern 19 about that vast number of poor people who are aged, diseased, or maimed, and I have been desired to employ my thoughts what course may be taken to ease the nation of so grievous an encumbrance. But I am not in the least pain upon that matter, because it is very well known that they are every day dying and rotting by cold and famine, and filth and vermin, as fast as can be reasonably expected. And as to the younger laborers, they are now in almost as hopeful a condition. They cannot get work, and consequently pine away for want of nourishment to a degree that if at any time they are accidentally hired to common labor, they have not strength to perform it; and thus the country and themselves are happily delivered from the evils to come.

20   I have too long digressed, and therefore shall return to my subject. I think the advantages by the proposal which I have made are obvious and many, as well as of the highest importance.

21   For first, as I have already observed, it would greatly lessen the number of Papists, with whom we are yearly overrun, being the principal breeders of the nation as well as our most dangerous enemies; and who stay at home on purpose to deliver the kingdom to the Pretender, hoping to take their advantage by the absence of so many good Protestants, who have chosen rather to leave their country than to stay at home and pay tithes against their conscience to an Episcopal curate.

22   Secondly, the poorer tenants will have something valuable of their own, which by law may be made liable to distress, and help to pay their landlord's rent, their corn and cattle being already seized and money a thing unknown.

23   Thirdly, whereas the maintenance of an hundred thousand children, from two years old and upwards, cannot be computed at less than ten shillings a piece per annum, the nation's stock will be thereby increased fifty thousand pounds per annum, besides the profit of a new dish introduced to the tables of all gentlemen of fortune in the kingdom who have any refinement in taste. And the money will circulate among ourselves, the goods being entirely of our own growth and manufacture.

24   Fourthly, the constant breeders, besides the gain of eight shillings sterling per annum by the sale of their children, will be rid of the charge of maintaining them after the first year.

25   Fifthly, this food would likewise bring great custom to taverns, where the vintners will certainly be so prudent as to procure the best receipts for dressing it to perfection, and consequently have their houses frequented by all the fine gentlemen, who justly value themselves upon their knowledge in good eating; and a skillful cook, who understands how to oblige his guests, will contrive to make it as expensive as they please.

Sixthly, this would be a great inducement to marriage, which all wise nations have either encouraged by rewards or enforced by laws and penalties. It would increase the care and tenderness of mothers toward their children, when they were sure of a settlement for life to the poor babes, provided in some sort by the public, to their annual profit instead of expense. We should see an honest emulation among the married women, which of them could bring the fattest child to the market. Men would become as fond of their wives during the time of their pregnancy as they are now of their mares in foal, their cows in calf, or sows when they are ready to farrow; nor offer to beat or kick them (as is too frequent a practice) for fear of a miscarriage.   26

Many other advantages might be enumerated. For instance, the addition of some thousand carcasses in our exportation of barreled beef, the propagation of swine's flesh, and improvement in the art of making good bacon, so much wanted among us by the great destruction of pigs, too frequent at our tables, which are no way comparable in taste or magnificence to a well-grown, fat, yearling child, which roasted whole will make a considerable figure at a lord mayor's feast or any other public entertainment. But this and many others I omit, being studious of brevity.   27

Supposing that one thousand families in this city would be constant customers for infants' flesh, besides others who might have it at merry meetings, particularly weddings and christenings, I compute that Dublin would take off annually about twenty thousand carcasses, and the rest of the kingdom (where probably they will be sold somewhat cheaper) the remaining eighty thousand.   28

I can think of no one objection that will possibly be raised against this proposal, unless it should be urged that the number of people will be thereby much lessened in the kingdom. This I freely own, and it was indeed one principal design in offering it to the world. I desire the reader will observe, that I calculate my remedy for this one individual kingdom of Ireland and for no other that ever was, is, or I think ever can be upon earth. Therefore let no man talk to me of other expedients: of taxing our absentees at five shillings a pound: of using neither clothes nor household furniture except what is of our own growth and manufacture: of utterly rejecting the materials and   29 instruments that promote foreign luxury: of curing the expensiveness of pride, vanity, idleness, and gaming in our women: of introducing a vein of parsimony, prudence, and temperance: of learning to love our country, in the want of which we differ even from Laplanders and the inhabitants of Topinamboo: of quitting our animosities and factions, nor acting any longer like the Jews, who were murdering one another at the very moment their city was taken: of being a little cautious not to sell our country and conscience for nothing: of teaching landlords to have at least one degree of mercy toward their tenants: lastly, of putting a spirit of honesty, industry, and skill into our shopkeepers; who, if a resolution could now be taken to buy only our native goods, would immediately unite to cheat and exact upon us in the price, the measure, and the goodness, nor could ever yet be brought to make one fair proposal of just dealing, though often and earnestly invited to it.

30   Therefore I repeat, let no man talk to me of these and the like expedients, till he hath at least some glimpse of hope that there will ever be some hearty and sincere attempt to put them in practice.

31   But as to myself, having been wearied out for many years with offering vain, idle, visionary thoughts, and at length utterly despairing of success, I fortunately fell upon this proposal, which, as it is wholly new, so it hath something solid and real, of no expense and little trouble, full in our own power, and whereby we can incur no danger in disobliging England. For this kind of commodity will not bear exportation, the flesh being of too tender a consistence to admit a long continuance in salt, although perhaps I could name a country which would be glad to eat up our whole nation without it.

32   After all, I am not so violently bent upon my own opinion as to reject any offer proposed by wise men, which shall be found equally innocent, cheap, easy, and effectual. But before something of that kind shall be advanced in contradiction to my scheme, and offering a better, I desire the author or authors will be pleased maturely to consider two points. First, as things now stand, how they will be able to find food and raiment for an hundred thousand useless mouths and backs. And secondly, there being a round million of creatures in human figure throughout this kingdom, whose sole subsistence put into a common

stock would leave them in debt two millions of pounds sterling, adding those who are beggars by profession to the bulk of farmers, cottagers, and laborers, with their wives and children who are beggars in effect; I desire those politicians who dislike my overture, and may perhaps be so bold to attempt an answer, that they will first ask the parents of these mortals whether they would not at this day think it a great happiness to have been sold for food at a year old in the manner I prescribe, and thereby have avoided such a perpetual scene of misfortunes as they have since gone through by the oppression of landlords, the impossibility of paying rent without money or trade, the want of common sustenance, with neither house nor clothes to cover them from the inclemencies of the weather, and the most inevitable prospect of entailing the like or greater miseries upon their breed forever.

I profess, in the sincerity of my heart, that I have not the least personal interest in endeavoring to promote this necessary work, having no other motive than the public good of my country, by advancing our trade, providing for infants, relieving the poor, and giving some pleasure to the rich. I have no children by which I can propose to get a single penny; the youngest being nine years old, and my wife past childbearing.

33

Discussing Content and Form

1. *What is the premise behind Swift's essay?*

2 *List in order the arguments that Swift's speaker uses to support his proposal: the number of children, the futility of their prospects in life, etc.*

3 *List some of the ways Swift satirizes people's attitudes toward money. How does he show his attitude toward the English government? Who are the "landlords" referred to in paragraph 11?*

4. *Examine the organization of the essay by grouping all the paragraphs into sections and determining what the chief function of each section is:*
a. *What is the special purpose of the first three paragraphs? Of the last three? What is the relationship between these two sections?*

b.   *Which paragraphs are given to the proposal itself? Which involve what might be called the practical matters of carrying it out? How many paragraphs deal with the advantages of the plan? How are these paragraphs introduced?*

c.   *It is common in argument to anticipate and answer possible counterarguments. Where do you find Swift's speaker answering objections to his proposal?*

d.   *How does the essay's organization contribute to the legalistic and formal tone of the monstrous proposal? What seems to be the connection between the organization and the irony behind the satire?*

5.   *What can you tell about the religious attitudes in Ireland during Swift's time?*

6.   *List some of Swift's criticisms of social conditions in Ireland. How do these conditions serve as background for the "proposal"? Where does Swift indicate what he thinks ought to be done about such conditions?*

Considering Special Techniques

1.   *Swift's essay is, of course, satire—his method is sustained irony. Throughout the "proposal" his fictitious spokesman makes monstrous suggestions that are the opposite of what is really meant. The writer of irony must give sufficient clues so that the reader does not take his statements literally.*

a.   *When do you first detect the irony? What clues lead to the recognition?*

b.   *What qualities in the character of Swift's speaker make him seem a convincing advocate of the "proposal"? How does he establish himself? Does he seem modest? Well-informed? Reasonable?*

c.   *The language and details of the selection are made carefully appropriate to the fictitious speaker; discuss the irony in these statements and find others which seem to you especially outrageous:*
"Infant's flesh will be in season throughout the year . . ."
(par. 13).
"This would be a great inducement to marriage, which all wise nations have either encouraged by rewards or enforced by laws and penalties" (par. 26).
"Men would become as fond of their wives during pregnancy as they are now of their mares in foal . . ." (par. 26).

2.   *What is the effect of the comment that the "helpless infants" must become thieves, "or leave their . . . country to fight for the Pretender in Spain, or sell themselves to the Barbadoes"*

(par. 1)? What is the effect of the references to the American friend (pars. 9 and 17)?

3. What is the effect of referring to children and their parents as if they are animals: "a child just dropped from its dam" (par. 4); "170,000 breeders" (par. 6), etc. Do you find it ironic to juxtapose this language with the references to the people as "souls"? Explain.

4. Words to learn and use: melancholy, importuning, sustenance *(par. 1);* prodigious, deplorable, grievance *(par. 2);* raiment *(par. 4);* apprehend, rudiments, proficiency *(par. 6);* nutriment *(par. 7);* eminent, collateral *(par. 13);* scrupulous *(par. 17);* expedient *(par. 18);* desponding, encumbrance *(par. 19);* vintners *(par. 25);* emulation *(par. 26);* exportation, propagation *(par. 27);* parsimony, animosities, factions *(par. 29);* effectual, inclemencies *(par. 32).*

Generating Ideas

1. From the essay, construct a mental picture of the person who is making the proposal. Then write a paper in which you describe his background, personality, and the attitudes and beliefs that may have led him to write as he does. Be sure that you use the essay itself for evidence to support your descriptive details.

2. Write a paper in which you discuss the language and style of the essay and show how they are related to the character who makes the proposal and to his purpose in the essay.

3. Write your own "modest" proposal for solving one or more of our present-day ills: unemployment, inflation, care of children and of the aged poor, export trade, armament, for example.

Index of Terms

Listed here are the various rhetorical and grammatical terms in the chapter introductions and study questions. Those terms used in the chapter introductions and study questions are cited by chapter number and page. Terms appearing in the study questions are indicated by author's name, page number, and question number. "Content" and "Techniques" refer respectively to the first and second groups of study questions, "Discussing Content and Form" and "Considering Special Techniques."